Animal Antics

BIRDS

Copyright © ticktock Entertainment Ltd 2007

First published in Great Britain in 2007 by ticktock Media Ltd.,
Unit 2, Orchard Business Centre, North Farm Road,
Tunbridge Wells, Kent, TN2 3XF

Author: Monica Hughes
Designer: Alix Wood and Emma Randall
Editor: Rebecca Clunes

ISBN 978 1 84696 498 5 pbk

Printed in China

This is Stanley.

He has a hat, a scarf and gloves to keep him warm.

How do YOU keep warm in the winter?

Stanley knows how some animals keep warm.

A whale has fatty **blubber**.

A polar bear has thick fur.

A mountain goat has lots of hair.

These animals don't need clothes!

Stanley likes the pigeons in his garden.

They have feathers
to keep them warm.

Did You Know?
All birds have two
legs, two wings
and feathers.

6

True or False?
All birds make nests.

Pigeons
fluff up their
feathers
in winter.

7

Stanley likes one
pigeon most of all.

He calls him Gordon.

Stanley knows that Gordon
is good at flying.

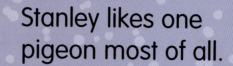

Did You Know?
Pigeons are fast fliers.
They can fly about
80 kilometres per hour.

Gordon can suck water up
his beak.

He calls 'coo, coo, coo!' but he
does not sing.

Stanley knows a lot about different birds.

He knows the ostrich is the **biggest** bird.

True or False?
An ostrich can run faster than a person.

An ostrich has feathers
and wings but it cannot fly.

Stanley knows that penguins are very good swimmers.

Their wings are like **flippers**.

They flap their wings as they swim.

Did You Know?

To move fast, penguins sometimes slide on the snow on their bellies.

Penguins can swim fast
but they cannot fly.

Stanley knows the hummingbird is the smallest bird.

It is the only bird that can fly backward.

It can also **hover** in the air.

Beak

Some hummingbirds have very long beaks.

They suck **nectar** from inside flowers.

Stanley knows there are thousands of different kinds of birds.

Kiwis have wings but can not fly.

Parrots have strong beaks so they can eat hard nuts and seeds.

Pelicans have big beaks to scoop up fish.

Peacocks have brightly coloured tail feathers.

Ostriches can run as fast as a car.

Stanley likes **birds of prey**.

They have curved beaks and sharp claws.

They are very good at flying.

Most birds of prey are strong.

They have very good **eyesight**.

Owl

Eagle

Birds of Prey

Falcon

Vulture

19

Most owls
hunt at night.

They have flat faces
and **big** eyes.

They can see and
hear very well.

Stanley wants
to fly.

Could he fly
with an owl?

Did You Know?
An owl can swallow a
mouse in one gulp.

True or False?
Some owls eat other owls.

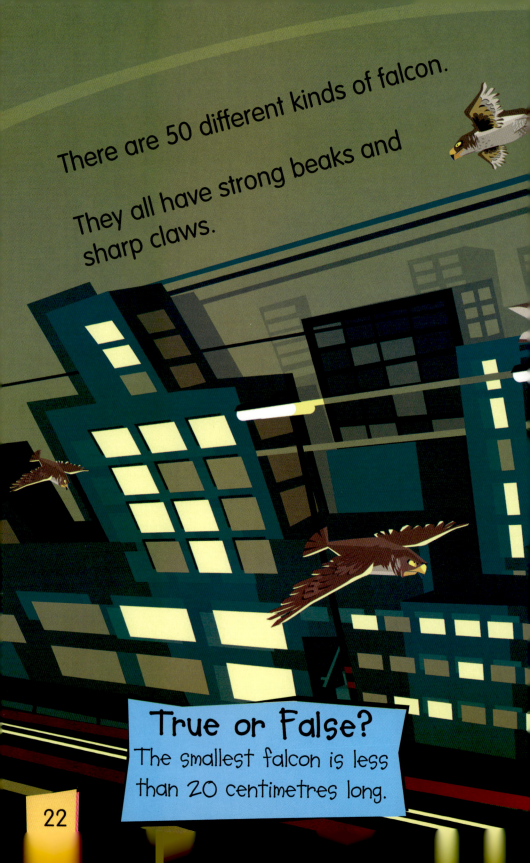

There are 50 different kinds of falcon.

They all have strong beaks and sharp claws.

True or False?
The smallest falcon is less than 20 centimetres long.

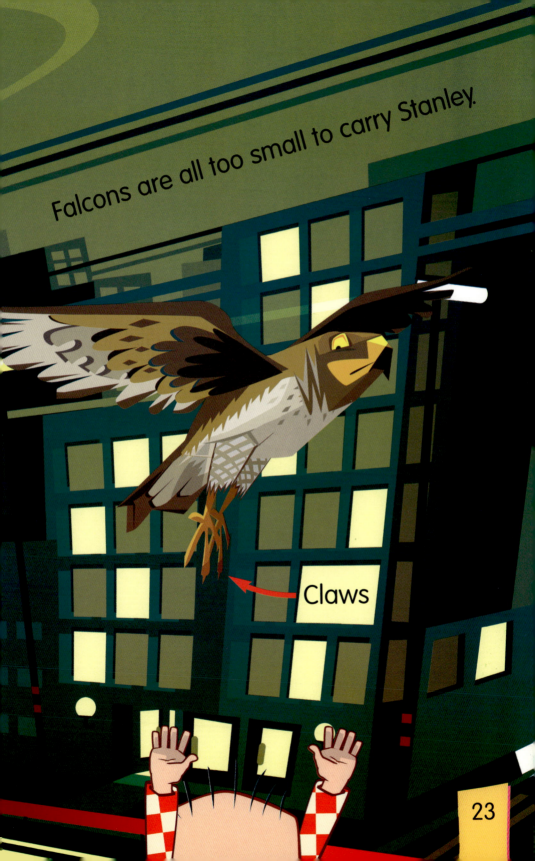

Falcons are all too small to carry Stanley.

Claws

Vultures have large wings and are good at **gliding**.

They do not hunt for food.

They feed on dead animals.

True or False?
Vultures don't sing,
they hiss and grunt.

Vultures have strong beaks to rip up their meat.

Beak

They eat everything except the bones.

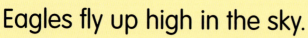

Eagles fly up high in the sky.

They are good at **gliding**.

Claws

They can see very well and are good at hunting.

Eagles bring food for their chicks.

Beak

Stanley likes eagles, but he would hate to be an eagle's dinner!

Stanley still likes Gordon best of all the different birds.

He knows pigeons eat seeds and fruit.

True or False?
Pigeons can take off with one flap of their wings.

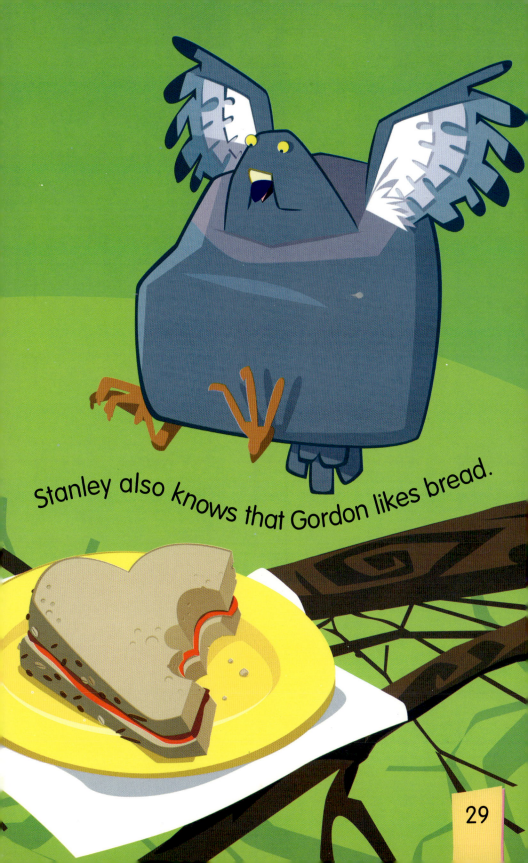

Stanley also knows that Gordon likes bread.

29

Stanley would still
like to fly like a bird.

But he can think of a
different way to fly.

Can YOU?

Glossary

Birds of prey Birds that hunt and kill for food.

Blubber The fat beneath an animal skin.

Eyesight Able to see.

Flippers Large flat parts of the body, good for swimming.

Gliding The way a bird can fly smoothly without flapping its wings.

Hover Stay in one place in the air.

Nectar Sweet liquid inside flowers.

True or False answers

Page 7   False
              Some birds lay their
              eggs in holes, on rocks
              or on the ground.

Page 10   True

Page 21   True

Page 22   True

Page 24   True

Page 28   True

THE MEDIA IN SCOTLAND

Edited by Neil Blain and David Hutchison

EDINBURGH UNIVERSITY PRESS

© in this edition Edinburgh University Press, 2008
© in the individual contributions is retained by the authors

Edinburgh University Press Ltd
22 George Square, Edinburgh

Typeset in 11/13 pt Monotype Bembo
by Servis Filmsetting Ltd, Manchester, and
printed and bound in Great Britain by
Antony Rowe Ltd, Chippenham, Wilts

A CIP record for this book is available from the British Library

ISBN 978 0 7486 2799 8 (hardback)
ISBN 978 0 7486 2800 1 (paperback)

The right of the contributors
to be identified as authors of this work
has been asserted in accordance with
the Copyright, Designs and Patents Act 1988.

Contents

Preface

The reason we have sought to publish *The Media in Scotland* is simple enough: although in the past thirty years several books on aspects of the Scottish media have appeared, cinema being particularly well served, there has been no attempt in one volume to cover the entire territory. (It is not false modesty which makes us say that the small volume of essays on the topic which one of us edited in 1978 was much narrower than the present undertaking.) It is desirable that there should be one book which offers readers a survey of as much of the field as possible, and does so in such a way that current concerns and debates are set in their historical contexts.

It is also appropriate, with the third Holyrood parliament well into its stride, that the strengths and weaknesses of the devolution settlement in the communications area are examined. As several of our contributors note, there is something a little bit lop-sided about cultural policy being devolved while broadcasting and media ownership remain exclusively the domain of Westminster. But however the devolution settlement might be modified, there are certain issues concerning the media which will still need to be addressed, not simply the legislative powers thereon of the Edinburgh parliament. The options open to a small nation with myriad calls on its budget, a nation, too, that is sensitive – some might say hyper-sensitive – about how it is portrayed, are both limited and challenging.

Something needs to be said at the outset about the title of the book, which is not perhaps as self-explanatory as might appear. To the average citizen, the media in Scotland do not comprise only those films, newspapers and broadcast programmes produced north of the border. To such a person exposure to, and consumption of, for example, cinema, will involve for the most part American films, with only occasional English or Scottish offerings – let alone those from elsewhere in the world – as part of the mix. Likewise in television, most of us who live in Scotland most of the time watch programmes from south of the border and from the USA. The situation in radio, however, is more complex, and with newspapers the indigenous dailies dominate the Scottish market – or at least they used to. As for the Internet, the click of a mouse has enabled us all to transcend geographical barriers, and often other barriers as well.

But the approach of this volume, while alert to the highly porous nature of national media boundaries, is nevertheless rooted in a strong sense of Scotland as a nation distinct in the political, economic and socio-cultural spheres (questions about its psychological distinctness arise intermittently in these contributions, too). Our book is focused on those parts of the media which are recognisably Scottish in terms of location, orientation and origin – ownership and control we realise are less open to such a commonsense test – and on the various ways in which they have engaged with the society in which they find themselves.

It was clear to us that a volume of this nature would of necessity be multi-authored. The field is far too broad for one or two individuals to cover it properly. Furthermore, there are real benefits in being able to draw on different expertises and varying perspectives. The authors are mainly, though not exclusively, academics, and the fact that as editors we were spoiled for choice is a reflection of the expansion of the study of the media in Scottish higher education. It is impossible to discuss contemporary culture adequately without sustained reference to the media. The past fifty years have witnessed a steady transformation of much of culture into media culture. Researching and studying the media have for long been as essential as studying economics, politics or psychology. The authors assembled in this volume bring a rich variety of expertise in media topics to the task of producing a comprehensive account.

The book is structured in what we hope is a logical fashion. It begins with three essays which seek to frame the discussion: one on the vexed issue of representation, the second on the approaches of the media to Scotland's linguistic diversity, and the third on the legislative and political complexities of the communications environment. These essays are followed by three chapters which – in broad fashion – chart the histories of the press, broadcasting and the cinema north of the border, highlighting emerging concerns as well as the key factors in the development of these media.

'Screen and Sound' groups five essays on the specific forms of television drama, soap opera, broadcast comedy, contemporary Scottish cinema, and radio and popular music. The contributions in 'Themes and Futures' are led by broader topics in which the media play important roles, starting with gender; then race and ethnicity; then questions of the Gaelic language; and then a comprehensive sweep across the field of Scottish media and politics. Given the centrality of this latter relationship, the topic is handled a little differently from the others, via three contributions: one is by an academic, and the other shorter chapters are written by two politicians of distinction – one recently re-elected to Holyrood and serving as a minister, the other now pursuing a variety of interests after an eight-year spell as a UK government minister – reflecting on their experiences. The volume ends with an analysis of current and impending technological and economic impacts on the national dimensions of sport, considering new media along the way.

It might seem trite to say that we look for a readership not only among academics and their students but also in the wider public sphere in Scotland. But we do genuinely seek that, and to this end have asked our contributors to write with both audiences in mind.

We thank our contributors for delivering their chapters on time (or at worst not too far beyond the deadline!) and for their patience and forbearance when we requested amendments and revisions in the interests of minimising duplication and ensuring wide coverage of the field. Where there are gaps, the fault lies with us, not our contributors. We are grateful to our publisher, Edinburgh University Press, and to its commissioning editor, Sarah Edwards, for backing the project so enthusiastically; all of us associated with the book hope that we have justified that commitment. We should also like to thank Janet McBain and the invaluable Scottish Screen Archive of the National Library of Scotland for their kind permission to use the cover photograph of the Palace cinema in Dunfermline.

Debate on both the Scottish media and on wider political and cultural concerns has been underway for a long time and is likely to intensify in the near future, not least as a consequence of the establishment by the new SNP administration of an inquiry into broadcasting in Scotland which was announced as we went to press. We would like to think that the book will contribute both to the specific and broader aspects of those ongoing discussions, by putting current concerns in context and raising others which merit more attention. Finally, we hope that taken together these essays offer a stimulating and enjoyable read.

Neil Blain, David Hutchison
August 2007

FRAMING THE DISCUSSION

1

A Cause Still Unwon: The Struggle to Represent Scotland

NEIL BLAIN AND KATHRYN BURNETT

As far as Mr Weir could make out, arriving when conversation was fairly floated, somebody (probably the LORD ADVOCATE) had devised and was administering a system of indentured labour in the Hebrides. The terms of engagement, he gathered, involved a condition of repatriation. Now that is a thing no Scot who respects himself and truly loves his country will submit to. He will cross the Tweed, come to London, become in turn Prime Minister and Leader of the Opposition, or vice-versâ. But repatriation he will not submit to. (Essence of Parliament, *Punch*, 20 February 1907: 140)[1]

ALL THAT'S BEST IN BRITAIN

An edition of *Lilliput* magazine[2] from precisely the middle of the twentieth century carries an advertisement for the Standard Vanguard saloon. It is part of a series of advertisements featuring 'All that's best in Britain' and features a half-page, low-angle, upper-body colour shot of a piper in semi-profile, in full Highland military dress with bearskin hat and a white cockade; his bagpipes fill most of the frame. Lit strongly to the face, he is framed against a background of blue sky. The copy fills the third quarter of the page, above a line drawing of a Standard Vanguard saloon:

All that's best in Britain . . .
Scotland, land of glens and lochs, of rich lowlands and thriving cities has reared on its soil a hardy, purposeful people – builders, explorers and engineers whose work forms part of our great British heritage . . . the

same qualities of craftsmanship and enterprise are to be found in the products of the Standard Motor Company, representing as they do in every
detail of their design 'all that's best in Britain'. (*Lilliput* July 1950: 109)

The 'All that's best in (or "from") Britain' strapline, which made reference to
the themes of the Festival of Britain on either side of that event, was also used
in an advertising series for the Triumph Mayflower and the Triumph Renown,
featuring various 'national' emblems such as a mounted guardsman, Morris
dancers, artisanal labour and royal pageantry. Another Standard Vanguard
advertisement in the series 'All that's best in Britain' features Saxon heritage:
'from time immemorial a horn has been blown each evening in the town of
Ripon . . . a survival of the Saxon Wakeman's curfew call . . . linking us with
a past that saw the building of the great cathedrals and manor houses by crafts-
men who strove for nothing less than the best' (June 1950: 8); the photograph
this time is a monochrome shot of the hornblower, in tunic and tricorn hat.

The dichotomy evident in much advertising of this period, between a
modern Britain boasting industrial and scientific capacity, yet also feeling a nostalgic yearning for a quieter time before the world wars, produces on the one
hand soporific images of the past, for example, a line drawing of a tranquil
cricket game on an English village green, for Regent Motor Spirit, under the
strapline 'The Spirit of the Nation'. On the other, we might find the 'Britain
leads' series for Wills's Gold Flake cigarettes, focusing not just on Britain's
accomplishments in the established technologies of shipbuilding and television
('research and inventiveness of a very high order enabled Britain to be the first
country in the world with television') but also in the developing field of jet
propulsion, looking forward to the economic struggles of the reconstruction
period.

Alongside this assimilative approach there is periodically revealed a glimpse
of an alternative account of Scottishness. A *Lilliput* cartoon of April 1950 features an elderly kilted Scotsman of forlorn appearance who has opened a letter
in his front hall, the caption reading 'Dear Sir, or Madam . . .'. He seems to be
considering these alternatives depressively (1950: 89).

Six years after Lovat's commando brigade had been piped ashore in
Normandy on D-Day, the piper in the Standard Vanguard advertisement represents a dimension of Britishness with a specific history, associated (say) with
those Highlanders, the sound of whose bagpipes brought (premature) hope to
the besieged inside the Residency at Lucknow. He operates as a conventional
symbol of Scotland, but his semiological functioning is more complex than it
appears, and his Highland garb is not the primary meaning of the text. We
discover at worst a less restrictive stereotype ('a hardy, purposeful people –
builders, explorers and engineers') than the image at first suggests, despite its

limitations. Though it is significant that a piper, rather than, say, an engineer, represents 'builders, explorers and engineers', this is a function of the general nostalgia of 'All that's best in Britain': 'industry', in another advertisement, is represented by a wheelwright rather than a jet propulsion engineer. The image is complex rather than simple (the cartoon, taking its Scottish identifiers from much the same reservoir of images, is merely a joke about a man in a skirt). The Standard Triumph advertisement, while framing the Scots as 'a people' (perhaps in this context 'an ethnicity') and therefore different from the English, simultaneously accounts for them as a component of Britishness and as producers of British heritage, whereas the cartoon belongs to a repertoire of difference.

Yet both Scottish texts assert difference. Ripon's hornblower is not constructed as belonging (say) to a gritty, resourceful Yorkshire 'people'; his Englishness is self-evident (his subjectivity is aligned with that of an English reader) and need not be accounted for. It is enhanced by reference to a 900-year-old extant tradition which 'began in Saxon times', the category of 'Saxon' being in such accounts coterminous with 'English'. In an alternative and more persuasive history, the Scots, Danes, Northumbrians and Normans all complicate this tranquil myth of Ripon's 'Saxon' continuities, but nation-building (and car sales) involve much simplification. These simplifications, however, create a durable currency.

GROUNDSKEEPER WILLIE AND THE BARON OF BRADWARDINE: CHARACTERISING SCOTLAND

'Hie to the house, Rose, and see that Alexander Saunderson looks out the old Châteaux Margoux (sic), which I sent from Bourdeaux to Dundee in the year 1713'. . .'We cannot rival the luxuries of your English table, Captain Waverley, or give you the *epula lautiores* of Waverley-Honour – I say *epula* rather than *prandium*, because the latter phrase is popular; *Epulae ad senatum, prandium vero ad populum attinet*, says Suetonius Tranquillus. But I trust you will applaud my Bourdeaux; *c'est des deux oreilles*, as Captain Vinsauf used to say – *Vinum prima notae*, the Principal of St Andrews denominated it. (Scott 1860: 178)

There's honey, Christmas cake, heather, a whole fruit bowl of citrus tones, smokiness, syrup, peat (usually fairly elusive, but poking its head out of the thickets of other tastes now and again), vanilla, leather, straw, ginger and even other sorts of wood beside the oak you'd expect in there; cedar is one, and I thought I smelled something like the balsa wood we used for the initial few lessons in first-year woodwork class.[3] (Banks 2003: 260)

Colour is a rusty, radioactive orange. Nosing reveals a bouquet of bubble gum and something vaguely citrussy, maybe tangerine? Carbonation is medium, and mouth-feel . . . well, you can almost feel the enamel dissolving on your teeth.[4] (*The Travel Book* 2005: 345)

Writer of *Trainspotting* to take up cudgels for deep-fried Mars bars in culinary book with Scottish slant.[5] (Gibbons: 2003)

Glasgow had in the 1890s a loose equivalent of *Punch*, namely *Quiz* magazine.[6] One of its correspondents notes that '*Punch*, or the "London Charivari", has often been able to crush by ridicule abuses and follies that seemed proof against argument. Why should not *Quiz*, or the "Glasgow Charivari", do likewise?' (*Quiz*, 22 August: 249). Glasgow's confidence blazes from the pages of *Quiz*, displaying a Victorian optimism and poise which in Britain now is thought of as an American characteristic. That parallel also applies to *Quiz*'s sparing focus on the appalling social conditions on which Glasgow's wealth was based: 'one of the regretful features of city life is a separation of the classes that seems to create a west-end and an east-end in feeling as in social position' (15 August: 236).

Its editorial (these are penned under the authority of 'Quiz Office') of 18 July 1890 focuses on the danger of steamers racing each other on the Clyde:

The Clyde has a reputation unequalled in the world for its river steamers. One only requires to sail on the Thames or the Mersey to see how far ahead we are in this matter. It is right that everything should be done to sustain this reputation, and the steamers that have recently been added to the fleet are undoubtedly in the line of progress. They are finer steamers than their predecessors and undoubtedly, take them all over, swifter as well. The outcome of the recent changes in the coast traffic has been a break-neck competition against which, when carried too far, Mr Quiz must protest. That it has been carried too far of late all who travel must have noticed. An amount of personal feeling has entered into it, and if some kind of check is not put on it, we may be carried to – the bottom, in a remarkably short time from the city. (p. 197)

A fortnight earlier (4 July), the editorial has sent a message of congratulations to the United States on the anniversary of the Declaration of Independence, speaking for Britain generally, noting that 'there is much in each country from which the other may learn, and in a healthy rivalry in the arts of peace between Britain and America much of the progress of the world lies'. 'May nothing', it concludes (p. 177) 'ever arise to affect the friendly relations now existing!' *Quiz* makes many references to American stories and events, New York being as much within its view as London. There are occasional nods to the large northern English cities as in some sense members of a community. Overall, *Quiz* is as often cosmopolitan as parochial, alert and engaged in the face of international currents and events. Its 'Under the Reading Lamp' column (14 March) typically notes that:

> Mr Arthur Severn[7] has given an authoritative contradiction to the malicious statement regarding Mr Ruskin made by the *New York Herald* recently. I should give a good deal to have Mr Ruskin's opinion on the style of journalism represented by the *New York Herald*. It would be a choice bit of English composition I feel certain (p. 19).

Wherever *Quiz* may be willing to acknowledge that Glasgow is still underdeveloped, it cheerfully assumes that the city will attend to it:

> Notwithstanding all those excellent features of our civic administration, which have caused Glasgow to be held up as an example to the world, we must admit that in the cultivation of what may be called the social side of our municipal life, on any large scale, we have hitherto been lacking . . . The significance of Tuesday evening's assemblage, in view of this, is important, and we have no doubt that the Lord Provost's ball, or some such gathering, will now be regarded as an institution while Glasgow continues to flourish. (14 March: 17)

Quiz generally presents a view of cultural life in which engagement with London is taken for granted, exhibitions and other London events being routinely handled. There is some ambivalence over the competitive aspects of the relationship. The column 'Town Tattle' (28 March) expresses the wish that when Glasgow's new art galleries are 'set agoing', they will have a Print Room similar to those in the British Museum or South Kensington. The framing of the matter barely dwells on Glasgow's as yet less developed state before briskly suggesting a solution: 'It is hard on the Provinces, that when any comparison falls to be made, it must of necessity be in London. Duplicates from British Museum or South Kensington might be arranged for' (p. 35). Even this modesty is intermittent. The same feature has reported a week earlier that *Century* magazine of that month contains an article which declares that Glasgow occupies 'not the second, but the first place among the communities of Great Britain' as a 'distinct and complete municipal organization' (p. 25). *Quiz Office* later reports (2 May 1890) that 'Greater Glasgow' will cover a municipal area of 25 square miles, with the combined populations of Manchester and Birmingham, 'and 180,000 more than Liverpool' (p. 86) and notes that Glasgow's claims to be capital of Scotland are strengthened by such great expansion. In another edition (23 May) the commentary generously congratulates the Corporation of Dublin on its erection of quality housing for the poor (p. 117), noting that

Glasgow could usefully follow suit, and likewise (29 August) on the occasion of a visit by Gladstone to Dundee, while regretting that he was not to 'come West, as was at one time expected he would', congratulates 'the citizens of Dundee on the visit they will have, and on their decision to present the right hon. gentleman with the freedom of the city. What a friend gets is not lost' (p. 257).

That 'east-end of feeling' which *Quiz* regretfully sees as an intrinsic feature of city life would eventually have more of the stage in Glasgow's representation, both of itself and by outsiders, than was imaginable in 1890. When Glasgow's newly formed anti-litter squad took to the streets in 2007, infamously, in knife-proof vests, in a city by then frequently characterised as the 'murder capital of Europe', Glasgow had already been the subject of extensive academic and journalistic discussion focusing, especially, on dual, contrastive late-modern accounts discernible by the start of the 1990s. Both these accounts display historical continuities. One, the pejorative Glasgow of multiple deprivation and crime, is continuous with a Glasgow which had from the time of its rapid nineteenth-century growth produced some of the worst social conditions in the world, with corresponding myths of the menace of the Gorbals and the post-war housing estates. The other, the postmodern city of service sector growth and cultural charms, is the downsized descendant of *Quiz's* Glasgow of progressive municipal development and investment in education and the arts.

There is no *prima facie* case for expecting that indigenous cultural production will produce positive accounts of local conditions, or that the typifications produced by outsiders will be negative. Cultural histories, of the novel, or the film, or of broadcasting, can be used selectively to prove both that proposition and the opposite. To generalise about the creative and gatekeeping mechanisms which engender or permit certain representations of cities and countries is difficult. Today, the crucial function of commissioning editors in broadcasting, who in the UK remain generally in London, is central to the decision about which kinds of productions (and with what contents and forms) reach public consumption of television (radio has more flexibility). In the newspaper press, including Internet publishing, editors, news agencies and journalists are all part of the process of selection, while magazines and consumer guides conform to their own editorial habits. The tendency wherein accounts of localities narrow to what are known as 'stereotypes' is very well established. A broader cultural conservatism which may be inherent in that narrowing is given further emphasis by editorial proclivities in the media, to stick with what is known, lest the audience desert.

If we try to understand why *Rab C Nesbitt* is to Glasgow what *Frasier* is to Seattle, the answer will be a complex mixture of economics, ideologies, politics, the expectations of commissioning editors, and half a dozen less accessible factors in the creative and production mix, including the headquartering of most of the Scottish media in Glasgow.[8] Rab C. is part of a much later industry of the demotic in Glasgow, and of a usurpation of Scottish identity by a stunted version of Glaswegian identity. If a waiter or a bartender in Hong Kong or Santa Fé should offer, as sometimes they will, his or her Scottish impression, there is a good chance it will be working-class Glaswegian (at least aspirationally; one of the present authors can attest to a stage production of *Brigadoon* in an American university of which the director – challenged on the authenticity of the pronunciation of 'up' as 'oop' – responded that the cast had listened very carefully to tapes of Scotty in *Star Trek*).[9] Some representations wield more power than others, and in different domains. For example, the American screen will tend to have disproportionate influence internationally. The comic grotesque Fat Bastard (one of a number of personae of Mike Myers in the *Austin Powers* series) may be placed in company with *The Simpsons*' Groundskeeper Willie, Mel Gibson's Wallace, Mrs Doubtfire, Shrek, and others, as figures egregiously bearing Scottish identity abroad without (as it were) permission. But whether there is anything more 'authorised' about *My Ain Folk, Cracker, One Foot in the Grave, Taggart, Morvern Callar, Red Road* or any other examples containing more apparently material Scottish dimensions is purely a matter of belief. What constitutes the 'national' dimension is in practice always hard to determine in film and television since the search implies looking for signs of cultural geography across many elements of production (commissioning, script, finance, location, creative and professional roles) and distribution. Fat Bastard's indigenous credentials do not seem quite as good as Dr Finlay's but that is only the beginning of an argument, for example about which of them better represents what, where, and to whom.

When the Baron of Bradwardine offers Waverley a bottle of his cherished Château Margaux, the authorial ironising on such a show of cosmopolitanism barely undermines the sense of culture which emerges from the display, a divergence and texture in Scottish history which the irony merely underscores. Shipped to Dundee six years after the Union, this wine holds a memory of a Scotland with its own European history, its ambassadors and schools and colleges in Paris and Rome. The visitor from England is juxtaposed beside European counters of Scottish identity. The quantity of forgetting involved in the narrow accounts of history and culture which are all that are generally now risked in broadcasting and most of the press in both Scotland and the UK is depressingly great. As time goes on, narrowcasting may in part be compensating for this, not least through the Internet, though it too has its limiting editorial habits (if and how radio may further develop in the DAB era is still to be seen). But where journalists and editors are prepared to work endlessly with the currency of banal and repetitive jingles, mapping 'deep-fried Mars bars' and fish suppers onto what is literally and figuratively a complex menu, they tend, as they do through their dependence on 'human interest' and celebrity culture, to treat real histories as a specialism not for their profession. Likewise, the caution of commissioning editors, unable, 400 miles away from the Central Belt of Scotland, to accept that more than the narrowest versions of Scotland make good drama or comedy, greatly restricts the accounts available.[10] There are parallels, too, for the financing of film;[11] and for the newsworthiness which Scotland can command in England. And when representations become based as much on other representations as on anything material in a local culture, they are both narrowed and exaggerated, seeming also to reach a critical mass which makes alternative discourses more difficult, for a variety of reasons, to venture.

Indigenous accounts from the eastern end of the Central Belt have been as savagely critical of Scottish culture as anything dreamt of in the west. The capital's most celebrated detective in literature and television, Ian Rankin's Rebus (a fish supper man, who really prefers tobacco and alcohol to food) is the bleakest of cultural observers both of his native Edinburgh and Scotland in general; and the celebrated and lethal strikes against Scotland and Scottishness in Irvine Welsh's *Trainspotting* (somewhere else not to eat out) are as succinct a response as possible to the bad faith inherent in Scotland's nego-tiation of its relationship with England. These attributions from within raise a further question.

A SCOTLAND IN WHOSE INTERESTS?

The BBC's independently produced *Restoration* (subsequently *Restoration Village*) TV project, which ran from 2003 until 2007, offered local communities the opportunity to enter endangered or dilapidated buildings (after local selection) into a 'national' contest, for viewers' votes, to win substantial Lottery funds for reconstruction or refurbishment. Central to the project was the need for management of 'local' and 'national' references informing the symbolic and economic commoditisation of each building. 'Placing' the past, through the selection of buildings and the narratives constructed in relation to them, required much the same duality as is at work in the piper's image in *Lilliput*. Buildings not in the Home Counties required to be framed as differentiated in terms of cultural geography and local history, so that they might offer sufficient interest and entertainment, formally presented within discourses of travel and tourism. Yet *Restoration*'s discursive practice requires the mediation of all 'oth-erness' such that 'local' and 'regional' particularities are wholly encompassed by an established national context within which to understand 'British' heritage. A building on Orkney requires to be at once relatively exotic, local and particular, and simultaneously to participate in a British heritage which includes a swimming baths in Manchester.

The fourteenth-century Portencross Castle sits between the small Ayrshire town of West Kilbride (about thirty miles southwest of Glasgow) and the Hunterston A and B nuclear power stations (the former now being decommissioned). The castle is roughly five miles north of the mini-conurbation of Saltcoats, Stevenston and Ardrossan (which contains significant multiple deprivation). *Restoration* visited the site in 2004, constructing a very different topography and cultural geography. The television sequence begins with a shot of the presenter in hilly terrain next to the Faslane nuclear base, relatively distant from West Kilbride, but apparently selected to initiate a military motif, beginning with glamorous *Top Gun*-style shots (with musical theme) of military helicopters and jet fighters (preceded by standard references to mountain, heather and 'endless vistas of glittering water'). We learn that all Britain's nuclear weapons are kept here because of the particularities of Scotland's access to the Atlantic.

The narrative then moves from Scottish, to British, back to Scottish military history in an almost undetectable slippage, the nuclear deterrent becoming an element in the continuity of Scottish defences of the Clyde estuary:

> The Clyde has in fact long been viewed as a vital strategic sea route. Even today it's home to the Faslane naval base. All of Britain's nuclear weapons are kept here because it's the ideal location for nuclear submarines to slink out into the Atlantic Ocean. But the military importance of the Clyde to the Scots is hardly a modern invention. And it's hardly surprising that as early as 1360 they decided to build a defensive watchtower to keep an eye on the sea routes favoured by the invaders.

This statement simultaneously conflates and confuses Faslane's Scottish and British dimensions. It also foreshortens Scottish history, since it had occurred to natives of Scotland to build coastal fortifications against invaders perhaps 1500 years before the Battle of Largs between the Scots and King Haco's invading Norwegians, which latter event occurred very near Portencross in 1263. Someone must have already built a watchtower there too or else the Scots (who won) would not even have known that the Norwegians were approaching. (As it happens Faslane, unlike Portencross, is in Argyll, which, having more coastline than France, required sea fortifications everywhere.)

A difficulty within London institutions, when defining the values attaching to Scotland's status within the UK, both preceded the Union and has more recently comprised a broader tendency to which media institutions, in some respects, merely conform. In *Restoration*, Scotland is a site for cultural visits, but an edition of 2004 focused upon one of Scotland's own explorers,

Dr John Rae. There is a developing history of the construction of a 'Scottish national' position on exploration (and indeed on science) from the first half of the nineteenth century. This position operated, however, within specific understandings of Britishness, and of Anglo–Scottish relations (Lewis-Jones 2002; Keighren 2005). Whether within the institutions of the admiralty, or of commerce and science, such Scottish figures conformed to British establishment habits and discourses of their time. Despite that, privileged institutions including the Royal Navy, *The Times* newspaper, and establishment pillars such as the Royal Geographical Society could, where necessary, construct a distinction between those who should be held at a distance (literally and figuratively) and those understood to be 'their own' (Burnett and Burnett 2004).

This is most strikingly exemplified in the media *cause célèbre* of the English explorer Sir John Franklin's ill-fated Arctic expedition of 1845 (fashionably determined to claim for Britain the fabled northwest passage from Atlantic to Pacific). Private allegations of an expeditionary party doomed (for various reasons) to failure were eventually to be coupled with a public outcry over the 'fate of Franklin's men'. After several search parties had been dispatched in 1848 and afterwards, it was subsequently alleged through news accounts that the men had not only perished unnecessarily but in a desperate attempt to survive had 'resorted to cannibalism'. Rae investigated the disaster soon after the event and unwittingly became the public bearer of the news. His report to his employers, the Hudson's Bay Company, contained descriptions of the men's fate provided by 'Esquimaux' (Inuit) who had discovered the bodies of the Franklin party and attested to cannibalism (an allegation subsequently validated by forensic testing decades later).

A letter of Rae's to that effect was published, without consent, in *The Times*. The ensuing squall was considerable. The media of the day refused to support such a slur, yet made much of running the story. Spurred on not least by Franklin's widow, newspapers including *The Times* and journals like Dickens's *Household Words* printed much on the topic of the Franklin story, debating the integrity of those involved, most notably focusing on Rae as the deliverer of the Franklin narrative, attacking the morality of the indigenous people and disparaging Rae (McGoogan 2001; Lewis-Jones 2002; Shu-chuan Yan 2006). Dickens himself, writing in *Household Words* in 1854, leaves little doubt that he finds Rae's conclusions to be ill-judged. But Dickens was a consummate media professional of his time and able to work the story more than one way to his own advantage as a public figure; and he magnanimously absolves Rae of blame, even for continuing to believe in the Inuit account ('the word of a savage is not to be taken for it; firstly, because he is a liar . . .', Dickens 1854: 392) noting among other compliments to Rae that readers should be 'proud of him as an Englishman' (1854: 361). Rae's reputation, however, failed to recover from less balanced assessments.

While Dickens was to observe in the same piece that 'we believe every savage to be in his heart covetous, treacherous, and cruel' (1854: 362), Rae's affinity with the Inuit – in his time he was thought to have 'gone native' – stands out in strong contrast.[12] His capacity to move beyond the ethnocentrism of his time is forever preserved in the remarkable form taken by his sculpted figure on the monument in St Magnus Cathedral in Kirkwall, displaying Rae as ever the fieldman, clothed in his Arctic work-gear, with his rifle, as though dozing after reading the book on which his rifle rests. Here is a man at one with his Arctic environment, yet reclaimed at the centre of his Orkney homeland (Burnett and Burnett 2004). Having lived until he was eighty, Rae died without a knighthood, quite exceptionally for an explorer of great achievement, not having been the beneficiary of an inclusiveness of vision to match his own.

In 2004, *Restoration* visited the Rae family home in Orkney, the Hall of Clestrain, in Orphir. As with Portencross, the question clearly arose for the producers of how best to construct the story of the house for the TV audience. *Restoration* combines two accessible sub-narratives. First, the history of this ruined private building acquires some personalisation, leading to an account of John Rae and his childhood at Clestrain, the biographical account of a boyhood life nurturing an ability for seafaring, exploration and an identity with 'the North', to explain Rae's later Arctic adventures.[13]

But this story in some respects competes with a separate cultural history of the House itself. The Hall of Clestrain is presented as an example of 'Georgian reach' to the 'remote' and 'unbelievable' (as one of the presenters puts it) location of Orkney. The interface of the local-national, or periphery-centre axis with the process of memorialising is demonstrated by the correspondence between the 'improbability' of this architectural gem so far to the north, and the 'remoteness' of Rae's achievement to the 'nation' – just as his exploits and their accounts were, in his own lifetime, situated at the margins, sometimes in clear opposition to an Anglo-British discourse and practice of exploration.

What we have seen of the Portencross story already demonstrates some uncertainties in the account of Scottish and British history emerging from London-based media output. However, the narrative which follows the Faslane introduction goes well beyond the merely peripheralising account of the Hall of Clestrain. It simply relocates Portencross wholesale within a fake construction designed to suggest the remote Highlands and Islands rather than the populated and much-visited Ayrshire coast (though the construction of the former as 'remote' is itself metrocentric). Portencross is televisually reconstructed as a castle of the Hebrides or the coasts of the northwest Highlands.

It is re-contextualised by shots of sea, and of mountains not in Ayrshire at all: the scene is set by a long lens shot of a mountain in Arran, an hour's boat trip away. All evidence of housing, industrial and recreation complexes on the surrounding Ayrshire coast is kept out of shot. Though Portencross and the coastal walk near it attract many visitors who drive there, and though the area was long ago assimilated within the recreational habits of many of the two million and more inhabitants of Greater Glasgow who can reach it in forty minutes, the programme's experts arrive by boat, constructing an imaginary sense of remoteness. *Restoration* on this occasion (it was more objective about its subjects in other instances) evidently required traditional Scottish spectacle to balance locations. But there must be cause for anxiety about the willingness of public-service broadcasters to treat localities outside London and the Home Counties with this degree of insouciance. This tendency has a long history. Part of it, as already noted, is about institutions.

There is a broader question illustrated by this fabrication, and it is one about the media, representation, and interest. The problems at the core of the 'nations and regions' policy adopted by the BBC, and other organisations, are the institutional counterparts of the difficulties evident in the regional vocabulary of television output. The 'nations and regions' tactic ('nations and regions' means 'not London') is a response from institutions reluctant to devolve real power, which construct this offering as a means to retain control in London. 'Nations and regions' proponents (including the regulator Ofcom) have traditionally been uncomfortable about real divergence across the UK. Regional cooking, local wildlife and folk culture are welcome as constituting difference, but ideological and political difference unnerve the ambassadors of the nations and regions policy. The contradictions at the heart of *Restoration's* treatment of locality partly mirror the asymmetrical relationships connecting media power and media output in Britain. *Restoration* was a series of visits (and thus highly characteristic) to the British regions from London, visits which generally comprise a one-way ideological and representative process, in which distance is also a one-way phenomenon, *from* London.

Alternatives to this exterior view do not need to be imagined: even a very modest indigenous approach to Scotland, such as Scottish Television's rural travelogue *Weir's Way*, which originated thirty years earlier, explored Scotland's internal dimensions both geographically and historically while aligning Scotland quite naturally with a larger world. Weir on one occasion visits Berwick Castle, for example, his narrative quietly suggesting the European dimensions and large scale of Berwick's history, reminding us of how drastically certain lengthy continuities within Scotland's wider identities have been obscured from present experience. The long-running BBC Scotland television series *Eorpa* has managed the difficult feat of using the Gaelic medium to thrive as the UK's most cosmopolitan current affairs programme. There is a divide of radical proportions between the Scotland of these indigenous programmes and the Scotland mediated by London.

All the while – and it is a matter of no small importance at a time when the relative economic power of London has further increased, and when competition among cities and regions in the UK to win investment is fierce – the BBC continues to market London nationally and internationally as though it were part of its mission. The Corporation's London-centric nature has seamlessly absorbed digital broadcasting, with offerings on BBC News 24 like *Dateline London* to place alongside the constant flow of images of London news locations. Streams of London-focused cultural programming on BBC Four Television are only periodically interrupted by visits to remote areas like Liverpool and Newcastle, often with an air of self-conscious adventure which seems perennially renewed. (Experiments by London broadcast producers with that most difficult of commodities for the BBC, the English regional accent, tend to favour caricature; but it is true that Scots broadcasters fare better, though often on radio.) Meanwhile, the Scots and Welsh have to assimilate endless references to 'the capital' with a sense of plurality never dreamt of in London.[14]

Sometimes parallel to the interest of public institutions, media industries in the private sector raise additional questions of purpose, which can include a more relentless focus on profit (representation solely with economic purpose) and, where the press is concerned, sometimes also the political will of proprietors and editors. In the world of professional politics, the issue of devolution of media matters to Holyrood, reserved in devolution legislation to Westminster, has been defended by Scottish Labour and is under attack by the SNP, and is therefore a matter of party political contention. Meanwhile, the fact that parts of the Scottish media in the private sector can still be considered Scottish in any sense is often a matter either of contingency, or belief, or both; in other words, where they are so it is only through circumstance, and to determine whether in reality they are or not often requires argument.

It was, however, noted earlier that indigenous cultural production is not linked in any predictable way with patterns of representation. Ideological processes can work to bring external value regimes to indigenous products. In both film and television it has not always been easy to distinguish economic forces from ideological forces in the process of fashioning Scottish screen products which can find a receptive market. Nor is production in Scotland any guarantee of quality. For example, it is arguable whether Scotland has come close to producing one quality newspaper with the substance of *The Irish Times*. It is true that Scotland has maintained the production of four regional dailies with broadsheet origins, as well as producing two serious Sunday newspapers, but a large question haunting demands for greater 'autonomy' for the Scottish media is one of quality.

Scotland exports media professionals, media entrepreneurs, and, by way of takeover by external companies, a number (not all) of its media businesses. This leaves a critical-mass question surrounding indigenous creativity, professionalism and production. The complex processes of globalisation, specifically of the cultural dimensions of nations, have been impacting upon Scotland in distinct ways. There are in particular very complicated patterns of cultural interchange with England, which seem to exhibit both increasing distance and proximity. Among the consequences are that (for example) if Scottish newspapers are not to their readers' satisfaction, then these readers will increasingly read London titles. This has co-existed with increasing demands for political autonomy and an increased sense of cultural separation. These developments are in accord with what we know of postmodern consumer behaviour, in which identities and choices are increasingly laid out like items on a delicatessen counter. (In Scotland, alas, grim inequalities exempt many from entering the store.)

CONCLUSION: FUTURE MEDIATION OF THE WORLD'S BEST SMALL COUNTRY

Weather aside, Scotland, like a fine malt, is a connoisseur's delight – a complex mix of history, culture and arts, festivals galore, feisty people and a wild and beautiful landscape – it should be savoured slowly. (*The Travel Book*: 345)

It is not difficult to misrepresent Scotland, and its representation has often been analysed selectively, too. When this is added to ethnocentric or otherwise ideological accounts of Scottish culture and history (in which anglocentric versions are often to the fore), the resulting discursive knots can be hard to disentangle. The available representations of Scotland form far too complex a range to be subject to careless generalisations. For such a very small country, Scotland has seemed both heavily and contradictorily productive of myth (Harvie 2002; Gifford and Riach 2004), at its most extreme being simultaneously the best and worst small country in the world.[15]

Now, however, the question for small national cultures is of visibility, not least to themselves, but also to others, and for a mixture of cultural, political, economic and psychological reasons. Though theoretically the multiple platforms of the digital media world ought to accommodate specialised requirements alike of consumers, producers and communities, digital space does not necessarily work to favour the needs of cultural geographies associated with small nations. 'Narrowcasting' for some specific taste communities (such as for sport, pornography or popular music) can produce revenue, proving commercially attractive (though spare bandwidth is thereby used to replicate, rather than vary, provision). But amidst massive digital expansion it is already evident that locality – depending on factors including critical mass – may lose its viability. Whereas it is commercially attractive, for example, to provide Asian television programming for large dispersed audiences from the Indian sub-continent, so that ethnic minorities in the UK and elsewhere may receive provision in their own languages, this is a function of the size of the audience and of specific cultural needs. Across the board, Scottish audiences already consume much of their media product, despite exceptions, from outside Scotland. One challenge posed to indigenous cultural producers in small nations is therefore related to critical audience mass in two ways, through size and preference.

Scotland will continue, probably, to export cultural commodities, including screen product, crucial for economic reasons of profit, infrastructural growth and employment. But it will be a struggle. The viability of media product which contains Scottish cultural themes and contents raises even harder questions (though landscape spectacle and specialised forms of quaintness will no doubt continue to offer their specific appeal). And it is on the Internet, and in mobile phone content, and within new and unpredictable forms of media convergence generally, that the relationship between representation and locality will really be tested. What will be the local contents available on future telephony-based product, for example? Amidst media consumption patterns of the future, the degree of visibility of traditional forms like television (as presently understood) is unpredictable. John Steinbeck's oft-cited riposte to Jackie Kennedy: 'You talked of Scotland as a lost cause and that is not true. Scotland is an unwon cause'[16] is still true in the age of globalisation, devolution and digital expansion.[17] The future role of the media in that process, however the cause turns out, is unclear. The media are not the only carriers of cultural identity, not by far, nor can they deliver their functions as guarantors of local democracy or political transparency in a predictable manner. However, they are politically and culturally very important, and their local dimension is crucial. The Scottish voice is as likely to get lost in the clamour of the digital age as to be heard through new forms of specialised provision. A Scottish media apparatus of sorts exists, unevenly viable across specific media, but its Scottishness is fragile. As with the rest of the apparatus of nationhood, there are large questions raised here, about political will, democracy, empowerment, accountability, resources and identity. As with other aspects of our heritage, there are important specific challenges, when faced with the risk of irreversible loss, to engage not only in conservation, but constantly in enterprise and reconstruction.

NOTES

1. The humorous and satirical magazine published from 1841 to 2002.
2. A small-format UK monthly magazine published from 1937 to 1960 with content ranging from humour to serious arts criticism and short stories, and with much photographic content.
3. These tasting notes refer to a thirty-year-old Macallan single malt.
4. Tasting notes for Barr's Irn-Bru, reprinted from Lonely Planet's *Edinburgh*.
5. On Irvine Welsh's 'defence of the fish supper and the deep-fried haggis'.
6. Published weekly by W. Weatherston & Sons, Glasgow, 1881–98; these samples are from the mid-point of its existence in 1890.
7. Arthur Severn: painter, friend of Ruskin, son of the painter and close friend of Keats, Joseph Severn.
8. How much more Mr Quiz would have revelled in a local incarnation of the Crane brothers, fighting over opera seats at the Theatre Royal! In his 'Advice to Cads', he affirms (25 July) that 'Glasgow flourished ere ever it saw you', requesting good behaviour of the anti-social when on visits beyond the city; and advising that 'you represent only a section of this community, and that, perhaps, the most con-temptible' (p. 206).
9. In fact, this pronunciation is not confirmed by further analysis of James Doohan's *oeuvre*.
10. The ability of Scottish TV producers to supply network content of high enough quality was controversially challenged by former BBC Chairman and ITV chief executive Michael Grade in 2007, echoed by the Director-General of the BBC.
11. Though there is a mini-tradition of Scottish film which finds in Europe part of its cultural landscape (Blain 2008).
12. Indeed his legacy has been his exceptional vision of Inuit indigenous knowledge.
13. Rae's autobiography (*Dr John Rae's Autobiography*, unpublished manuscript, Scott Polar Research Institute, ms 787/1) details his island upbringing, positioning this as crucial to his character development and his exceptional capacity for physical challenge (also addressed in his account, 'Roughing It', Boy Life in Orkney, *Orkney Herald*, 16 February 1887, Orkney Archives).
14. This would have been doubly a source of anguish to Mr Quiz in Glasgow, who rather assumed that his city was Scotland's real capital.
15. Scottish airports having first greeted arrivals with the message that Scotland is the 'best small country in the world', it was thereafter dubbed 'the worst small country in the world' by sections of the media in 2007 when it came at the foot of a league comparing performance indicators in small countries in Western Europe.
16. In a letter of 28 February 1964. An expanded quotation offers a fuller perspective on the matter. 'I have been thinking about what you said regarding lost causes. And it is such a strange subject. It seems to me that the only truly lost causes are those which win. Only then do they break up into mean little fragments. You talked of Scotland as a lost cause and that is not true. Scotland is an unwon cause.' Steinbeck continues, now referring to the United States: 'Probably the greatness

of our country resides in the fact that we have not made it and are still trying' (Steinbeck and Wallsten 1975: 795). This framing of the matter makes the prospect of perpetual struggle seem relatively attractive.

17. By the time Gordon Brown became Prime Minister, and Alex Salmond, First Minister of Scotland, 300 years after the Union (and 100 years after *Punch* satirically reflected on how little Scots and Scottish politicians cared for repatriation) the pursuit of another 'unwon cause' had begun to make its force felt in calculations about the future of the UK – namely that of England.

REFERENCES

Banks, I. (2003), *Raw Spirit: In Search of the Perfect Dram*, London: Century.

Blain, N. (2008), 'The visibility of small countries: the Scottish dimension in film and television', in C. Harvie and K. Veitch (eds), *Scottish Life and Society: A Compendium of Scottish Ethnology*, vol. 8: *Transport, Communications and the Media*, Edinburgh: John Donald, forthcoming.

Burnett, K. A. and R. Burnett (2004), 'Scottish polar exploration and the representation of national heroic endeavour (1880–1914)', paper delivered to Visual Culture and Taste in Late Victorian and Edwardian Britain Conference, Centre for Visual Culture in Britain, University of Northumbria, July 15–16.

Dickens, C. (1854), 'The Lost Arctic Voyagers', *Household Words*, 2 and 9 December.

Gibbons, F. (2003), 'Writer of *Trainspotting* to take up cudgels for deep-fried Mars bars in culinary book with Scottish slant', *The Guardian*, Tuesday, 19 August 2003.

Gifford, D. and A. Riach (eds) (2004), *Scotlands: Poets and the Nation*, Manchester: Carcanet Press, and Edinburgh: The Scottish Poetry Library.

Harvie, C. (2002), *Scotland: A Short History*, Oxford: Oxford University Press.

Keighren, I. M. (2005), 'Of poles, pressmen, and the newspaper public: reporting the Scottish National Antarctic Expedition', 1902–4, *Scottish Geographical Journal* 121 (2): 203–18.

Lewis-Jones, H. (2002), *Peripheral Vision: Aspects of Science in the Canadian Arctic, 1840–1890*, University of Cambridge, unpublished M.Phil thesis.

McGoogan, K. (2001), *Fatal Passage: The Untold Story of John Rae, the Arctic Adventurer Who Discovered the Fate of Franklin*, Toronto: HarperCollins.

Lilliput magazine vol. 26, nos 1–8, issues 151–8, January–August 1950.

Punch, or The London Charivari magazine, vol. CXXXII, January–June 1907.

Quiz magazine, March 1890–August 1890.

Scott, W. [1814] (1860) *Waverley*, Edinburgh: Adam and Charles Black.

Steinbeck, E. and R. Wallsten (eds) (1975), *Steinbeck: A Life in Letters*, London: William Heinemann.

The Travel Book: A Journey Through Every Country in the World (2005), Victoria, Australia: Lonely Planet Publishing.

Yan, Shu-chuan (2006), 'Voyages and visions: imag(in)ing the Arctic in the Victorian periodical, 1850s–1870s', *NTU Studies in Language and Literature* 53, no. 16 (December, 2006), 53–82.

2

Scots, English and Community Languages in the Scottish Media

JOHN CORBETT

The story of Gaelic in the modern Scottish media can be presented as the coherent narrative of a relatively successful campaign to win acknowledgement and support, from the 'condescending paternalism' of the *BBC Handbooks* to the Gaelic Language Act of 2005 (Cormack, this volume). The story of Scotland's other languages in the media is a less coherent one, complicated as it is by a number of factors. As the majority language of contemporary Scotland, English requires neither definition nor legal support; its nature, status and role are taken for granted. Scots, if taken as the general term for a set of language varieties that are, given goodwill, mutually intelligible with English, is not so easily presented as a single, distinctive language whose users are entitled to linguistic rights. Its presence in the media is diffuse and ranges from 'broad Scots', that is, densely textured regional or social varieties served up in drama or light entertainment, to the token phrase and mock Caledonian accents adopted by transatlantic imports such as *Star Trek's* 'Scotty' and *The Simpsons*' 'Groundskeeper Willie'. Although they are more easily defined than Scots, community languages such as Urdu, Chinese, and increasingly Polish have weaker claims to being historical factors in the construction of a Scottish identity, and the presence of these languages is often seen less as a resource to be nurtured than as simply a communicative obstacle to be overcome (Herrington and Kendall 2005). This chapter can only, then, offer a sketch of the complex relationship of Scots and English in the modern Scottish media, and touch fleetingly on the rise in provision for speakers of community languages.

SCOTS AND ENGLISH

The story of Scots in the media has been obscured for a number of reasons, one of which is alluded to above. Historically, Scots is distinguished from English by a distinctive vocabulary, grammar and accent. However, much vocabulary and grammar is shared between Scots and English, to the extent that the two language varieties are usually mutually intelligible. In addition, since the late sixteenth century, there has been a marked shift in Scotland towards the adoption of English conventions for formal writing, a process strengthened by the gradual development of written, standard English and the rise of mass education. Since the eighteenth century, southern English norms have also modified the speech of the Scottish upper and middle classes to the extent that a 'polite' middle-class Scottish accent emerged (Jones 1995). By the turn of the twentieth century, broad Scots writing was confined to literature and some journalism (Donaldson 1986), and broad Scots speech was the domain of the rural peasantry and urban working classes. Since the decline in the functional range of written Scots predated the rise of a standard written English, no widely accepted and taught standard variety of Scots developed. Scots now exists largely as the sum of regional and social varieties spoken by particular communities in Scotland, and in those areas of Northern Ireland where speech patterns were strongly influenced by the 'plantation' of Scottish economic migrants in the seventeenth century (Jones 1997; Montgomery 2005). Nevertheless, broad Scots remains a distinctive marker of Scottish regional, social and national identity and, often, nationalist politics, although in Northern Ireland Ulster-Scots is generally taken to be a linguistic marker of the Unionist community.

Since the eighteeenth century there have been regular 'vernacular revivals' or 'renaissances' in literary Scots, whose most famous proponents – Robert Burns, James Orr, Walter Scott, Robert Louis Stevenson, Hugh MacDiarmid – have alternated between broad Scots and English in their published work. Consequently, Scots in modern times can be seen less as a separate language from English, though Scots language activists argue otherwise (for example, Purves 2002), and more as a set of regionally and socially diverse dialects of English, with restricted social functions. Furthermore, because of the gradual association of Scots with the urban working classes and the rural peasantry, and possibly because the use of broad Scots can signify resistance to the Anglophone establishment, many traditional Scots features can be caricatured merely as English slang. The presence of Scots in the print media ranges from the totemic use of an individual Scots word in an otherwise English article, to the occasional feature article written wholly in broad Scots. In the broadcast media the presence of Scots can range in intensity from the minimal presence of a 'polite' middle-class Scottish accent, almost indistinguishable from English Received Pronunciation, to a highly differentiated literary medium charac- terised by a dense use of distinctive vocabulary and grammatical features.

SCOTS IN THE PRINT MEDIA

In his revisionist account of Scottish fiction in the nineteenth century, Donaldson (1986: 148) makes large claims for the cultural importance of the Scottish press, arguing, for example, that in the period between 1860 and 1900 the press published 'more than 5,000 full-length Scottish novels'. Donaldson asserts that for half a century the popular press dealt with the full spectrum of contemporary life through features and fiction, much of which was written in Scots; a selection is given in Donaldson (1989). Other critics remain sceptical of the value of this literary revival (for example, Gifford 1988: 236) and an accurate assessment of its significance remains elusive, partly since the mater- ial that Donaldson champions is still largely unexplored, and partly because the source materials were not designed to be other than ephemeral, and so little found its way into book form.

In the later twentieth century, serialised fiction in the local press was less common. Where used as the vehicle for communication, broad Scots in the mainstream press in central Scotland tends now to be confined to discussions of its own linguistic status. Papers with a strong regional identity more regu- larly carry features, poetry and fiction in a broad Scots specifically associated with that place, such as Robbie Shepherd's weekly columns in Doric for the *Press and Journal* (a sample of these is anthologised in Shepherd 2006). Since the latter part of the twentieth century, print outlets for poetry and prose in Scots have been confined largely to the 'little magazines' such as *Lallans* and *Chapman*.

Isolated Scots linguistic features are used more generally in the Scottish press (Douglas 2000; 2008). They tend to crop up in feature articles, sports report- ing, humorous columns and diary entries, rather than in main news articles or main editorials, and they serve several functions:

- Markers of readership's class, regional and/or national identity, depending on the context. A tabloid newspaper will use a particular set of Scots colloquialisms, while the broadsheets will use a different set to bond with its readership. Some expressions, like the universal 'wee', are shared between the two and are also frequently used in the English press, often to indicate 'Scottishness', particularly in colloca- tions like 'wee dram', as in 'A wee dram cuts obesity risk? It's not that simple' in *The Guardian* (17 December 2005).

- Markers of communities of practice; for example, Scots terms associated with football are occasionally used in sports sections to ally the newspaper with its readership, for example 'England sunk by Batty's blooter' in the *Daily Record* (1 July 1998).
- Markers of others' social identity. Colloquial Scots can be used as a means of indicating, or often mocking, out-group stereotypes, as in the *Daily Mail* headline (7 December 2004): 'By yon manky banks: National Park is a rubbish-strewn haven for city neds, say locals'.

To summarise, where the Scots language is found in the print media in Scotland today, it reflects the nation's ambivalence about its status and its value in performing functions other than marking regional, social and national identity. Scots continues to serve the latter functions, not on the whole by producing accurate and consistent representations of regional, social and national speech patterns, but by contributing shibboleths that can either be read by the readership as celebrating their own identities, or as mocking the identities of out-groups in the community, out-groups characterised as 'teuchters', 'keelies', 'schemies' or 'neds'. Where a more extended use of Scots is offered, it tends to be restricted to the spheres of poetry, fictional prose, the discussion of language issues, or light-hearted or humorous columns, often by popular entertainers.

SCOTS IN THE BROADCAST MEDIA (RADIO)

The advent of radio in 1923 allowed listeners the potential of direct access to Scottish voices, rather than to their representation in written form. However, as has been well documented, the early years of public broadcasting in the UK were characterised by the promotion – by a Scottish director-general, John Reith – of a homogeneous southeastern pronunciation as the typical 'BBC accent'. The resilient mythology that a single variety of language guarantees intelligibility, as articulated, for example, in Alford (1864), is evident in an apologia for the first fifteen years of the output of the 'Scottish Region', compiled and edited by the BBC's public relations officer, George Burnett. A contribution by a radio announcer, Aidan Thomson, addresses the language issue in a paternalistic fashion that is typical of the period and some time thereafter (Burnett 1938: 124):

> Now, the 'accent' question. We speak to all kinds of people who themselves speak all kinds of ways, and therefore are naturally in favour of their own way, tending to lump together all other ways as 'wrong'. But language is the instrument of communication: if you don't talk the same or nearly the same language as your auditor, your ideas will not reach him.

We cannot have an announcer for each variety of Scottish speech, so we must look for something which will be intelligible to everybody and will displease as few people as possible. In practice, we try to find and use a lowest common denominator of educated Scottish speech.

If in the broadcast media, as in the news and editorials pages of the Scottish print media, the registers of power were denied to Scots speakers, there were still places where local and literary varieties of Scots were welcome and even celebrated. In August 1923, the first Scottish radio play broadcast was a version of *Rob Roy*, produced by and starring R. E. Jeffrey. Scots voices featured in other genres, such as the Scottish Children's Hour's 'series of trips on an imaginary train', the 'Radio Express' (Christine Orr, in Burnett 1938: 96). As with the print media, then, in the early decades of radio broadcasting there were spaces for the Scots language in features, entertainment and drama. Indeed, it might be fair to say that Scottish radio drama output during much of the twentieth century parallels newspaper literary production of the latter half of the nineteenth century as a site of largely neglected cultural activity. This neglect might be partly due to the fact that in the context of a largely Anglophone output, the Scots element is so small that it can easily be overlooked. A post-war report into the breadth and quality of radio output in 1947 and early 1948 estimated that 'the amount of "Scottish Time" on the Scottish Home Service . . . over a particular year . . . is according to one computation rather less than one-fifth of the total listening time' (Highet 1949: 15). From the perspective of the twenty-first century, a Scottish broadcaster which devotes even 20 per cent of its time to Scottish-produced and themed programmes might be viewed rather less critically than the BBC was then. Furthermore, increasingly today the relatively few broadcasts featuring Scots speech can easily be lost in the flood of Anglophone voices on the airwaves.

A metropolitan perspective on the relationship of the centre to the 'Regions' (which, despite protests, included Scotland) was given in 1956 by then Head of Drama (Sound), Val Gielgud. While generally supporting the principle that drama with a local origin should be produced locally, he goes on to argue that dramatists whose work is of a high enough quality – such as Bridie – must be considered 'National not Regional' and so their work should be produced in London (Gielgud 1956: 128–9). The turf wars between London and BBC Scotland for the cream of Scottish drama would continue well into the 1970s (Hetherington 1992: 20–3).

Even so, following the initial airing of its version of *Rob Roy*, the BBC broadcast programmes that used one or another variety of Scots to a greater or lesser extent. Often the Scots was confined to peripheral, working-class characters such as the maid in James Bridie's otherwise middle-class play, *The Switchback* (Bridie 1942: 20–1). Other plays and adaptations, such as Bridie's adaptation of Chekhov's *The Proposal*, 'transposed' into Scots, used a broader idiom more consistently in what is essentially a fifteen minute sketch about a bickering couple on the road to marriage. More of a sustained impact was made by *The McFlannels*, an immensely popular comedy series about a Glasgow family, written by Helen W. Pryde. It began in 1939 and continued through the 1940s, each episode being broadcast three times per week during its seasonal runs. Much of its success lay in its use of lively Glaswegian speech, as in the opening of the second episode 'The Flitting' (Pryde 1939: 1):

> WILLIE: Here, is there nae sign o' that coalman yet? Folk'll soon no' get intae the close, it's that bung-fu' o' oor furnicher.
>
> PETER: Here 'e is, daddy. Here's the coalman! Here's the coalman! Here's . . .
>
> WILLIE: Well, you come doon affa that jawbox or ye'll be fa'in through the wundy. Come on, noo, Peter, when ye're tell't.
>
> PETER: Can Ah get carryin' somethin'?
>
> WILLIE: Mebbe. We'll see. Jist you keep oot the road for a wee.

If rare, other dramatic voices in Scots were not wholly absent from the airwaves. *Ferm Deem* by Jessie Kesson, broadcast in 1948, was one of numerous radio scripts she wrote over thirty years, many of which had a strong Doric flavour. *Ferm Deem* was further distinguished by presenting the playwright in the part of Rose, a young farm-servant taken in from the poor-house by an unsympathetic couple, Mr and Mrs Dobie (Kesson 1948: 4):

> MRS DOBIE: Rose! Are ye beddit yet? Rose! (*Mrs Dobie opens bedroom door*) Na! Na! nor beddit! Nae wunner she cannae rise in the mornins . . . (*walks away to confab with Burnie on Rose's defects*) Sair's my trauchle wi' her! Deems! They're a' the same . . . gweed for naethin' lumps . . . I've nivir got ane tae suit me yet! I canna think fats come ower . . .
>
> BURNIE: (*shortly*) Weel, weel, dinna harp on aboot her! Jist ye get rid o' her. She's a skookin' futtret o' a craittur onywye . . . I canna think fat wye ye ivir fee'd her at a'!

In 1950, Robert Kemp, himself an accomplished playwright in Scots as well as a BBC producer, wrote and produced *The Guid Scots Tongue*, a twenty-four-part series that invited listeners to 'brush up on your knowledge of Scots words and phrases'. In the programmes, a refined, fictional character, 'Jean', played by actress Joan Fitzpatrick, travelled the country, learning about the history and local varieties of Scots, by way of explanations, readings and scripted interviews with characters fictional and real, historical and contemporary. The series was repeated, with some variation in content, in 1954.

Despite Highet's reservations about the quantity – and quality – of the Scottish output in the late 1940s, the ten years after the end of the Second World War were later perceived by BBC radio veterans as a 'golden age' (McDowell 1992: 88–9). Throughout the latter half of the twentieth century, the role of radio as a provider of a full range of mass entertainment diminished, and it began gradually to provide niche markets with specialised services and targeted audiences. There were consequently fewer resources for radio drama in Scots. Even so, a celebratory season of the previous decade of Scottish drama, broadcast on BBC Radio Scotland weekly between October 1980 and January 1981, could combine new productions and repeats of theatrical adaptations (Oliver 1980).

By the time BBC Radio Scotland was launched in 1978, it had to compete not only with television but also with BBC community stations and commercial ones. The range of language varieties now heard on Radio Scotland covers everything from Scots-accented English to broad Scots. If there are fewer of the descendants of the patrician tones of Aidan Thomson and his ilk, an educated Central Scottish accent is still preferred for news announcements and current affairs. Reporters, commentators and contributors to phone-in programmes and other *vox pop* segments, however, have a wider range of regional and social pronunciations and it is in these types of broadcast that the nation arguably comes closest to hearing itself speak in something approaching its actual diversity. Urban accents predominate in football programmes such as *Off the Ball*, but there are also notable broadcasters from the heartlands of regional Scots, such as Robbie Shepherd, who continues to fly the flag for Doric language and culture, and Cameron Stout, *Big Brother* victor, whose Orcadian accent is equally distinctive. A regular, rich diet of Orcadian can be heard on Radio Orkney, which, like Radio Shetland and other Scottish local opt-out stations, broadcasts daily.[1] However, Cameron Stout notwithstanding, the distinctive language of the northern islands is seldom heard in the Scottish mainstream media.

Indeed, only a handful of programmes over the past five decades have followed the lead of Kemp's radio series on *The Guid Scots Tongue* and systematically sought to bring broad Scots to the mainstream radio schedules. In Scotland these have been largely associated with the producer and writer Billy Kay, whose *Odyssey*, an award-winning oral history series about working-class Scots, was broadcast on Radio Scotland, and also on the UK network, in the early 1980s. It was followed by a series dedicated to the history of the language, *The Scots Tongue* (which had a television counterpart, *The Mither Tongue*; see below), a series of conversations in Scots, *Amang Guid Company*, and a number of other programmes that often had a connection with Scottish literature, Scots language and oral traditions. Kay's broadcasting is distinguished by his willingness to use Scots himself as a narrator and interviewer, a trait he shares with Conal Gillespie and Liam Logan, presenters of BBC Radio Ulster's *A Kist o Wurds*, a half-hour magazine programme celebrating Ulster-Scots culture. Its website blurb gives a taste of the density of the Scots on offer: 'Gie yer lug tae a kist fu o yairns, music, wittins an crack bi Ulster Scots folk oan the shew that's the hame o the hamely tongue.'[2] It is ironic that, at the time of writing, the radio programme with the most consistent track record of using broad Scots over the past few years is produced and broadcast in Northern Ireland.

SCOTS IN TELEVISION AND FILM

The shift from radio to television that gathered momentum from the mid 1950s onwards saw greater constraints on writers and producers wishing to make pro-grammes in Scots. Since they are more expensive to produce, television pro-grammes have to reach a larger audience than radio programmes, and so the lack of a widely accepted, homogeneous identity for Scots can be seen as one factor in its relative lack of visibility on television. Where television pro-grammes with Scots content were broadcast in the 1950s and 1960s, they adopted the low-risk strategy of following formats that had already proved suc-cessful in theatre, music hall and radio. In the 1970s, there was a blossoming of television plays in Scots that had been adapted from theatrical productions, such as Bill Bryden's *Willie Rough*, John Byrne's *The Slab Boys*, John McGrath's *The Cheviot, the Stag and the Black, Black Oil*, and Robert Kemp's adaptation of Molière's *The Laird o' Grippy*, starring Rikki Fulton. The tradition was later followed by Scottish Television with its adaptation of the popular standard *The Steamie*, by Tony Roper. In this respect, television was mimicking the pattern set by successful radio adaptations of Scottish theatrical drama (Oliver 1980). In more recent decades, work that includes some Scots, from a light sprinkling to a heavier dusting, continues to be adapted from canonical novels or suc-cessful contemporary fiction, like Robert Louis Stevenson's *Weir of Hermiston*, and Iain Banks's *The Crow Road*, or commissioned from writers with a strong literary pedigree, for example Irvine Welsh's *Wedding Belles*.

By the 1970s, BBC Scotland was in competition with better-resourced London-based production units who were responsible not only for the adapt-ation of McGrath's successful stage play, but also original television drama like Peter MacDougall's *Just Another Saturday* (Hetherington 1992: 20–3). Higher production values and the advent of Channel 4 in 1982 blurred the distinction between television drama and theatrical film. While space here is too limited to discuss the Scots language in film in detail, it is worth noting that from the 1980s, television companies have been closely involved in the co-financing of films that contain some distinctive Scots voices – for example, Scottish Television backed *A Sense of Freedom* and *The Big Man*, the BBC financed or co-financed other Peter McDougall productions, including *Down Where the Buffalo Go* (Dick 1990) and, more recently, the critically acclaimed *Ratcatcher* and *Red Road*. Among Channel 4's Scottish output were the adaptations of Jessie Kesson's *Another Time, Another Place* (which had previously been a successful radio play and novel), Gareth Wardell's play *Conquest of the South Pole* and of course, Irvine Welsh's best-seller *Trainspotting*. Given the stereotypical gritty realism associated with televised and filmed Scottish drama, most of the Scottish voices heard in films are more or less diluted versions of urban Central Scots. For North American audiences, this dilution was furthered by the dubbing of some theatrical and DVD versions. In *Trainspotting*, lexical substitutions for the American market included UK-wide terminology and slang, for example 'mail' for 'post' and 'girl' for 'bird'; Scots 'Ken' was dubbed as 'know' and 'smack' was even used for the less common U.S. slang, 'skag.'[3] The tension between authenticity and comprehensibility is an ongoing concern for productions that are shown outside Scotland. This concern intensified in 2005 when Ken Loach's *Sweet Sixteen* was shown with subtitles on national UK television, which resulted in viewers in Greenock seeing their own speech subtitled. The earlier theatrical release of this film in England had included subtitles in the first reel to make the audience 'comfortable' (Stein 2005).

While the idioms of urban districts such as Greenock or Leith do enjoy occasional airings, subtitled or not, more traditional or rural varieties of broad Scots are visible in fewer productions aimed at a mass market. Some opportunities for exposure were afforded by the picaresque adventures of the characters in John Byrne's two series for the BBC, *Tutti Frutti* and *Your Cheating Heart*. In the latter, for example, Frank and Cissie, the Glaswegian hero and heroine, encounter a Doric-speaking character, 'The Toad', a biker from the 'Loons of the Apocalypse' (Byrne 1990: 174–5). The scene plays on the stereotypical mutual incomprehensibility of different varieties of Scots:

THE TOAD: . . . I didna ken ye wur a Loon, ken.
FRANK: Yeh, right. [*To Cissie*] What's a 'Loonken'?
THE TOAD: [*Leering over Cissie*] Fit Chapter ye wi'?
CISSIE: [*To Frank*] You tell him.
FRANK : Chapter? Aw . . . er . . . The Devil-dogs . . . Carfin.
CISSIE : [*To The Toad*] Chuck oglin' us.
THE TOAD: [*To Frank*] Fit'd she say?
FRANK : [*Apologetically*] I think it's your after-shave. [*Sotto voce, to Cissie*]
D'you want us to die?

THE TOAD:	Ho!
	He leans forward and pokes Frank.
THE TOAD:	[*Close to Frank's face*] S'nae a bad-lookin' quine . . . if I ever loss the errial aff me sickle I'll ken far tae come till.
	He winks and swings off along the Waltzer.
CISSIE :	What'd he say?
FRANK:	Biker talk . . .

The language of rural Scotland has been an acknowledged source of humour at least since James VI of Scotland instructed his court poets on the fitness for comic poetry of *uplandis* or country speech in the late sixteenth century (Jack and Rozendaal 1997: 465). Over the past century, rural Scots speakers have been joined by working-class urban Scots-speaking characters as the butt of jokes in a string of television comedy programmes, several of which are discussed elsewhere in this volume. The best-known caricature of Glaswegian Scots is probably still the series of sketches that the entertainer Stanley Baxter performed on several television and radio series, 'Parliamo Glasgow'. In these sketches, 'The Professor' tutors the home audience in the pronunciation of Glaswegian expressions such as *Izat a marra on yer barra, Clara?* ('Is that a marrow on your barrow, Clara?'). The humour of 'Parliamo Glasgow' derives partly from its satire on the stiltedness of early television language programmes, and partly from the contrast between the ridiculous but euphonious Glaswegian expressions and their polite English equivalents.

In his poem sequence 'Unrelated Incidents', Tom Leonard condemns the regressive attitudes that demarcate 'the language of the gutter' from 'the language of the intellect'. He reserves particular contempt for those who would argue that only one language can be associated with truth, power and authority in programmes like 'The Six O'Clock News' (Leonard 1984: 86, 88). Leonard's satirical critique of comic Scots resonates with an anxiety that the success – both domestically and on the UK network – of series like the 1990s' *Rab C. Nesbitt* associates Scots speech too closely with comedy and, implicitly, trivialises it. On the other hand, part of the success of *Rab C. Nesbitt* lies in its protagonist's habitual undercutting of the affectations of such middle-class speakers of standard English as his relative 'Shug', the now-gentrified 'Hugh'. *Rab C. Nesbitt* also uses comedy to confront intransigent attitudes to language. In the episode 'Offski', for example, Rab visits London and lambasts its natives for finding the Australian of *Neighbours* comprehensible while his Govan accent leaves them perplexed. In one scene, his dialogue is subtitled in a fashion that both recalls the 'Parliamo Glasgow' sketches and anticipates the row over *Sweet Sixteen* (Pattison 1990).

Despite the skill with which comic creations like Rab C. Nesbitt raise serious concerns about linguistic prejudice, while Scots is restricted in genre, its speakers run the risk of being stereotyped and marginalised. In the sixteenth century, comic verse using *uplandis* speech co-existed with the use of broad Scots in a range of other literary and non-literary genres. The gradual reduction in the range of genres articulated through Scots, and the virtual elimination of the non-literary genres, functionally constrain the speech communities that continue to use a variety of Scots, and increase the danger of stereotyping. And when the dominant surviving genre is comedy, the line between celebration of the vitality of an idiom and the mockery of those who speak it is often a fine one.

Two non-comic genres that find some space for Scots-inflected voices, at least, are crime drama and soap operas. With a few exceptions, such as *Sutherland's Law*, a London-based BBC production following the adventures of a procurator fiscal in North Argyll, Scottish crime drama tends to fall into the 'urban realism' school, from Eddie Boyd's private eye series from the 1970s, *The View from Daniel Pike* starring Roddy McMillan, through the various incarnations of Glasgow-based *Taggart*, to the adaptations of Ian Rankin's Edinburgh-set *Rebus* novels. The Scots language, in these popular helpings of tartan *noir*, adds local colour, a dash of humour and hard-man threat: 'Pike, ya chantywrassler!' cries an unseen antagonist in the opening moments of 'Four Walls', an episode of *The View from Daniel Pike* (Boyd n.d.: 2). The dramatisations of M. C. Beaton's *Hamish Macbeth* in the mid-1990s adroitly combined elements of Kailyard, crime and comedy.

More folksy is the language of soaps and soap-influenced series, from the village life of *Dr Finlay's Casebook*, in its BBC and commercial manifestations, through the long-running *Take the High Road* (or, latterly, until its demise in 2003, *High Road*), to the picture-postcard, neo-Kailyard of *Monarch of the Glen*. By contrast, the transposition from rural Glendarroch, Glenbogle or Lochdubh to urban Shieldinch, the fictional locus of *River City*, which brings together a cast and characters of geographically and linguistically diverse origins, raised considerable practical issues. *River City*, launched in 2002, suffered from early criticism that its language was inauthentic, a problem that might have arisen from the lack of agreed conventions for writing Scots, and the consequent difficulty, in a genre that demands teamwork, of achieving consistency in the representation of Scottish characters' different varieties of speech (O'Donnell, this volume).

In the mid-1960s, Scots of a more literary register found its way on-screen in a modest number of programmes, such as a short series called *Poems and Places*, which featured photographs, taken by Alan Daiches, illustrating readings of poems commissioned from several Scottish poets of note. Adaptations remained a pillar of drama with a literary Scots flavour, with such productions as the perennial favourites *Weir of Hermiston*, *Rob Roy*, and *Huntingtower*. A highlight was Lewis Grassic Gibbon's trilogy, beginning with a serialisation of

Sunset Song (which had also enjoyed success as a radio drama in the 1940s) and continuing with *Cloud Howe* and *Grey Granite*. Grassic Gibbon's prose is marked by a lilting, poetic lyricism that gave a strong impression of authenticity while remaining accessible to non-Scots audiences (Corbett 2005), and this quality was evident also in the adaptations.

Following Robert Kemp's exploration of *The Guid Scots Tongue* on radio in the 1950s, there have been several television series specifically devoted to educating viewers about the history, status and prospects of Scots. In the 1980s, BBC Scotland's *The Mither Tongue* set a pattern later followed by *Scots: The Language of the People* (also BBC Scotland), *Haud Your Tongue* (Channel 4) and *Reid About Scots* (Scottish Television). These series were characterised by charismatic presenters – Billy Kay, Jimmy Reid and Carl MacDougall – touring the country and interviewing speakers of different Scots varieties, to a background chorus of talking heads. In 2005, BBC Wales spearheaded an ambitious UK-wide multimedia project, *Voices*,[4] across a range of platforms: television, radio and the web. Overall, the *Voices* project saw a systematic, if temporary, attempt to celebrate linguistic diversity in Scotland and the UK as a whole.[5]

COMMUNITY LANGUAGES IN THE SCOTTISH MEDIA

Punjabi, Urdu, English and Scots feature in the fictional narrative of Zaf, a Glasgow-based DJ whose last broadcast on Radio Chaandni forms the substance of Suhayl Saadi's debut novel, *Psychoraag* (2004). The novel is inspired by community radio stations given licences to transmit for temporary periods, such as Radio Ramadhan in Glasgow and Multi Ethnic (ME) FM based in Aberdeen. From modest beginnings, more permanent stations have grown, including Awaz FM, which 'serves the Asian population in Glasgow, broadcasting in Urdu, Punjabi and English delivering entertainment, news, local, national and community information in a bi-lingual format'.[6]

The relative lack of investment in money and expertise required to set up a temporary community radio station allows for niche marketing and a diversity of languages. One of the founders of Radio Ramadhan, Imran Alam, talks about relying on word of mouth to advertise the new station when it began, and deliberately varying the languages to capture specific groups of listeners:

> obviously there was a lot of non-English speaking, particularly women, living amongst the Muslim population in Glasgow, so we tried to change the timetable so we could get English, Arabic, Urdu and even in some cases Gujarati shows, or slots, onto the daily timetable. That way we could reach across to a wider audience.

To some extent, Asian audiences had been targeted by earlier bilingual mag-azine and music programmes, such as BBC Radio Scotland's *Eastern Echoes, Chinese Times* and *Ghetto Blasting* in the early to mid 1990s, as well as by locally produced newsletters and magazines; however, the advent of community licences has allowed members of the ethnic communities greater agency in har-nessing the broadcast media more fully to reflect the linguistic and cultural diversity of present-day Scotland.

CONCLUSION

This chapter has shown that there has been a proportionately small, yet persist-ent presence of Scots language in the Scottish print and broadcast media, and that this has been joined in recent years by voices from the ethnic communities in Scotland. The Scots presence has been largely ad hoc, it has often dealt in comic, criminal or couthy stereotypes, and it has been heavily slanted towards the central belt with only occasional diversions elsewhere, principally to the northeast. The mainstream media have hedged their bets when presenting mate-rial in broad Scots, by adapting formats that have worked in other spheres, such as books, plays and, very occasionally, even poems. As programming for the main-stream media becomes ever more expensive to deliver, the guerrilla nature of cheap, cheerful and increasingly sophisticated digital technology might well be the future hope for both broad Scots and minority language provision.

NOTES

1. For Scottish regional services, see: www.bbc.co.uk/scotland/radioscotland/view/show.shtml?news.
2. Source: www.bbc.co.uk/northernireland/radioulster/a_kist_o_wurds.
3. Source: http://imdb.com/title/tt0117951/alternateversions.
4. Source: http://www.bbc.co.uk/voices.
5. Some of the original recordings made for radio programmes included in the *Voices* project have been archived and are available online from the Scottish Corpus of Texts and Speech, www.scottishcorpus.ac.uk. The full text of the interview with Imran Alam is also available here.
6. Source: 'History of Awaz FM' on www.radioawaz.com.

REFERENCES

Alford, H. (1864), *A Plea for the Queen's English: Stray Notes on Speaking and Spelling,* London.

Boyd, E. (n.d.), *The View from Daniel Pike: 'Four Walls',* unpublished television script: Scottish Theatre Archive.

Burnett, G. (1938), *Scotland on the Air*, Edinburgh and London: The Moray Press.

Bridie, J. (1942), *The Switchback*, unpublished radio script, Scottish Theatre Archive, University of Glasgow.

Byrne, J. (1990), *Your Cheatin' Heart*, London: BBC Books.

Corbett, J. (2003), 'Ecstasy controlled: the prose styles of James Leslie Mitchell and Lewis Grassic Gibbon', in M. P. McCulloch and S. Dunnigan (eds), *A Flame in the Mearns: Lewis Grassic Gibbon, A Centenary Celebration*, Glasgow: ASLS, pp. 89–103.

Dick, E. (ed.) (1990), *From Limelight to Satellite: A Scottish Film Book*, Glasgow and London: Scottish Film Council and British Film Institute.

Donaldson, W. (1986), *Popular Literature in Victorian Scotland: Language, Fiction and the Press*, Aberdeen: Aberdeen University Press.

Donaldson, W. (1989), *The Language of the People: Scots Prose from the Victorian Revival*, Aberdeen: Aberdeen University Press.

Douglas, F. M. (2000), *The Role of Lexis in Scottish Newspapers*, unpublished PhD, University of Glasgow.

Douglas, F. M. (2008), *Scottish Newspapers, Language and Identity*, Edinburgh: Edinburgh University Press.

Gielgud, V. (1956), *British Radio Drama 1922–1956: A Survey*, London: Harrap.

Gifford, D. (1988), 'Myth, Parody and Dissociation: Scottish Fiction 1814–1914' in D. Gifford (ed.), *The History of Scottish Literature Vol. 3: Nineteenth Century*, Aberdeen: Aberdeen University Press, pp. 217–60.

Herrington, M. and A. Kendall (eds) (2005), *Insights from Research and Practice: A Handbook for Adult Literacy, Numeracy and ESOL Practitioners*, Leicester: National Institute for Adult Continuing Education.

Hetherington, A. (1992), *Inside BBC Scotland 1975–1980: A Personal View*, Aberdeen: Whitewater Press.

Highet, J. (1949), *Scotland on the Air: Aspects of Scottish Broadcasting*, Glasgow: Department of Economic and Social Research, University of Glasgow.

Jack, R. D. S, and P. A. T. Rozendaal (eds) (1997), *The Mercat Anthology of Early Scottish Literature 1375–1707*, Edinburgh: Mercat Press.

Jones, C. (1995), *A Language Suppressed? The Pronunciation of the Scots Language in the Eighteenth Century*, Edinburgh: John Donald.

Jones, C. (ed.) (1997), *The Edinburgh History of the Scots Language*, Edinburgh: Edinburgh University Press.

Kesson, J. (1948), *Ferm Deem*, unpublished radio script: Scottish Theatre Archive, University of Glasgow.

Leonard, T. (1984), *Intimate Voices: Selected Work 1965–1983*, Newcastle: Galloping Dog Press.

McDowell, W. H. (1992), *The History of BBC Broadcasting in Scotland, 1923–1983*, Edinburgh: Edinburgh University Press.

Montgomery, M. (2005), *Ulster-Scots Language, Yesterday and Today*, Dublin: Four Courts.

Oliver, C. (1980), *A Decade's Drama: Thirteen Plays from the 1970s*, Glasgow: BBC Radio Scotland.

Pattison, I. (1990), *Rab C. Nesbitt: The Scripts*, London: BBC Books.

Pryde, H. W. (1939), *The McFlannels Rub Along, Episode 2: The Flitting*, unpublished radio script: Scottish Theatre Archive, University of Glasgow.

Purves, D. (2002), *A Scots Grammar*, 2nd edn, Edinburgh: Luath.

Ramsay, P. (1979), 'Radio Scotland: The Second Blueprint', *Scotsman*, 15 September, p. 8.

Saadi, S. (2004), *Psychoraag*, Edinburgh: Black and White.

Shepherd, R. (2006), *Robbie Shepherd's Doric Columns*, Edinburgh: Birlinn.

Stein, E. (2005), 'Misunderstood', *The Independent*, 10 June [http://findarticles.com/p/articles/mi_qn4158/is_20050610/ai_n14663255].

3

Communications Policy

PHILIP SCHLESINGER

SCOTLAND'S COMMUNICATIVE SPACE

Communications policy has acquired a particular meaning of late inasmuch as it relates to the formerly separate but now increasingly 'converged' fields of broadcasting, telecommunications and wireless communications. These have become a single object of policy intervention because of regulatory change in the UK since the coming into effect of the Communications Act 2003. Communications policy is formally distinct from cultural policy. However, as I shall argue below, there are de facto overlaps. It is, in any case, increasingly plain that legal, technological and economic changes are redefining the nature of tradeable 'cultural content' and putting older institutional distinctions under severe strain.

Scotland occupies a distinct communicative space within the United Kingdom. If we start by thinking of Scotland's space in terms of traditional media, we might note that the country has long had an indigenous press, which continues to exercise a strong grip on the country's readership, despite increasing inroads made by the Scottish editions of London-based titles. Most Scottish national titles (whether indigenous or editions of London papers) are published in Glasgow, Scotland's media capital. Significant papers are also published in Edinburgh, Dundee and Aberdeen; and there is also a well developed local press.

In the field of public service radio and television, the whole country is served by BBC Scotland, headquartered in Glasgow. Also regulated on public-service lines is SMG Television's Channel 3 station, STV, which is the main commercial station in Scotland. In the south, ITV Border serves a small segment of the Scottish audience. EMAP and GMG are the dominant players in commercial radio in Scotland, with high audience reach in the central belt. The BBC, Channel 3, Channel 4 and Channel 5 all have legal obligations to spend varying proportions of their programme-making budgets outside of London on first-run productions. Part of this 'quota' expenditure occurs in Scotland and is crucial to sustaining the country's creative economy. Indeed, looked at from a 'creative industries' perspective, communications and cultural policies become subordinate to a wider framework that also takes in business, education and science policy (Schlesinger 2007). Scotland is one of the UK's leading broadcasting production centres in the 'nations and regions' of the UK, with Glasgow as the linchpin. However, the BBC's aim to build up capacity in Greater Manchester looks set to offer a challenge to Glasgow's position in the nations and regions of post-devolution UK, although at the opening of the BBC's new Glasgow headquarters in September 2007, the Director-General, Mark Thompson, committed the Corporation to enabling BBC Scotland to increase its network television figure very substantially.

Scotland's communicative space needs to be mapped on to its political space. Devolution has thrown into relief institutional relations that were once left relatively implicit. The Scotland Act 1998 distinguished between 'devolved' and 'reserved' matters. Broadcasting – central to the Communications Act 2003 – was expressly reserved to Westminster.

Telecommunications is also identified as a reserved matter in the Act. Some key powers over the press (most notably, in respect of cross-media ownership and concentration) are also reserved, coming under UK regulatory bodies. Those powers not under statutory regulation are under the self-regulatory purview of the London-based Press Complaints Commission.

Scotland, however, retains considerable autonomy over cultural policy. Scottish Screen, the screen agency for Scotland, has responsibility for developing all aspects of the national screen culture and industry. The arts more generally come under the remit of the Scottish Arts Council. Until recently, the business development end of the creative industries has been handled by Scottish Enterprise. This picture will change, with the abolition of Scottish Screen and the Scottish Arts Council and their replacement by the new strategic body for the creative industries, Creative Scotland (Scottish Executive 2006a).

Cultural and communication policies in Scotland, therefore, are asymmetrically subject to distinct Scottish and UK jurisdictions. But devolution has created a new political system north of the border with the capacity to debate matters that still remain London's exclusive legislative and regulatory prerogative. Whereas cultural policy has been an indisputably legitimate and exclusive matter for Holyrood to discuss and legislate on, from time to time questions about communications, both Scottish and UK-wide, have also been debated in the Scottish Parliament. For instance, when the Communications Bill was passing through the Commons, there was also some debate at Holyrood, the main issue addressed being Scottish representation on the new regulatory body, the Office of Communications, Ofcom (Scottish Parliament Official Report 2002).

For most of its existence, the Scottish Parliament's pre-eminent concern about the media has been rather narrowly focused on its own image in Scotland, although there have been occasional forays into the economic dimensions of film and broadcasting, for instance. And perhaps there are current signs of heightened interest in a broader agenda. In January 2007, the Enterprise and Culture Committee convened a round-table discussion on Creative Scotland that necessarily spilled over into areas of UK policy-making (Scottish Parliament Official Report 2007). Any discussion of 'creative industries' issues (central to the UK government's drive to achieve global competitiveness) is bound to find the border bypassed.

To date, the fact that communications is a reserved matter has arguably inhibited thinking about broader policy questions in both an Executive and a Parliament dominated from 1999 to 2007 by the Labour-Liberal Democrat coalition. Although during that period, the Scottish National Party (SNP) periodically advocated greater control over broadcasting north of the border, on the whole political discussion of the communications agenda has been limited and sporadic. With an SNP minority government installed in May 2007, culture in a broad sense (including broadcasting) looked likely to rise up the agenda. This was signalled by directly situating the post of Minister for Europe, External Affairs and Culture in the Office of the First Minister, Alex Salmond.

TENSIONS IN BROADCASTING

Because of its prominence in everyday life, broadcasting (especially television) tends to be a focus of jurisdictional tensions. These emerge occasionally and often unpredictably – most often in the field of news and current affairs programming, which is at the heart of politics.

The most notorious recent row occurred in 1998, the year before devolution became a reality. The main lines of the story have been aired elsewhere (Schlesinger et al. 2001). The heart of the matter was whether or not BBC Scotland should be allowed to broadcast its own 6–7pm hour of news and current affairs on BBC1. This would have entailed an opt-out from network news to follow an agenda ordered according to Glasgow's priorities, as had been the case with Radio Scotland's news output for the previous twenty years.

For London, this was too much. For some – including John Birt, the BBC's then director-general – the 'Scottish Six' was but one step away from the dissolution of the realm and '[t]he end of a single common experience of UK news' that would 'encourage separatist tendencies' (Birt 2002: 484).

Senior ministers, mostly Scots, and the Prime Minister, were persuaded by this alarmist vision. Contrariwise, by the end of the various press campaigns, almost 70 per cent of Scots were said to be in favour of a Scottish Six (Schlesinger et al. 2001: 46). What is so interesting about this case is its translation from a rather arcane and essentially private broadcasting row, debated for months between the Broadcasting Council for Scotland, one of the four advisory bodies which until recently operated in the nations and regions, and the BBC Executive in London, into a major Scottish political story. The Scottish Six became a thoroughly national matter: one of having 'our' news denied to us by 'them'. And for the London-based opponents (the key ones being top Labour Party Scots), BBC Scotland's policy could easily be tarred with the brush of nationalism, and therefore dismissed. Although there was to be no 'Scottish Six', BBC Scotland was allowed to launch *Newsnight Scotland*, a late-night opt-out from *Newsnight*, on BBC2.

For a while, the political heat dissipated. A little-noticed inquiry by the Scottish Affairs Committee at Westminster in spring 2002 showed no concern about the Scottish Six (Scottish Affairs Committee 2002). Further skirmishes, however, came in autumn 2003 when it was reported that BBC Scotland had been producing pilot programmes for the BBC1 6–7pm news and current affairs slot as part of BBC Scotland's review of its journalism output (Russell and Macintosh 2003: 48–9).

These tussles were but the preamble to the publication on 17 December 2003 of BBC Scotland's *Journalism Review* (BBC Scotland 2003). Amongst a range of findings, what grabbed the headlines – predictably enough – was the report's virtual interment of the Scottish Six. While the research uncovered some doubts about the relevance of news from London, the conclusion was that while 'the case for an integrated Scottish news hour does not appear strong enough to justify the change being made, the position should remain under review' (BBC Scotland 2003: 17–23).

Irrespective of what the corporation might decide, others have kept the matter on the agenda. On 8 March 2004, the Scottish Consumer Council (2004) published a brief riposte to the BBC's research. Its report, based on a survey of attitudes towards BBC news provision, found that a majority of respondents favoured the creation of a Scottish Six. Paul McKinney, then head of news and current affairs at Scottish Television, also took up the cudgels. He argued (with SMG's endorsement) that Scottish broadcasters should broaden their horizons and put out an international, UK and Scottish news programme on Channel 3 in the slot currently occupied by ITN's late night news (Fraser 2004). As the digitisation of television supply proceeds, the grounds of debate seem certain to shift. If launching a Gaelic television channel is feasible, so too is setting up a Scottish one. In the era of downloads and podcasts, not to speak of a wide range of niche stations on digital platforms, there is certainly no technological bar to making a news programme on the lines of the Scottish Six widely available. Its viability, of course, would depend on audience demand and adequate finance, and political considerations would doubtless come into play.

Scotland's distinctive political map and electoral cycle occasionally throw up other complications. Even before devolution, the country's political culture created the odd difficulty for London-based schedulers. Post-devolution, the same inherent tensions have persisted. When the ITV network broadcast *Ask the Prime Minister* in winter 2000, it faced protests about impartiality. The programme was due to be screened before a Westminster parliamentary by-election in Falkirk West. Speculation was then rife about whether there would be a UK general election the following spring. Putting on an access show of this kind featuring Mr Blair meant that, in order to ensure due impartiality, ITV had to reschedule its programmes in Scotland. It also added a special edition of the election programme, *Hustings*, to meet the objections of the SNP. Such incidents tend to attract much press *Sturm und Drang*, some parliamentary expostulations, and, from a Scottish point of view, serve to rattle the cage of a presumed, homogeneous Britishness.

Network broadcasters have had to rethink aspects of programming and scheduling in the wake of devolution. However, the continuities are more striking than the changes. London-based programme teams in the current affairs field have made adjustments to established formulae to meet Scottish needs, while at the same time keeping the entire UK audience in mind (McNair et al. 2003).

AFTER THE COMMUNICATIONS ACT 2003

On 17 July, the Communications Act 2003 received Royal Assent. This has shaped the context for the development of Scotland as a communicative space, as it has for the rest of the UK.

Both political and economic calculations were behind the refusal to devolve powers over the media. Politically, notably in relation to broadcasting, there has been a fear in key government circles and amongst some senior broadcasters that parcelling out powers will lead inevitably to separatism and the collapse of the Union.

The UK government conceives of increased economic competitiveness as occurring within a 'convergent' digital electronic environment: broadcasting, telecommunications and computing are to come together to create the basis for a 'knowledge' or 'information' society. For British policy-makers, the key reference point is the global economy and building 'UK plc's' strength within that context. Permitting the emergence of bigger players – for instance, a unitary ITV to replace most of the old federal system – easing cross-media ownership rules, and encouraging foreign investment have all been part of this picture. The Communications Act 2003 was strongly driven by such considerations.

The passage of the Act was preceded by a lengthy period of consultation. First there was a White Paper, *A New Future for Communications*, in December 2000. This was followed by the draft Communications Bill, on which public consultation began in May 2002. That consultation was paralleled by the pre-legislative scrutiny of a joint committee of the two Houses at Westminster, chaired by the Labour peer Lord Puttnam. The committee reported in August 2002. The government accepted a substantial number of amendments, and a revised Communications Bill was issued at the end of 2002. The relatively open consultation process allowed a variety of lobbies to intervene.

However, little public debate took place in Scotland during the Act's lengthy gestation. The Voice of the Viewer and Listener (a UK interest group) held a public conference on the Bill in Edinburgh in 2002, and there were occasional newspaper articles (Galbraith 2002; Kemp 2002; Schlesinger 2002). There was just one, rather unfocused, parliamentary debate in October 2002. More typical, apart from direct lobbying in London by a variety of interests, was the convening of small private meetings, such as a Glasgow gathering in February 2002 sponsored by the Scottish Consumer Council (SCC). The discussion on that occasion showed that visiting London policy-makers had given little thought to the implications for Scotland of their legislative proposals. The expression of strong views did at least put Scottish concerns onto the agenda. The SCC itself also worried about how market consolidation would affect 'regional identity, plurality and choice' in broadcasting and that Scotland was falling behind with respect to the Internet and digital television take-up (Scottish Consumer Council 2002).

While at one level there are intense pressures on broadcasting to face outwards and address the global market, inherited constraints have meant that audiences in the nations and regions are still served in ways largely continuous with the past. A principled argument to retain 'regionality' was propounded by the outgoing regulator for commercial television, the Independent Television Commission (ITC), in its *Charter for the Nations and Regions* in 2002.

This stance had an influence on the climate of opinion during the legislative process. The ITC also argued strongly for the retention of offices in the nations and regions. Its own research was used to bolster the arguments, identifying a considerable appetite for news provision that addressed local and regional concerns and indicated that regional programming was regarded as a vital service by the majority of viewers (Hargreaves and Thomas 2002; Kidd and Taylor 2002).

Independent producer interests were effectively pursued by their trade organisation, PACT, which was instrumental in ensuring that favourable programme supply conditions were established as the Bill was debated (ITC 2002; PACT 2002). Independent television production for BBC Scotland, ITV and Channel 4 (and other broadcasters) has contributed to building capacity in Scotland, particularly in Glasgow. The Communications Act 2003 endorsed the demand for some continued decentralisation of the broadcast economy. But (as previously) the present order does not uniquely favour Scottish interests as against those of any other nation or region. Ultimately, the performance of the broadcast economy in Scotland will be decided by its competitiveness within the wider UK framework – with, as noted earlier, the Greater Manchester area destined to be a major competitor in the near future.

The Screen Industries Summit for Scotland was held in Glasgow in November 2003 precisely to consider Scotland's competitive position. The participants were drawn mainly from broadcasters, independent production companies and Scottish development agencies. Attended by over 150 people, this was the largest meeting to discuss the future of the audiovisual industries in Scotland for well over a decade. Of the UK's total of £4.8 billion audiovisual content production in 2001, Scotland accounted for £240 million, or 5 per cent (Graham and Associates 2003).

Subsequently, the Screen Industries Summit Group (SISG) was formed. It described itself as 'a cross-industry group which seeks to increase network and international presence and growth in production across all areas of the screen industries in Scotland' (SISG 2005: n.p.).

Meetings held in early 2004 identified key objectives for a Scottish lobbying exercise in the fields of television, film, the games industry and research and development. This move involved collaboration between a range of Scottish media interests and the Scottish Executive. From the Executive's standpoint, 'SISG was established to report to Scottish Ministers. It has acted as a high level task group to make recommendations on the key actions needed to ensure growth and sustainability for the screen industries in Scotland' (Scottish Executive 2004: n.p.). SISG's views on the need to promote 'the national aspect of the Scottish screen industries', the need for 'critical mass in production, commissioning and broadcasting', a 'proportionate share' of funding, public service broadcasting competition for BBC Scotland, and support for Gaelic broadcasting were all endorsed by the Executive in a submission to phase one of Ofcom's review of public service television broadcasting (PSB review). The

Scottish Executive also registered concern about the loss of talent from Scotland and supported the move of some broadcast commissioning from London to Glasgow.

The SISG has continued to make representations in the Scottish interest. For instance, in response to the Department of Culture, Media and Sport's (DCMS) Green Paper consultation during the BBC's Charter Review as well as expressing its views during phase three of Ofcom's PSB review (SSIG 2005).

It is hard to assess how effective the Scottish lobby has been in fighting its case. It is sometimes difficult for such a coalition to speak with one voice. For instance, in 2006 pressure from producer interests in the SISG to increase the quantity of Scottish-based programme production by ITV, Channel 4 and Five (in line with the BBC's nations and regions commitments) met with an unenthusiastic response from the broadcasters concerned (Vass 2006).

REGULATION AND THE REGULATORS

The distinct Scottish interest in communications has long been recognised, and in certain instances institutionalised, at the UK level. Until 2003, and the launch of Ofcom, the reigning model had been a politically inspired one, based on the seat in the UK cabinet accorded the Secretary of State for Scotland. As that territorial office was demoted in political significance during the summer of 2003, congruent changes took place in the world of communication regulation (Trench 2004).

The BBC's Board of Governors – since 1 January 2007 replaced by the BBC Trust – long had 'national' members for Scotland, Wales and Northern Ireland. This system recognised the territorial distinctiveness of the smaller nations in the UK state. The practice was extended – by statute – to the other regulatory bodies, the ITC (and its predecessor bodies, the ITA and the IBA), as well as to the Radio Authority. The Broadcasting Standards Council also statutorily followed the same model. In the field of telecommunications, there was a Scottish Advisory Committee on Telecommunications (SACOT), with a statutory duty to advise the then regulator, Oftel, on the needs of telecoms consumers in Scotland.

Before Ofcom, therefore, regulatory bodies dealing with broadcasting had Scottish representation at their highest levels. Scottish ire was aroused when it was decided that Ofcom's main board would drop the territorial principle for this strategic level of decision-making. It was obvious from repeated ministerial statements, as well as the blank wall encountered during lobbying lunches such as that organised by the SCC, that the principle was not going to be conceded. The Office of Communications Act 2002, which set up the Ofcom board in advance of the Communications Act 2003, made no provision for territorial representation on the board of nine members.

The Puttnam committee, which reviewed the government's draft Bill, expressly considered the 'representation of nations and regions'. It supported the UK government's approach to the composition of the main board. However, the committee asked that existing provisions in respect of the two key subordinate committees – the Content Board and the Consumer Panel – be strengthened. The committee was open to lobbying on this question and recommended that 'Ofcom be placed under a statutory duty to maintain offices in Scotland, Wales and Northern Ireland'; the regulator was also to report specifically on its activities in the nations (House of Lords, House of Commons 2002: 20–1).

Peers, MPs and MSPs were vigorously lobbied by SACOT (2002) to strengthen the rather weak provisions on representation agreed by ministers. The Scottish Executive lobbied on similar lines. The First Minister, Jack McConnell, took exception to the lack of representation on the Ofcom main board, but Tessa Jowell, the Westminster Secretary of State for Culture, Media and Sport, rejected his argument. Mr McConnell also raised the issue with Helen Liddell, the Scottish Secretary. The Scotland Office, according to some insiders, toed the DCMS/DTI line, which was hostile to any statutory provisions being made for Scottish representation.

At the end of 2002, the revised Bill required offices to be set up in each of the UK's nations. The Content Board and Consumer Panel would each have a member for Scotland. SACOT argued that this was not enough to attend to the country's needs and that 'the Bill should be amended to provide for a Committee for Scotland, reporting to the Ofcom Board, with input to and from both the Content Board and Consumer Panel'. The Committee for Scotland amendment was resisted by the Ofcom Board 'on the grounds that it was something they were going to do anyway. It was also resisted by the Government up to the final stages of the debate in Lords.'[1] Lobbying efforts, however, which included amendments to the Bill drafted by SACOT, resulted in provision for a statutory Scottish national committee, and ensured that other national committees were also set up. Statutory status has entrenched the Scottish committee's functions. This status had to be fought for, and represents one clear outcome of Scottish lobbying.

Since its inception, Ofcom has been a key policy actor as well as regulator. Its central focus is on questions of competition, and consequently its role in pursuing citizen as opposed to consumer interests has become an object of public discussion (Harvey 2006; Livingstone et al. 2007; Smith 2006). Its public interventions exemplify the 'evidence-based' style so beloved of New Labour, and in its Southwark HQ it disposes of considerable expert firepower. From the start, Ofcom has produced detailed annual plans and reports and has undertaken a series of major 'strategic reviews' of public service television broadcasting and telecommunications. It has also published extensive analyses of digitisation and of spectrum and has provided influential annual surveys of the communications market. Some of its attention has indeed focused specifically on the nations and regions, although these are at the margins of its concerns (Ofcom 2006a).

In line with the Communications Act 2003, national offices and advisory committees were established. Ofcom's Scottish director, Vicki Nash, was appointed in March 2004. Ofcom Scotland's key role is to transmit Scottish perspectives on policy issues to its London HQ. The Scottish office also implements Ofcom's regulatory policy in Scotland and networks with a wide range of Scottish political, economic, cultural and social actors. The political class at Holyrood, the Scottish Executive civil service and major industrial players are regarded as important 'stakeholders'. The Advisory Committee for Scotland (ACS) also came into operation in March 2004 and has drawn together a range of skills across broadcasting and telecommunications with a membership that reflects Scotland's regional diversity.

Dr Nash chaired the ACS for its first year, reflecting Ofcom's initial caution about the workings of its advisory committees. In 2005, ACS member Joyce Taylor (an experienced former television executive) became chair. In 2006 she was appointed as the Scottish member of Ofcom's Content Board and replaced by another ACS member, Thomas Prag, previously Scottish member of the Radio Authority. The ACS meets at least every quarter and addresses a wide range of communications issues on which it may make submissions to Ofcom from a Scottish perspective. The Scottish members of the Content Board and Consumer Panel and the chair of the Gaelic Media Service often attend ACS meetings. It is one of the few expert spaces in Scotland in which the rapidly transforming communications policy agenda can be addressed in the round, although it is difficult to assess the extent of the ACS's influence on policy-making.

CURRENT ISSUES

Major policy developments in UK broadcasting form the essential backdrop to what is happening in Scotland. There was the influential PSB television review carried out by Ofcom in 2004–5. One of the key outcomes for production in the nations and regions was the decision to reduce ITV's obligatory hours of regional, children's and religious programmes, although the reduction – until digital switchover – will be less in Scotland, Wales and Northern Ireland than in England (Ofcom 2005: 13).

Furthermore, the UK government's Review of the BBC's Charter (2003–6), much in line with Ofcom's thinking, redefined the corporation's public purposes. In the corporation's Charter and Agreement 2006, these are specified as sustaining citizenship and civil society; promoting education and learning; stimulating creativity and cultural excellence; representing the UK, its nations, regions and communities; bringing the UK to the world and the world to the UK. The BBC is also tasked with helping to bring the benefits of emerging communications technologies and services and taking a leading role in the switchover to digital television – the replacement of the analogue terrestrial transmissions network with an all-digital terrestrial one by 2012. This last purpose is a key item of UK government policy and central to Ofcom's agenda. In line with a government policy shift that it had anticipated, the BBC also changed its form of governance, replacing the governors with the BBC Trust – in effect, installing a more distanced quasi-regulator.

The 'modernisation' of the BBC's regulatory system – unlike Ofcom's – has not led to the abandonment of the territorial principle. Jeremy Peat, the Scottish national governor appointed in 2005, became the Trust member for Scotland in January 2007. The Broadcasting Council for Scotland (as is the case in the other nations) was replaced by an Audience Council for Scotland. This has a consultative role on the BBC's effectiveness in promoting its public purposes and serving the interests of licence fee payers.

The development of Gaelic broadcasting is discussed elsewhere in this volume but what should be noted here is that support for Gaelic is officially both a matter of Scottish cultural policy and an embryonic Scottish broadcasting policy, and provides a good example of how hard it sometimes is to draw clear lines between the two. Precisely in this vein, the then Scottish Executive Culture Minister, Patricia Ferguson, underlined the Executive's 'commitment to Gaelic broadcasting' and 'the importance of the language to our history and culture'. 'Gaelic digital television', she said, 'should have a significant impact on the status and use of the language, boosting the confidence of Gaelic native speakers and learners' (Scottish Executive 2007).

The development of Gaelic broadcasting shows that the devolved/reserved distinction is not immutable and that where there is a will to cooperate across the different levels of government in the UK (as well as a pressing necessity to do so) solutions can be found.

Across the UK as a whole, Ofcom has had a key role in policing the terms of trade for regional production that falls within a public service broadcaster's target (Ofcom 2006b). The quota system is the life-blood of dispersed production capacity in the UK. The Scottish independent production companies – with few exceptions – are small and low in capitalisation. Recent industry reports have stressed the need to improve the business skills of independents and to make them more market aware (The Research Centre 2002, 2003). For some, enhancing indies' business capacities now means making them fit for sale in a consolidating and concentrating market.

The recent buy-ups of IWC Media (in 2005) and The Comedy Unit (in 2006) by London-based RDF Media Group suggest there are limits to growth in Scotland: a successful indy's marketability makes it fair game for purchase. While the quota system exists, there is a sound commercial logic to having Scottish subsidiaries of UK operations as this eases access to the nations and regions money pool. But what are the longer-term implications of a south-wards shift of control for Glasgow's continued development as Scotland's broadcasting hub?

The passage of the 2003 Act shortly preceded the creation of a merged ITV, effectively ending the period of the regional-federal commercial model in force since 1955. That framework was transformed by the concentration of ownership. Only UTV in Northern Ireland and STV in Scotland remain as residues of the old system.

In recent years, the future of SMG has been increasingly questioned, fol-lowing the sale of its newspapers and then a key part of its radio assets to address its debt problems. A takeover by UTV was mooted throughout 2006 and early 2007. After a boardroom coup in March 2007, the new management team appears to have opted to consolidate the STV brand and to concentrate on tele-vision production (Laurance 2007: 13; Vass 2007).

As we head towards the government's goal of a complete digital switch-over for television broadcasting by 2012, those who wish to argue for a different model of commissioning public service production, and for changing radically the nature of its distribution, point to the impact of new technology. Digitisation expands the capacity for universal delivery. If a large number of channels were to become universally accessible, in principle the delivery of public service programming could be put out to tender on different principles from those that now obtain. Conditional access technology could transform the nature of payments for services. Such arguments raise fundamental ques-tions about the licence fee. Should it be maintained, top-sliced or distributed by a new public service broadcasting agency across a wider range of recipients, of which the BBC would be only one, even if the most significant?[2] Ofcom has again mooted the idea of a Public Service Publisher (first floated in 2005). This entity is intended to harness digital technologies' capacity to distribute public service content. It is not clear how this new capability would be organ-ised. Nevertheless, a PSP would doubtless offer competition to the BBC, and would probably bid for a share of the licence fee (Ofcom 2007).

Increasing numbers now buy broadcast entertainment and mobile telephony as a matter of course, making unquestioned future public support for the licence fee more and more doubtful. Longer-term changes in media consumption patterns – particularly among young people – are fertile ground for those who would argue that public service tax-based revenues should be shared rather than earmarked for the BBC. How individual choice can be mobilised to sustain a public good has become the new heartland of debate about public service broadcasting.

WHERE CULTURE AND COMMUNICATIONS POLICY MEET

In June 2005, the Cultural Commission – set up in response to the then First Minister Jack McConnell's St Andrew's Day Speech in 2003 – reported at some length (Cultural Commission 2005). Mr McConnell had stressed the centrality of culture to Scotland's government and public life. The Cultural Commission undertook a major inquiry into how to effect change and was chaired by James Boyle, formerly head of BBC Radio Scotland and also previously controller of BBC Radio 4.

Although broadcasting is a reserved power, devolution is a process. Seven years on, the Cultural Commission's stance raised questions about the position set out in the Scotland Act 1998. The Commission's approach was premised on assumptions about buttressing Scottish national identity, national renewal through culture and bolstering economic development through the creative and cultural industries. Its report dramatised the tension between the pursuit of a national – that is, Scottish – cultural policy and the rolling-out from London of a UK broadcasting policy (now conceived as a branch of communications policy).

As defined by the DCMS (1998) – and Scottish Executive policy has signed up to this conception – the creative industries do include broadcasting. The Cultural Commission affirmed that 'BBC Scotland is a constituent part of Scottish culture'. By doing so, it laid claim to television and radio as necessary parts of a coherent cultural policy. Scottish ministers were asked to introduce 'an element of devolution of broadcasting' and told that there was 'a strong case for the establishment of at least one channel based in Scotland' (Cultural Commission 2005, Annex G: 5). The Commission challenged the constitutional status quo by suggesting that a Scottish channel might become the responsibility of Holyrood.

The Commission's report implied that broadcasting policy (as part of a broader creative industries strategy) is properly subordinate to a national cultural policy. If this were followed through, it would mean rethinking the present division of powers between London and Edinburgh and also current regulatory arrangements. In its response to the Cultural Commission, the Scottish Executive gave the recommendation short shrift. It underlined that it was 'not attracted' to the idea of a Scottish channel:

> Broadcasting is a reserved matter and is the responsibility of the Department for Culture, Media and Sport. It would also be a costly way of increasing opportunities for Scottish broadcasting and creative talent. We consider that our efforts and resources would be better spent on securing the future of Gaelic broadcasting, continuing to work to increase TV production in Scotland and encouraging broadcasters to improve coverage of Scottish issues on existing channels rather than trying to set up a new one. (Scottish Executive 2006b: 43)

That response exemplified the Executive's reluctance to explore the boundaries between the devolved and the reserved. The spectre of independence has haunted the calculations of devolutionist politicians, perhaps precluding more adventurous thinking.[3] If followed through, the SNP's manifesto commitments in the May 2007 election campaign will put serious pressure on the status quo. The party called for a 'dedicated news service and more quality programming made in Scotland'. The spectre of the 'Scottish Six' has thereby again raised its head. The SNP has also said that it will 'push for the devolution of broadcasting powers to the Scottish Parliament' and that it wants the BBC 'to retain more of the licence fee raised in Scotland' (SNP 2007). In August 2007 First Minister Alex Salmond set up the Scottish Broadcasting Commission under the former head of BBC Scotland's news and current affairs department, Blair Jenkins, with a broad investigative remit. This represents a frontal attack on the present operation of broadcasting powers: it is a challenge to both the present regulatory system and the flow of broadcast finance.

To conclude, it is plain that Scotland's institutional frameworks for handling culture and for dealing with media and communications are asymmetrical and inconsistent. That we cannot imagine a neatly bounded national space is one of the inherent complexities of the devolved Scottish condition. Although the image of the nation as a self-contained communicative space no longer reflects the realities of cultural flows in the era of 'globalisation', it does point to something important. The levers of statehood may still afford decisive policy advantages that those of mere autonomy within a state do not (Schlesinger 2000).

ACKNOWLEDGEMENTS

This chapter builds on revisions of earlier work. My thanks to Lindsay Paterson, editor of *Scottish Affairs* 47 (2004), and to Bill Miller, editor of *Anglo-Scottish Relations from 1900 to Devolution and Beyond*, Oxford: Oxford University Press (2005), for permitting the successive re-use of my original contributions. I have drawn on research conducted for an AHRC-funded project (2006–8) on 'Creativity: policy and practice', ID No. 112152. Although I am presently a member of Ofcom's Advisory Committee for Scotland, this chapter has been written purely in a professional and personal capacity.

1. Personal communication from Jeremy Mitchell, Chairman of SACOT, 4 September 2003.
2. See Elstein 2004 and Cox et al. 2004; for comments, see Schlesinger 2004 and Wells 2004. More than twenty years ago, the Peacock Committee (1986) proposed a model that dispersed public service broadcasting services across the market place. Neither the technology nor the market conditions then existed to make this proposition easily realisable.
3. The special advisor John McTernan (2003: 26), writing as both a Westminster and Holyrood insider, has commented: 'Scotland has a Parliament because it is a nation, albeit one within a larger political unit. But because of the strength of nationalism over the last thirty years, there remains a residual fear that doing anything to build national identity is a gift to separatists.'

REFERENCES

BBC Scotland (2003), *Journalism Review 2003*, www.bbc.co.uk/scotland.

Birt, J. (2002), *The Harder Path: The Autobiography*, London: Time Warner.

Cox, B., T. Gardam and A. Singer (2004), 'How to save shows like Operatunity', *Media Guardian*, 15 March, pp. 2–3.

Cultural Commission (2005), '*Our next major enterprise*': Final report of The Cultural Commission, Edinburgh: Scottish Executive.

DCMS (1998), *Creative Industries Mapping Document*, London: DCMS.

Elstein, D. (chairman), Broadcasting Policy Group (2004), *Beyond the Charter: The BBC after 2006*, London: Premium Publishing.

Fraser, D. (2004), 'STV news chief gives backing to independent "Scottish Six"', *Sunday Herald*, 14 March, p. 10.

Galbraith, R. (2002), 'What happened to the principles of independent TV?', *Sunday Herald*, Business, 9 June, p. 7.

Graham, D. and Associates (2003), *Audit of the Screen Industries in Scotland*, Glasgow: PACT in Scotland.

Hargreaves, I. and J. Thomas (2002), *New News, Old News*, London: BSC and ITC.

Harvey, S. (2006), 'Ofcom's first year and neoliberalism's blind spot: attacking the culture of production', *Screen*, 47:1, 91–105.

House of Lords, House of Commons (2002), *Joint Committee on the Draft Communications Bill, Draft Communications Bill*, Volume I – Report, HL Paper 169–I; HC 876-I, London: The Stationery Office, Session 2001–2, 25 July.

ITC (2002), *UK Programme Supply Review, A Report by the Independent Television Commission to the Secretary of State for Culture, Media and Sport*, November 2002, London: Independent Television Commission.

Kemp, K. (2002), 'Broadcasting bill will promote regional identities', *Sunday Herald*, Business, 23 June, 2002, p. 8.

Kidd, M. and B. Taylor (2002), *Television in the Nations and Regions*, London: ITC.

Laurance, B. (2007), 'SMG will focus on TV after the coup', *The Sunday Times*, Business, 15 April, p. 13.

Livingstone, S., P. Lunt and L. Miller (2007), 'Citizens, consumers and the citizen-consumer: articulating the citizen interest in media and communications regulation', *Discourse & Communication*, 1:1, 63–89.

McConnell, J. (2003), St Andrew's Day Speech, Royal Scottish Academy of Music and Drama, Glasgow, 30 November, Scottish Executive News Online, https://194.247.95.101/pages/news/extras/p_00017600.aspx.

Macleod, A. (2002), 'McConnell fight for Scots voice in broadcasting body', *The Times*, Scottish edition, 22 May, p. 10.

McNair, B., M. Hibberd and P. Schlesinger (2003), *Mediated Access: Broadcasting and Democratic Participation in the Age of Mediated Politics*, Luton: Luton University Press.

McTernan, J. (2003), 'Too late review?', *Holyrood*, 8 September, p. 26.

Ofcom (2005), *Ofcom Review of Public Service Television Broadcasting*, London: Ofcom.

Ofcom (2006a), *The Communications Market: Nations and Regions*, London: Ofcom.

Ofcom (2006b), *Review of the Television Production Sector: A Consultation*, London: Ofcom.

Ofcom (2007), *A New Approach to Public Service Content in the Digital Media Age: The Potential Role of the Public Service Publisher, Discussion Paper*, Ofcom: London.

PACT (2002), *PACT Submission to the ITC Review of the Programme Supply Market*, London: Producers Alliance for Cinema & Television.

Peacock, Professor A. (chairman) (1986), *Report of the Committee on Financing the BBC*, Cmnd. 9824, London: HMSO.

Russell, M. and K. Macintosh (2003), 'Nations and regions: Should there be a Scottish Six?', *Holyrood*, 1 December, pp. 48–9.

SACOT (2002), 'UK Communications Bill: Briefing for all MSPs', December, SACOT: Edinburgh.

Schlesinger, P. (2000), 'The nation and communicative space', H. Tumber (ed.), *Media Power, Professionals and Politics*, London and New York: Routledge, pp. 99–115.

Schlesinger, P. (2002), 'Bill's new world order could be the death of regional diversity', *Sunday Herald*, Business, 2 June, p. 8.

Schlesinger, P. (2004), 'Anti-Beeb brigade with a charter to work mischief', *Sunday Herald*, 1 February, p. 12.

Schlesinger, P. (2006), 'Creativity: from discourse to doctrine?', *Screen*, 48: 3, 377–87.

Schlesinger, P., D. Miller and W. Dinan (2001), *Open Scotland? Journalists, Spin Doctors and Lobbyists*, Edinburgh: Polygon.

Scottish Affairs Committee (2002), *Post Devolution News and Current Affairs Broadcasting in Scotland*, Third Report of Session 2001–2, House of Commons, HC 549, London: The Stationery Office, 21 March.

Scottish Consumer Council (2002), *Reaching Out: The Consumer Perspective on Communications in Scotland*, Glasgow: Scottish Consumer Council.

Scottish Consumer Council (2004), *BBC News and the Scottish Six: Scottish Consumers' Views on Value for Money and the Licence Fee*, Glasgow: SCC.

Scottish Executive (2004), The Scottish Executive Submission to Phase One of Ofcom's Review of Public Service Broadcasting, Cultural Policy Division, The Scottish Executive, July 2004, unpaged.

Scottish Executive (2006a), *Draft Culture (Scotland) Bill Consultation Document*, Edinburgh: Scottish Executive Education Department.

Scottish Executive (2006b), *Scotland's Culture*, Edinburgh: Scottish Executive.

Scottish Executive (2007), 'Financial support for Gaelic broadcasting', news release, www.scotland.gov.uk, 23 March.

Scottish Parliament Official Report (2002), 'Broadcasting and the Print Media', Thursday 31 October 2002, www.scottish.parliament.uk/S1/official_report/session-02/sor1031-0.htm#Col14999-14810.

Scottish Parliament Official Report (2007), 'Creative Scotland', Enterprise and Culture Committee, col. 3597–3528, Edinburgh: Scottish Parliamentary Corporate Body.

SISG (2005), 'Response by Scotland's Screen Industries Summit Group (SISG) to the DCMS Green Paper: Review of the BBC's Royal Charter – *A strong BBC, independent of government*', March, unpaged.

Smith, P. (2006), 'The politics of UK television policy: the making of Ofcom', *Media, Culture & Society*, 28:6, 929–40.

SNP (2007) 'Supporting culture and creativity', www.snp.org/policies.

The Research Centre (2002), *Risky Business: Inside the Indies*, Glasgow: The Research Centre for Television and Interactivity.

The Research Centre (2003), *Inside the Commissioners*, Glasgow: The Research Centre for Television and Interactivity.

Trench, A. (2004), 'The more things change, the more things stay the same: intergovernmental relations four years on', in A. Trench (ed.), *Has Devolution Made a Difference? The State of the Nations 2004*, Exeter: Imprint Academic, pp. 165–92.

Vass, S. (2006), 'Channels urged to look beyond England', *Sunday Herald*, 2 April, http://www.findarticles.com/p/articles/mi_qn4156/is_20060402.ai_n16197412.

Vass, S. (2007), 'Victor in SMG boardroom battle outlines plans for more focused future', *Sunday Herald*, 15 April, www.sundayherald.com.

Ward, S. (2004), 'Demand grows for a "Scottish Six"', *The Scotsman*, 9 March, p. 9.

Wells, M. (2004), '£1bn culture cost in ending TV licence fee', *The Guardian*, 25 February, p. 7.

THE HISTORICAL CONTEXT

4

The History of the Press

DAVID HUTCHISON

Of the three traditional media – press, broadcasting and cinema – it is the press which has the longest history, stretching back, as it does, for over 300 years in Britain and in Scotland. In what follows there will be an attempt to analyse the changes which have taken place over that period, and to locate these in their social, economic and political contexts. For this purpose the history will be divided into three periods, the first running from the earliest times until the middle of the nineteenth century, the second until the middle of the twentieth, and the third covering the past fifty years. The approach will be broad brush, and, in the hope that present experience can be illuminated by the past, there will be some movement back and forth in time.

ORIGINS UNTIL 1855

Among the earliest documents, which can be regarded as the forerunners of newspapers, are the *Acta Diurna*, posters detailing social and political events in classical Rome, and newsletters produced in the late Middle Ages by European merchants for their colleagues. Print utilising moveable type was developed in the West by Johannes Gutenberg in the mid-fifteenth century in Mainz (the Chinese had invented the process in the eleventh century). Gutenberg's Bible of 1455 was produced on paper (another Chinese invention dating from the second century), a material then derived from rags, and much more economical for manufacturing books than the animal skin required for parchment. William Caxton introduced the technology to England in 1477, but it was 1508 before it reached Scotland, when Andrew Myllar and Walter Chepman opened a printshop in Edinburgh.

Relatively cheap multiple copies were now possible, and, alongside books, various irregular news-sheets began to appear in different European countries. It is generally believed that the first Scottish newspaper was an Edinburgh reprint of the London *Diurnal Occurrances Touching the Dailie proceedings in Parliament from the 27 of December to the third of Januarie, 1642.* The proceedings in question reflected the struggle between Charles I and his legislature which would shortly lead to the Civil War and Charles's execution. The *Mercurius Caledonius* of 1661 is regarded as the first Scottish title proper, although it had a very short life and was suppressed by the Scottish Privy Council. The abolition of that body in 1708 paved the way for a somewhat less draconian approach by the authorities to the circulation of information, and various titles then began to be established, including *The Edinburgh Evening Courant* (1718–1871), the *Caledonian Mercury* (1720–1867), *The Glasgow Advertiser/Herald* (1783–), Aberdeen's *Press and Journal* (1748–), the oldest Scottish title extant, Dundee's *Courier* (1816–), *The Scotsman* (1817–), *The Inverness Courier* (1817–) and the *Dumfries and Galloway Standard* (1843–).

These papers did not appear on a daily basis but less frequently, and were heavily dependent on material lifted from London titles, which arrived some days after publication via mail coach (the London titles themselves contained 'intelligence' from Europe which was inevitably out of date). They printed what would now be called hard news, and a significant amount of advertising; their circulations were in the hundreds, although their readerships were much larger, as a consequence of their availability in coffee houses; they were, however, subject to a range of government measures explicitly designed to limit their impact and confine their perusal to 'responsible' sections of society.

Because they were printed on paper produced from rags, rather than the wood pulp which became the norm in the latter part of the nineteenth century, copies of these titles have survived in better shape than later papers, and it is possible to study them in libraries,[1] and indeed to purchase copies from specialist dealers.

Edition 10,128 of *The Edinburgh Evening Courant*, for example, appeared on Saturday, 14 December 1782 and consists of four pages of relatively small print, the pages the same length but slightly narrower than those in *The Guardian's* current Berliner format. There are no illustrations apart from one crudely drawn peacock over an advertisement for ladies' dresses. The front and back pages and one column of page three consist of advertising – houses, land and clothing are offered to readers, as are the services of a doctor and a chimney sweep; public and legal notices also appear. On the other pages are a report of a House of Commons debate which took place on 9 December, and 'Foreign Intelligence' from Paris dated 1 December. An editorial comments on the negotiations then underway to end the war with France and the United States which had stemmed from the American Revolution; there is also information about ships which had arrived on the Clyde (6 December) and Leith (10 December).

Edition 1,228 of *The Glasgow Courier* (1791–1866), published on Thursday, 4 July 1799, is of a similar size. It also has four pages, of which the fourth and most of the third consist of adverts similar to those in the Edinburgh title, although one difference is the large number of announcements from ships offering passage for goods and persons to the United States and the West Indies, reflecting Glasgow's position as a major Atlantic trading centre. Pages one and two contain reports of parliamentary proceedings on 28 June, and foreign reports from France (12 June), with which Britain was again at war, Germany (12 June) and Turkey (25 May). Local shipping news and a case underway in the Court of Session are also covered.

In the press of this period domestic news was not over-emphasised, and it was not until the later nineteenth and early twentieth centuries, particularly when mass-market titles began to appear, that Scottish news began to assume the importance it currently enjoys.[2]

Newspapers then also allied themselves to specific political causes. Cowan in his pioneering study of early Scottish titles describes the *Edinburgh Advertiser* (1764–1859) and the *Courant* as 'dully orthodox Tories' and remarks of *The Glasgow Courier* that 'for seventy years [it] . . . was to be diehard Tory' and, unlike the more tolerant *Herald*, 'a defender of the West Indian slave owners' (Cowan 1946: 20–1). *The Scotsman* was founded in 1817 specifically to give voice to Edinburgh liberalism in the face of conservative press hegemony. However, it has to be emphasised that political debate in such papers did not penetrate beyond elite groups. Although the cover prices were only a few pence, that was high relative to income. Furthermore, beginning in 1712, British governments imposed a range of press taxes – on adverts, paper itself and on individual copies sold. By 1776 stamp duty, as this last tax was known, was one and a half pence per copy, by 1797 three and a half pence. Thus, through the price mechanism, circulations could be restricted, and, since it was illegal to market unstamped titles, prosecutions could be mounted by the authorities against those producing and selling them. This situation led to a massive campaign against the 'taxes on knowledge', with radical papers openly defying the authorities by refusing to submit to the stamping system. Consequently, noted proprietors, such as Henry Hetherington of the London-based *Poor Man's Guardian* (1831–5), were jailed on several occasions. Joel Wiener notes that in the period 1830–6 hundreds of periodicals and newspapers circulated without stamps, despite constant government attempts to close them down (Wiener 1969). Glasgow, like Manchester, was at this time a centre of industrial and social agitation and several illegal periodicals, including the *Loyal Reformer's*

Gazette (1831–8) *The Scottish Trades Union Gazette* (1833) and *The Tradesman* (1833–34), appeared. The proprietor of the last-named was Alexander Campbell who has been described as 'the founding father of the Scottish labour movement' (Fraser 1996: 35). Campbell was charged with evading stamp duty and, despite claiming that he accepted donations not payment, was convicted. He avoided jail at that juncture but his involvement with another unstamped paper subsequently led to a two-month period of imprisonment. Wiener demonstrates that similar publications in Edinburgh were rather less radical in tone, reflecting the lack of a large industrial proletariat in the capital.

With the extension of the franchise initiated by the 1832 Reform Act, it became clear to all but the blindest reactionaries that the 'taxes on knowledge' were not only ineffective and unjustifiable, but also a barrier to the growth of cheap papers, which might well serve to reconcile the vast majority of working people to the constitutional status quo, with its promise of reform rather than revolution. So in 1853 the advertisement tax was abolished, in 1855 stamp duty and in 1861 the tax on paper itself. The consequences were several. Mainstream newspapers were now much cheaper and therefore more likely to be within the financial reach of working people, they could attract more advertising (radical titles always struggled to secure adverts for obvious political reasons), since the advertiser no longer had to pay a tax in addition to the cost of insertions. New titles aimed directly at the working class benefited too from the steady increase in the ability to read, a trend consolidated by the Education Act of 1872. In 1845 twenty-five Scottish burghs had newspapers; fifteen years later the figure was fifty. In addition several existing titles moved to daily publication (Donaldson 1986: 3–6). As papers expanded their frequency and size, invested in new technology and extended their journalistic resources, both start-up and running costs increased substantially. The radical press struggled in the new situation. Curran and Seaton, noting that most of the local dailies established mid-century in Britain were affiliated to the Tory or Liberal parties, comment that 'The early radical stress on moral regeneration through social reconstruction became a celebration of moral improvement through the spread of middle class enlightenment' (Curran and Seaton 1997: 39).

It is arguable, however, that the social transformation which took place was caused by several factors, and that the decline of the radical press needs to be understood in a much wider context than the impact of cheap papers aimed at the working class. Nonetheless the decline is remarkable. Cowan calculates, using the official records of stamps issued, that in 1837 the circulation of Edinburgh's legal papers amounted to 12,941 copes per issue, Glasgow's 6,408, Dundee's 1,350 and Aberdeen's 2,592 (Cowan 1946: 169–70). Circulation figures for Scottish radical titles are hard to obtain, but evidence from south of the border suggests that, at the height of their success, the total circulation of such papers in some areas equalled and perhaps exceeded that of the stamped press. In Scotland the tradition did not disappear entirely and was carried on in the twentieth century by the weekly *Forward* (1906–56), which was initially managed and edited by Tom Johnston, later a distinguished Secretary of State for Scotland. Johnston overcame the problems endemic in such publications – lack of finance, inadequate staffing, the difficulties in attracting advertising and securing reliable distribution – and the paper led an independent existence for fifty years before merging with the UK-wide *Socialist Commentary*; by 1912 its sales had reached 20,000 per week (Campbell 1978: 33). The *West Highland Free Press*, which was established in 1972 in Skye by a team of young journalists led by Brian Wilson, who later became a Labour minister, has consciously sought to continue the radical tradition, while also cannily providing its readers with the kind of material they would expect from a regional weekly.

It could not be argued that Scotland's newspapers achieved very much during this early period which was particularly distinctive on the UK scene. However, that is not true as far as magazines were concerned. At the beginning of the nineteenth century the *Edinburgh Review* (1802–1929) was founded as a quarterly dedicated to progressive Whig politics and to literature. The *Review* pioneered the long critical essay, the like of which is found today in publications like the *London Review of Books*, the *TLS*, and, on occasion, in the recently established *Scottish Review of Books* (2004–). It paid its contributors well and enjoyed a reputation for making and breaking literary careers; by 1815 its print run was 13,000 copies per issue (Finkelstein 2007: 206). Its success encouraged the establishment in London of the *Quarterly Review* (1809–1967), a Tory journal which was enthusiastically promoted by the novelist Walter Scott who disapproved of the Edinburgh publication's politics – and of a hostile notice of his poem *Marmion*. The *Edinburgh Review* was followed by the monthly *Blackwood's Magazine* (1817–1980), which secured UK-wide success with its mixture of politics, arts and literature; it printed in serial form fiction by writers such as George Eliot, Trollope and Conrad. William Chambers's weekly *Edinburgh Journal* (1832–53) enjoyed equal success when it sought a different audience with its more varied bill of fare and enthusiastic promotion of self-improvement.

1855 TILL 1955

In the second half of the nineteenth century British newspapers not only found themselves free of government taxes – though legislative constraints such as the laws of seditious libel remained, and would be added to later by such statutes as the Official Secrets Act of 1911 – but also the beneficiaries of major technological innovation. Wood pulp replaced paper derived from rags as the basic raw material; paper itself was manufactured by machinery rather than hand (an early nineteenth-century development). The first rotary press had been used in London by *The Times* in 1814 and had an output of 1,100 sheets per hour; by 1865 the first roll-fed rotary press had been built in the USA and it produced 12,000 complete newspapers per hour. By the end of the nineteenth century linotype machines were employed in composing pages, and illustrations employing various techniques were commonplace. Photographs were introduced to newspapers at the beginning of the twentieth century and colour photography in the latter part of the twentieth.

Technological change external to the press also had a major impact. The electric telegraph came into being in the 1840s, in 1851 a cable was laid across the English Channel, and in 1866, after an earlier failed attempt, across the Atlantic. Alexander Graham Bell invented the telephone in 1876, and in 1891 a cable was laid between England and France, although it was not until 1956 that the first transatlantic cable began operating, not least because Marconi transmitted the first radio signal across the ocean in 1901 and paved the way for wire-less communications over vast distances.

All of these developments transformed the collection of news. It was no longer necessary to rely on road or on the burgeoning railway system for the transmission of information over long distances. The German entrepreneur, Julius de Reuter, exploited the growth of telegraphic services, initially on the continent, then in London in 1851, in order to supply business data. However, Reuter expanded into the provision of foreign news to British papers in London and elsewhere in the country, thus providing access to reports far sooner than had previously been the case, and at a price much lower than if they all had been obliged to employ their own correspondents abroad. The company he founded continues to operate as a news agency today (though the bulk of its revenue, as in its earliest period, derives from its business services), alongside other agencies including the American Associated Press and Agence France Presse. While in time the metropolitan titles employed a growing corps of foreign correspondents, that was never really an affordable option for Scottish papers, which to this day continue to draw heavily on agencies for their foreign reports. The Press Association (PA), which was founded in 1868, is owned by Britain's non-metropolitan titles and provides them with a service of UK national news. At an early stage Reuters entered into an agreement with PA to supply it with international news for its clients in return for a substantial payment and the provision of domestic news which Reuters could then distribute overseas.

Railways revolutionised life to an extraordinary degree, since goods and people were now able to travel overland at thitherto undreamed of speeds. As far as the British press is concerned, the impact ultimately worked to the advantage of London-based titles and the disadvantage of provincial ones. The capital's papers could now be printed late evening and early morning and dispatched by train to most parts of England and Wales in time to be sold the next day. Since metropolitan titles were produced in the political and commercial heartland of the UK, they were not only closer to government, but they often had far greater resources at their disposal than provincial ones, not least because of the size of their London base markets. As a result, many provincial papers, once secure in their own areas, faced intense competition which only a few were able to resist in the long term. That is why the non-London press in England and Wales today largely consists of evening papers and local weeklies, many morning and Sunday titles having gone to the wall, although there are a few doughty survivors such as the Leeds-based *Yorkshire Post* (1866–) and the Cardiff-based *Western Mail* (1869–).

Paradoxically, Scotland's newspapers benefited from the limitations of the railway system. In the latter part of the nineteenth century, when London-based morning papers were making life very hard for English provincial titles, it was difficult for newspaper trains to reach Scotland in time for the titles to be on sale throughout the country alongside the Scottish ones. Even when printing centres linked through the telecommunications system to London were opened in the north of England, distribution problems remained. Scottish papers were given a long breathing space not available to their English provincial counterparts in which to build up reader loyalty. All four of the country's major cities acquired significant press industries and, despite the predominance of Glasgow-based titles, retain them today.

The developments just discussed were accompanied by a growth in the number of journalists and in the professionalisation of that trade. The Institute of Journalists was formed in 1884 and the National Union of Journalists in 1907. The latter is more like a traditional trade union than the former but both seek to ensure that appropriate standards are maintained in the profession. Arguments continue to rage about the best preparation for the job – apprenticeship, university courses, a combination of the two, or even immersion in the so-called 'university of life'.

By the end of the nineteenth century then, newspapers had become large-scale businesses requiring substantial investment. There was little room for the small-scale operation beyond the local level and, as the twentieth century progressed, even local titles found themselves bought up by acquisition-hungry chains.

Although newspapers now offered a much wider agenda than they had done previously, with crime, human interest, sport, entertainment and, increasingly, feature material aimed at women readers being part of the regular mix, particularly in titles which sought mass-market appeal, politics remained a central concern. But as Stephen Koss has argued, an important change took place during the period. Whereas from the mid-nineteenth century until the beginning of the twentieth, newspapers had allied themselves closely to particular political parties or factions, sometimes regardless of the damage caused to their own commercial interests, that ceased to be the case in more recent times.

> By the middle of the twentieth century newspapers had been divested either by choice or by circumstance of the political role in which they had been cast for the better part of a hundred years. To be sure, they usually continued to favour one party over another and to take partisan stands, particularly at the time of general elections. But they had abandoned and, in certain cases, repudiated the avowedly political objectives to which they had been dedicated through and beyond the second half of the nineteenth century. (Koss 1984: 3)

The contemporary reader might immediately retort by citing the *Daily Mail* (1896–) and *The Daily Telegraph* (1855–) as papers clearly committed to the Conservative cause, or the *Daily Record* (1895–) as one committed to Labour. In fact, the *Telegraph* was once allied to the Liberal politician, William Gladstone, despite its current manifestation as the voice of the non-strident middle-class Tory voter, and readership surveys tell us that a significant proportion of its readers do not vote Conservative. Furthermore, the *Telegraph* cannot be relied on to support the Conservatives regardless, as several recent leaders of the party can ruefully testify. Similar points can be made about the *Daily Mail* and the *Daily Record*. The latter may in recent years have been denounced by Labour's opponents in Scotland on account of its alleged willingness to attack these other parties ferociously, but in some circumstances the *Record* has been happy to run a campaign against particular legislative proposals emanating from the 1999–2007 Lab/Lib Dem Holyrood coalition. The way in which *The Sun* (1964–) shifted its political allegiance, after it was acquired by Rupert Murdoch's Newscorp in 1969, from Labour to Mrs Thatcher's Tory party, then to Tony Blair's New Labour, while along the way its Scottish edition briefly supported the SNP, illustrates the same point. Newspapers have become fickle friends of political parties, if they are friends at all.

As was noted earlier, Scotland's major cities all have an extant title dating back to the eighteenth or early nineteenth centuries. However, the higher circulation mass-market titles are a more recent phenomenon. The *Daily Record* appeared in 1895 and was owned by a company formed by Alfred Harmsworth; it was followed by the *Sunday Mail* in 1919. Harmsworth moved on from the *Record* to establish the *Daily Mail* which first appeared in 1896, and within four years reached the then unprecedented daily circulation of one million. Three years later Harmsworth founded the *Daily Mirror* (1903–) which, after a poor start as a title aimed at women, became a paper noted for its use of pictures, at a time when press photography was in its very early stages. By the outbreak of World War One the *Mirror's* circulation was rivalling that of the *Mail*. Harmsworth, who became Lord Northcliffe, was an early example of the powerful proprietor who sought both commercial success and political influence, though that did not involve slavishly toeing a party line. The Canadian Max Aitken, later Lord Beaverbrook, was a comparable figure. He acquired the *Daily Express* (1900–), a rival of the *Mail*, in 1911, and launched the *Sunday Express* in 1919. Beaverbrook ensured that his papers supported his pet political causes, in particular Empire Free Trade.

Such proprietors have not disappeared, as mention of Rupert Murdoch has indicated. Murdoch heads a vast business enterprise with interests in press, broadcasting, film and beyond. But, unlike his fellow colonial of Scottish descent, Beaverbrook, who pursued causes dear to his heart, Murdoch seems more interested in using his titles to advocate policies of potential benefit to his commercial activities, which may in part explain their frequent political re-alignment. On the other hand, Robert Maxwell, the Czech-born business-man, who in 1984 acquired the Mirror Group, including its Scottish titles, did indeed use his papers to mount various short-lived campaigns, while at the same time he plundered his employees' pension fund. His was a brief career as newspaper baron and it ended with his apparent suicide in 1991.

The two most successful Scottish press companies, D. C. Thomson and Johnston Press, have been led over the years by much less flamboyant charac-ters. Thomson is a Dundee-based business which in 1905 acquired the long-standing *Courier*, and then proceeded to build up a company whose publications include *The Sunday Post* (1914–), which in the post-World War Two period had a circulation of over one million, a record no Scottish paper has surpassed. In addition, Thomson produces a range of comics and maga-zines, including *The Beano* (1938–), *The Dandy* (1937–), *The People's Friend* (1869–) and *The Scots Magazine* (1927–). The comics, which are targeted at the UK market rather than the Scottish one alone, have specialised in the kind of subversive anti-authority humour which appeals to young children, and in Dudley D. Watkins, creator of Desperate Dan and Lord Snooty (also Oor Wullie and The Broons of *The Sunday Post*), and Leo Baxendale, progenitor of The Bash Street Kids, it had artists of remarkable talent and invention. *The People's Friend*, for its part, began life as a literary offshoot of John Leng's leftish *People's Journal* (1858–1990), but in Thomson's hands it has become a repository of homely tales and helpful hints. *The Scots Magazine* is a popular ethnic title tar-geted at domestic and expatriate readerships. The Johnston Press was estab-lished in Falkirk in 1767 and for much of the period under review was a modest undertaking. Its transformation into the local/regional giant it has become is a relatively recent phenomenon.

In the early 1950s the Scottish newspaper scene was a vibrant one. *The Glasgow Herald* and *The Scotsman* were solid broadsheet titles, each thirled to its home area but with pan-Scottish aspirations, albeit partially realised ones. In 1953 the Edinburgh title had been purchased by the Canadian Thomson Corporation, a newspaper company headed by Roy Thomson, another colonial tycoon of Scots extraction. The seller was Kemsley Newspapers, then the largest chain in Britain, which at that time owned *The Daily Telegraph* and *The Sunday Times* (1821–), and the previous year had sold the *Daily Record* and the *Sunday Mail* to the Mirror Group. The *Record* and the *Scottish Daily Express* (the quasi-independent edition of the London Beaverbrook title which had been established in 1928) were engaged in a fierce circulation war, while the Aberdeen and Dundee mornings continued to dominate their respective markets. The age of television had begun, but so far it was the cinema rather than the press which had felt its competitive force.

1955 TO THE PRESENT DAY

The history of broadcasting in Scotland is discussed elsewhere in this volume, but what needs to be noted here is the wary reaction of British newspapers when radio began in the 1920s, a reaction which manifested itself in a hostility to on-air news bulletins and a reluctance to publicise broadcast programmes. But it was not long before a *modus vivendi* was established when newspapers found that they could not only exist alongside their new competitor but could also use its activities as the basis for material of interest to readers. The combination of words and pictures has been more difficult to deal with, although its effects took time to make themselves felt.

Evening papers were the section of the press which proved most vulnerable to the challenge of television, specifically early evening news bulletins, whether from BBC Scotland, which began broadcasting as part of the UK network in 1952, or from the ITV stations, STV, which came on air in 1957 (one day after BBC Scotland, in a pre-emptive strike, launched a brief early evening domestic news summary), and Grampian and Border, which followed in 1961. By 1963 Edinburgh had lost the *Dispatch* (1886) while the *News* (1873–) survived. Glasgow lost its *News* (1875–1957) and *Citizen* (1864–1974), and that city too has only one remaining title, the *Times* (1876–). The one-city/one-title pattern is common throughout the UK, and the evening papers which survive struggle constantly against declining circulations.

Local weeklies have enjoyed mixed fortunes, and there has been much consolidation, with companies such as Johnston and Scottish and Universal

Newspapers being dominant in the field; titles owned by the latter, which for much of the period was part of George Outram, publishers of *The Glasgow Herald*, have passed to Trinity Mirror. Very few local newspapers are now owned by a company based in the area concerned. This is true on both sides of the border, so the Scottish-based Johnston now vies on the acquisition trail with Trinity Mirror, Northcliffe (Daily Mail and General Trust) and Newsquest (a subsidiary of the US company Gannett). The limited regulatory powers available to the state against concentration have been applied only very intermittently. Local newspapers remain very good investments, for they do not pay journalists particularly high wages, they often enjoy monopoly status in their areas and they continue to attract large volumes of advertising. As we have seen, advertising revenue has been crucial to the press for hundreds of years, and currently a mass-market daily would expect 50 per cent of its revenue to derive from that source, while for an upmarket one – and local titles – the figure is nearer 70 per cent. The chains look for a profit level of up to 30 per cent of turnover, and beyond, a figure undreamed of by many industrial companies and rarely achieved by national papers.

Commercial television and commercial radio – the latter began in the early 1970s in the UK – have clearly taken revenue from the press, although new media can and do have the effect of increasing total advertising spend. A major challenge facing all newspapers at the beginning of the twenty-first century is how to deal with the increasing importance of on-line advertising, particularly in the lucrative classified field, at a time when on-line sources of news are also proliferating. Newspapers can of course set up their own websites and seek to attract advertising in that way, but significant profits from such endeavours have so far been hard to come by. Raising cover prices is another option but might that course of action simply drive more readers to on-line and broadcast sources of news?

One supposed solution has been the introduction of give-away morning titles (free local weeklies packed with advertising and anodyne editorial content having existed for several decades). The Swedish Kinnevik company has been the free mornings pioneer throughout Europe and has based its operations on urban transport networks, through which distribution is relatively easy. In Scotland the publishers of the *Daily Mail* are responsible for *Metro*, an advertising-financed tabloid which offers a digest of news, much of it in snippet form, alongside extensive entertainment listings. *Metro*, in contrast to its owner's paid-for national titles, is devoid of editorial comment and analysis. Despite the commercial success of *Metro*, it is highly doubtful if it is possible to run a serious newspaper which is willing to challenge those in authority solely on the basis of advertising finance. And *Metro*, particularly for young people, seems like another good reason not to pay for a paper. Furthermore, the spread of such titles saps the goodwill of newsagents and other outlets on which newspaper companies continue to rely for distribution of their products.

Despite the difficulties evening titles encountered in the new television age, other segments of the market were more buoyant. The Scottish edition of the *Daily Express* reached a circulation of over 650,000 in the late 1950s, and when the *Daily Record* became the leading morning in the 1970s, it managed to sell over 700,000 copies per day. However there were setbacks: the demise of *The Bulletin* (1915–60); the ill fortune which attended the *Scottish Daily News*, the attempt in 1975 to create an employee-owned paper after Beaverbrook drastically curtailed its Scottish presence; the short lives of the *Sunday Standard* (1981–3) and *Business AM* (2001–3). Nonetheless, two upmarket Sunday titles, *Scotland on Sunday* (1988–) and the *Sunday Herald* (1999–) were founded and are now well established, with their current owners, Johnston and Newsquest, apparently committed to their survival. Significantly, both titles appeared after Newscorp's 1986–7 victory over the print unions at Wapping in London, which led to the widespread introduction of computer-based production techniques and substantial cost savings throughout the industry. Until the two new Scottish papers made their debuts, there was a real gap in the Sunday market in Scotland, for although the *Post* and the *Mail* enjoyed very large circulations relative to the country's population, they did not offer the kind of service provided by the English broadsheet Sundays, which is one reason why *The Sunday Times* continues to sell well north of the border, despite the erosion of its market share by the new arrivals. These two titles represent a maturing of the Scottish newspaper market. Paradoxically, the amount of space they and their daily stable mates give to the discussion of public affairs and the arts makes it even less likely that a Scottish weekly journal along the lines of the *New Statesman* or *The Spectator* will ever emerge. Several quarterlies such as *The Scottish Review* (1995–), *Scottish Affairs* (1992–) and the revived *Edinburgh Review* (1969–) do provide opportunities for in-depth debate about politics, culture and the arts, while ethnic and specialist magazines flourish in their niche markets, but it is noteworthy that the fortnightly *Holyrood* (1999–), which focuses on Scottish politics and local government, is only available on – a rather expensive – subscription. It is not targeted at the general reader.

The range of Scottish-based titles may have been extended but the overall trend has been one of decline. In the mid-1970s Scottish-produced titles represented almost two-thirds of the dailies and Sundays purchased in Scotland, 64 per cent and 66 per cent of 1.7 million and 2.7 million copies respectively.[3] By 2006, however, the situation had changed markedly: the daily and Sunday totals were now lower, at 1.5 million and 1.6 million respectively, and English titles had eroded the shares of the indigenous papers. Some had done so by introducing editions substantially different from those on sale south of the border. Newscorp was to the fore here and, with a printing plant and substantial editorial presence in Glasgow, it was able to produce *The Scottish Sun*, the *Scottish News of the World*, and *The Sunday Times Scotland*. Enough account is taken of Scottish readers' interests – not least in sport, football in particular – and the political and social contexts in these papers to justify the mastheads. The *Scottish Daily Mail* has gone down a similar route: it was selling 124,000 copies in the second half of 2006, three times its 1970s figure, and not far short of the combined circulations of *The Scotsman* (58,000) and *The Herald* (70,000), which in the mid-1970s were selling 90,000 and 109,000 respectively. The most spectacular success has been that of *The Scottish Sun*: its non–editionised version sold 155,000 in 1976 compared to the *Record's* 676,000, but in mid-2006 *The Scottish Sun* managed 394,000 against the *Record's* 384,000. This was achieved by both editorial flair and price cutting, with *The Sun* selling for a next-to-nothing ten pence against the *Record's* thirty five pence, a *prima facie* case, it might be argued, of predatory pricing. It will be noted that the overall sale of the two papers combined has declined in the period by 6 per cent; however, given the annual slide of 2 per cent plus in overall circulations, which has become the norm in recent years in the UK – and in North America and much of Western Europe[4] – this can be regarded as something of a success, particularly when it is remembered that in Britain as a whole it is the tabloids which have suffered the steepest declines ('broadsheet' and 'tabloid' are used here in their traditional senses rather than as descriptive terms for page sizes). In Scotland sales of broadsheet dailies – Scottish and English in origin – have declined by 19 per cent overall since the 1970s, while Sunday broadsheets have seen an increase of 35 per cent; the daily tabloid market has declined by 9 per cent and the Sunday one by 46 per cent. Scotland has diverged from UK trends, in that in Britain as a whole there has been an overall increase in broadsheet daily sales and a much sharper decline in the tabloid daily market.

English titles, with or without a kilt, (a Scottish edition), now account for 55 per cent of daily sales and 44 per cent of Sundays. The four Scottish-based daily broadsheets – the *Courier*, *The Herald*, the *Press and Journal* and *The Scotsman* – have seen an absolute decline of 30 per cent in sales, while English-based titles have enjoyed a 65 per cent increase; within that market segment there has been a 12 per cent shift in share from the one to the other. In the tabloid sector the decline in Scottish titles (the *Daily Record*) has been 43 per cent, with English-based titles gaining 30 per cent on their previous figure; the market-share shift is 20 per cent, almost double that to be found in the broadsheet segment. As far as Sundays are concerned, there were no Scottish broadsheet titles in 1976 and the two new titles now have a 49 per cent share, English titles having suffered a 31 per cent decline. In the Sunday tabloid sector, the decline in the sales of the two Scottish titles is a remarkable 56 per cent, while

English titles have declined by 20 per cent. The shift in market share from Scottish to English titles is 14 per cent. The political sea change which led to devolution does not appear to have strengthened the loyalty of Scottish readers to Scottish newspapers; in fact, the opposite has happened. Marketing and price-cutting have played roles but something else must be at work. Perhaps there is a Holyrood-induced *ennui*, perhaps a desire for a wider perspective, or simply a belief that English titles with greater resources from both advertising and sales can offer a better service than Scottish ones, particularly if they editionise in more than a perfunctory fashion. If an English broadsheet daily were to increase its Scottish content substantially, that could create serious problems for its Scottish counterparts. And the oft-mooted proposal that *The Herald* and *The Scotsman* should merge to form one well funded pan-Scottish title, perhaps on the model of *The Irish Times*, might well come to be seen as the only viable alternative to continual decline in the face of the advance of the English broadsheets north of the border. It is worth noting, however, that the press in the Irish Republic also finds itself under pressure currently from editionised English titles, particularly Newscorp ones.

The relationship between the media and politics is explored elsewhere in this book. What should be noted here is that, as Scotland has become a country less attracted to the Conservative party, so the press has responded to that change in mood. *The Sunday Post* remains a very traditional paper, and its precipitate circulation decline in the past thirty years owes something to that fact, although the *Post* has long since sought to adopt a more plural approach to politics than it did in the past. And *The Herald*, once derided by the Labour establishment as the 'Scottish Tory *Pravda*' – a reference to the then Soviet Union's leading title – which during the 1979 General Election declared that it was vital for the nation's future that Mrs Thatcher be elected, has abandoned support for the Conservative cause, in favour of a left-liberal stance, the kind of approach which the distinguished expatriate journalist Andrew Neil finds so irritating and sought to counter when the Barclay Brothers put him in charge of Scotsman Publications (Hutchison 2006: 38).

The Barclays purchased the Edinburgh titles from the Thomson Organisation in 1995 when that company began to withdraw from newspapers in Canada and elsewhere, but ten years later the Barclays sold the papers to the Johnston Press, which in *The Scotsman* and *Scotland on Sunday* acquired pan-Scottish titles for the first time. Northcliffe, which purchased its Aberdeen titles from Thomson at the same time, sold them to Dundee's D. C. Thomson in 2006. The Scottish Media Group, owner of STV and, latterly, Grampian, acquired *The Herald* and the *Evening Times* in 1996, founded the *Sunday Herald* in 1999, then, faced with mounting debts after an ill-advised series of acquisitions in England, sold them in 2002 to Newsquest/Gannett. At the time of writing, it is not clear whether

Trinity Mirror, which is struggling to meet its investors' profit expectations, intends to retain the *Daily Record* and *Sunday Mail*. For the moment there is something of an east coast/west coast split in ownership, with Scottish companies in control in the east and an English and an American company in the west. Almost certainly that pattern will change, though in which direction is hard to predict.

Newspapers, whether mass- or up-market, entertain, stimulate and divert their readers, but they also provide information and provoke discussion about what is happening in their own society and beyond. At their best they challenge those in authority, elected and unelected. Newspapers are businesses but they are far more than businesses. It can only be hoped that the current and future owners of the Scottish press will continue to be aware of their responsibilities not only to their shareholders but also to the wider public good.

ACKNOWLEDGEMENT

My thanks are due to the Special Collections staff of Glasgow Caledonian University.

NOTES

1. For holdings see Mackenzie, A. (1994), *Report of the Newsplan Project in Scotland*, London: British Library.
2. For a discussion of this development see Myra Macdonald's chapter in Hutchison, D. (ed.) (1978), *Headlines: The Media in Scotland*, Edinburgh, Polygon.
3. The 1976 circulation figures are drawn from my chapter in *Headlines*, and 2006 ones from the Audit Bureau of Circulations.
4. See Hutchison, D. (2007), 'The EU and the press: policy or non-policy?', *European Studies* 24, for a discussion of general trends on a wider canvas.

REFERENCES

Campbell, B. (1978), 'Forward: the radical press in the early twentieth century', in D. Hutchison (ed.), *Headlines: The Media in Scotland*, Edinburgh: Polygon, pp. 30–8.
Cowan, R. M. (1946), *The Newspaper in Scotland: A Study of its First Expansion 1815–1860*, Glasgow: George Outram.
Curran, J. and J. Seaton (1997), *Power Without Responsibility*, 5th edn, London: Routledge.
Donaldson, W. (1986), *Popular Literature in Victorian Scotland*, Aberdeen: Aberdeen University Press.
Finkelstein, D. (2007), 'Periodicals, Encyclopaedias and Nineteenth Century Literary Production', in S. Manning (ed.), *Edinburgh History of Scottish Literature*, Volume 2, Edinburgh: Edinburgh University Press, pp. 198–21.

Fraser, W. H. (1996), 'Alexander Campbell' and 'Alexander Campbell and some "lost" unstamped newspapers', *Scottish Labour History Journal*, 31, pp. 35–50.

Hutchison, D. (2006), 'Ownership, Control and Cultural Policy', *Edinburgh Review*, 116, pp. 35–45.

Koss, S. E. (1984), *The Rise and Fall of the Political Press in Britain, Volume 1*, London: Hamish Hamilton.

Wiener, J. H. (1969), *The War of the Unstamped*, Ithaca: Cornell University Press.

5

The History of Film and Cinema

DAVID BRUCE

The three words 'Scottish', 'film' and 'industry', have never sat comfortably together. Indeed there have always been plenty of people, most famously the great John Grierson, ready to deny the possibility of such a conjunction having any meaning at all.[1] Yet there is no denying that Scottish film production and Scottish cinema exhibition have had many successes, some of them quite outstanding and far-reaching in their effects.

Whatever else may be said about the history of film in Scotland, one thing is obvious: this is no story of a smooth trajectory from small beginnings to final grand triumph. Rather, it is a tale of stops and starts, of false dawns and the occasional blazing comet, of overblown expectations and disproportionate despair. It is probably significant that, to date, there has been only one comprehensive, scholarly chronicle, Duncan Petrie's *Screening Scotland*.

In the work of the men and women directly involved in the making and showing of Scottish films, there is much to admire. The contributions of individual Scots to the film culture of this and other lands are so notable that they demand to be celebrated. As to the systems, the politics, the context in which they have had to operate, that is another matter – yet there are many significant achievements there, too.

With all the advantages of hindsight, it is possible to identify times in this erratic history when with luck or better management things could have been quite different. Arguably, there were such key moments in 1946, 1960, 1980 and 1995. For example, in the mid-1990s, when the centenary of cinema was being celebrated, there was a burst of enthusiasm for Scottish film. In 1995, Peter Capaldi's short film *Franz Kafka's It's a Wonderful Life* had just won an Oscar; two major movies with greater or lesser degrees of Scottishness,

Braveheart and *Rob Roy*, were on the list for the next year's prizes, the former winning no less than five Academy awards; *Trainspotting* was breaking box-office records; there were several other Scottish-based movies in the pipeline including Lars von Trier's *Breaking the Waves*; the UK's new National Lottery was dispensing money for film projects; a new agency, Scottish Screen, was being established to amalgamate the existing film bodies; there were rumours of several projects to build studios, leading to foolish newspaper stories about 'Hollywood on the Clyde' (or in the Highlands); and so on.

There is no denying that there was much in that time which constituted real advance for film in Scotland, but in the longer view the question has to be asked as to whether the potential that such activity represented was properly understood. And although this was opportunity on a greater scale than before, it was not the only time this kind of situation had arisen.

THE EARLY YEARS

Broadly speaking, the history of Scottish film can be divided into three periods. The first lasts from the invention of the medium in the late nineteenth century until about 1930, the era of so-called 'silent' cinema. The second, from then until the end of the 1970s, was characterised by the domination of documentary production. The third, continuing to the present day, has seen the establishing of fiction film as the main mode of Scottish cinema.

Scotland did not invent the movies, though we will of course lay claim to midwifery at the birth thanks to William Kennedy Laurie Dickson (1860–1935) whose work in the USA with Thomas Edison included designing the Kinetoscope and establishing 35mm as the norm for the gauge of moving film. Admittedly, Dickson was born in France and died in England, and appears never to have lived in Scotland despite being proud of his Laurie ancestry.

At the beginning, movies were the province of the travelling showmen. There could be as many as a dozen or more film tents at one fair. The first film screening in Scotland was probably at Christmas 1895 at the Carnival Ground, Gallowgate, Glasgow. Then, on 13 April 1896 a version of Edison and Dickson's Kinetoscope was the system used in the Empire, Nicolson Street, Edinburgh (now Edinburgh Festival Theatre). Lumière's *Cinematographe* was first shown on 26 May 1896 by Arthur Hubner in the building in Sauchiehall Street, Glasgow, that was successively the site of a panorama, Hengler's circus, the Waldorf dance hall, and the Regal cinema.

As film shows became increasingly popular, whether in temporary structures or as novelty items in musical halls, so the impermanence of tents and vans was replaced by custom-built premises. Whatever the original venues they had used, the showmen, such as Kemp in Ayrshire, Poole in Edinburgh, Green in

Glasgow, Biddall in the Borders, soon moved into permanent buildings designed specifically for film. That transition was relatively rapid. Fifteen years after the invention of the medium, there were cinemas in every part of Scotland. Sadly, only a very few of these survive as cinemas, or anything else, to this day – Campbeltown's New Picture House (1913) being a rare and precious example – and the casualty list is a very long one.

These new buildings were often the antithesis of the temporary structures they replaced. For example, the La Scala in Helensburgh which opened in 1913 was a replacement for a 'corrugated iron and wood' building put up in 1911. The La Scala, like many other similar cinemas, expressed a clear statement that cinema was now a classy form of entertainment. With its elegant art deco interior and tip-up seats (one of the first in Britain to install them), the La Scala was considered one of the finest of its type outside London but like so many of its era, its significance seems to have bypassed the consciousness of host communities and latter-day planners until too late.[2] An even earlier custom-built establishment was the Vitagraph in Sauchiehall Street, Glasgow, which opened in 1910 with the remarkable novelty of Kinemacolor, a system in which every individual frame was coloured by hand.

To begin with, both film-making and the exhibition of films might be practised by the same people. The showmen would mostly present what they could buy in, but since cine cameras were available to purchase from 1896, they could, and often did, make their own movies. The principal self-generated genre was the 'local topical' which guaranteed an audience because it contained images of the audience itself. This was a good strategy, for who could resist the chance to see themselves on the big screen? That impulse or compulsion to stare or wave at the camera, to claim the most fleeting of celebrity as though to prove personal existence, continues to this day as a staple of television.

The value of these seemingly primitive 'topicals' is easy to underestimate. As documents of how people looked and moved they are beyond price. We have the Gordon Highlanders marching in Aberdeen in 1899; William Walker's footage of Queen Victoria and her family at Balmoral; the pre-evacuation St Kilda films; the Paisley cinema queue of 1929 with babes in arms (free entry) scarcely smaller than the child carrying them which also includes the images of two children who would die in the infamous Hogmanay fire-scare stampede in the Glen Cinema only weeks later. Or again, there was James Hart, manager of the Grosvenor cinema in Byres Road, Glasgow, whose 'Great Western Road' filmed on a Sunday morning in 1915 contrasts so movingly with his post-war repeat of the exercise seven years later. There is even a rather bizarre piece of work that is possibly unique and not for general consumption. In March 1896, Dr John McIntyre, a pioneer of X-rays in the service of medicine, made moving X-ray pictures of a stomach and of frogs' legs. These films and many others, fortunately mostly preserved in the Scottish Screen Archive, are national treasures.

In the newly established cinemas, for the most part what Scottish audiences saw was in line with that shown elsewhere in the United Kingdom and therefore the story is not significantly divergent from what can be found in any good history of silent cinema in Britain.[3] There were of course very individual Scottish experiences of cinema. Robert Garioch's account of his mother as 'pianny wumman' at the Picturedrome in Easter Road in Edinburgh is a nice example of how local circumstances could make the experience of cinema-going memorable for a child, and no doubt for an adult as well, but to find any peculiarly Scottish dimension to film in the period before the coming of sound, we have to look to the production end of the business (Garioch 1979: 49).

In the first decades of the twentieth century, two factors positively favoured indigenous film production. Before the advent of sound, the processes were relatively cheap. As we have seen, projectable films could be made by cinema owners and managers, and they pulled in the local audience merely by shooting what was happening in the streets. Story-telling films were not that much more difficult to produce. The second advantage was the universality of the medium so long as it came without sound and therefore language.

Small film studios appeared across Britain, with, in one Glasgow instance, some evidence of success. James Bowie's Rouken Glen studio was the base for the three-reel *Rob Roy* (1911), directed by Arthur Vivian and starring John Clyde and Theo Henries. 'Ace Films' took over the studio in 1919 and produced a five-reeler, *The Harp King*, and when they went bankrupt 'Broadway Cinema Productions' made *Fitba Daft*. Sadly, none of these films survives, and traces of what was possibly a significant episode in Scottish film history are equally difficult to find. Was there, as might be suggested, a still-born Scottish feature film industry?

What is not lacking is evidence of the popularity of Scottish subjects as raw material for everyone else's film industry. From the very beginning, our allegedly romantic quaint selves, our glorious landscapes and (more legitimately) our store of tales and epics from the pens of Scott, Stevenson, Barrie and the others made our culture a happy hunting ground for those who had the entertainment of the worldwide cinema-going public as their aim.

From the primitive *Scotch Reel* (1898), *The Effects of Too Much Scotch* (1903), *McNab's Visit to London* (1905) and *The Amorous Scotchman* (1909) to the more seriously intentioned *Lochinvar*, *Macbeth*, and *The Bride of Lammermoor* (all also 1909), the list is astonishing.[4] Just as remarkable is the proportion of Scottish-related material that derives from the work of the aforementioned authors. Richard Butt reckons that as many as a quarter of such films in the period before 1920 are based on the work of just those three writers, a total of over 150 releases. Only Shakespeare, of English-language writers, is in the same league (Butt 2007: 53).

By the end of cinema's first thirty years, a familiar pattern had been established in Scotland. Cinema-going was popular; the product was almost entirely imported; the indigenous output, such as it is, was at cottage industry level; there were no big players based in the country. There was certainly a significant Scottish contribution to world cinema but already that was being made by Scots abroad, most conspicuously in Hollywood. There, the expatriate actors included Eric Campbell from Dunoon, a giant of a man who as Chaplin's foil in *Easy Street* and other films achieved a stardom of his own before his tragic death in a traffic accident in 1917.[5] One of the greatest directors, too, was a Scot. Frank Lloyd (1889–1960) would gain Academy awards and nominations for several of his films including *Cavalcade* (1932) and *Mutiny on the Bounty* (1935).

In one significant regard, however, there was a difference from later times. There was no state involvement in the business of film. Indeed, the only major reference to government involvement is in the tragic case of the Glen Cinema disaster in which seventy children died in an unnecessary panic when they believed wrongly that the building was on fire. That event led directly to legislation on cinema safety with far-reaching consequences for the industry throughout Britain. However, the role of government in film-making would become increasingly important in the next period of Scotland's film history, the decades which saw the great rise in cinema attendance, the lowest production of indigenous fiction film, and the dominance of documentary.

TALKING FILMS

The coming of sound changed everything. For thousands of musicians this was bad news as their services were no longer required to accompany silent films. For exhibitors, the capital investment required not only for the systems but the buildings themselves was now very considerable. The Playhouse, on Edinburgh's Leith Walk, opened in 1929 with an auditorium which seated some 3,000 and yet was not the biggest in Scotland, that honour being held by Green's Playhouse in Glasgow with 4,200 seats. Scotland was already well established as a consumer country for the movies, a position it would maintain until television and domestic central heating changed all that forty years later.

Scots figured prominently in the growth of cinema chains, no one more so than John Maxwell (1877–1940). As is the case with the 'Hollywood Scots', Maxwell's contribution is largely based on what he did beyond Scotland's borders. It is true that his origins and first successes were in Scotland but his main contribution was to wider British cinema in the founding of Savoy Cinemas, British National Pictures (the company that made the first British talking picture, Hitchcock's *Blackmail* (1929)), and finally, the exhibition chain, Associated British Cinemas. Maxwell undoubtedly had an impact on Scotland but only as a consequence of his endeavours in London. His colleague and fellow Scot, Robert Clark, did at least have a direct involvement in specifically Scottish film exhibition as chairman of Caledonian Associated Cinemas alongside Sir Alexander B. King and Robert Wotherspoon, but it is Maxwell who is the most important figure.

Take also the case of John Grierson (1898–1972). Although he certainly influenced Scottish film-making and the thinking about film in Scotland, his greatest achievements were from London and Canadian bases. And yet, as a fine paradox, we can argue that Alexander McKendrick (1912–94), an American citizen born in Boston, who died in Los Angeles and whose finest film was set in New York, was Scotland's greatest film-maker. The simple conclusion is that Scotland was, and is, too small a country to contain its talents in practically any sphere of life that has an international dimension, and few pursuits are more international than film.

In one regard, Grierson and Scotland are inextricably linked; it is not merely that 'the father of the documentary' made both of the only two films he actually directed in Scotland – *Drifters* (1929) and *Granton Trawler* (1934) – nor that he was involved in the Films of Scotland Committees of 1938 and 1954 and in the founding of the Edinburgh International Film Festival, it is also his psychology. The son of a rural dominie, Grierson had the ability to bring phenomenal energy and intellect to whatever matter was in hand.[6] His work ethic, as well as his gruff determination to succeed whether by fair means or subversion, his acute political awareness and a permanently radical position marked him out as unmistakably a Scot of the most virulent type.

Grierson was primarily a propagandist concerned with mass communication (Grierson 1990: 65). Documentary film was his medium (later it would be television) because that was the way to get to people (Hardy 1966: 289). 'Documentary' was not 'reportage'. 'Reality' was the raw material to be treated 'creatively' to get the message across. So if some of the postmen in the GPO Film Unit's *Night Mail* (1936) were actually actors hired for the movie and if the interior of the train was shot in a studio, so what? The story of the journey of the postal express from London to Scotland, the message about the expertise and even excitement of the seemingly banal moving of letters up the track, is not only clear but is, like the mail itself, amazingly delivered.

Indigenous Scottish film production in the period 1930 to 1979 was almost exclusively in documentary. There were exceptions, particularly towards the end of the period when ambition on the part of some film-makers and of those who sponsored them led to one or two story films. There were other occasional forays into fiction such as *The Little Singer* (Elder Productions, 1956) but Scotland in fiction on the big screen was found only in the efforts of non-Scots companies and individuals or, at best, in the hands of Scots directors, writers and actors working for English or American producers.

In the otherwise rather thin bibliography of Scottish film,[7] the one subject area concerning film and Scotland which has produced relatively substantial and serious critical writing is, of course, representation. Although our sensitivity on the matter of how the world sees us seems to be slightly less hysterical post-devolution and there has been a realisation that blaming others for our ills is no longer such a simple option, there is no doubt that it would take a monumental degree of detachment not to feel discomfort, even outrage, at much of the film product claiming to be about Scotland and the Scots. Of the 150 or so 'Scottish' films which made it to cinemas between 1930 and 1975, it is doubtful if more than a handful would meet with unqualified approval by a modern Scottish audience.

The nearest thing to Scottish cinema, then, is in the fairly small number of films made with substantial participation by Scots. There had been some at the end of the silent era including two starring Harry Lauder: *Huntingtower* (1927) and *Auld Lang Syne* (1929). Similarly, it is probably legitimate to set aside the many examples of Scott-derived, adapted Stevenson productions, the pseudo-biographical, historical – mainly Hollywood – versions of the life of Mary Queen of Scots, the Barrie-esque Kailyardery and so on, to concentrate on the handful that in some degree relate genuinely to Scotland's culture.

Michael Powell was no Scot – in fact he was a quintessential Englishman. However, he became a devoted Scotophile, and of his Scottish films – *Red Ensign* (1934), *The Edge of the World* (1937), *The Spy in Black* (1939) and *I Know Where I'm Going* (1945) – at least two should be willingly adopted by us, even though they are about an outsider's perception of our country. They are extraordinary films which should be included in a Scottish filmography.

By the same token, that list must also include the story of the Knockshinnoch mining disaster, *The Brave Don't Cry* (1952) from Group 3, directed by Philip Leacock but produced by Grierson in his rather unlikely and not very successful spell in feature film; and *The Brothers* (1947), David Macdonald's much under-rated but strongly cast black Highland story. Some would argue that *The Gorbals Story* (1950) should also be included but as, in effect, a filmed play with little sense of cinema, it is hard to bracket it in the same category. Hitchcock's *The Thirty-Nine Steps* (1935) is one we would dearly like to adopt as ours but great Buchan yarn as it is, its relation to Scottish culture and Scottish film is slender.

Other obvious exclusions are easy to name: *Brigadoon* (1954) heads the list, of course, and we could indulge ourselves by remembering how awful some of the others were, but they are at best footnotes to a Scottish film history, or should be. Far better to concentrate on works and artists whose orientation and intentions eschew exploitation of the stereotype Scotland and tell stories with which we can reasonably identify.

Two names stand out here, Alexander Mackendrick and Bill Douglas, the latter's work being better discussed when we examine the emergence of genuine Scottish feature film-making later. Mackendrick, however, is of great significance in the story of Scottish film. With *Whisky Galore* (1949) and *The Maggie* (1954) he created something new, a comedy genre based on a kind of recognisable if exaggerated Scottish culture but layered with issues of a much more universal sort, especially those concerning the nature of community and authority. In this, Mackendrick's films belonged within the Ealing Studios tradition and transcended it. Objectively, these two films may not have been Mackendrick's best work – *Sweet Smell of Success* (1957) must surely be that – but they did demonstrate, as perhaps only *The Brothers* did before, that in cinema a Scottish context does not have to be inhibiting and merely colourful.

Whisky Galore begins with a mock documentary. This is not by chance, for as we have noted earlier, documentary was a powerful form of cinema at the time. It had been particularly important during the war years, for informational and propaganda reasons, but its place in cinema schedules, usually as a supporting short, had been established long before then.

To think of documentary as a peculiarly Scottish form of film-making is simplistic but forgivable. The Grierson connection makes for a solid claim, of course, and for most of the middle of the twentieth century the only film-making which was truly indigenous to Scotland and which therefore gave a decently reliable representation of our country and ourselves, was in the output of a few native film production companies working in documentary.

Ironically, the first instance of an organised attempt to represent Scotland by documentary film involved virtually nothing from Scottish production companies, and though many of the creative personnel were Scots, they were London-based. The first Films of Scotland Committee was formed in anticipation of the 1938 Empire Exhibition in Glasgow. The idea was Grierson's and though not all the seven films were of the finest quality (*Scotland for Fitness* being hilarious in its awfulness), nonetheless they demonstrated what a serious approach to the representation of Scotland on film could achieve. *The Face of Scotland* (1938) and *Wealth of a Nation* (1938) in their honesty and rigour were cases in point.

That essentially Griersonian ethic is very apparent in the films made in Scotland during the war and in the period immediately thereafter. These films, mostly made for public information ('propaganda' seems too strong a term given the content) qualify as indigenously Scottish by virtue of being originated by an enlightened Scottish Office. There, they were overseen by

Grierson's biographer Forsyth Hardy, later to become director of the second Films of Scotland Committee. Of these films, Donald Alexander's *Children of the City* (1944), about 'juvenile delinquency' and the legal system, is perhaps the most recognised, but there were others well worth a viewing today, such as *Highland Doctor* (1943).

It was Hardy's and Grierson's ambition which led to the formation of the second Films of Scotland Committee in 1954, but before that came a strange episode. In 1946, Scottish National Film Studios set up office in Glasgow. The grand title conceals the fact that it was the brainchild of a small group of people motivated more by nationalism, it seems, than by ambition for film (Bruce 1996: 159–61). Among the objectives of the company were the building of a studio in the Highlands and the establishing of a training school, a university chair of cinematography and an archive. In the event, the only film made was a road safety short with the deliciously appropriate title of *Someone Wasn't Thinking* (1946). The enterprise collapsed in a year, its obituary being uttered by one of its backers, Sir Hugh Roberton, the famous conductor of the Orpheus Choir, who declared, 'Films are chancy anyway'.

There is, however, one important point to be noted about this particular debacle. Unlike the first Films of Scotland Committee, Scottish National Film Studios had no connection with government, no route to the public purse, and it is indeed that relationship (or lack of it) between film and state which becomes key to the story of Scottish film from then on.

The second Films of Scotland Committee is the great case in point (Sherington 1996). It was technically a sub-committee of the Scottish Council for Development and Industry and yet received no government funding, its start-up being financed by a £10,000 loan from its treasurer, the millionaire draper Sir Hugh Fraser. Its job was to 'stimulate and encourage the production of Scottish films in the national interest'. It was given, as the chairman, Sir Alexander B. King, famously remarked, 'A remit without a remittance'.

It is therefore quite astonishing and an extraordinary tribute to Forsyth Hardy (1910–94) who was the committee's director from its inception until 1974, that even under such a seemingly hopeless constraint, the committee not only produced 168 short films but in effect bred a considerable portion of the film-making talent in Scotland for the next forty years. The committee's greatest triumph was the winning of an Oscar for live action short subject in 1960 for *Seawards the Great Ships*, but there were more prizes for it and for many of the other films, and if not all of the output was of that quality, the overall standard was remarkably high.

The question as to how, without government funding, this body of work could be achieved is simply answered. Hardy, who was on long-term secondment from the Scottish Office, was able to elicit sponsorship from companies, public and local authorities and other agencies to pay for films promoting their interests on the promise of cinema screenings, often negotiated by Sir Alex King in his other capacity as chairman of Caledonian Associated Cinemas. Added to that, Hardy's careful husbandry meant that Films of Scotland could deploy the money earned to make the occasional non-sponsored film, even to the point that latterly it was able to produce two short fiction films, *The Duna Bull* (1972) and *The Great Mill Race* (1975), both of which provided valuable experience for the film-makers. However, by that time, one or two of them had already had some experience of the genre through short fiction films produced for the Children's Film Foundation, then headed by the Dundee-born Henry Geddes.

But in the end, it was inevitable that Films of Scotland would be overtaken by history and by television as that medium became the natural home of documentary. It is rather poignant that *Seawards the Great Ships* was almost the last of the major cinema documentaries for many years (before the recent revival of the genre in different guise) and that its subject was an industry also on the point of sharp decline. Neither Scottish film-making nor shipbuilding could survive without state intervention. Perhaps if, on winning the Oscar, Films of Scotland had been put on the public payroll, the subsequent history of Scotland and film might have been very different, but that possible window of opportunity stayed shut.

Before leaving the documentary period, it should be noted that a more personal form of film-making was also practised in Scotland, some of it with great distinction. For example, three film-makers with, coincidentally, strong island connections should be mentioned: Jenny Gilbertson (a Grierson *protégée*) in Shetland, the poet-film-maker Margaret Tait of Orkney and the German Werner Kissling with his essentially anthropological study of Eriskay, *A Poem of Remote Lives* (1935).

It should also be registered in something more than a footnote that during this time, the only other source of Scottish story films was the amateur movement, an area easily overlooked by historians. With its enthusiasm, its competitions and festivals, it fulfilled an important function, not least as the breeding ground for talent, such as the great animator Norman McLaren, spotted by Grierson at the International Amateur Festival of 1936 and later taken by him to Canada. Laurence Henson, Eddie McConnell, Mike and Keith Alexander and others of Scotland's most successful film-makers also emerged from that background. In addition to Grierson, the Amateur Festival's prestigious adjudicators included Victor Saville, Anthony Asquith, Alberto Cavalcanti, Michael Powell and Alfred Hitchcock.

But the landscape of cinema and film was changing. Starved of investment, the great movie palaces and many of the lesser halls were in decline or closed.

The high point of cinema attendance post-war, which had risen to an astonishing 1,400 million admissions in the UK in 1951, was past. By 1984 admissions were only 53 million. The next generation of cinemas, reversing the trend, would be the multiplexes with their emphasis on maximum choice, flexible timings and popcorn, so that by 1998 attendance was back up to 123 million.

INTO FICTION

It might well seem strange to a casual observer of Scottish culture that with such a rich heritage of stories – everything from folk tales to high literary achievement – the Scots have been so poor at mining it to make movies, leaving that to others to do so at will and in quantity. They might even note with some bemusement that when Scottish film-makers do make a movie, it is very unlikely that the screenplay will be based on established literary work. It is true that there are exceptions to such a general observation, but they are few and most are recent, for example, *Rob Roy* (1995) – though it is at some removes from the original by Sir Walter Scott; *Trainspotting* (1996) based directly on the novel by Irvine Welsh; and *Young Adam* (2003) from the book by Alexander Trocchi.

But before we chastise ourselves any further, we should consider the difficulty of making any kind of story film at all in Scotland. Even our southern neighbours, with ten times the population and a long tradition of corporate film-making, have had their difficulties. In England, in the years after World War Two, there were many people deeply concerned by the lack of 'serious' film-making. 'Free Cinema', with such as Lindsay Anderson (who considered himself a Scot), Tony Richardson and a small group of their contemporaries, effected a transition from radical documentary to the feature films of Woodfall with extreme difficulty. What chance then for such a thing to happen in impoverished Scotland with no film infrastructure or feature tradition to build on?

At least there was a tradition in documentary and that was to prove very important, but truly indigenous story film in Scotland, when it emerged, did so in an unexpected way. Bill Forsyth's *That Sinking Feeling* (1979), a gentle comedy about unemployed youngsters and a robbery that goes wrong, was followed by his *Gregory's Girl* (1980), and suddenly there was a Scottish film industry – or at least that was what the newspapers said. The truth was rather different, but what Forsyth (born 1947) had achieved was genuinely very important. He had demonstrated that while others were agonising about the lack of Scottish feature film, or about the dreadful way in which Scotland was portrayed onscreen,[8] it was just possible, with sufficient determination, to make a movie that lots of people would pay good money to see.

Although Forsyth very properly receives the credit for his courage and not least for making two expert and highly enjoyable films from in effect a standing start, there was a kind of precedent in a different genre. Bill Douglas (1934–91) was, according to Lindsay Anderson, 'A poetic film maker whose feeling for moment and the intensity of the image makes him unique'. His films were 'torn out of him'. Douglas's British Film Institute-funded trilogy *My Childhood* (1972), *My Ain Folk* (1973), and *My Way Home* (1978) scarcely count as feature films in their duration (at forty-three, fifty-five and seventy-two minutes respectively), but their power is greater than that of most films twice their length. Most importantly, in their autobiographical way, unmediated by commercial or other external concerns, they spoke directly of real lives and circumstances. In this, they were more nearly related to documentary than any cinema fiction of the time, certainly anything made with a Scottish content.

The late 1970s and early 1980s were also the time when writing and debating about Scottish cinema (and the lack of it) became fashionable. Two events shaped much of the thinking of the period – 'Film Bang' in 1976, a gathering organised under the auspices of the Association of Cinema and Television Technicians (ACTT), and 'Cinema in a Small Country' in 1977, a conference mounted by the Association of Independent Producers (Scotland) and the Scottish Arts Council. They came about mainly because of the justifiable frustration felt by film-makers who, having matured and proved their skills in the documentary movement, now wanted a fair opportunity to move on, and for that there needed to be money. One contentious issue was whether there should be a devolved allocation to the Scottish Film Council (the publicly funded agency whose remit was mainly educational) of a portion of the British Film Institute's Production Fund. On a single vote during 'Cinema in a Small Country', the idea was rejected on the grounds that it was better to pitch for the larger pot.

In any case, the funding of British film making was in process of fundamental and positive change thanks to cinema's enemy, television. The arrival on the scene of Channel Four in 1982 and the subsequent involvement of BBC and other broadcasters in the production of films whose initial screenings would be in cinemas before they were broadcast, made for a new scene entirely.

The other matter which occupied, indeed often dominated, debate was the familiar one of the representation of Scotland on screen. The 'regressive tradition of Tartanry and Kailyard' was the recurring theme. 'Scotch Myths', the splendid Edinburgh Festival exhibition and film (1982) by Murray and Barbara Grigor, and 'Scotch Reels', a collection of essays edited by Colin McArthur, were the main manifestations and text. *Brigadoon* was the key movie (McArthur 1982, 2003). Shamefully, Bill Douglas's films were not quoted in the debate as they did not fit with the argument.

It has to be said that the majority of the practising film-makers felt that 'the Brigadooners', who were mostly academics and writers, were doing them no great favours. The real issues were money, structures and how to gain the influence to shape film-making in Scotland. To most of the film-makers, the cultural debate, particularly in its retrospection, was simply irrelevant, a distraction even, when they were struggling to find the cash to make a movie.

Meanwhile, Bill Forsyth had done the impossible. *Gregory's Girl*, to the disbelief of most Scots, had proved an international hit. A film about teenagers in the unlikely setting of Cumbernauld, a Scottish new town, reportedly 'had them queuing round the block in Tokyo'. Comedies about young people in Scotland were suddenly bankable. A genre was born, and *The Girl in the Picture* (1985) and *Restless Natives* (1985) followed. Forsyth's former colleague in documentary, Charles Gormley (1937–2005), made *Heavenly Pursuits* (1986), and Forsyth himself was to continue with probably his best work, *Local Hero* (1983), *Comfort and Joy* (1984) and *Housekeeping* (1987).

Nor was it only comedy. A much darker strand of 'hard man' movies emerged. A television film starring David Hayman, *A Sense of Freedom* (1981) was the first, but *Silent Scream* (1989) and *The Big Man* (1990) set a trend. Indeed, one of the problems of cinema in a small country is that one swallow does tend to make a summer. To the despair of those with such concerns, 'Scottish cinema' seemed only to equate to light comedy for a year or two, then it was exclusively West of Scotland violence. Fortunately, as a greater diversity of product and talent has emerged, that kind of stereotyping has gradually lessened.

The growth of film-making with various degrees of Scottishness has not eliminated the traditional forms in which Scotland's contribution is limited to the scenery and a few token Scottish actors. Of many possible examples, the Ted Danson vehicle *Loch Ness* (1996) will do, but while the exploitation of one of our finest myths may be acceptable, the distortion of our history is another matter. There is an interesting comparison to be made between *Braveheart* (1995) by the Australian Mel Gibson, and *Rob Roy* (also 1995) directed by the Scot Michael Caton-Jones. Though the former was based on historical events of great importance in our history and the latter derived essentially from the novel by Walter Scott, it was Caton-Jones's that was clearly the more authentic and the better film – though at ten Oscar nominations and five actual awards for *Braveheart* to one Oscar nomination for *Rob Roy*, the Mel Gibson $70-million epic, clearly was the more important, in the American view at least.

As we have noted earlier, the mid-1990s was one of the key periods in the history of Scottish film. In addition to the historical epics, other very different films were being made. As Bill Forsyth's *That Sinking Feeling* had caused a stir for being a genuinely home-made Scottish story film in 1979, so fifteen years later Danny Boyle and Andrew MacDonald's *Shallow Grave* (1994) came as something of a shock, and not just because of the content. The surprise of a *film noir*, and one of such quality, coming from Scotland was only trumped by the arrival of *Trainspotting* from the same team a year later.

Since then, Scottish film-making has continued to diversify. New names, new configurations have appeared. Actor-director Peter Mullan is perhaps the best example of those whose talents can earn them international employment and recognition while still remaining very close to home. Worldwide transport and communication are such that the need to migrate permanently to the hotspots of production, as earlier generations did, is no longer pressing. Craig Armstrong, in Glasgow, can write scores for Hollywood films such as *Moulin Rouge* or *World Trade Centre*; Robbie Coltrane or Tilda Swinton can still live in Scotland when in earlier days that would not have been a practical proposition.

Despite such changes, one factor remains constant. Just as much as talent and ideas, money is the root of all film-making, and it is in the economy of Scottish film that success and salvation will always lie. Grierson's dictum – referred to earlier – that there never was, never could be, a 'Scottish film industry' was qualified to the extent that the reason was that it would require 'the public authorities to be persuaded' – and they never would be 'because it was not in the Presbyterian soul'. Setting aside the rhetoric, Grierson was right.

Governments, local and central, have never been very keen to support film, perhaps because of an ancient belief that the medium is a creature of the fairground, but it is a fact that almost no film of truly Scottish origin in the past twenty-five years has come about without the financial support of the public authorities including the broadcasters. Indeed, with such as *Mrs Brown* (1997) supported by the BBC, or any of the examples of Channel Four financing, it is quite possible to argue that only with the public purse open, whether through the National Lottery or any other route, is it conceivable that there is any Scottish film at all.

Despite all the difficulties, there is plenty to be cheerful about. The celebration of film itself is something we do rather well. The Edinburgh International Film Festival is the longest continuing event of its kind in the world; in the Edinburgh Filmhouse, Glasgow Film Theatre and the other publicly funded cultural cinemas throughout the country, Scotland provides excellent access to world cinema. Media education, archiving and professional training which did not exist in Scotland forty years ago are now all of high quality.

Scottish talent on both sides of the camera now has greater success and achieves higher status than ever. Where Sean Connery (and Eric Campbell, long ago) triumphed in Hollywood, many Scottish actors have followed – Brian Cox and Ewan McGregor outstandingly so – and there are many more to be found on the international screen, including the aforementioned Peter Mullan as well as Billy Connolly, Billy Boyd, James McAvoy, Robert Carlyle, Dougray Scott, Martin Compson and plenty of others. Directors, producers, writers, composers, cinematographers, designers, animators – Scotland seems to be able to breed them all. Maybe our efforts in film and cinema do not add up to 'an industry' but as a small nation contributor to the world scene Scotland does reasonably well. The only thing that rankles is that given a fairer wind (but that means politics and money), we might do even better.

NOTES

1. See Grierson's letter to the Editor, *Saltire Review* (June 1960).
2. See www.cinematreasures.org/theater.php/13973.
3. See, for example, Barnes, *The Rise of the Cinema in Great Britain*.
4. See McBain, 'Scotland in feature film: a filmography', in Dick (ed.), *From Limelight to Satellite*.
5. Bruce, *Scotland the Movie*, p. 65.
6. See Hardy, *John Grierson, A Documentary Biography*.
7. See Murray, *That Thinking Feeling: A Research Guide to Scottish Cinema 1938–2004*.
8. See, for example, McArthur (ed.), *Scotch Reels*.

REFERENCES

Barnes, J. (1983), *The Rise of the Cinema in Great Britain*, London: Bishopgate Press.

Bruce, D. (1996), *Scotland the Movie*, Edinburgh: Polygon.

Butt, R. (2007), 'Literature and the screen media since 1908', in Ian Brown (ed.), *The Edinburgh History of Scottish Literature, Vol. 3: Modern Transformations*, Edinburgh: Edinburgh University Press.

Dick, E. (ed.) (1990), *From Limelight to Satellite*, Glasgow and London: Scottish Film Council and BFI.

Garioch, R. (1979), 'Early Days in Edinburgh', in Maurice Lindsay (ed.), *As I Remember*, London: Hale.

Grierson, J. (1960), letter to the Editor, *Saltire Review*, Edinburgh: Saltire Society, June 1960.

Grierson, J. (1990), *Eyes of Democracy*, Stirling: University of Stirling.

Hardy, F. (ed.) (1966), *Grierson on Documentary*, London: Faber and Faber.

Hardy, F. (1979), *John Grierson, A Documentary Biography*, London: Faber and Faber.

McArthur, C. (ed.) (1982), *Scotch Reels*, London: BFI.

McArthur, C. (2003), *Brigadoon, Braveheart and the Scots*, London: I. B. Tauris.

McBain, J. (1990), 'Scotland in feature film: a filmography', in Eddie Dick (ed.), *From Limelight to Satellite*, Glasgow/London: SFC/BFI.

Murray, J. (2004), *That Thinking Feeling: A Research Guide to Scottish Cinema 1938–2004*, Edinburgh: Edinburgh College of Art/Scottish Screen.
Petrie, D. (2000), *Screening Scotland*, London: BFI Publishing.
Sherington, J. (1996), *Films of Scotland*, Glasgow: Scottish Film Council.
www.cinematreasures.org/.

6

Broadcasting: From Birth to Devolution ... and Beyond

MAGGIE SWEENEY

INTRODUCTION

Prior to the establishment of a Scottish Parliament in July 1999, there were increasing calls from some quarters that in addition to acquiring legislative powers on matters relating to health, education, economic development, law, transport, and the arts, a substantial element of authority over broadcasting should also be wrested from Westminster control. Delivering the Edinburgh Festival's MacTaggart Lecture in 1996, the then Director-General of the BBC, John Birt, hinted that the BBC would 'be sensitive to the creation of a Scottish Parliament' (Smith 1997: 30). For some, this appeared to signal that, with the re-shaping of the UK political landscape, would come also a re-structuring of the centralised approach to broadcasting, which has dominated in Britain since the inception of the BBC in 1922. However, post-devolution the degree of 'sensitivity' accorded the broadcasting institutions and the concomitant needs of their audience has yet to be fully realised, within the contexts of both day-to-day programming output and the potential benefits to the wider economy.

Such concerns have, of course, been recognised within the Scottish media sector itself. The 1998/1999 BBC Scotland *Annual Review* reported that the number of hours produced by BBC Scotland for network television had increased by a third on the previous year. This was in part attributed to commissioning success and the diversity of programme output. In the area of arts (*Film 99*), drama (the BAFTA award winning *Mrs Brown*), entertainment (*Rab C. Nesbitt*) and children's programming (*Fully Booked*), BBC Scotland productions had performed consistently well across the network. Similarly, Radio Scotland saw an increased investment in its commissions from both

Radio 3 and 4, with an unprecedented sixty hours of drama and readings, whilst two science series, *Patient's Progress* and *Life After Darwin*, received particular critical acclaim.

In spite of that however, audience feedback suggested that some elements of BBC Scotland's output represented 'an unsatisfactory compromise which tried unsuccessfully to straddle the needs of Scottish and UK audiences in one pro- gramme'. Such criticism brought into question the specificity regarding the role of broadcasting from a distinctive Scottish perspective and its relationship to the wider UK audience. For, as stated in the Review's conclusion, the objectives for the BBC in post-devolution Scotland would entail that the Corporation:

> Strengthen the performance of the BBC as a whole in Scotland, increas-
> ing overall market share and reach of viewing and listening, and enhanc-
> ing public perception of the value of BBC services by introducing a
> pattern of network programme supply from Scotland, which brings
> Scottish talents and experiences to audiences across the UK. (BBC
> Scotland Annual Review 1998/99: 24)

These sentiments have, of course, been echoed elsewhere, most recently in the BBC Scotland *Annual Review* 2005/2006. Recent contributions from BBC Scotland to the network have been well received, by both audiences and the Broadcasting Council for Scotland (replaced by the new Audience Council in 2007), with series such as *Monarch of the Glen*, *Sea of Souls* and *Still Game* com- plimented for providing alternative representations of contemporary Scottish culture. Nevertheless, the Review suggests that greater efforts should be made to increase the range and formats across the network, whilst at the same time, due consideration should be given to issues of cultural representation. In that respect it is suggested that:

> BBC Scotland should seek to offer programmes and content that would
> be relevant to and link with local needs via the introduction of local on-
> demand service . . . and at the same time, increase the range and number
> of programmes from Scotland on the network. (p. 6)

Additionally, a key strategic development for the future involves a nurturing of creative talent within the Scottish media sector. Not only is this of central importance from an institutional point of view, but is of equal relevance to sus- taining and contributing to the long-term local media economy.

Underlying these policy initiatives is the recognition that, as the key public service provider in Scotland, the BBC is required to deliver diverse quality programming which accurately reflects Scottish culture in all its manifestations, to both local and national audiences. However, in addition, there is also an acknowledgement that such initiatives must give due consideration to maximising value for money in return for the publicly funded licence fee. In that sense, financially successful programme investment is not only of economic importance in the development of future output, but is of equal significance in maintaining and sustaining audiences, long term. As we shall see, such concerns are not new.

NATION OR REGION: THE BBC AND THE LIMITS OF CENTRALISATION

When discussing the nature of broadcasting within Scotland and the wider UK in general, there is an occasional tendency to overlook the fact that in the early stages of development, radio was the sole medium in operation. Although there was experimentation with television in the later 1920s by a number of companies, including one led by the Scottish engineer John Logie Baird, radio was the dominant medium until the post-war period. The British Broadcasting Company was founded in 1922 as a government-sponsored organisation and initially transmitted in the London area, but soon stations were established elsewhere in the UK: in Scotland, the first operational station was opened in Glasgow at 202 Bath Street on 6 March 1923. Subsequent stations were opened in Aberdeen, Edinburgh and Dundee between October 1923 and November 1924. By that year all the company's stations throughout the UK were linked by land line to allow simultaneous broadcasting, and a brief era of local autonomy came to an end (Briggs 1985).

The initial uptake of the service was limited, owing to the costs of the licence fee and radio sets, together with the crude nature of the technology. However, by 1927, when the Company was reconstituted as the British Broadcasting Corporation (BBC) under Royal Charter, more and more of the population began to recognise the attractions of the medium. Similarly, the first Director-General, the Scottish Presbyterian John Reith, was quick to realise the potential benefits that an effective broadcasting system could deliver to its listeners. For Reith, the guiding principles were shaped by three core elements – namely that the service should, in the words of the first and subsequent Charters, provide 'information, education and entertainment'. However, of equal importance to Reith was the notion that above all else, the BBC should be a public service, free from both commercial pressures and interference from external forces, in particular government (Scannell 1990).

Broadcasting soon came to be considered as one of the most significant influences on the social life and cultural fabric of the nation (Cardiff and Scannell 1991). Programmes gave structure and routine to people's daily lives, but in spite of this, the output failed to reflect the diverse range of local and regional cultures in any significant fashion. And whilst the advent of the Regional Scheme in 1929 (discussed below) was viewed as a progressive development for both BBC staff and audiences, in practice any moves towards decentralisation of responsibilities were met with considerable resistance from the hierarchy in London. Indeed, as highlighted elsewhere (McDowell 1992), such resistance was even to be found north of the border with concerns being aired by the Scottish Regional Director himself, David Cleghorn Thomson, after the proposal for the Regional Scheme was announced.

Of particular concern to Thomson was the notion that in providing Scotland with greater autonomy, the result might be a duplication of programming material emanating from the national network in London. From his perspective, the content and style of some Scottish programming was of such 'inferior' quality that it could simply not compete on equal terms when compared with the national service – he noted specifically that the distinctive cultural mix of the Scottish audience was not always reflected on the airwaves. Accordingly, in a broadcast to Scottish listeners in October 1929, he outlined the key policy strategy which would underpin output within the region. Significantly this was to result in a reduction in the number and frequency of programmes transmitted from Scotland on the basis that it was neither economically nor creatively viable to continue as before. These perceptions contributed to the reinforcement of the Corporation's justification in maintaining a policy of centralisation (McDowell 1992: 24).

By the late 1920s however, despite the kind of reservations articulated by Thomson, it had become apparent that the one-service provision was increasingly unpopular throughout Britain, and so in response to criticisms, a full dual programme service, regional and national, was introduced. Transmission began from the Scottish high-power mast at Westerglen in June 1932. Now listeners in Scotland had access to two alternative services: the National Programme from London and the Scottish Regional Programme. Whilst this new arrangement had certain advantages in terms of the quality of reception, and in providing listeners with an alternative to the National Programme, that was offset by the fact that financial control remained with London. Not only that, the London regional service supplied a substantial part of the output to all the other regional services, particularly outside the evening peak hours, although there was some limited programme exchange among the non-metropolitan regions, Wales, West, North, Midland, Northern Ireland and Scotland (Scannell 1993). But clearly the stranglehold of centralisation was still firmly in place. Inevitably, north of the border this impacted upon levels of staffing, technical resources and the ability to produce an increased variety and quantity of programming, for both regional and national services (McDowell 1992).

Debate about centralisation continued within the BBC. In a report submitted to the Corporation in January 1936, Charles Siepmann, the Director of Regional Relations, stated:

Centralisation represents a short-sighted policy. The provinces are the seed ground of talent and the ultimate source of our supply for London programmes. The existence and development of our Regional work provides an effective insurance policy against the drying up of resources of supply for our programmes. (cited in McDowell 1992: 35)

Siepmann specifically advocated that greater provision should be made for the Scottish Regional Service to expand its output. Whilst his recommendations were reinforced by the Ullswater Report of 1936, and additionally supported by the government, the BBC's corporate response, however, was less enthusiastic. Although it accepted that, as the national broadcaster, it had a duty to reflect the disparate nature of UK society, it was determined to maintain a policy of centralised control, stating that it had 'no desire to replace the metropolitan by regional centralisation' (cited in McDowell 1992: 38).

It is apparent that such sentiments and attitudes still prevail. In 2006 as part of the Charter Renewal process, the Department of Culture, Media and Sport (DCMS) published its new Agreement with the Corporation and felt obliged to remind the BBC Trust, which was replacing the Board of Governors, that:

In . . . representing the UK, its nations, regions and communities the BBC Trust must seek to ensure that the BBC (a) reflects and strengthens cultural identities through original content at local, regional and national level; and (b) promotes awareness of different cultures and alternative viewpoints, through content that reflects the lives of different people and different communities within the UK. (DCMS 2006: 4)

It is significant that at the time of Charter Renewal, there were growing concerns about the extent of cutbacks being implemented within BBC Scotland, particularly in news and current affairs (MacMillan 2006).

On the outbreak of war in 1939, regional broadcasting was suspended and in its place a single Home Service was established. The move to a national service transmitting on synchronised transmitters was considered necessary for security reasons, the fear being that German aircraft when entering British airspace might use separate transmission frequencies as navigational aids. In 1940 a second national service, the Forces Programme, was introduced. Although the Home Service provided regular news bulletins, talks and readings, the Forces Programme was dedicated to more popular, light entertainment such as jazz music, variety and sports. Significantly, the proportion of Scottish items on the Home Service was initially considerably reduced to a weekly 'Scottish Half-Hour'.

During this period the Corporation recognised that the skills and expertise required to run a wartime broadcasting service were markedly different from those called for during peacetime. Therefore, following a period of consultation, the BBC decided to appoint two Director-Generals: Sir Cecil Graves, who oversaw programme production, and Robert Foot, who focused on the financial re-structuring of the institution. Of the two appointees, Foot was eager to promote a greater output of material from the regions, recognising the overall advantages that this would bring for both staff and listeners. Accordingly, the range and quantity of Scottish items – features, Scottish news, current affairs and Gaelic programmes – were increased during his tenure. With Foot, there was a growing recognition that post-war re-structuring of the service would necessitate the provision of greater opportunities for regional output. Subsequently, in July 1945, the Scottish Regional Programme was replaced by the Scottish Home Service which was allocated its own wavelength (McDowell 1992).

This was part of a tripartite restructuring, the planning for which was underway before the war ended (Crisell 2002). The new structure consisted of the Light Programme, a replacement for the Forces Programme; the Home Service, which would continue as the key network provider which regions could opt in and out of; and the Third Programme, which was launched in 1946 and offered a more intellectually demanding range of output.

Listeners to the Scottish Home Service were now provided with renewed opportunity to opt out of London programming. In addition, the shape and content of output expanded considerably and ranged from drama, news, children's programming, talks and features through to sport, current affairs and variety. The period of post-war activity is often referred to as the 'golden age' of Scottish broadcasting, with programmes such as *The McFlannels*, *Sportsreel*, and *Children's Hour* proving particularly popular with listeners. Nevertheless, the new service was not universally lauded. The Saltire Society for its part was critical of the use of the term 'region' which, from its perspective, failed to acknowledge Scotland's unique status as a 'nation':

> The term 'Regional' should be dropped entirely so far as Scotland is concerned. Strictly speaking it should only apply to the English provinces. Scotland is a nation containing at least five 'Regions' in the proper sense of the term, and its use to describe the whole of Scotland causes both annoyance and confusion. (cited in McDowell 1992: 59)

And, perhaps not surprisingly, any attempt by the BBC hierarchy to assuage such concerns was usually met with derision and further complaints. Of greater significance to the Corporation was listener feedback, which in the main was highly positive and responsive to the post-war output. The content of programming seemed to reflect Scottish culture in all its variety and in turn to resonate with the listening public. Inevitably, however, with the advent of television, and then the demise of the BBC's monopoly, this 'golden age' of radio came to an end.

VISION ON – THE POST-WAR ERA

Early demonstrations of television took place in Selfridge's department store in London in 1925. During these pioneering days, the technology and equipment were fairly crude and rudimentary. However, following the recommendations of the Selsdon Committee in 1934, the BBC Television Service finally went on air on 2 November 1936. Transmitted live from Alexandra Palace in London, the service was initially confined to the metropolitan area, 'reaching approximately 400 households within a radius of forty to 100 miles' (Crisell 2002: 77). With the outbreak of war in 1939, however, the service was suspended and did not resume until 1946. As in its infancy, the service was still primarily available in the London region. Nevertheless, with improvements in design and technology, it spread across the UK, arriving in Scotland with the opening of the Kirk O'Shotts transmitter in 1952.

Whilst television was clearly a rival to radio, an even greater concern to the Corporation was the looming threat of commercial broadcasting. With the publication of the Beveridge Report on Broadcasting, in January 1951, came the first signs that the continuation of the BBC monopoly was increasingly anachronistic in post-war Britain. Although the report and the subsequent Government White Paper on Broadcasting did support the monopoly, there was a growing sense with the upsurge in leisure activity, together with advances in technology, that such a situation was becoming increasingly untenable (Briggs 1985). Prior to its final deliberations, the Beveridge Committee had received a variety of submissions challenging the BBC's dominance. One such submission from the left-wing Fabian Society, whilst upholding the principles of public service broadcasting and the continuation of the licence fee, refused to accept that broadcasting output should reside exclusively within the remit of one organisation (Beveridge Committee 1951).

In addition, the report also made clear that whilst the Committee had concerns regarding the implementation of commercial broadcasting, they bore little relation to the objections submitted to them by the BBC:

> We regret as a guiding principle in broadcasting competition for numbers of listeners. But we do not accept the assumption underlying the BBC Memorandum that the only alternative to monopoly is degrading competition for listeners, and that in broadcasting a monopoly alone can have high standards and social purpose. (Beveridge Committee 1951: 43)

In the light of subsequent events – particularly with the advent of increased competition following the Broadcasting Act of 1990, and the publication of Ofcom's report into public service broadcasting in 2005, *Competition for Quality* – such remarks appear somewhat anachronistic in the contemporary broadcasting environment, where notions of 'standards' and 'social purpose' have arguably become secondary to the pursuit of profit and ratings.

The Beveridge Report was of some significance to Scotland, insofar as recommendations were made that London should decentralise some of its responsibilities, and that regional services be accorded more programming autonomy. In line with this recommendation, Broadcasting Councils for Scotland and Wales were established in 1953 – the Northern Ireland Council was not set up until 1981. Although in their infancy they functioned in a purely advisory capacity, they represented an encouraging step towards greater independence for the so-called National Regions. Crucially, however, financial control continued to remain in London.

Direct challenge to the BBC's monopoly finally came about as a result of the election of a Conservative government in October 1951. It took a different approach from that of its Labour predecessor, and within seven months published a White Paper on Broadcasting, which argued that a degree of competition would be beneficial to both audiences and industry. The result was the Television Act of 1954, which gave the green light for commercial broadcasting to be introduced to the UK. (The advertising-financed English-language Radio Luxembourg, which had beamed to the UK since the 1930s and attracted substantial audiences for its populist fare, was based in the Grand Duchy.) Approximately a year later, on the evening of 22 September 1955, ITV came on air – at that stage confined to the London area (Sendall 1983).

Since its inception, ITV has been viewed as constituting a commercially funded model of public service broadcasting, which is sustained by advertising revenue. Therefore, in that respect, it clearly differed from the organisational and structural formation associated with the early years of the BBC, which was funded by the public via the licence fee, a compulsory tax on receiving equipment. In addition, as has been noted above, the BBC had allowed the national network to dominate the schedules at the expense of regional services. However, the Independent Television Authority (ITA), the regulatory body responsible for the new sector, expected a greater regional input from the contractors to which it awarded franchises. STV (Scottish Television) went on air in August 1957 as the first contractor in Scotland. The chairman of the company which won the central Scotland contract, Roy Thomson, (in)famously quipped that an ITV franchise was a 'licence to print money'. STV was followed on air in September 1961 by Border and Grampian Television, which meant that the ITV service was now available to all of Scotland.

It is notable, nevertheless, that when awarding a franchise to STV, the ITA did so with the proviso that the new operator should generate a minimum of 15 per cent of programming itself, with the remainder of its output to be acquired from the network providers such as Associated Rediffusion, Associated Television and Granada. (But even 15 per cent of indigenous output meant that STV, in company with BBC Scotland, was offering an opt-out service in television in which the bulk of what viewers were offered was produced elsewhere in the UK, a pattern which continues to this day.) With programmes such as *Here and Now*, *Scotsport* and *The One O'Clock Gang*, STV were in some respects pioneers in developing innovative, original formats. Whilst Grampian also catered to the needs of its indigenous audience, Border (owing to its geographical position) was never fully recognised as a distinctly Scottish service. The programming approach of the ITV companies was generally more populist in terms of style and content, in recognition of the *zeitgeist* of the post-austerity 1950s. And whilst this met with audience approval, for STV and for the commercial sector as a whole, such an approach was to work to their disadvantage on the publication of the Pilkington Report on Broadcasting in 1962. Roy Thomson's financial boast was not of much help either.

Chaired by Sir Harry Pilkington, the Committee on Broadcasting was highly critical of ITV's output, noting that much of its programming was 'trivial', 'debased' and 'derivative'. This was in contrast to the BBC which, overall, received a more favourable assessment and whose programming was viewed as being more 'serious' and of 'higher' quality than that of its commercial competitors (Pilkington Committee 1962: 34). Interestingly, ITV was also criticised for its limited output of regional programmes, on the grounds that much of what was produced in the regions failed to reflect, particularly in Scotland's case, the distinctive, local culture in any detail and was screened outwith peak viewing times:

> Thus, though the smaller independent television companies produced more hours of programming than did the BBC Regions, items of local appeal still formed only a small part of each company's programme: and most of these items were shown at off-peak hours. (Johnson and Turnock 2005: 22)

Whilst the report had little impact on ITV's long-term profitability, this was offset considerably by the awarding of the licence for a third channel to the BBC; BBC2 opened in April 1964 in the London region, with all of Scotland finally coming within transmitter range by 1969; colour transmissions north and south of the border began, initially on the new channel and with limited geographical coverage, in 1967.

Britain was now entering a new period of economic prosperity and rejuvenation. By the mid-1960s, society was undergoing a sea change, both socially and politically, with the advent of the 'teenager', changing attitudes to personal behaviour and the election of a Labour government in 1964 after thirteen years of Conservative rule. Radio as a medium was in decline whilst television was in the ascendancy, and the BBC was gradually forced to respond and adapt to the challenges which lay ahead. The introduction of VHF transmission in the 1950s facilitated the development of local radio, as it created additional space on the waveband. The first experiments took place in Bristol in 1961, followed by Dumfries in March 1962. However, there was little evidence to suggest that there was a substantial demand for local radio (Briggs 1965). On the other hand, pop-music-orientated 'pirate' stations – for example Radio Caroline (1964) and Radio Scotland (1965) – were proving to be highly successful and represented a recognisable threat to BBC services.

With the introduction of the Marine Broadcasting (Offences) Act in 1967, such forms of broadcasting became illegal. By that stage, under government pressure, the BBC had responded by re-structuring its services. This culminated in the re-branding of the Light, Third and Home Services as Radio 2, Radio 3 and Radio 4 respectively. In addition, in order to capture the youth market, the first BBC station devoted largely to the broadcasting of 'pop' music was established in the form of Radio 1. Meanwhile, Scotland was still receiving the bulk of its output from the network stations, although the Scottish Home Service continued to opt out of Radio 4 and mount its own programmes for several hours a day. A fully stand-alone Radio Scotland (as we know it today) did not come into being until 1978. Like many of the BBC's innovations, it arose to some extent as a response to perceived competition from the commercial sector. And it was part of an initiative which saw the establishment of similar stations in Wales and Northern Ireland. In England, despite initial misgivings, the BBC did develop local radio, beginning with Radio Leicester in 1967, and there are now forty stations in the country. (Local television, despite some interesting experiments, has not developed in the UK, although the availability of additional spectrum when analogue television is switched off may enable it to become a reality.)

The Conservative government of Edward Heath, elected in 1970, was broadly sympathetic to the possibility of introducing Independent Local Radio services (ILR), financed by advertising, alongside the growing BBC sector. And in June 1972 the Sound Broadcasting Act reached the statute book; by October the following year, Britain's first ILR station, London Broadcasting Company (LBC), went on air. Before the year was out, Scotland would also have its own ILR in the form of Radio Clyde, which began broadcasting on New Year's Eve 1973. Since that time, the independent sector within Scotland has proved particularly successful, with the establishment of additional stations throughout the country, most notably Radio Forth (1975) in Edinburgh, and Northsound (1981) in Aberdeen (see Garner, this book). In spite of these inroads by the commercial sector, the most recent annual figures for radio indicate that the demand for the BBC's output is still high, with over a quarter of the population tuning in at some juncture each week (BBC Scotland Annual Review 2006).

In its submission to the Annan Committee on the future of broadcasting in 1974, the Scottish National Party remarked:

> Scottish broadcasting suffers from being neither fully 'National', nor purely 'regional'. There is [*sic*] too little cash, too few facilities, and too much duplication of effort. So long as BBC London and the ITV Big Five dominate programme schedules and sign the cheques, Scottish broadcasting will remain provincial. (cited in McDowell 1992: 225)

These comments made over thirty years ago are similar to much of the criticism that has been levelled at Scottish broadcasting since its inception. The Annan Report, it should be noted, was sympathetic to Scotland's case, suggesting that both BBC and ITV regional companies should produce more material for the networks. However, the Committee rejected outright any notion of a separate broadcasting authority being established north of the border. The Government's response to the report was roughly in line with Annan's recommendations, with the additional requirement that the Broadcasting Council for Scotland should be accorded greater self-governing powers.

Both the BBC and ITV regional companies, including STV, were advised by Annan to increase their production operations in Scotland and provide a greater percentage of programme material to the networks. In principle, this was to be commended. Nevertheless, it is important to remember that Scottish Television has historically, by dint of its size, location and audience demographic, been at a distinct disadvantage when compared with its larger competitors from the south, such as Granada. (The situation for both Grampian and Border has been even more disadvantageous.) Difficulties in generating levels of advertising revenue comparable to those achieved by its southern competitors have inevitably affected STV's ability to compete on a level playing field in terms of programming output. Additionally, the economic significance of – the basic need for – network sales for BBC Scotland and Scottish Television cannot be overlooked in assessing their long-term financial viability.

CABLE, SATELLITE AND THE ADVENT OF THE INTERNAL MARKET

As Scotland entered a new political era in the 1980s, innovations in technology and the rapid expansion of satellite and cable services began to impact upon the post-war duopoly. Competition for audiences and listeners became intense within the broadcasting environment. Driven by neo-liberal Thatcherite policies, broadcasting now became closely aligned with the market economy. Furthermore, from 1982 the BBC and ITV had to contend with an additional terrestrial competitor in the shape of Channel 4. These changes intensified the move towards a more rationalised industry, particularly within the BBC, where between 1986 and 1990, 7,000 staff became redundant. This inevitably had an impact on Scotland, as it did elsewhere in the UK, and was to be further compounded with the appointment of John Birt as Director-General in 1993 (Crisell 2002).

Under Birt's stewardship, the BBC was to be exposed to the full force of the market economy. Policies such as 'producer choice' and the 'internal market' became central to the BBC's *modus operandi*. What this meant in practice was that every production unit had to compete for funding against other units, and then purchase resources, from inside the Corporation or from independent suppliers, depending on which offered the better deal. In addition, the 1990 Broadcasting Act had stipulated that the BBC and ITV contractors were to ensure that not less than 25 per cent of their total programming output was obtained from the independent sector. A policy document published by the BBC in 1992, entitled *Extending Choice*, stated:

> In the past, as a dominant provider, the BBC had an obligation to cover all audiences and broadcasting needs: in the future it will have an obligation to focus on performing a set of clearly defined roles that best complement the enlarged commercial sector. (cited in Goodwin 1998: 130)

In terms of policy, the shift in emphasis was clear – the BBC had now fully accepted the ideology of the market place, though it was seeking to retain a very important position within that market place. The adoption of this approach was to have significant ramifications for broadcasting in Scotland and, as highlighted earlier, still resonates today within the sector.

Indeed, examination of the political machinations which formed the background to the 1990 Broadcasting Act suggests that (to an extent) policy initiatives were shaped specifically to undermine the role of the BBC and its primary position within the broadcasting environment. Whilst Thatcherism placed an emphasis on deregulation, privatisation and minimal state interference, the government, fearful of television's political influence, was reluctant to leave broadcasters, particularly the BBC, to their own devices (Crisell 2002: 244).

So, with the 1990 Act it clearly sought to diminish the power of both the Corporation and the large ITV companies.

Subsequently, there was significant upheaval within the commercial television sector. Under the Act, the renewal of ITV franchises was put out for competitive tendering, though with a built-in 'quality threshold'. However, this approach resulted in some of the key players within the industry losing out as a result of the inadequacies in the criteria governing the tendering process:

> The government had originally favoured the idea of an auction partly because 'cash' is a more transparent and measurable criterion than 'quality'. But the belated reintroduction of 'quality' bedevilled the whole process, reducing the auction to something of a lottery and a farce. (Crisell 2002: 247)

This situation is best illustrated by examining the eventual outcome of the process in relation to some of the key industry players. Carlton TV's successful bid for the London weekday franchise, for example, was the highest at £43 million, and it resulted in the then incumbent Thames Television losing the franchise by £10 million. At the other extreme, and owing to a lack of interest from prospective rivals, Scottish Television (like Central Television in the Midlands) was able to renew its franchise with 'a contemptuous £2,000' (MacDonald 1991).

Throughout the 1990s ITV was marked by a period of continuous consolidation. Increased competition from cable and satellite channels, together with a downturn in advertising revenue, began to hamper developments throughout the industry, including the Scottish sector. As we entered the twenty-first century, this increasing instability and uncertainty began to impact considerably on the quality and quantity of programming produced. Following the controversial takeover of Grampian Television by STV in 1997, Scottish Media Group (SMG) was now firmly established as the key player within the region. However, the rapid expansion of the company's portfolio, resulting in the acquisition of the *Herald* newspaper group, Virgin Radio and the cinema advertising company, Pearl and Dean, was perceived to have a detrimental impact on staffing and future programme development. This was compounded by the company's strenuous efforts to accommodate both the needs of its shareholders and audience expectations.

At the time of writing, following increasing criticisms from shareholders and industry personnel, SMG has appointed a new chief executive, Rob Woodward, who in a newspaper interview gave a clear indication of the future policy direction which would underpin Scottish Television. Woodward envisages that the main focus of the business will be television, for which the plan will be twofold: 'to revive local programming and make more productions for

the ITV network and other major broadcasters' (Vass 2007). Indeed, as highlighted by Woodward, one of the major flaws which contributed to SMG's
woes was a decision by the previous regime to have STV's minimum programming commitments reduced. For them, opting out of the network was
not economically viable as the digital era beckoned. But Woodward disagrees
with that decision:

> It depends on your confidence in your programming . . . When STV opt
> out, from *Scotsport* through to the local news, it consistently beats the
> network slot. We will be looking at what types of programmes will enable
> us to do more of that. (*Sunday Herald*, 15 April 2007)

Although network commissions are currently worth in the region of £20
million per year to STV, such a policy could be economically advantageous.
In addition, plans to sell off Virgin Radio and Pearl and Dean would further
offset the current debt of £150 million (ibid). Whilst these moves might contribute to the future long-term benefit of shareholders, it is equally possible
that the Scottish audience could also reap rewards from such disinvestments.
With a reduced debt, additional income generated from the network and
greater confidence from shareholders, combined with improvements to the
overall quality and volume of programming, Scottish Television may be on the
path to recovery. Currently, its two most successful network productions
are the long-running crime dramas *Taggart* and *Rebus*, which demonstrate that
the expertise, skills and creative impetus are available but that significant
financial investment is required in order for the industry to be sustained within
Scotland.

SO WHAT NOW? SCOTLAND'S BROADCASTING FUTURE

In a memorandum produced in 1975, the Broadcasting Council for Scotland
remarked:

> To those who are not Scots it should be said that the Scotland that we
> seek to project is not only the known land of romance and matchless
> scenic beauty but also the newer Scotland of off-shore oil, industrial
> growth, artistic renaissance and self-government – not parochial, but
> outward-looking and international in its approach. (BCS 1975: 16)

When we examine the history of broadcasting in Scotland, however, the
picture that emerges is one where, despite the attempt to be 'outward-looking
and international' in approach, all too often broadcasters have fallen into the
trap of parochialism. This is not to blame those pioneers of the medium within
Scotland, who made strenuous efforts to push the boundaries in terms of

programming output. For it is important to recall that any examination of Scotland's contribution to broadcasting entails due consideration being given to the wider social and political landscape of the UK.

During the BBC's infancy, its output was very much dictated by policy directives from London. This centralisation of the decision-making process, combined with controls over finance, has inevitably placed severe limits on operations in Scotland, particularly in relation to news and current affairs. Whilst the flagship programme *Reporting Scotland* provides the main regional news to the whole country (*Scotland Today* being its commercial equivalent) and *Newsnight Scotland* has made promising in-roads in the coverage of the wider Scottish political scene, the 'Scottish Six' has yet to materialise (Schlesinger 2004).

As suggested earlier, the tensions which have existed within Scottish broadcasting down the years can in part be attributed to how Scotland has been perceived by senior executives in London. Although a 'national region' in broadcasting terms, Scotland is *de facto* a nation and as such has always sought special status. Examination of the long interaction between London and Scotland over the years clearly reveals the extent of the reluctance on London's part to confer greater autonomy on Scotland within both the BBC and the commercial sector – the constant fear being that there would be an inevitable dilution in the quality and scope of output. And it has to be said that similar anxieties continue to be expressed from time to time north of the border too.

Whilst within this chapter it has not been possible to offer a very detailed account of Scotland's place within broadcasting, it is hoped that some sense of the country's contribution to the medium has been provided. Scotland now has a minority SNP government at Holyrood. From the Nationalist perspective the only way forward is for Scotland to acquire full political autonomy. In the event of that outcome, it can be argued that broadcasting would be a significant beneficiary. Or would it? For inevitably such changes to the political shape of the UK would in themselves raise a whole host of issues about the future of Scotland's broadcasting industry.

Indeed, as I have suggested throughout, Scotland's position within the media sector and in some respects the very survival of its media institutions, are dependent on the financial resources available. Whilst the BBC's new developments at Pacific Quay in Glasgow, together with a possible upturn in SMG's fortunes, are to be welcomed, it is questionable whether either of these organisations could compete long term, at both the Scottish and global levels, from bases in a small independent country. It is of course stating the obvious to say that programme-making requires a critical mass of talent and creativity, and in that respect Scotland is well resourced. But long term the production of news, drama, sport, or music requires not only a nurturing of creative talent, but also considerable financial investment, a point highlighted within the BBC Annual Review 2005/2006. Currently it is debatable whether or not the Scottish economy could sustain what might be a short-term surge in the sector's output on a long-term basis.

As Scotland moves into its ninth year of devolution, questions remain too about what we the audience want and expect from our broadcasting institutions. This is a question which has not gone unnoticed by the BBC in Scotland, which commented, in the BBC Scotland *Annual Review* 2005/2006, that:

> BBC Scotland fully understands that as a broadcaster dependent on the licence fee, it must listen to audiences and deliver the highest standards of efficiency in its operations: priorities for the year ahead include strengthening accountability to audiences, and delivering BBC Scotland's savings and business change plan to maximize value for money for licence payers. (BBC 2007: 1)

These observations perhaps indicate the complexities of the future relationship between audiences and broadcasters. Audiences want 'quality' programming but at a price that is affordable. And therein lies an additional problem in terms of Scotland's commitment to broadcasting output, for questions of 'quality' have never easily sat alongside notions of 'efficiency', and 'savings'. As ITV has discovered, cost-cutting can lead to derivative and unedifying forms of programming.

So what of the future? The SNP government in Holyrood may well seek to acquire legislative powers on broadcasting issues. Of equal importance is the necessity to attract the additional, inward investment required to compete at both the local and global levels. Not only will such investment, if it can be obtained, contribute to sustaining a recognisable model of public service broadcasting within Scotland, but it will also help to nurture the kind of supportive environment which facilitates creative energy. Whatever the outcome of current moves, it is to be hoped that Scotland will not lose its position within the wider broadcasting community, but will be able to build on what has been achieved to date and thereby project an 'outward-looking, international' approach to broadcasting in the twenty-first century.

REFERENCES

Annan Committee (1977), *Report of the Committee on the Future of Broadcasting* (1974), Cmd 6753, London: HMSO.
BBC (2000), *BBC Scotland Annual Review: 1998/1999*, Glasgow: BBC.
BBC (2007), *BBC Scotland Annual Review: 2005/2006*, Glasgow: BBC.

Beveridge Committee (1951), *Report of the Broadcasting Committee* (1949), Cmd 8116, London: HMSO.

Briggs, A. (1965), *The History of Broadcasting in the United Kingdom: Volume II – The Golden Age of Wireless*, London: Oxford University Press.

Briggs, A. (1985), *The BBC: The First Fifty Years*, Oxford: Oxford University Press.

Broadcasting Council for Scotland (BCS) (1975), *Memorandum to the Committee on the Future of Broadcasting*, Glasgow: BBC.

Cardiff, D. and P. Scannell (1991), *A Social History of British Broadcasting. Vol 1, 1922–1939*, Oxford: Basil Blackwell.

Crisell, A. (2002), *An Introductory History of British Broadcasting*, London: Routledge.

Department of Culture, Media and Sport (DCMS) (2006), *Broadcasting, An Agreement Between Her Majesty's Secretary of State for Culture, Media and Sport and the British Broadcasting Corporation*, London: HMSO.

Goodwin, P. (1998), *Television under the Tories: Broadcasting Policy 1979–1997*, London: British Film Institute.

Johnson, C. and R. Turnock (2005), *ITV Cultures: Independent Television Over Fifty Years*, Berkshire: Open University Press.

MacDonald, C. (1991) 'Scottish eye on networks', *Glasgow Herald*, 17 October.

MacMillan, A. (2006), 'Outrage as axe looms over BBC Scotland's flagship programmes', *Scotland on Sunday*, 23 July.

McDowell, W. H. (1992), *The History of BBC Broadcasting in Scotland, 1923–1983*, Edinburgh: Edinburgh University Press.

Ofcom (2005), *Ofcom Review of Public Service Television Broadcasting Phase 3 – Competition for Quality*, 8 February, www.ofcom.org.uk/consult/condocs/psb3/pdf.

Pilkington Committee (1962), *Report of the Committee on Broadcasting*, Cmd 1753, London: HMSO.

Scannell, P. (1990), 'Public service broadcasting: the history of a concept', in A. Goodwin and G. Whannel (eds), *Understanding Television*, London: Routledge.

Scannell, P. (1993), 'The origins of BBC regional policy', in S. Harvey and K. Robins (eds), *The Regions, the Nations and the BBC*, London: BFI.

Schlesinger, P. (2004), 'The new communications agenda in Scotland', *Scottish Affairs*, 47.

Sendall, B. (1983), *Independent Television in Britain: Volume 1, Origin and Foundation, 1946–62*, London: Macmillan.

Smith, N. (1997), 'Broadcasting and a Scottish Parliament', *Scottish Affairs*, 19.

Ullswater Committee (1936), *Report of the Broadcasting Committee*, Cmd 5091, London: HMSO.

Vass, S. (2007), 'Victor in SMG boardroom battle outlines plans for more focused future', *Sunday Herald*, 15 April.

SCREEN AND SOUND

7

Three Ring Circus: Television Drama about, by and for Scotland

JOHN R. COOK

'It's shite [*sic*] being Scottish.' So began a vituperative article by Tom Little in *Scotland on Sunday* on 19 November 2006. Having just watched the highlights of the 2006 BAFTA Scotland awards on TV, Little was moved to quote Renton, Ewan McGregor's character in the film version of *Trainspotting* (1996). Where, asked Little, was the quality of BBC Scotland's drama output to justify its current £180 million a year licence fee income? Looking back to the earlier success of adaptations such as that of Iain Banks' *The Crow Road* ten years before (BBC TV 1996) and rejecting current BBC Scotland claims that it was fulfilling its role as a drama-maker for Scotland through production of its twice-weekly soap *River City* (BBC TV 2002), Little asked three pointed, if harsh, questions:

> Question one: what was the most innovative drama serial broadcast on the BBC in 2006? Answer: *Life on Mars*. Question two: what was the most interesting drama serial broadcast on the BBC in 2005? Answer: the revived *Dr Who*. Question three: what connects the two shows, other than the slavish devotion of the sort of sci-fi anorak who describes his religion as 'Jedi' in the national census? Answer: they were massive critical successes, earned vast amounts of money in overseas sales – and they were both made by BBC Wales. And, as far as I am aware, the Beeb in the principality has not had to cancel its own soap opera, *Pobol y Cwm*, which has run since 1974, to pay for these commissions. (Little 2006)

Judging by the many e-mail responses to this article, posted on the *Scotland on Sunday* website, Little did not seem to be alone. The overwhelming majority of correspondents agreed: 'Dour and uninteresting doesn't begin to describe the current state of Scottish TV and filming', ran one post; while another stated that what was needed was a right good clearing out of that 'tiny and self-sustaining clique commissioning programmes from each other in a monopolistic orgy of mediocrity and self-congratulation' (web responses to Little 2006).

These are strong feelings but are they justified? Is Scottish television drama output so poor, compared, for example, to that of Wales? How did we get to the present situation and where might things be heading in the future? This chapter will try to explore these questions by offering a broad survey of the history of TV drama production with reference to Scotland, picking out key moments and developmental shifts. At the outset, however, this phrase 'with reference to Scotland' needs a little explanation and contextualisation. Television drama may be 'about' Scotland but that does not necessarily mean, always, that it has been produced 'by' Scotland, or that Scottish interests and influence have been paramount in shaping the resulting images and representations. Likewise, even if the dramas are 'about' Scotland and have been produced 'by' Scottish broadcasters, it does not necessarily follow that this means they are principally 'for' Scotland, in the sense of serving the exclusive interests of the Scottish public, whether in public service or commercial terms. Drama production has always been the most expensive form of television, and Scotland is, of course, a small country of only five million people.[1] The consequent pressures on indigenous programme-makers to recoup costs via networking to the whole UK or sales further afield are obvious and these pressures can have direct effects on the kinds and quality of images of Scottish life circulated via TV drama. Representations of national identity through such high-resource forms as television drama are always a kind of three ring circus: the 'by', 'about' and 'for' of the chapter title.[2] While these rings may overlap in mutually beneficial ways and in a happy consensus serving all the various interests involved, they may not do that, and it is always wise to bear this in mind.

One can start to see the three ring circus in operation from the very advent of television in Scotland and through the subsequent history. As noted elsewhere in this volume, television came to Scotland in 1952 and the first Scottish-originated television drama was transmitted nationally by BBC TV on 19 March 1952. *The Old Lady Shows Her Medals* by J. M. Barrie and starring Andrew Keir was a televised production from the Glasgow Citizens' Theatre performed by the Citizens' company. In these early years of essentially theatrical relay, the Citizens' provided much of the play material. Numerous pieces by the theatre's co-founder, James Bridie (1888–1951) were televised, and during this period Pharic Maclaren emerged as Scotland's leading and most prolific TV drama producer. By the end of the decade, he was producing television plays from BBC Scotland's recently opened Glasgow television studio.

Early examples of these included *Act of Living* by Douglas Rae (tx. BBC TV, 9 January 1958) and *Murder in Mind* by T. R. McKay (tx. BBC TV, 20 November 1958). However, *The Times* newspaper, reviewing both plays, sniffily complained of 'the mediocre output of the Scottish studio'; it was only when Maclaren applied his skills to comedy drama, with the original series of *Para Handy – Master Mariner* (BBC TV 1959–60, adapted from the tales of Neil Munro and starring Duncan MacRae as Para Handy), that the newspaper felt able to lavish praise for the 'cohesion' of this particular Scottish production (Anon. 1959: 9).

Given this hostile context, providing familiar images from Scottish culture like *Para Handy* was always going to be an easier task in terms of winning production resources and network acceptance than challenging with the new and the unfamiliar. It was perhaps a lesson not lost on Maclaren himself who, while he went on to produce a range of drama output for BBC Scotland, later became well known for his adaptations of Scottish literary classics mounted from Scotland for the network, starting in the early 1960s with Robert Louis Stevenson's *The Master of Ballantrae* (BBC TV 1962) and continuing into the 1970s with Stevenson's *Weir of Hermiston* (BBC TV 1973), Sir Walter Scott's *Rob Roy* (BBC TV 1977) and John Buchan's *Huntingtower* (BBC TV, 1978) as well as *Sunset Song* (BBC TV 1971) – the first of Lewis Grassic Gibbon's trilogy 'A Scots Quair' – for which he is today best remembered.[3]

During the 1960s network interest in Scotland was not confined to the single TV play. In 1962, BBC TV launched *Doctor Finlay's Casebook* (BBC TV 1962–71), the drama series that would perhaps do most to define images of Scottishness for the UK television audience during this period. Based on the writing of doctor-cum-novelist A. J. Cronin, *Doctor Finlay's Casebook* portrayed life in the medical practice of fictional Tannochbrae, a small community in the lowland Scottish countryside. The original series was set between the wars, thus safely distancing it from any direct contemporary reference to the post-war National Health Service.[4] This quality of nostalgia coupled with the Scottish rural settings and the series' playing-out of compromise and conciliation between the generations – young, idealistic Doctor Finlay (played by Bill Simpson) learns to work with and respect older Doctor Cameron (Andrew Cruickshank), all the time watched over and advised by trusty Presbyterian housekeeper Janet (Barbara Mullen) – helped to make *Doctor Finlay's Casebook* a much-needed ratings banker for the BBC during the 1960s as it struggled to compete for the popular audience with ITV. The series ran for 178 episodes throughout the whole of the decade, and in January 1964, after becoming a huge ratings success, it was moved to the prime drama slot of Sunday evenings. Thus, *Doctor Finlay's Casebook* helped to initiate a tradition of 'feel-good' Sunday night UK network drama, involving warm-hearted storylines and loveable characters in nostalgic rural settings, a tradition which persists to this day.

In terms of its Scottishness, it is important to realise that while the principal cast members were certainly Scottish (though Barbara Mullen, who played Janet, was US-born) and episodes were recorded at Glasgow's Studio 'A' (McDowell 1992: 211), most of the key personnel behind the camera were from network centre in London, including writers Vincent Tilsley and Donald Bull; directors Gerard Glaister and Julia Smith; and producers such as Andrew Osborn, who was also Head of BBC TV Drama Series during this period. In other words (and in keeping with the 'three ring circus' typology), this was drama 'about' Scotland but very much 'for' the consumption of the rest of the UK. The images of Scottish life were essentially the familiar and comforting ones of a couthy, small town or rural parochialism that would later come to be so hotly critiqued as 'Kailyard', in the famous 1982 *Scotch Reels* analysis of media representations of Scotland.[5]

There was, however, one significant intervention during this period from London, which did strive to unsettle and challenge how the Scots were represented both to the wider UK and also to themselves. Not strictly speaking a drama but a documentary (it was produced under the then Head of Documentary and Music, Huw Wheldon), Peter Watkins' 1964 BBC TV film *Culloden* (tx. BBC-1, 15 December 1964) eschewed romanticised versions of the various Jacobite uprisings and re-enacted the 1746 battle of Culloden using documentary-style techniques. In so doing, the film challenged conventional 'shortbread tin' views of Scottish history by portraying the battle as the effective genocide of Highland culture and of an alternative way of life.

Culloden was widely acclaimed on transmission and its influence is discernible in subsequent work. Though later critical of some of Watkins' techniques such as his preference for non-professional actors,[6] playwright and director John McGrath echoed many of his *Culloden* themes in the 1974 TV version of his 7:84 theatre production of *The Cheviot, The Stag and The Black, Black Oil* (1st tx. BBC-1 *Play for Today*, 6 June 1974). Written by McGrath and directed by John MacKenzie, the TV play strikingly and provocatively contrasted historical re-enactments of the events of the Highland Clearances following 1746, with documentary reportage on North Sea oil exploitation in the 1970s, cross-cut with footage of the 7:84 touring theatre company performing the stage version of the play to a Highland community audience. The implication was that the Highlanders, disinherited in the eighteenth century, were being disinherited all over again – along with their fellow Scots – through having no control over their own land nor of the North Sea oil that was starting to flow in the 1970s.

While the BBC was regularly producing works both about and from Scotland during this period, the situation within Scottish commercial television was more patchy. STV (covering the Glasgow, Edinburgh and Central Belt areas) had launched in 1957, followed in 1961 by Grampian (covering the north) and Border (covering the Scottish-English border). Production resources in these companies were limited, their main function being to maximise profitability by attracting advertisers in their respective areas via the networking of the most popular productions of the big English ITV companies, while augmenting this with a diet of local news, sports and other types of low-cost studio-based output. In 1968, STV, however, did dip its toe into the water of the 'redcoats in the heather' sub-genre, producing *Flight of the Heron*, based on D. K. Broster's 1925 novel, followed up in 1970 by an adaptation of Scott's *Redgauntlet*. Both were essentially children's drama, networked by ITV in appropriate slots.

By the 1970s, STV began to be more adventurous in its drama policy. As Hugh O'Donnell outlines in this volume, STV experimented with locally produced soap opera such as *High Living* (STV 1968–71) and *Garnock Way* (STV 1976–9). It also produced a range of single plays including, in 1978, networked productions by Stephen Poliakoff (*City Sugar*, tx. ITV, 6 August 1978) and Ian Curteis (*Hess* tx. ITV, 30 September 1978). As Jeremy Potter documents in his *History of Independent Television in Britain*, an advertising squeeze which had hit the company hard financially earlier in the decade had begun to rectify itself by the mid-1970s, and with one eye to convincing the IBA to renew its franchise at the 1980 review, STV began to plough money into prestige programming (Potter 1990: 154). One notable success was a highly praised, networked serial version of Muriel Spark's novel *The Prime of Miss Jean Brodie* (STV 1978). Another was 1979's *Charles Endell Esquire* which took its title character, a Glasgow gangster originally based in London, from a successful series made by another ITV company: London Weekend Television's early 1970s hit *Budgie* (LWT 1971–2). As played in both series by Scots actor Iain Cuthbertson, Endell was a smooth, Machiavellian gangster who, in the sequel, returned to his native Glasgow after seven years in prison.

Iain Cuthbertson was one of the most recognisable Scottish actors on TV in the 1970s. Having achieved success in *Budgie*, he also starred for BBC Scotland as a small-town procurator fiscal in its successful network drama *Sutherland's Law* which ran for three series between 1973 and 1976. Cuthbertson's memorable presence on each side of the law underscores how many Scottish TV dramatic representations of this period revolved around crime and had a kind of hard-boiled quality. Another notable example was writer Edward Boyd's BBC2 series *The View from Daniel Pike* (BBC TV 1971–3) which was set in contemporary Glasgow and starred Roddy McMillan as the eponymous Pike, a tough private investigator and debt collector. While in one sense a refreshing change from the Tartanry and Kailyard stereotypes so bemoaned by the *Scotch Reels* project, these hard-boiled images, with their sub-*film noir* excitement and their playing-up to 'no mean city' images of Glasgow to gain acceptance from network audiences, can be seen to have had their own inherent weaknesses and limitations from the very start: a masculinist discourse of urban hardness and violence which critics would later come to associate with some of the more negative aspects of 'Clydesideism' (Petrie 2004: 17).[7]

In television, the undoubted 'bard of hard' (Burnside 2004) during this period was writer Peter McDougall. Despite (at the time of writing) not having had any new TV work produced since 1993, McDougall probably remains the most significant dedicated television playwright to have emerged from Scotland. Born in Greenock, he left school at fifteen and worked in the shipyards before moving to London in the mid-1960s (Petrie 2004: 21). Encouraged to write his experiences down by playwright and actor Colin Welland, McDougall made his transmission debut on *Play for Today* with *Just Your Luck* (tx, BBC-1, 4 December 1972), which centred around a pregnant teenage girl living on a depressingly sectarian council estate in Greenock. Here, suddenly, there appeared to be an authentic new voice documenting lived working-class experience, exactly the prevailing *Play for Today* ethos of the period.

All the themes, settings and actors of McDougall's 1970s *Plays for Today* were Scottish; however, he was produced out of London and his themes were controversial.[8] His next work, *Just Another Saturday*, was actually the first TV play he wrote but had originally been rejected in favour of *Just Your Luck* because it had dealt directly with sectarianism, tracing as it did a long Saturday in the life of a young lad who twirls the mace at the head of the annual Protestant Orange Day parades through the streets of Glasgow. With religious intolerance a live issue as a consequence of the Troubles in Northern Ireland, the reasons for the BBC's nervousness were clear. Following the transmission of *Just Your Luck*, the play was eventually produced (1st tx. BBC-1, 13 March 1975) and garnered acclaim for McDougall, director John MacKenzie and the BBC when it won the International Prix Italia award for Drama in September 1975.

McDougall and MacKenzie ended their TV drama collaboration at STV with *A Sense of Freedom* (1980), a filmed adaptation of the autobiography of convicted murderer Jimmy Boyle which was a high-profile success for the company. Indeed, 1980 was something of an *annus mirabilis* for STV's fiction production – not only did it produce *A Sense of Freedom*, it also contributed half the £200,000 budget of Bill Forsyth's 'break-out' Scottish cinema hit, *Gregory's Girl* (1981). Meanwhile, it began commissioning no less than thirty-three single TV plays for six series of its *Preview* slot, which were all produced for the local STV audience (Macdonald 1990: 203). Clearly, in terms of the 'three ring circus' typology, this was TV drama designed solely 'for' Scotland,

and as Gus Macdonald, Managing Director of STV between 1990 and 1997, noted in a 1990 essay, many writers got 'a chance on *Preview*' (Macdonald 1990: 203).

One writer, in particular, who got his chance would put his mark on the next decade in Scottish television, a decade which would see Scottish broadcasting, and that of the rest of the UK, alter radically in response to the enormous political and cultural changes wrought by Thatcherism. This writer was Glenn Chandler, a former pathologist, who subsequently went on to create *Taggart* (STV 1983 to date), the most successful of all Scottish television dramas. At the time of writing, it has been sold for broadcast in over eighty countries, putting the drama's Glasgow setting on the world stage (SMG Productions 2007).

The initial idea for *Taggart* arose from Robert Love, then Controller of Drama at STV, who needed a drama proposal 'which the ITV network could not refuse' (SMG Productions 2007) and hit upon the concept of a Glasgow detective, commissioning Chandler to write a pilot. If this underscores the difficulties STV encountered arousing network interest in its ideas in a broadcasting environment which was getting more and more commercial in the 1980s, the resulting three-part serial, *Killer* (STV 1983), did sufficiently well in the ratings for the ITV network to green-light a full series. This began transmission under the title *Taggart* in 1985.

The continuing success of *Taggart* should not be sniffed at since, as Gus Macdonald noted, 'finding such a winning format in UK network drama is [a] difficult event' even for the big players, let alone a smaller company such as Scottish Television (Macdonald 1990: 197). Nevertheless, it is interesting that in the same essay, as he looked back on the *Preview* single-play slot, Macdonald recorded with a certain wistfulness: 'Purely Scottish productions like these were lost in the otherwise welcome advance to networking in the 1980s which produced the *Taggarts* . . .' (Macdonald 1990: 203). Here, there was a sense that in the transformations of the previous ten years to a much more commercially-driven environment, something had been lost; that now, there was far greater reliance on the tried and trusted formula which could sell to the widest possible international market, rather than anything of greater risk or expense that nevertheless might contribute something of cultural value to the local Scots audience. Seen in this light, the longevity of *Taggart*, together with STV's attempts to repeat its network and international success through subsequent *Taggart*-like crime series including *McCallum* (1995–8) and the various *Rebus* adaptations from the Edinburgh novels of Ian Rankin (2000, then 2006 to date), can be seen to denote a basic conservatism; a narrowing of the range of drama produced in response to the commercial imperatives acting upon the broadcaster.

The launch of Channel Four in 1982 also saw profound shifts in the type and range of screen fiction produced about, by and for Scotland. The channel's ambitious *Film on Four* initiative in which it eschewed single plays in favour of funding production of a slate of British films which gained theatrical release prior to television transmission, changed the ecology of British television drama production forever. By the mid-1980s, the BBC felt it had to follow suit, its predominantly studio-bound television plays no longer seeming adequate by comparison. *Play for Today* ended in 1984, to be replaced with the more amorphous single film drama slots, *Screen One* and *Screen Two*. ITV, meanwhile, had more or less abandoned single TV play production by the early 1980s. Only in radio does the single play still thrive.[9]

For Scotland, the launch of Channel Four initially seemed a godsend. Writing in 1990, John Caughie stated that 'it would be hard to overestimate the extent of the transformation it has brought about in Scottish and British film and programme production'. Suddenly, it was not uncommon for Scottish films and programmes to be seen and Scottish accents to be heard, particularly on television. Channel Four had helped create not only more diverse films and programmes but crucial to the development of a more diverse culture, 'audiences for representations' that equated to 'a national or regional culture as much as a film and television culture' (Caughie 1990: 21). The list of Scottish films wholly funded or co-funded by Channel Four in the period 1982–1990 alone included *Heavenly Pursuits* (1986), *Conquest of the South Pole* (1989), *Silent Scream* (1989) and adaptations from novels by Jessie Kesson (*Another Time, Another Place* (1983)) and Christopher Rush (*Venus Peter* (1989)).

Yet while Channel Four helped fund or co-fund a dozen Scottish features during the 1980s and stimulated the emergence of an infrastructure of Scottish independent production, there was a downside. The move to film tended to mean commissioners and creative practitioners alike privileged the servicing of cinema audiences, rather than television viewers. Film was far more costly to produce than even the old single play (which had hitherto been TV drama's most expensive form). This meant fewer productions could be made in any one year and they took longer to produce and to reach the TV screen, thus militating against topical material. Also, the risks attached in trying to produce films for the international cinema market first and the home television market second, tended to work against the new and untried, whether in relation to giving new writers their 'chance', or dealing with political or controversial subject matter that might be of particular interest to local audiences. It is perhaps telling that Peter McDougall, who achieved such success in the 1970s on *Play for Today*, struggled much more in the 1980s and beyond, and has had (at the time of writing) only three more TV scripts successfully produced since *A Sense of Freedom* in 1980.

One last gasp for the single television play form came in 1984 when the associate director of the National Theatre, Bill Bryden, was appointed Head of TV Drama at BBC Scotland, a post which Bryden combined with his South Bank responsibilities until 1993. One of the first fruits of Bryden's tenure was the production of his own play *The Holy City* (tx. BBC-1, 28 March 1986), a re-imagining of the life and death of Christ set in contemporary Glasgow. Starring David Hayman as a mysterious stranger preaching a message of love and hope, the play aimed to present the Christian story as relevant to contemporary Scottish working-class experience. In doing so, it made a number of polemical points about the death of shipbuilding on the Clyde and the domination of Scotland by England.

It was, however, for a production which eschewed traditional images of 'Clydesideism' that Bryden's tenure would come to be most remembered. *Tutti Frutti* was a six-part serial by theatrical playwright and painter John Byrne, first transmitted in the spring of 1987. It would go on to win great acclaim for BBC Scotland, including no less than six awards at the 1988 BAFTA ceremony (amongst them best serial/series award, and best actress award for Emma Thompson) and is still remembered to this day by its fans in Scotland and further afield. The idea came from Bryden who telephoned Byrne to remind him of 'The Poets', a Glasgow rock 'n' roll group who had troubled the lower reaches of the charts in the 1960s with one hit before disappearing into obscurity. 'Where are they now?' Bryden asked. According to Byrne: 'He provided the hare . . . and I set the dogs on it' (Brennan 1987).

The resulting *Tutti Frutti* is a comedy drama tale centring on 'The Majestics', an ageing obscure rock 'n' roll outfit who reform for a twenty-fifth anniversary tour, only to hit disaster when their leader, Big Jazza McGlone, inconveniently perishes in a car crash. McGlone's brother, Danny (played by Robbie Coltrane), comes over for the funeral from New York where he has been ekeing out a living as a piano player. As the doppelganger of Big Jazza, Danny is drafted in to front the band by the Majestics' shady manager Eddie Clockerty (Richard Wilson), as the group begins a dispiriting tour around small-town venues in places like Shotts, Methil and Buckie. Interwoven into this comic narrative are Danny's attempts to find romance with Suzi Kettles (Emma Thompson), and it is this relationship and her involvement which finally save the day as she joins the band and the group starts to turn a corner, culminating in a 'triumphant' gig at Glasgow's Pavilion Theatre.

At the heart of *Tutti Frutti* is an implicit repudiation of 'Clydesideism'. As Duncan Petrie has pointed out, the drama 'exposes the failings of traditional conceptions of masculinity in order to bury the stereotype of the "hard man" once and for all' (Petrie 2004: 57). Key to this is the character of Vincent Diver (Maurice Roëves), the band's guitarist and self-styled 'hard man of rock' who is always clad in black leather. His hard-man persona is comically undermined. As the drama progresses, he is bandaged, hospitalised, stabbed in the throat and testicles, and confined to a wheelchair with a neck brace, eventually having to struggle to the group's climactic Glasgow gig on crutches. The ultimate undermining of his masculinity is when his wife Noreen reveals to him that the real reason they have never been able to have children is his low sperm count. In a final act of self-destruction, he douses himself in alcohol and sets himself alight on stage at the Pavilion (Petrie 2004: 58).

Tutti Frutti explored all this in highly comic ways but its deconstruction of Scottish masculinity can be seen, in retrospect, to mark it out as a drama in keeping with its Thatcherite times. The production used humour to make its points about aspects of tragedy and harshness in Scottish life, aiming to entertain its audience and cajole them, rather than to shock or politicise them as, perhaps, had been the case in previous works by McDougall or Bryden. The serial's valorisation of the feminine principle as the saviour of men from the flaws of their own masculinity, in the shape of Suzi Kettles – the strong woman who brings out the best in Danny and eventually saves the band – also seems very much in keeping with a 1980s feminist *zeitgeist*. Despite its bittersweet treatment of the topic, the drama, too, traded on the familiarity and appeal of American popular culture and of rock 'n' roll to draw in audiences. For all these reasons, it is perhaps no surprise Byrne has been labelled the 'first postmodernist from Paisley' (National Theatre of Scotland 2007).[10]

Yet despite the numerous awards and the support of the then Director of BBC Television Programmes, Michael Grade, who ensured a prime-time slot for it on BBC1 and a BBC2 repeat the following year, *Tutti Frutti* did not do well in the ratings, gaining only 3.3 million viewers across the UK as a whole on first showing (Macdonald 1990: 198). Part of the problem seemed to be difficulties that some southern viewers had in dealing with and relating to the Scottish accents at a time, in recent history, when the north–south cultural and economic divide had perhaps never been so stark. Nor did Byrne's follow-up serial for BBC Scotland, *Your Cheatin' Heart* (BBC TV 1990), revolving around country and western music, do so well in critical or audience terms.

In the 1990s, however, the cultural climate began to shift in Scotland's direction as the political situation started to change, too. By the mid-1990s, there was what might be called the *Shallow Grave* (1995) and *Trainspotting* (1996) effect: two successive Channel Four-funded Scottish film hits from the talented director/writer/producer trio of Danny Boyle, John Hodge and Andrew Macdonald. Suddenly, these films, coupled with the release of *Braveheart* (1995), Mel Gibson's Oscar-winning Hollywood epic on the life of William Wallace, helped put Scotland on the international cultural map, making it a 'cool' place about which to produce films and television programmes. This new confidence amongst a rising, more assertive generation of Scots could also be seen at BBC Scotland with the appointment of Andrea Calderwood as Head of TV drama in 1994. At the time, it was a controversial choice as she was a young (then twenty-eight), relatively inexperienced producer. Peter McDougall famously dismissed her as a 'wee lassie' (Smith 2004). The appointment, however, was an indicator of the changing face of television and the fact that, 'wee lassie' or not, women television executives were a new powerful force to be reckoned with. Given the changing economic and power relationships between men and women over the previous few decades, not least the fact that 'women control the remote',[11] and now comprise the majority of the TV drama-watching audience, this development is hardly surprising. In this context, it is perhaps easy to see why Peter McDougall's work, with its ultra-masculinist emphasis, has struggled to find a place on television since 1993.

Calderwood reflected the new freedoms there were in the 1990s to produce both television and film and to move easily between them. During her tenure between 1994 and 1997, she trebled the output of the department, counting amongst her successes an Oscar-winning film for BBC Scotland (*Mrs Brown* (1996) starring Judi Dench as Queen Victoria), alongside the creation of a Sunday-night network hit, *Hamish MacBeth* (BBC TV 1995–7), featuring rising star Robert Carlyle in the leading role. *Hamish MacBeth* was essentially a continuation of the kind of Sunday-night feel-good television which *Doctor Finlay's Casebook* had pioneered in the 1960s – in this case it is not a doctor but a Glasgow policeman who is relocated to a fictional Highland town, Lochdubh, there to encounter the distinctive ways of the locals. Based on the books by M. C. Beaton, there was, however, an undercutting quirkiness to *Hamish MacBeth* which, though mild, owed something to cult American TV drama of the early 1990s such as *Twin Peaks* (ABC 1990–1) and *Northern Exposure* (CBS 1990–5), both of which had depicted the essential weirdness underlying small-town life. This was not just a function of the casting of Carlyle (best known for grittier fare such as Ken Loach films and Granada's *Cracker* series) but also the fact that his character, Hamish MacBeth, was a pot-smoking policeman unusually attached to his West Highland terrier, wee Jock, and who did not take the letter of the law too seriously. His one ambition was to try to avoid promotion since that would mean having to leave Lochdubh. As a result, he would often let others take the credit for solving the crimes he in fact had solved.

Having overseen these and other productions, Calderwood quickly moved on to become Head of Production at Pathé Pictures in 1997. She later went on to set up her own company, Slate Films, and to produce the Oscar-winning *The Last King of Scotland* (2006). Her successor at the BBC, Barbara McKissack, continued the tradition of feel-good drama with *Two Thousand Acres of Sky* (BBC TV 2001–3), which revolved around a single mum who relocates to the fictional island of Ronansay, and perhaps most successfully, *Monarch of the Glen* (BBC TV 2000–5). The latter dealt with the lives and loves of the inhabitants of the fictional Glenbogle estate in the Scottish Highlands and continued the Sunday-night tradition where *Hamish MacBeth* had left off. *Monarch of the Glen* ran on the network for seven series and was sold to many countries around the world. If the ratings and commercial appeal of producing such fare is obvious, it is interesting to note the ambivalence shown towards it by John McCormick, the then BBC Scotland Controller, when he was interviewed on his retirement:

> *Monarch of the Glen* does raise interesting issues. I just came back from Australia where it's playing on a Saturday at 7.30 and getting record audiences. And you have that kind of feeling like 'is that what they think contemporary Scotland is like ?'. . . I'm kind of ambivalent to *Monarch*. It's a tremendous success, international success. It earns revenue for the BBC which comes back into Scotland. Of course, if you could get eight million viewers for a gritty contemporary social challenging drama at 8 o'clock on a Sunday night on BBC1, then you may feel more creatively satisfied. (McCormick 2004: 281)[12]

Nevertheless, as McCormick stated in the same interview, the institutional and business imperatives behind *Monarch of the Glen* were clear: BBC Scotland needed 'a returning series on Sunday nights' since popular drama was required to sustain a department in order that the single films or one-off dramas which win prestige and garner awards could continue to be produced. This cannot be done unless there is a department behind them earning its keep:

> So if you have a £1.2 million film scheme on the one hand and you've got a popular drama, you've got signature series for BBC2 or BBC4, challenging work being commissioned, and you've got a soap, then you've got a rounded department. All that can happen from that is you develop in strength and underpin that. People come to you. It also means that you give a lot of people work opportunities in Scotland. It allows them to do other work in Scotland. That's the business aim. (McCormick 2004: 280)

The launch in 2002 of BBC Scotland's *River City*, a Scottish soap opera for the local audience that picked up the mantle from STV's dying *Take The High Road* (1980–2003), was part of that same strategy. *River City*'s executive producer Barbara McKissack said at the time: 'I think it's great to have something that is just for Scotland itself' (Adair 2003).

Yet if in the three ring circus of Scottish production, this was drama designed principally 'for' Scotland, to what extent was it truly serving Scotland? As the comments cited at the start of this chapter make clear, *River City* and the policy which spawned it have generated much criticism. John McCormick's view that popular drama could help sustain a diverse and rounded department is undermined to an extent by the fact that the bulk (£10 million) of the £14 million drama budget given to BBC Scotland, as part of network centre's aim of spreading production across the 'nations and regions', had been spent on a soap, and as a consequence of that soap's very local nature, would never be recouped through networking or international sales. So are Tom Little and his *Scotland on Sunday* supporters correct, therefore, in saying that Scottish TV drama in the 2000s has become an inferior and inward-looking backwater? What can the history, sketched out here, tell us?

For one thing, it shows that the heritage is a rich one and that for most of its history, BBC Scotland had a far greater presence on the network than BBC Wales.[13] While Wales, once dismissed as localised and parochial, has forged ahead in recent years, both in network and overseas sales terms, with the production of hit fantasy series for the network, BBC Scotland's decision to allocate the bulk of its resources to *River City* has led to an inevitable turning inwards to focus on its home audience.[14] Nor has there been much competition from STV of late – from the *annus mirabilis* year of diversity in 1980, STV's range has considerably narrowed to detective series like *Taggart* and *Rebus*. This is not surprising given the considerable pressures commercial broadcasters are now under to maintain audience share and advertising revenue in the digital age of multi-channel choice.

Hence if there is to be a diverse future for Scottish TV drama, the best hope probably lies with the BBC, given its secure licence-fee income. But a new factor is at work, since the costs of drama are falling and in an increasingly globalised world, new digital technologies are facilitating distribution to potential audiences of millions around the world via the Internet. The universally interconnected world we are moving into arguably needs new thinking about what producing a 'Scottish' TV drama might mean. Whilst the old three ring circus traced here may have been concerned with questions of TV drama 'about', 'by' and 'for' Scotland, in the new world, the three rings are being rapidly redefined as 'local', 'national' and 'global' marketplaces. To survive and prosper, producers in the future will not be able to afford to concentrate on just one of these – the 'local' – because in the digital age they are all increasingly interconnected. They will need to service all three.

NOTES

1. Current typical costs for BBC TV drama range from £500,000–£900,000 per hour spanning low-cost/mid-range to high-end/expensive drama (source: 'Commissioning', http://www.bbc.co.uk/commissioning/tv/business/tariffs).

2. The title, 'Three Ring Circus', is inspired by an experimental TV play of the same name, written by Jack Gerson. Produced and directed by James MacTaggart in 1961 from Glasgow, its critical success led to MacTaggart being invited to London to lead a number of narrative experiments in play production which eventually saw him promoted to be producer of the first 1965 season of the famous *Wednesday Play* slot. MacTaggart's former colleague, Pharic Maclaren, also contributed a number of BBC Scotland-produced plays to *The Wednesday Play* slot in the 1960s, including Edward Boyd's *A Black Candle for Mrs Gogarty* (tx. BBC-1, 25 October 1967) and Welsh writer Ray Jenkins' *Patterson O.K.* (tx. BBC-1, 8 October 1969). My thanks to Lez Cooke (Manchester Metropolitan University) for clarification of research details concerning *Three Ring Circus*. A paper by Cooke analysing this play was delivered by him at the July 2006 *Screen* Studies international conference in Glasgow.

3. Adaptations of the other works in Grassic Gibbon's 'Scots Quair' trilogy, *Cloud Howe* and *Grey Granite*, were later produced by BBC Scotland in 1982 and 1983 respectively.

4. *Doctor Finlay* was later revived by STV between 1993 and 1996, this time starring David Rintoul as the eponymous doctor. Interestingly, the setting was updated to post-World War Two and the foundation of the National Health Service, this having become safely 'period' by the 1990s.

5. See McArthur, Colin (ed.) (1982), *Scotch Reels*, London: British Film Institute. Another BBC TV London-produced drama of the period in the mould of *Doctor Finlay* was *This Man Craig* (BBC TV 1966–7), starring John Cairney as a scientist teaching physics in a contemporary secondary school in the fictional Scottish town of Strathaird, who was as idealistic about education as Doctor Finlay was about medicine. It lasted for only two series on BBC 2.

6. See McGrath's comments on Watkins' use of non-professional actors in an interview for *Ex-S – Culloden: Making Reel History* (1st tx. BBC 1 Scotland 15 April 1996).

7. As Petrie puts it, 'Clydesideism' projected a Scotland that was 'urban, industrial and working class in character' in reaction to the discourses of Tartanry and Kailyard. However, its potential progressiveness was also 'compromised by its overtly masculine associations with hard physical labour, . . . gambling, excessive drinking and violence' (Petrie 2004: 17–18).

8. Post-*Play for Today*, later McDougall BBC works would be produced by BBC Scotland – for example, *Down Where the Buffalo Go* (tx. BBC-1, 19 January 1988) and *Down Among the Big Boys* (tx. BBC-1, 19 September 1993).

9. Although the single play is rarely seen on television today, it is still alive and well on BBC Radio 4, and to a lesser extent BBC Radio 3, and Scottish-based producers and writers continue to make a significant contribution to this output.

10. US popular culture and its bittersweet refraction in Scottish lives have been constant themes of John Byrne's stage work, most notably in 'The Slab Boys Trilogy' (1978–82), a trio of autobiographical plays examining the influence of American popular culture and of rock 'n' roll on the lives of three Paisley boys as they grow

up from the late 1950s to the 1970s. In 2006, Byrne also oversaw a successful revival of *Tutti Frutti* as a stage production.

11. Jane Tranter, BBC Television Controller of Drama Commissioning (2000–6), interview, *The South Bank Show – TV Drama Stories Part Two* (tx. ITV1, 8 February 2004).

12. An example of the kind of 'gritty contemporary social challenging' BBC Scotland drama which McCormick might have had in mind here was *Tinsel Town* (BBC TV 2000–2). Set in a Glasgow dance club/drugs den, it featured much strong language, sex and drug-taking scenes. It aired late night on BBC2.

13. For a review of the history of the relationship of BBC Wales TV drama to the UK network, see Blandford, S. (2005), 'BBC Drama at the Margins', in J. Bignell and S. Lacey (eds), *Popular Television Drama: Critical Perspectives*, Manchester: Manchester University Press, pp. 173–8.

14. Julie Gardner, Head of BBC TV Drama in Wales from 2003, presided over the successful revival for the network of *Doctor Who* (BBC TV 2005 to date) and the hit time-travelling cop show, *Life on Mars* (BBC TV 2006–7). Her success saw her promoted in 2006 to overall Head of Drama Commissioning for the entire BBC TV network. BBC Scotland's only recent foray into this fantasy field, *Sea of Souls* (BBC TV 2004 to date), a Saturday-night network drama series revolving around a parapsychology unit, has had less of a public impact.

REFERENCES

Adair, T. (2003), 'River City – waving or drowning ?', *The Scotsman*, 6 September 2003, http://news.scotsman.com/topics.cfm?tid=917&id=979982003.

Anon., (1959), 'Amiable rogues on shipboard', *The Times*, 12 December 1959, p. 9.

Brennan, M. (1987), 'Return of the geriatric rockers', *The Sunday Times*, 1 March 1987, http://web.lexis-nexis.com/professional/form?_index=pro_en.html&_lang=en&ut=3359560165.

Burnside, A. (2004), 'Bard of hard sounds off', *The Sunday Times*, 21 November 2004, http://www.timesonline.co.uk/tol/newspapers/sunday_times/scotland/article392919.ece.

Caughie, J. (1990), 'Representing Scotland: new questions for Scottish cinema', in E. Dick (ed.), *From Limelight to Satellite*, Glasgow and London: Scottish Film Council and British Film Institute, pp. 13–30.

Little, T. and web responses (2006), '£180m a year . . . and the best that we get for it is *Happy Birthday Broons*', *Scotland on Sunday*, 19 November 2006, http://scotlandonsunday.scotsman.com /index.cfm?id=1712542006.

Macdonald, G. (1990), 'Fiction friction', in E. Dick (ed.), *From Limelight to Satellite*, Glasgow and London: Scottish Film Council and British Film Institute, pp. 193–206.

McCormick, J. (2004), 'An interview with John McCormick, former Controller, BBC Scotland (conducted by Christine Geraghty and Ian Goode)', *Journal of British Cinema and Television*, 1: 2, 275–86.

McDowell, W. H. (1992), *The History of BBC Broadcasting in Scotland 1923–1983*, Edinburgh: Edinburgh University Press.

National Theatre of Scotland (2007), '*Tutti Frutti Live*: John Byrne Q & A', http://www.nationaltheatrescotland.com/content/default.asp?page=s224.

Petrie, D. (2004), *Contemporary Scottish Fictions: Film, Television and the Novel*, Edinburgh: Edinburgh University Press.

Potter, J. (1990), *Independent Television in Britain – Volume 4: Companies and Programmes, 1968–80*, Basingstoke and London: Macmillan.

SMG Productions (2007), '*Taggart*', http://www.smgproductions.tv/content/default.asp?page=s2_2_15.

Smith, A. (2004), 'Big boys don't cry', *Scotland on Sunday*, 18 April 2004, http://scotlandonsunday.scotsman.com/review.cfm?id=435102004.

8

'Nae Bevvying, Nae Skiving': Language and Community in the Scottish Soap Opera

HUGH O'DONNELL

INTRODUCTION

The soap opera was one of the great cultural phenomena of the twentieth century. Appearing first on American radio during the Great Depression of the 1930s – its name deriving partly from the fact that the programmes in question were sponsored by large corporations such as Colgate-Palmolive and Procter & Gamble which produced, among other things, detergents – its key structural element was its serial format. In other words, episodes were open-ended and, in contrast to series where each episode is structured around its own self-contained narrative, in the soap opera narratives rolled, potentially endlessly, from one episode to the next. The longest-running soap opera in the World, *The Guiding Light*, began on American radio in 1937, made the transition to television in the early 1950s, and continues to this day, seventy years later.

The first country outside the United States to adopt the soap opera format was the UK with radio soaps such as *Mrs Dale's Diary* (1948–69) and *The Archers* (1950–), and the first television soap, *The Grove Family*, running from 1954 to 1957. Though these productions were broadcast throughout the UK, they were in fact English rather than in any meaningful sense British. Domestically produced Scottish soap operas would not emerge until much later, and once they did they would consistently lag in popularity behind the English soaps broadcast north of the border. This chapter will examine that apparent conundrum.

THE SCOTTISH SOAP OPERA

Scottish television serial productions which clearly fulfil the requirements of the soap opera format can be listed as follows:

High Living	STV	1968–71
A Place of Her Own	STV	1971
Garnock Way	STV	1976–9
(Take the) High Road	STV	1980–2003
Machair	STV	1993–9
River City	BBC	2002–

Of these *Machair* was (mostly) in Gaelic, and it is dealt with elsewhere in this volume (see Cormack). In this chapter I will deal only with those productions using various combinations of Standard English, Standard Scottish English (SSE) and Scots.

HIGH LIVING AND A PLACE OF HER OWN: THE MISSING LINKS

High Living was set in Glasgow, in a high-rise block of flats, and featured Eileen McCallum in the lead role. Though individuals in their fifties and over still retain memories of this studio-bound serial with its four sets (including the laundry room in the basement), somewhat surprisingly no physical trace of it remains, with neither STV, Scottish Screen nor the BFI having any copies in their archives. It is, therefore, impossible to provide any kind of analysis here, though the production's clearly urban location was important, as was its strongly working-class feel. *High Living* was followed by the short-lived *A Place of her Own*, in which Eileen McCallum appeared as councillor Kate Crombie. As with the earlier production, no episodes remain.

GARNOCK WAY: THE CHANGING FACE OF SCOTLAND

Garnock Way, STV's third soap, ran for three years from 1976 to 1979, clocking up over 300 episodes before being stopped, more or less without warning, to allow production facilities to be transferred to the forthcoming *Take the High Road* (Elder 1990: 18). It was a relatively cut-price production, shot almost entirely on video in the studio with the very rare location shooting done on film. It also starred Eileen McCallum – this time in the role of Jean Ross (indeed, this actress has appeared in every single soap opera made in Scotland) – and is in a somewhat more privileged position in that some episodes do in fact remain. The first episode opened with a black and white shot of a pithead, panning to a road sign showing the village of Garnock to be twenty-three miles from Glasgow and twenty-eight from Edinburgh (a location further strengthened by the fact that the local paper is the *Roxburn and District Observer*, a less than subtle reference to the village of Broxburn in West Lothian). We then switch to the village's mercat cross, with all filming in colour from that point on. We move inside Jean's house, where she puts the paper on the table revealing the headline 'Central Scotland Pit Closures May Affect Wilderness Pit'.

Garnock Way is perhaps the most overtly political soap opera the UK has ever seen. It starts with rumours of pit closures and threats by shop steward Sandy Menzies – the physical resemblance to Jimmy Reid, famous for the Upper Clyde Shipbuilders occupation of the early 1970s, is surely no coincidence – to bring out the whole of Scotland, in fact the whole of the UK if that was to happen. When boatyard owner Mr McDougal asks Alex Ross to take over as yard manager, he offers him a rise of six pounds a week 'keeping within the government's limits', and his first task is to achieve 'economies' by cutting down pilfering of materials among the workers.

The programme dealt forcefully with the significant changes affecting the Central Belt in the 1970s. Though the pit struggled on, many of the miners lost their jobs (including Jean's son Hugh) and had to find alternative work. The very nature of Garnock was threatened with the proposed construction of Garnock New Town, and later episodes featured town hall struggles with officials travelling through to Edinburgh to argue their case against high-density housing with the Secretary of State. Sandy Menzies and Alex Ross eventually both became councillors (though, in typical soap opera fashion, no mention was ever made of which party they might have stood for), a change which saw Alex in particular move to a suit and tie and briefcase. Moral dilemmas then arose when he had to decide whether to vote for or against rises in council house rents. In terms of personal relationships, members of the older generation had to learn how to live with separations and divorces, and to cope with a combative younger generation to whom their values often seemed alien.

As a particular focus of this chapter will be how the language issue (see Corbett, this volume) is played out in Scottish soaps, I would like to say a little about the particular patterns present in *Garnock Way*. What is most striking is the gender division in operation. On the one hand, all the female characters in the soap speak SSE – in fact, Jean and Alex's daughter Ginny is 'perjink' to the point of being totally unrealistic in terms of where the production is supposedly set, speaking a kind of SSE one would be more likely to associate with Bearsden. On the other hand some of the men at least – Sandy Menzies and taxi-driver Howie Watson in particular – speak a more or less consistent Scots, while the others use the kind of tokenised Scots to be found in *Taggart*, for example. While a tendency among women towards greater linguistic 'correctness' is a well-known sociolinguistic phenomenon (Trudgill 1974: 85), the gap between the speaking styles of the members of the same family at times strains realism beyond breaking point (Govan and Bearsden in the same living room). But this tension between how groups represented on television actually speak and how television *itself* speaks is one which remains largely unresolved in Scottish broadcasting to this day. The question of 'what to do with Scots', whether to have it at all, and if so which characters to have speaking it, is one that will recur throughout this analysis.

In Alex Ross's case, moreover, his elevation to the status of councillor meant a much more wholehearted embrace of SSE as well as of a suit and tie. In addition, this lack of realism was compounded by the fact that what Scots was spoken was Glasgow rather than West Lothian Scots. Whatever its timbre, Scots operates to suggest working-class origins, lack of education, and even lack of ambition.

TAKE THE HIGH ROAD: AMBLING THROUGH THE RYE . . .

Scotland's longest-running soap to date has been *Take the High Road* – earlier name suggestions had included *The Glendhu Factor* and *High Road Low Road* – launched by STV in 1980 in response to an invitation from the ITA for a soap from one of the UK 'regions' which could be shown throughout the ITV network (Elder 1990: 12), and running till 2003. Though always lagging some way behind *EastEnders* when it launched in 1985, in terms of the number of viewers it was able to attract in Scotland (Kingsley 1988: 425), *Take the High Road* must be considered a successful production since, unlike any Scottish soap opera before or since, it had an audience not only in England and Northern Ireland – though not always at the same point in the schedule – but latterly also in Australia.

Take the High Road featured a number of the actors from *Garnock Way*, but as very different characters and in a very different location. The initial contrast with *Garnock Way* could not possibly be more striking: while the former was set in a mining community about to be dwarfed by a high-rise new town, *Take the High Road* was set in the fictitious village of Glendarroch (location shooting was in the actual village of Luss on the west bank of Loch Lomond, renamed Loch Darroch in the fictional world). For the first decade at least anything related to city or even town life seemed very far away. Framed as it was by its picturesque setting – on average around half of any episode consisted of location shooting – and by a heavy focus on the vagaries of village life with such key characters as the minister, the laird, the over-zealous bobby, the sleazy local newshound and the busybody Mrs Mack, all dominated by the Big House, it was a long-running televisual version of the Kailyard. Perhaps in view of its location, we might describe it as a form of 'Tartan Kailyard' since, with its craggy views and lilting accents, *Take the High Road* was closely aligned with the discourse of Tartanry which works essentially to offer a romanticised representation of Scotland to a mainly non-Scottish audience.

Ghastly things happened from time to time, of course – infidelities, deaths, murders, fires and so on, all standard soap-opera fare – but the community called on all its resources to pull through. There were spats over fishing rights, turf wars between rival estates Glendarroch and Letir-Falloch (settled in gentlemen's clubs in London), even turf wars between neighbouring ministers, but everything remained essentially unchanged as the 1980s with their Thatcherism, yuppies, miners' strikes and de-industrialisation came and went.

Given its (mock) Highland setting – the name Glendarroch is an anglicisation of the Gaelic 'Gleann Darach' (Glen Oak) – the language question (what to do with Scots) never really raised its head since, as is well known, Scots was never spoken in those parts of Scotland which used to belong to the Gaeltacht. A range of varieties of English was on display, but all the characters spoke Standard English or SSE of one kind or the other: indeed, this was seen as a requirement for its acceptability to other ITV regions.

. . . BECOMES *HIGH ROAD*: THE GORBALS OF THE HIGHLANDS?

However, winds of change began to blow through the sedate world of *Take the High Road* as it entered the 1990s. A storyline in that year incorporating the new golf course at Luss offended some viewers who felt that it was not compatible with the soap's overall 'rural' feel (Elder 1990: 95). The title was changed to *High Road* to bring it more in line with the 'punchier' titles of other UK soaps. However, the greatest catalyst for change was the decision by a number of members of the ITV network to drop the programme in 1993, as a result of which STV announced in 1994 that it would be ceasing production. Consternation ensued, a sizeable demonstration led by the cast and the production team filled George Square in the centre of Glasgow, and STV backed down. It was a victory for the fans perhaps, but one which would, in the long run, prove to be Pyrrhic.

Although production continued, some important changes took place, including a reduction in the number of episodes broadcast from two to one per week. However, the most important changes took place inside the narrative world. The titled incomers disappeared, along with their patrician accents, and a number of younger characters came on board. These included gangly teenager Dominic Buchan, first fostered and later adopted by the Ramsays, and his girlfriend Sally, accompanied by the opening of the obligatory nightclub (complete with debates over the relative merits of rave versus techno), and twenty-somethings such as Tiffany Bowles, the beautician, one of whose first remarks was to announce that 'even little villages have to move with the times'. West-of-Scotland working-class accents became more common with characters such as good-for-nothing layabout and, briefly, mobile-shop operator Gary Macdonald, but above all with the arrival of taxi-driver-cum-general-handyman (and arrant coward) Chic Cherry, played by well-known Scots comedian Andy Cameron, who initially spoke a fairly consistent Scots completely unknown in *Take the High Road* prior to that point, but of course already very familiar to television viewers through *Rab C Nesbitt*, the BBC Scotland sitcom, which had been running for four years. There was even a black character for a short while, the Reverend Ben from Nigeria.

Perhaps the greatest change of all was the rapid increase in prominence of neighbouring town Auchtarne. A thirty-minute bus journey from Glendarroch, Auchtarne, though it defies identification with any real-life Scottish location, was large enough to host a sizeable comprehensive (attended by Dominic and Sally), a further education college (where Eddie Ramsay worked for a while as an IT lecturer), a hospital (which the Ramsays attended in relation to their fertility problems), and even a 'tough' housing scheme which produced not only club barman Victor (who described it as 'the Gorbals of the Highlands') but also petty criminal and thug (later turned garage mechanic) Paul Lafferty. Though neither Glendarroch nor its rural atmosphere went away, all of this worked to give the soap a much more 'urban' feel with its storylines of schoolyard bullying, exam stress, even taxi wars. *High Road*'s engagement with 'issues' was also stepped up considerably from its days as *Take the High Road*. As the second half of the 1990s rolled on, there were storylines of male infertility, male breast cancer, student prostitution, rape, stalking, lesbianism, even anti-Englishness, alongside more rural issues like sheep worrying or attacks on local wildlife. These changes were, in fact, the outer signs of a much more fundamental transformation which was taking place: from 1994 on *High Road* no longer thought of itself primarily as a UK soap, as a result of which it also moved from a mainly Kailyard discourse to one with more visible elements of Clydesideism.

Though viewing figures in Scotland had crept up to the one million mark by the end of the 1990s, the 'victory' of 1994 proved to be merely a stay of execution. In 2000 STV announced that the show would be axed and, although all those involved in the production apparently continued to believe that a reprieve would be forthcoming (as a result of which the scriptwriters did not bring *High Road* to any kind of orderly end), this time there was to be no way back. Insider accounts suggest that *High Road* was simply overcome by economic logic: the cost of the broadcasting licence had risen to over £2 million pounds after several years in which, thanks to the vagaries of the blind

bidding system introduced in the 1990 Broadcasting Act, STV had been broadcasting virtually licence-cost-free. *High Road*, at £60,000 per episode, represented a substantial outlay, particularly in view of the loss of the English
regions; and in the end it was sacrificed on the altar of corporate efficiency. No
doubt there is something in this, and perhaps in the end the equation was too
easy for STV's accountants, with suitable encouragement and prompting, to
ignore, but it seems unlikely that this is the whole story.

The move from two episodes to one per week had placed *High Road* in the
extremely unusual situation – at least for a soap opera – of experiencing a
yawning gap between its production schedule and its broadcast schedule, to
such an extent that when production finished in 2000, there was a large enough
backlog of episodes to continue broadcasting for another three years. However,
most UK soap operas are shot six to eight weeks ahead of screening, and one
of their essential characteristics is to be broadly in the same 'time frame' as their
viewers. Perhaps this would have mattered less had the production maintained
its *Brigadoon*-like features of the 1980s, but when it became more issue-
oriented in the 1990s, the scriptwriters found themselves in the position of
absorbing issues into the narrative knowing that the viewers would not be
exposed to them for two or three years, by which time they might well have
moved out of public debate. But perhaps more importantly, despite the influx
of younger characters with their fresh faces and energetic outlook on life – and
a number of them would in fact eventually leave the production – *High Road's*
dramatic centre remained its older and increasingly ageing characters. In the
second half of the 1990s there were four romantic attachments leading to marriage – between Isabel and Alun, Effie and Jockie, Tom and Morag, and Mairi
and Lachie – all involving people in their late fifties or sixties. Perhaps a soap
where so much of the sexual chemistry is concentrated in that section of the
age scale was already doomed to a lingering death. In any case, it is difficult to
reconcile with the profile of a station which saw itself as energetic, dynamic
and facing the future.

RIVER CITY: GLESGA BELANGS TAE WHO?

BBC Scotland's first ever soap *River City* had its genesis in an allocation of
some £14 million made to the station by the then BBC Director-General
Greg Dyke as part of a plan to encourage the production of drama in the so-
called 'nations and regions'. The bulk of that £14 million (£10 million) was
used to launch this new production. This was a brave decision, since everyone in the industry knew that *High Road* had ceased production. A rural soap
was clearly out of the question and, after some hesitation (Leith in Edinburgh
was at one point floated as a possibility), the decision was taken to set the new

'gritty, urban' soap in Glasgow. It was to be in the fictitious borough of Shieldinch (an amalgam of the real-life place names Shieldhall and Whiteinch) on the banks of the Clyde (a boatyard is part of the permanent backdrop of the purpose-built ten-acre set in Dumbarton) and was to represent a city in a phase of transition from an industrial past to a 'fashionable' and even 'trendy' future.

River City opened on 24 September 2002, and is still on the air. Its trajectory has not always been an easy one. Its first episode attracted around 750,000 viewers – a very respectable score – but this quickly fell away. In early 2003, when it was (suicidally) scheduled against *Coronation Street*, its viewing figures reached an all-time low of 160,000, leading it to be dubbed 'River Shitty' in the Scottish tabloids. However, the investment was simply too great for BBC Scotland to pull the plug on this production so early. Wholesale changes followed, including the appointment of a new director, new scriptwriters, the elimination of a whole raft of characters (including the entire Malik family) and the recruitment of a number of high-profile new members of the cast (including Lorraine McIntosh, former singer with the band *Deacon Blue*, and Stefan Dennis, an Australian actor who had previously appeared in the highly popular Australian soap *Neighbours*). *River City* did eventually rally, and has now settled down at just under half a million viewers per episode, including around 100,000 for its weekend omnibus. Though this is still short of the audiences achieved by the likes of *EastEnders* and *Coronation Street* in Scotland, *River City*'s future – despite the fact that the hoped-for network exposure has not yet been achieved – now seems secure, at least in the medium term.

In its short existence *River City* has had a truly multifarious cast coming and going in a rapid turnover, and no more than a handful of the original characters remain. Despite its Glasgow setting, characters have hailed from many other parts of Scotland – most notably the Aberdonian Roisin speaking a strong northeast Scots – and it has featured a significant number of non-white characters of Indian, Pakistani or Chinese origin, some born in Scotland, and some immigrants, including more recently migrant workers from Eastern Europe. After a slow beginning, the programme's engagement with issues has been extraordinarily intense, matching or even outdoing *High Road* in its final phase (a number of scriptwriters have in fact worked for both productions). There have been storylines about stalking, Internet pornography, sexual abuse of minors, alcoholism, mental illness, homophobia (one of the central characters is gay), racist violence, even lapsed priests, along with the usual soap opera gamut of infidelities, separations, divorces, murders and deaths. With its small-scale industrial heritage and its residually working-class feel, with its kenspeckle local personalities and at times somewhat claustrophobically parochial range – characters seldom venture furth of Shieldinch – *River City* combines some residual elements of the Kailyard with a somewhat larger dose of watered-down Clydesideism. If *High Road* was a form of 'Heelan Kailyard', perhaps *River City* could best be described as a form of urban Kailyard, a contradictory amalgam reflecting its ambivalent attitude to its public.

While *High Road*'s Highland setting had allowed it to sidestep the question of Scots for most of its existence, given the broadly realist discourse of British soaps as a whole, the question of Scots simply could not be avoided in *River City* since this is the standard mode of communication of the majority of the population of Glasgow. The first few episodes would make the role allotted to Scots quite clear. The high point of the opening episode was the wedding of Tommy Donachie and Eileen Henderson. Tommy had previously worked in the shipyards, where he had been a shop steward. When the shipyards closed, he used his redundancy money to open a pub, The Tall Ship, together with Eileen, thereby moving from the working class to the petite bourgeoisie (more on this below). His change of status was immediately apparent when he opened his mouth. He began his wedding speech by pretending that he was actually addressing a mass meeting of shipyard workers. His first words, echoing Jimmy Reid's at the onset of the UCS work-in, were 'Comrades! There'll be nae bevvying, nae skiving, nae . . .'. 'Realising' that he was in fact addressing his wedding guests, he then paused and added 'Oh, sorry, wrong speech'. In that brief pause he changed from Scots to English, since, had he continued to speak Scots, he would have said 'Oh, sorry, *wrang* speech'.

It is widely claimed, in both academic and journalistic writing, that British soaps are about the 'working class' (see O'Donnell, 1999: 206–11 for a detailed analysis of this claim). This is not in any simple sense the case, since the vast majority of the characters who populate British soap operas (there are of course some exceptions) belong to the petite bourgeoisie: they are publicans, shop-keepers, café and restaurant owners, small business owners and the like. It is this class rather than the working class proper which constitutes the moral centre of British soaps, and in this respect *River City* is no exception, most of its main characters owning small businesses ranging from pubs and cafés to shops and garages or building firms. The crucial difference between *River City* and the other UK soaps, however, is that in those soaps the language of the petit-bourgeois characters is by definition the language of the soap. Characters who do not, for example, speak with a cockney accent in *East Enders* or with a Lancashire accent in *Coronation Street* are immediately identified as geographical outsiders – what we might term a form of 'vertical' segregation – though, providing they meet certain, broadly-speaking, moral standards, they can be accepted by the soap community. The common language of the central characters both signals their shared class origin and values and acts as a barrier which ensures that outsiders are granted admittance only on the community's terms. While the language/class barrier is one which surrounds the community in other UK soaps, in *River City*, by contrast, there are internal frontiers – forms of 'horizontal' segregation – regarding the speech of characters coming from the same geographical area, frontiers which simultaneously constitute an *internal* class hierarchy.

The broad outline of this hierarchy is as follows: well-educated young 'entrepreneurs' and professionals mostly speak SSE, with only the occasional and highly tokenised nod in the direction of Scots at the very most; traditional (mostly middle-aged) petit bourgeois characters speak a bizarre mixture of SSE and Scots in which SSE clearly dominates, with typically Scots forms such as 'cannae' or 'didnae' or the occasional 'doon' or 'aboot' thrown into the mixture; working class and underclass characters speak west-of-Scotland urban Scots similar to that used earlier by Rab C Nesbitt, in the eponymous sitcom. Unlike other British soaps, therefore, *River City*'s community is split along class lines, a split which is clearly reflected in the way characters speak, and a split which, we might note, aligns the working class with the underclass.

Perhaps the clearest example of this hierarchy at work has been the varying fates of the characters Derek (Deek) Henderson and Bob Adams, also known by his nickname Shellsuit Boab, since he originally made money for himself by stealing and reselling shellsuits (a working-class fashion item currently much despised in middle-class circles in Scotland). In the opening episodes Deek and Boab are still at school, and conform visibly to the stereotype of what is widely known is Scotland as the 'ned'. At the beginning of the second episode they meet up in an abandoned gap site where Boab sells Deek a shellsuit he has stolen from a local store. Their conversation goes as follows:

> DEEK (*smoking a cigarette*):   Huv ye goat it then? (*Boab gives him a shellsuit*). Excellent! (*He gives Boab money*)
> BOAB: Ye know, if ye want [w+ant] anythin else oot ay there, trainers or whitever, the security guy's useless. (*He kisses the money Deek has given him*)
> DEEK: Ye cannae start daein trainers an aw.
> BOAB: How no?
> DEEK: Ye're Shellsuit Boab. Ye'd huv tae cheinge yer name.

As can be seen, at this point in *River City* both of these (in fact disreputable) characters are speaking recognisable forms of Scots.

Subsequent developments, however, were to take the two characters in very different directions. After leaving school Deek went on a Business Studies course at university, and after graduating joined the young entrepreneur group by becoming the manager of the Lazy Rays tanning salon owned by his uncle Raymond (Ray), at which point his name reverted to Derek. Boab became a garage mechanic (this is about as 'working class' as it is possible to be in a British soap) and, though he eventually became joint owner of an extremely precarious garage business with his brother, he remains the most overtly proletarian of the characters along with the other members of his immediate family. In March 2005 the following exchange took place between Derek and Boab when the former agreed to share a flat with him to help him get over the fact that his girlfriend Michelle had left him:

DEREK: Look at this place. If Bob Geldof saw it he'd start a charity. Even that Kim and Aggie wouldn't set a foot in here.

BOAB: Ach, it's no that bad. Ah tidied up the other day.

DEREK: Well, you didn't make a very good job of it, did you?

BOAB :   So it goat messy again.

DEREK: Aye, that's why we've got to keep on top ay it.

BOAB :   Look, when Ah come hame fae work Ah'm knackered.

DEREK: And I'm not?

BOAB :   Ah jist want [w+ant] tae chill oot!

DEREK: So do I, but I can't when the place is a tip.

BOAB: Aw right, aw right. If ye're goanae keep naggin oan like an auld wifie. Whit dae ye want [w+ant] me tae dae?

This conversation ends with Boab somewhat ruefully informing Derek: 'See that university, it's startin tae cheinge you'.

Though Derek continues to make a few concessions to Scots (concessions he does not normally make when speaking to other characters), it is clear that his language is now predominantly SSE, while the uneducated Boab continues to speak in Scots as before. It is also absolutely clear that the difference in language reflects a difference in authority between the two characters, with Derek adopting an almost schoolmarmish attitude in relation to Boab. Beyond that, Boab's family, in particular his mother Scarlet – like Rab C Nesbitt and Chic Cherry before them – are coded overwhelmingly in the mode of comedy, a mode frequently strengthened by their outlandish gesturing and posturing and (quite deliberately overacted) facial expressions.

In his discussion of linguistic exchanges between speakers from different classes, French sociologist Pierre Bourdieu argues that these cannot be understood in purely linguistic terms (1991: 67):

the linguistic relation of power is not completely determined by the prevailing linguistic forces alone: by virtue of the languages spoken, the speakers who use them and the groups defined by possession of the corresponding competence, the whole social structure is present in each interaction (and thereby in the discourse uttered).

The force of such an argument can easily be appreciated in exchanges such as that between Derek and Boab above, since not only is the entire weight of the educational establishment lined up behind Derek, so also are centuries of language division in Scotland which have produced a situation which Kay describes as follows:

> The status of Scots at the beginning of [the twentieth] century derived very much from trends established in the eighteenth century and hardened in the nineteenth century. The language came to be regarded as a working-class patois, despised by the increasingly anglicised upper and middle classes. (1986: 125)

CONCLUSION

Given the current proliferation not only of channels but also of platforms, it seems unlikely that the soap opera will continue in the twenty-first century to be quite the force it was in the twentieth. Nonetheless, its days are by no means numbered, and soaps continue to fill most, if not all, of the top ten places in UK viewing figures every week. But the fact remains that, when compared with that of its English counterparts, the story of the Scottish soap opera has not been one of unqualified success. The early productions were relatively short-lived (and in some cases apparently not deemed worthy of preservation), *High Road* was unable to survive in the longer term, and *River City*, though now fairly well established, has been unable to outperform its English rivals. How are we to explain the fact that the Scottish television viewing public still continues to prefer English productions to what we might call 'its own'? The answer, I would like to suggest, may well lie in Scotland's continuing schizophrenic relationship with its own languages whereby, far from being viewed as equals, SSE is seen as the language of the educated and the public sphere, and, as Kay argues, Scots is seen, even by many of its own speakers, as inferior and even as a sign of narrow horizons.

Given that Scots is – despite the well-known problems in arriving at reliable figures – almost certainly the normal mode of communication of a majority of the population of Lowlands, the dilemma facing broadcasters producing a realist genre such as soap operas is precisely 'what to do with it'. Three strategies have emerged at different times:

1. Ignore it (*Take the High Road* in its 'UK' phase).
2. Attach it to male members of the working class, simultaneously identifying them as 'stuck in the past' since the educated and the upwardly mobile quickly abandon it (*Garnock Way* and *High Road* in its 'Scottish' phase).

3. Attach it to both male and female members of the working and under-class, but within a framework of perhaps understated, but nonetheless perfectly visible comedic effect (*High Road* and *River City*)

As I have argued elsewhere (O'Donnell 1999), UK soaps are fundamentally about community: indeed they are a cultural space where the concept of community has lived on long after it has been dethroned from political practice (if not entirely from political rhetoric). The unresolved issue of 'equal rights' for Scots means that, for the time being at least, the circle of notions of community and requirements of realism simply cannot be squared, since realism requires the presence of Scots, yet the presence of Scots splits the community. Sociolinguist Peter Trudgill argues that discrimination against a child's dialect within the education system can only have negative consequences: 'To suggest to a child that his language, and that of those with whom he identifies, is inferior in some way is to imply that *he* is inferior' (1974: 74). If we change 'child' to 'viewer' in that observation, it surely continues to make sense. As productions such as *Rab C Nesbitt*, *Chewin' the Fat* and *Still Game* have shown, speakers of Scots are more than capable of laughing at themselves when they are clearly presented in the mode of fun. However, it is a very different matter to find oneself presented as an object of amusement or condescension in a format purporting in one way or another to be some kind of 'reflection of reality' (a very common claim made by producers of soaps everywhere).

There can be little doubt that the presence of Scots on television in Scotland has increased dramatically in recent years, but this cannot be seen in any straightforward sense as an unproblematic victory as regards the representation of that language. Its emergence has taken place within the discourses of language and class that continue to be dominant within educated circles in Scotland as a whole – circles from which, needless to say, both BBC Scotland and STV recruit many of their decision-makers. Of course individuals in both organisations continue to fight rearguard battles in favour of Scots (Paisley 2003), but the odds are massively stacked against them. The problem is not so much one of Scottish broadcasting as one of Scottish society, and until that problem is resolved, Scottish soap operas will probably continue to lag in popularity behind those produced south of the border.

ACKNOWLEDGEMENTS

This chapter draws partly on research funded by the Generalitat de Catalunya and the Anglo-Catalan Society and carried out in 2007 by Enric Castelló of the Universitat Rovira i Virgili, Tarragona, and myself. I would like to thank the following for giving of their time to speak to us: Jack Dickson (scriptwriter, *River City*), Mark Grindle (producer, *High Road*), Sandra McIver (executive producer, *River City*), Janet Paisley (scriptwriter, *High Road/River City*) and Marc Pye (scriptwriter, *High Road/River City*). Thanks also to STV Head of Library Services, John Rushton, for providing archive episodes of *Garnock Way* and *High Road*.

REFERENCES

Bourdieu, P. (1991), *Language and Symbolic Power*, London: Polity Press.

Chapman, M. (1978), *The Gaelic Vision in Scottish Culture*, London: Croom Helm.

Elder, M. (1990), *Ten Years of Take the High Road*, London: Boxtree.

Kay, B. (1986), *Scots: The Mither Tongue*, Edinburgh: Mainstream Publishing.

Kingsley, H. (1988), *Soap Box: The Papermac Guide to Soap Opera*, London: Papermac.

O'Donnell, H. (1999), *Good Times, Bad Times: Soap Operas and Society in Western Europe*, London: Leicester University Press.

Paisley, J. (2003), '*Whit wey fur no?* Scots and the Scripted Media: Theatre, Radio, TV, Film', in J. M. Kirk and D. P. Ó Baoill (eds), *Towards our Goals in Broadcasting, the Press, the Performing Arts and the Economy: Minority Languages in Northern Ireland, the Republic of Ireland, and Scotland*, Queen's University Belfast: Belfast Studies in Language, Culture and Politics, 10.

Trudgill, P. (1974), *Sociolinguistics: An Introduction to Language and Society*, London: Penguin Books.

9

Broadcast Comedy

IAN MOWATT

Despite being a very small country, Scotland has produced, in Harry Lauder and Billy Connolly, two of the best, internationally known comedians of the twentieth century. Both Lauder (1870–1950) and Connolly (1942–), made significant, if very different, contributions to comedy broadcasting in this country. It is, therefore, important to acknowledge that the discourses of Lauder and Connolly have played a crucial part in other people's perceptions of Scotland.

There were significant variations in the substance and narratives of Lauder and Connolly – when Lauder died in 1950 the swear word 'fuck' which is employed throughout Connolly's act was not acceptable on stage anywhere in the UK, let alone on the airwaves, and would not be for decades to come. Lauder was 'couthy' by comparison with Connolly and his popular jokes about Scottish stinginess played very much second fiddle to his songs, although he was not averse to stopping a song like *I love a Lassie* two-thirds of the way through to play a comic turn about losing an engagement ring (Attic Archives, *The Great Entertainers*, BBC: 1985). Connolly's superb monologues examining the ludicrous minutiae of everyday life or dissecting the small-ads columns in newspapers are far more important than his music. There is also a difference in the way their audiences received the two performers. Yet there are similarities in their careers. Like many entertainers, both had difficult, unhappy childhoods. Lauder's career coincided with the popularity of the gramophone and he was probably the first British artist to sell more than a million records (Jack 2006); half a century later Connolly's big break into the British media – when he told a joke about a murderer burying his dead wife face down so he could park his bicycle in her 'bum' on *Parkinson* (BBC 1975) – coincided with the introduction of the domestic video recorder. Both Lauder and Connolly far preferred broadcasting with live audiences as opposed to studio work. Both also emerged into the entertainment industry having first undertaken harsh manual jobs. Lauder was a coal miner for nearly ten years, Connolly a welder on the Upper Clyde. Both would invest a large part of their earnings in Highland estates, and, between flurries of engagements, enjoyed playing the part of the rural laird. But the main difference between the two – and indeed one of the great divides in twentieth-century Scottish comedy and Scottish broadcast entertainment as a whole – is that while Connolly occasionally wears a pair of tartan 'troos', Lauder was clad in tartan from head to toe, carried a crooked stick at all times when on stage, and is thus held by many cultural critics to be responsible for perpetrating worldwide the lasting image of a backward, inward-looking, Tartanry-besmirched image of the Scot which has lasted until the present day.

Lauder's main contribution to BBC Radio was in the early period, not in Scotland but in England. Hence we find him giving, on Boxing Day 1925, what is described by *The Scotsman* newspaper as 'a very successful broadcast from 2LO' (*The Scotsman*, 27 December 1925; 2LO was the BBC's first transmitter). On the following day, Lauder met a journalist at Euston and inquired 'with the keenest anxiety' how his broadcast had been received. In the following year, this time on Hogmanay, Lauder capitalised on his radio programme to send a message to his Granny Vallance (the mother of Lauder's wife who had died earlier that year), who was hard of hearing but who could make out Lauder's voice when she heard him on the radio if she was wearing headphones (*The Scotsman*, 1 January 1927). Almost a year later, on 9 November, *The Scotsman* reports – note, once again from London – a national broadcast:

> There was more hearty laughter at Savoy Hill yesterday than there had been for many months. Solemn-faced BBC officials rocked in No. One Studio when Sir Harry Lauder rehearsed his fifth and last broadcast performance which was given last night, before he leaves on a tour of New Zealand.

Thereafter, the radio performances decline. They return, occasionally, in the 1930s when Lauder was over sixty, and during World War Two he broadcast extensively on the home front; an audio copy of a very moving visit to a Clydebank shipyard, not long after the blitz, is still in the archives of BBC Scotland (BBC Scottish Archive, 25 December 1942).

Lauder spent thirty years travelling the English-speaking world with his act, covering Australia, New Zealand, the USA and Canada – the last two being visited twenty-two or twenty-three times (accounts vary). Whilst touring America and Canada, he travelled about in a personal train. Often he would put on three shows a day. In his study of music hall in Scotland, Paul Maloney asks himself why Lauder broke through to iconic status and world fame, and concludes:

> In cultural terms, whatever the views of his detractors, Lauder's stage persona undoubtedly resonated for the working expatriate Scots who came to see him. However much he consorted with millionaires . . . he retained a down-to-earth demeanour, and a classless, inclusive appeal that suited the New World. On a professional level, he was by all accounts a charismatic performer, one of the very few thought by his peers to embody something close to genius. (Maloney 2003: 176–7)

Billy Connolly was born in a room and kitchen in Anderston, Glasgow in 1942 (Stephenson 2001: 4–5). His mother abandoned him and his sister Florence when Billy was four and he was brought up by two aunts, one of whom, Mona, disliked him. His father also beat and molested him (Stephenson 2001: 62). After secondary school Connolly served a five-year apprenticeship as a welder. His break into comedy came about by accident: when he was performing with a group called the Humblebums, the group's manager, Nat Joseph, suggested that he concentrate on comedy rather than music.

The extent of Connolly's worldwide success is not dissimilar to Lauder's but has obviously been enhanced by air travel, proper archives, and the invention of the video and DVD recorders. There are only a few scraps of film remaining of Lauder's stage performances while almost every routine of Connolly has been recorded in sound or vision. He is best known in Britain for his four extremely popular 'World Tours' of Australia, New Zealand, and Scotland, and of England, Ireland, and Wales, all of which were screened on BBC1. In these series Connolly meets interesting personalities and offers witty commentaries on what he encounters. He has also been a frequent guest on the 'chat show' of his friend Michael Parkinson (eight appearances). In America, apart from doing big-venue stand-up comedy, he has recently been earning $1million per movie (Harlow 2003). He has also appeared on many chat shows, featured in the sitcom *Head of the Class*, and then in his own sitcom *Billy* (January–July 1992).

The main reason why Lauder and Connolly have been so successful, despite the major differences in their material, is that regardless of how vast the audience in front of them, they were obviously capable of making every single member of it feel that they were singing or talking just to them. Of the other major Scottish comedians of the twentieth century, Jimmy Logan and Rikki Fulton, though extremely successful in Scotland, were not much known outside of it. Stanley Baxter, on the other hand, was a popular national UK entertainer for many years on London Weekend Television and BBC1, although he was not known internationally.

BROADCAST COMEDY

Broadcast comedy nowadays throughout the UK falls into fairly distinct categories such as sketch shows, sitcoms, specials, and chat shows. The former two are intended to be funny throughout, while the latter two only partially so. As far as Scotland is concerned, broadcast comedy in general and sitcom in particular have never been in a stronger position than they are today. The protagonist in this scenario is Colin Gilbert. While Ewan Angus is currently responsible for commissioning comedy for BBC Scotland, it is Gilbert's independent production company, The Comedy Unit, which makes most of it. Gilbert came to Scotland in 1980, having spent two useful seasons working as a researcher on the hugely successful sketch programme *Not the Nine O'Clock News*. In the spring of 1981 Gilbert produced seven weekly radio programmes called *Naked Radio* for BBC Radio Scotland. The purpose of this series was to develop a team of writers and performers who could go on to make programmes for television that could eventually be good enough for the network. The first writer to emerge was Bob Black who subsequently wrote five series of the sitcom *City Lights*, all of which were later repeated UK-wide on BBC2. Although *City Lights* was neither original nor uproariously funny, it marked an important step forward in terms of the representation of Scottish people in comedy. The series was set in a bank where nobody wore a kilt, and in a city far from any Kailyard. Hitherto there had been few normal-looking people in Scottish comedy. Indeed, despite two moderately successful series of adaptations of Neil Munro's Vital Spark/Para Handy stories[1] (which were sketches originally meant to be read in the tram or train in the Glasgow *Evening News* in the early years of the twentieth century and were never really suitable for being extended into television programmes), the most outstanding series produced by any channel in Scotland had been the BBC's *Stanley Baxter Show* of the 1960s and early 1970s in which the comedian enjoyed excellent support from Una MacLean, not only in the famous 'Parliamo Glasgow' sketches, but in a range of other material. Later, more lavishly funded LWT programmes made by his last Scottish BBC producer, David Bell, would establish Baxter as one of the most versatile impressionists and entertainers of his generation. In Scotland, however, productions of comedy had been irregular and largely disappointing. To establish the cause of this, it is necessary to go back to the early days of the history of broadcasting and to examine the low premium placed on comedy in general and Scottish comedy in particular.

In *A Social History of British Broadcasting*, Scannell and Cardiff point out that throughout the BBC:

> There was, by the early thirties . . . as yet no coherent policy for broadcast entertainment. At the same time, entertainment on radio could not

rely either on simply getting artists into the studio to do their turns, or in relaying live shows from the halls. On the whole they did not work and they were not funny. Even when relays of stage shows were allowed they often made awkward broadcasting: loud applause might overpower the microphone and gales of laughter might engulf the point of the gag. (Scannell and Cardiff 1991: 229)

These problems extended to the entirety of BBC output including Scotland where, in 1948, the retiring Controller, Melville Dinwiddie, made the additional point:

Visits to many military stations and units revealed the fact that the universal need was for light music and amusing items. Items that would make men laugh were most sought after, especially if they were mixed with modern dance music. There just weren't enough comics to go round. The great personalities of the Variety world, Sir Harry Lauder, the late Will Fyffe and Harry Gordon did great work. The sad fact is that many Scots Comics do not suit radio, however well they may do on the Music Hall stage. (Dinwiddie 1948: 19)

EARLY COMEDY BROADCASTING IN SCOTLAND

An examination of the programme schedules for radio broadcasting in Scotland from the mid-1920s until the outbreak of hostilities in 1939 allows some characteristics of Scotland as a region to become clear. First, it is apparent that amateur local drama groups played an important part in the schedule on offer. As early as April 1925, the Glasgow station aired *Poached Eggs and Pearls*, a comedy in two scenes by Gertrude Jennings, presented by the Aberdeen Amateur Dramatic Company. Later that year an amateur group from Dundee were given their opportunity. These programmes tended to occupy slots in the middle part of the evening from forty minutes to an hour and a half in length. However, most of the comedies originated in London and were beamed to the whole of the UK, for example, the musical comedy *Dear Little Billie* was relayed throughout the UK from the Shaftesbury Theatre London (*The Scotsman* Archive). But despite the prominence of London, there continued to be regular musical and comedy productions from mainly amateur but also professional groups in Glasgow, Edinburgh, Dundee and Aberdeen. What there appears to have been a distinct shortage of nationally, and in Scotland, is the more down-to-earth traditional singers and comedians so popular in the variety theatre, who might have appealed to the less well-off and less educated sections of society. Gradually, as the 1920s became the 1930s, the BBC began to realise that unless it began to make some concessions to variety, sales of receivers might fall.

One good example of a proper broadcast variety show (as opposed to half an hour relayed from a theatre) comes from June 1930. Listeners throughout the UK were treated to a vaudeville programme from 7.45 until 9.00 pm featuring Jose Collins, a well known musical comedy artist. Collins was a frequent radio performer and starred two years later in a programme of seventy minutes duration when she was supported by G. H. Elliott, the Chocolate-Coloured Coon (sic), Nosmo King and Partner, the Black-Faced Comedians and, at the bottom of the bill, Will Fyffe, the Dundonian who, it can be argued, lied his way to success by singing *I Belong to Glasgow*. (Blackface acts were popular in the UK for about 150 years from around 1830 until the end of the Black and White Minstrel Show in 1978.) Apart from her radio performances, Collins appeared in five Broadway productions and eleven movies, so clearly radio could attract top-line performers.

THE MCFLANNELS

The first step towards genuine broadcast comedy in Scotland (as opposed to the broadcasting of variety acts) was a programme called *The McFlannels*. *The McFlannels* was described as a serial by the BBC. There are, however, strong elements of comedy embedded in the scripts by Helen W. Pryde. The programme ran on radio in Scotland for several years from 1939, and was transferred to television in 1958. All of the families in the series were named after a different fabric. In the main working-class family, Mr McFlannel is a foreman, Mrs McFlannel a housewife, their daughter Maisie a schoolteacher, and their son Peter seems to work with his father. The only remaining episode in existence, *Papering the Parlour* (BBC Scottish Archive, 14 October 1958), is one of the television series from 1958, recorded on a single camera with appropriate interludes (John Corbett's chapter in this volume discusses scripts published). This was recorded on film since videotape had not yet been invented. *The McFlannels* gave important breaks to three actors who would go on to play a very prominent role in broadcasting. Russell Hunter played Mr McFlannel, Molly Weir was Poison Ivy McTweed, and Rikki Fulton made his broadcasting debut as the Scottish church minister, the Revd. David McCrepe. Ian Christie (a former BBC Producer) believes that the reason *The McFlannels* did not work on television was that listeners had formulated their own ideas on what the different characters looked like and found the visual incarnations difficult to accept. Another variety programme broadcast on radio at about the same time as *The McFlannels*, *Number Seventeen Sauchie Street*, starring Andy Stewart and Margo Henderson and featuring Stanley Baxter and Jimmy Logan, was also popular during its four-year run.

THE COMING OF TELEVISION

In the first year of Scottish transmissions, 1952, the BBC broadcast through-out the UK from Glasgow's Metropole Theatre a television show starring the nationally known singer Gracie Fields, supported by three very experienced Scottish comedians, Dave Willis, Harry Gordon and Jack Radcliffe. Shortly afterwards *Highland Fling*, a variety show starring Chic Murray and his foil, Maidie, was broadcast from Rutherglen Repertory Theatre. Ian Christie also remembers working closely on several comedy series with the immensely popular comedian Lex McLean between 1955 and 1971, during which time McLean performed for six months a year at the Pavilion Theatre, doing two shows a night.

> With the arrival of commercial television in September 1955, broadcast-ing entered a new phase of development. BBC programme policy was now formulated in the absence of the monopoly, but the Corporation did have the advantage of control over both radio and television which was denied to its competitor. (McDowell 1992: 121)

Because of its powerful position in the Central Belt, Scottish Television (STV), serving both Edinburgh and Glasgow, was described by its owner, Roy Thomson, the Canadian press magnate, as 'a licence to print money' (McDowell 1992: 128). Although a rather tactless remark, this did indeed prove to be the case, but the main competition to the BBC came from ITV pro-grammes made outwith Scotland rather than from STV's own productions. Admittedly, there was some original programming including a lunchtime light-entertainment daily feature, *The One O'Clock Gang*. This was screened five days a week and lasted for ten years. It bolstered the careers of the comedian Larry Marshall, the multi-instrumentalist Jimmy Nairn, the support comic Charlie Sim, and a teenage singer and comedienne, Dorothy Paul, who would later go on to play a leading role in the television adaptation of Tony Roper's superb play about Glasgow in the 1950s, *The Steamie*. Although much of this programme was improvised and of variable quality, it was a success with many viewers.

The next piece of comedic programming should have ensured STV's future as a comedy broadcaster. It secured a contract for a series with Jack Milroy and Rikki Fulton for the first television version of *Francie and Josie*. The original idea, which was Fulton's, had been to create two Glasgow teddy boys who would bounce off each other on stage in the Glasgow Alhambra's *Five Past Eight* shows which the pair were headlining in 1960. The shows had been a huge success and the television series ran, on and off, for three years. The language of the duo, particularly 'Hullawrerr' instead of 'hello', and jokes about the 'Palais de

Dance' – 'Are you dancin?' – 'No it's just the way I'm staunin' – played by Fulton as the male and Milroy as the sought-after female, became immensely popular throughout Scotland. Fulton claimed in his autobiography that a mother only had to call that 'Francie and Josie were on the telly and in seconds the streets were cleared of children' (Fulton 1999: 277). At Milroy's funeral in 2001, Fulton admitted that their quickfire Glasgow patter was often made up on the spot – 'On stage I didn't know what Jack was going to do or say next, and he didn't know what I was up to' (Our Glasgow Story, www.ourglasgowstory.com).

Fulton would eventually spend almost the last twenty years of his career as the starring comedian in the BBC's *Scotch & Wry* television series which saw out Hogmanay just before the New Year programme. His Supercop sketches and those of a lugubrious Presbyterian minister in 'Last Call' stick in the minds of many viewers as classic Scottish humour.

STV's next comedic move was a highly unusual and exceptionally memorable one for rather unusual reasons. Between 1958 and 1968 BBC Scotland had networked a Highland song and dance show throughout the UK. The host was Andy Stewart who held the show together introducing the various acts – fiddlers, accordionists and many dances all performed by ladies wearing white dresses with tartan shawls and gentlemen in kilts. Stewart also sang, after a fashion, and enjoyed considerable success with a comic number, *Donald Where's Your Troosers*, and a mawkish ballad, *A Scottish Soldier*. The programme he starred in, *The White Heather Club*, was very popular, and its peak audience throughout the UK touched ten million viewers. Despite Stewart's perky personal style, the music, solo performers and dancers were all introduced in a respectful manner.

STV had previously been responsible for a similar production entitled *Jigtime* but now in the 1970s it offered *Thingummyjig*, an irreverent country music ceilidh presented with colossal enthusiasm by a businessman and part-time DJ called Jack McLaughlin. Describing himself as the 'Laird O' Coocaddens' (the district of Glasgow where the STV studio was), McLaughlin's typical intro would go as follows: 'Greetings fans in single ends and but and bens, grannies in crannies, streakers in Twechar – it's time to tickle your tartan tonsils'. He would then introduce the acts such as the skiffle group the Vindscreen Vipers, a pair of elderly sisters known as Fran and Anna wearing tights and mini–kilts and described by McLaughlin as the 'Gruesome Twosome'. Other more conventional acts like Jim Johnstone's dance band might follow. The highlight of the evening, however, was a song by Sidney Devine, a country and western singer from Ayrshire whose voice, in certain high notes, has been compared to the cry of a cat undergoing strangulation. Before the first series had ended, *Thingummyjig* had become compulsory viewing. There have been few worthwhile comedy programmes to come out of STV since that time. Apart from

Thingummyjig, there was a series by Una MacLean in 1967, which was partially networked but not shown in London. STV should have been able, on the back of its success with *Francie and Josie* and *Thingummyjig*, to build its comedy output but it failed to do so. Whether this was deliberate or not is unclear. What is not in doubt is that since soaps expanded to occupy four or five nights a week, the demand for comedy on the ITV network as a whole has declined. It is also possible, of course, that STV would claim that their money has been better invested in the hugely popular *Taggart* (1983–) or the potentially world best-selling television series of Ian Rankin's *Rebus* (2000–) novels. After all, *Taggart* has now been running for twenty-four years and a major share of its costs is recouped by STV from international sales. Only thirteen episodes of *Rebus* have been made to date but Ian Rankin is an author with a global audience and, despite his assertion that his current *Rebus* will be his last, there are still several novels to fall back on, not to mention possible narratives utilising the character, as happened with the *Morse* (1987–2000) series. In this respect, STV may have demonstrated wisdom rather than recklessness.

Because STV has abandoned comedy for most of the past thirty years, the major producer in Scotland has been The Comedy Unit and the major broadcaster the BBC. One respect, however in which the commercial channels in Scotland have made a distinctive contribution to comedy involves an Aberdonian trio known as *Scotland the What*. Comprising Stephen Robertson, Buff Hardie and George Donald, the trio first met at university in Aberdeen and have attracted sell-out audiences in that area and elsewhere in Scotland for over a quarter of a century. Their sketches and songs were performed in 'the doric', the dialect of the northeast of the country. Many of their performances at His Majesty's Theatre, Aberdeen were screened on Grampian Television and several have also been shown on STV. Their humour is very dry and sometimes hilarious while their witty songs are reminiscent of a barbershop quartet.

COLIN GILBERT AND THE COMEDY UNIT

Colin Gilbert worked for the BBC for twenty years before leaving to found The Comedy Unit in 1995 with his colleague April Chamberlain. His departure came during the John Birt era when producers in Scotland were experiencing substantial difficulties in finding executives to whom they could pitch their ideas. Before establishing The Comedy Unit, Gilbert had produced/directed five series of *City Lights* (1987–91) for BBC Scotland. These sitcoms starred Gerard Kelly as a not very bright young man with literary aspirations who worked in a bank. The programmes were shown firstly in Scotland, then repeated at different times south of the border. Kelly has subsequently gone on to become the lead performer in Glasgow pantomimes, following in the footsteps of Baxter, Fulton and Logan who all played principal dame regularly. The *City Lights* cast also included a number of other comic performers who, through it, received their first major breaks on television, such as Andy Gray, Elaine C. Smith and Jonathan Watson, who currently appears in his own sketch show, *Watson's Wind Up* on Radio Scotland on Saturday mornings. *City Lights* was good for Scotland, as previously argued, because it was a modern urban comedy with immediately recognisable 'types' in the cast. Bob Black, the writer, now scripts pantomimes and indeed *City Lights* eventually began to resemble a rather ramshackle pantomime as it progressed. However, it was the first comedy in Scotland with a contemporary setting since *The McFlannels* and there were several excellent minor characterisations.

RAB C NESBITT

The second series undertaken by Gilbert was *Rab C Nesbitt* (1988–99), which gave Gregor Fisher his first leading role as an unemployed alcoholic living with his family in the working-class Glasgow district of Govan. Initially the BBC's head of comedy in London disapproved of the way *Nesbitt* had been shot – on a single camera (widely regarded nowadays as the best way of recording a situation comedy as opposed to the traditional multi-camera studio set-up). One of Gilbert's constant irritants is what he regards as the ignorance of senior broadcasting staff. He recalls that he was once in a meeting along with Paul Jackson (producer of *The Young Ones* and *Three of a Kind*) and, after a while, he realised that the two of them were the only people in the room who had actually made a comedy programme.

Rab C Nesbitt, which ran for over a decade, has touched a number of raw nerves: some English viewers claim they cannot understand the language, while some Scottish viewers dislike the way it represents this country and its citizens. There is also an interesting sociolinguistic divide on which Colin McArthur has commented:

> In order to heighten the vernacularity (Scottish) of the central characters . . . the series operates non-naturalistically by having many of the authority figures, even the working-shopkeepers and licensees speak with (sometimes) rather posh, Received Pronunciation-based Scottish accents. (McArthur 1998: 110)

McArthur comments further:

> Such darkly accomplished writing and playing may seem odd in what is after all, a situation comedy, but one of the benefits of writer Ian Pattison, producer/director Colin Gilbert and the excellent ensemble cast having

worked together over several series, is that they are able to take chances. (ibid: 120)

Gilbert responds to this comment thus:

> Yes, that's probably fair enough. The thing about *Rab C Nesbitt* that was the secret of his success is that Ian Pattison writes really dark (material) and had written many sitcoms before that were devoid of hope, but what Gregor Fisher does with the script is make you realise that Rab is not defeated. Then Ian saw Gregor do it and realised he could write more for him. So he wasn't just a big buffoon and not about to slit his wrists.[2]

Rab C Nesbitt was a highly original, black comedy in which, despite the eponymous hero's miserable condition, he philosophises eternally about the nature of life in post-industrial, postmodern Glasgow. It has also been the most durable situation comedy ever produced in Scotland. When it is at its best, in several episodes – but especially episode six of series one, *Holiday* – it is as funny and beautifully constructed as any situation comedy anywhere in the world. But sitcoms are made to engender laughter and the grimness of *Rab C* can be an obstacle to that, though it is worth noting that series one sold 60,000 copies in its first week when issued on video. An extremely important revenue stream for The Comedy Unit – and other companies – is the sale of DVDs of their productions.

STILL GAME

One of the great current successes of The Comedy Unit is *Still Game* (2002–) written and performed by Ford Kiernan and Greg Hemphill. This situation comedy, which originally took the form of a stage show, and later formed the basis of a regular item in the performers' sketch show *Chewin' the Fat* (1999–2001), ultimately emerged as a sitcom in its own right in 2002. The title refers to the antics of two Glaswegian pensioners, Jack Jarvis and Victor McDade, who live in Craigland, a fictional district of the city. Six series have been broadcast on BBC1 Scotland to great acclaim but only since series four have the shows been screened south of the border, on BBC2.

A distinguishing feature of this sitcom, which now extends to thirty-five episodes, is that almost all of the central roles are played by actors approximately thirty years younger than their characters. This gives *Still Game* a surreal quality, almost as if it is prophesying the inevitability of senescence. The programme has also featured several well known guest stars. In this respect, it has more in common with American sitcom than the average UK sitcom. However, although *Still Game* is excellent, it breaks no new ground. It is very well written and acted and the scripts confer real dignity on the elderly pair. However, *Last of the Summer Wine* (1973–), *One Foot in the Grave* (1990–2000) and *Waiting for God* (1990–4) preceded it by several years in dealing humorously with the problems of old age. It does, however, introduce an Asian shopkeeper for the first time in a Scottish comedy, a development which is long overdue. Another offshoot of *Chewin' the Fat* which has not attracted the same degree of acclaim is *The Karen Dunbar Show* (2003).

SCOTS COMEDY VS ENGLISH COMEDY VS AMERICAN COMEDY

No programme made in Scotland can yet compare with the best English productions such as *Steptoe and Son* (all scripts sold to America),[3] *Porridge* (twenty-two scripts sold to America), *Till Death Us Do Part*, *Only Fools and Horses*, and *Hi De Hi*. All of these had original qualities. *Steptoe* replaced the father/daughter relationship with an abrasive father/son relationship; *Porridge* was the ultimate in character comedy; *TDUDP* was highly politicised; *Only Fools*, whose principal character, Del Boy, acquired almost folkloric qualities, is the only sitcom ever to have attracted half of the British population to watch its final episodes, while *Hi De Hi* focused on an entourage of failures trying to run a holiday camp. Class, and its power to unite and divide in English society, were explored in many of these series. In Scottish comedy, class is rarely engaged with explicitly since the protagonists are almost invariably working class. Occasionally in *City Lights* or *Rab C Nesbitt*, some middle-ranking official wearing a tie will speak rather affected Standard Scots English – usually to general derision. It is also the case that in England, however, there have been many comedy programmes like *Life with the Lyons* (1955–60), *The Good Life* (1975–8), *Terry and June* (1979–87), *To the Manor Born* (1979–81), *Keeping Up Appearances* (1990–5), and *The Vicar of Dibley* (1994–6) which are clearly set in exclusively middle-class surroundings; Scotland has no comparable series to date.

American comedy, in contrast to both Scottish and English comedy, is big business. A successful situation comedy – for example *Friends*, where the main actors were being paid $1 million per episode near the end of its ten-year run – will be sold overseas and syndicated in the USA for the foreseeable future and will make multi-millionaires of the stars, several of the writers (twelve writers, working in pairs, is normal for an American sitcom) and a number of the producing and directing staff. Guest stars are more common in US sitcom compared with Britain, and spin-offs are also popular. *The Mary Tyler Moore Show* (1970–7) had two spin-offs, *Rhoda* (1974–8) and *Phyllis* (1974–5). Although some critics regard situation comedy as frivolous, it can be argued that certain themes are better handled within a comic form than a more overtly serious one. The theme of war was sensitively explored in

MASH (1972–83), women's rights in the *Mary Tyler Moore Show* (1970–7), family life and its ups and downs in *The Simpsons* (1999–), the ludicrous nature of serial drama itself in the sitcom *Soap* (1987–91), or social catharsis in the Jewish humour of *The Jack Benny Programme* (1950–65), *The George Burns and Gracie Allen Show* (1950–8), *Seinfeld* (1989–98) and *Curb Your Enthusiasm* (2000–).

American situation comedy is also the opposite of Scottish when it comes to class. US productions are almost exclusively set in middle-class milieux. Stanley Aronowitz has argued that 'there are no longer direct representations of the interactions among workers on American television' (Beattie 1995: 1). Although at the beginnings of American television there were two series, *Amos' n Andy* (1951–3) and *The Honeymooners* (1955–6), with working-class settings, since 1990 there have been only two worthy of mention, *Roseanne* (1988–97) and *Grace Under Fire* (1993–8).

CONCLUSION

So, our great performers Lauder and Connolly apart, Scottish broadcast comedy plays very much third fiddle to England and the USA. This is partly to do with money and the relative smallness of the country, partly because the pool of actors and writers is bigger in England and enormous in America. Recently, though, the number of situation comedies in the American TV top twenty has dropped from an average of five over the past two decades to just two in the season 2006–7. This may be a one-off, as has happened before in 1985 but, as Caryn Mandabach, the respected producer of the *Cosby Show* and *Roseanne*, recently pointed out, an average cost of $2 million per pilot, compared with the relatively inexpensive nature of talent shows where the talent comes free, is making life increasingly uncomfortable for the mirth-makers (*The Guardian*, 4 June 2007). At least the set-up here in Scotland remains much better than it was twenty years ago.

The Comedy Unit was taken over in August 2006 by RDF Media, makers of popular television reality shows like *Wife Swap* (2003–) and *Ladette to Lady* (2005–), but Colin Gilbert sees this as an asset, since RDF has influence and representation in the south which have already provided useful contacts for the Scottish team. It is to be hoped that his optimism will be justified. However, in 2007 the BBC and ITV – commissions from which accounted for an important 21 per cent of RDF's £99 million revenue in 2006 – temporarily suspended new proposals from the company, pending the results of an inquiry into how misleading footage was included in a preview for a documentary about the Queen; the footage suggested that the monarch had stormed out of a photoshoot. At the time of writing therefore RDF's future looks a little uncertain.

ACKNOWLEDGEMENT

I would like to thank Kirsty Crawford, Colin Gilbert, Peter Mills and Ian Christie for their generous help in enabling me to write this chapter.

NOTES

1. A further nine fifty-minute series of the *Tales of Para Handy* starring Gregor Fisher and directed/produced by Colin Gilbert was shown on BBC1 (1994–5).
2. Personal interview with author.
3. American networks rarely buy complete programmes. Instead it is more normal to purchase the script and adapt it for American audiences.

REFERENCES

Bettie, J. (1995), 'Roseanne and the changing face of working class iconography', *Social Text*, 45.
Bland, B. (2007), 'Queen and BBC row haunts RDF', *Daily Telegraph*, 20 July.
Briggs, A. (1965), *A History of Broadcasting in the United Kingdom V: The Golden Age of Wireless*, New York: Oxford University Press.
Dinwiddie, M. (1948), *Twenty-five Years of Scottish Broadcasting*, Edinburgh: BBC.
Fulton, R. (1999), *Is It That Time Already?*, Edinburgh: Black and White Publications.
Harlow, J. (2003), 'Connolly joins the $1M a film club', *The Sunday Times*, 14 December.
Jack, I. (2006), 'From bad to good', *The Guardian*, 27 May.
Maloney, P. (2003), *Scotland and the Music Hall*, Manchester: Manchester University Press.
Mandabach, C. (2007), 'How America stopped laughing', *The Guardian*, 4 June.
McArthur, C. (1998), 'The exquisite corpse of Rab (elais) C (opernicus) Nesbitt', in M. Wayne (ed.), *Dissident Voices: The Politics of Television and Cultural Change*, London: Pluto Press.
McDowell, W. H. (1992), The *History of Broadcasting in Scotland 1923–1983*, Edinburgh: Edinburgh University Press.
Scannell, P. and D. Cardiff (1991), A *Social History of British Broadcasting (Vol 1, 1922–1939)*, Oxford: Blackwell.
Stephenson, P. (2001), *Billy*, London: HarperCollins.
Digital sources: *The Scotsman, Guardian Unlimited, Times Online*.
Archival material: BBC Scotland Archive.

10

Contemporary Scottish Cinema

SARAH NEELY

In an article in the Scottish cultural magazine, *The Drouth*, Mark Cousins provocatively bemoaned the lack of a vibrant film culture in Scotland. Putting Iran's cinematic achievements forward as a – perhaps surprising – example, Cousins identifies several reasons for Scotland's underdevelopment, most of which revolve around a lack of experimentation and a general absence of interest in exploring the capabilities of the film form. This he puts down to the dominance of an accomplished literary tradition and the consequent development of oral culture rather than a visual alternative. Blame is also laid on various training schemes and funding initiatives espousing the rigid frameworks of mainstream film-making practices without allowing much room for new forms and practices to emerge (Cousins 2006: 12–13).

That diagnosis seems hard to accept when considering the diversity of recent films made in and about Scotland. Contemporary offerings include films skilfully working within mainstream genres but also films that push the boundaries of dominant forms and representations. However, this sort of experimentation, or even what might be called an avant-garde approach, is not necessarily a new development in Scottish cinema. On the contrary, there is a history of an avant-garde in Scottish cinema that has often been overshadowed by critical accounts and debates concerned with more dominant modes of representation. This chapter aims to reassess the development of a Scottish Art Cinema (Petrie 2000) alongside a consideration of avant-garde film-making practices. In addition to discussing recent Scottish film offerings, stretching across a wide variety of genres – both art house and mainstream – the chapter will refer to the largely ignored work of the experimental film-maker, Margaret Tait, in order to illustrate some of the key tensions presented within Scottish film-making and the body of criticism surrounding it.

Historically, Scottish film criticism expressed an urgency for debunking the myths of Tartanry and Kailyard. In collections such as Colin McArthur's *Scotch Reels* (1982), or Eddie Dick's *From Limelight to Satellite* (1990), films with Scotland as their subject matter were scrutinised for these types of representations; the depiction of Scotland was seen as limited to narratives of fantasy, more often projected from outside the country rather than from within. These types of representation continue to provide a source of tension between what political bodies and governmental industries promote and what are considered in other spheres to be acceptable representations. The tension is not unique to Scotland: Ruth Barton has pointed to a similar double-bind in Ireland where certain representations of the past are promoted and denied simultaneously (Barton 2000).

The other often-cited myth, Clydesideism glorifies the strength of the working-class male. Throughout the history of Scottish literature and film criticism, heavily masculinised narratives, drawing from 'hard man' mythology, and overlooking the woman's perspective in favour of the working-class male's, have also been the focus of lively debate (Lea and Schoene 2003; Schoene 2000, 2004). John Hill's examination of British cinema in the 1990s, including Ken Loach's multiple filmic representations of Scotland, suggests similar points of contention, mainly that the films' meditation on the erosion of working-class culture and their nostalgic attempts to return to traditional representations, ignore other social groups (2000).

Scotch Reels was important for various reasons, not least of which was the serious attention it paid to the representation of Scotland on film. Nevertheless, it paved the way for a subsequent body of criticism that foregrounded debates around the specified discourses at the expense of other forms of representation. Some years later, John Caughie reflected on how the critical approaches in McArthur's book had been somewhat narrow in focus and ultimately restricted the accuracy of the writers' conclusions (Caughie 1990). In *Scotch Reels* discourses of Tartanry and Kailyard were labelled 'pathological', with only 'realistic' feature films being suggested as a 'progressive' route for future film-making (McArthur 1982: 2–3). The tracks thus laid down literally left little to the imagination; fantasies were eschewed in favour of representations strongly tied to the 'material' realities of Scotland. The over-emphasis on realist discourses as a positive route forward was further reinforced by the significant attention to documentary film-maker John Grierson, and the work of the Films of Scotland Committee.

Grierson's influence on Scottish cinema is profound. His mass communication background, his preference for pragmatic, collective, political approaches to film-making, and a general disregard for the artifice and invention of fictional narratives can be traced through to contemporary film-making practices. Although Grierson does not entirely escape without criticism in *Scotch Reels*, his influence is a key strand of debate throughout. The dominance of the debates around realism and the opposing fantasies of Tartanry and Kailyard resulted in the marginalisation of discussion of other film-making practices. Although a detailed account of the Workers' Film Society movement is provided (Allen 1982: 93–9), only brief consideration is given to the amateur film movement. More astonishingly, Bill Douglas is largely ignored. Glasgow School of Art graduates Helen Biggar and Norman McLaren are signposted, but mainly in terms of their politically motivated rather than artistic efforts (Allen 1982: 96; Hill 1982: 110). In the volume's timeline of Scottish film culture, the retrospective of McLaren's work at the Edinburgh film festival in 1971 is mentioned, but another retrospective organised in 1970 by Murray Grigor (one of the volume's contributors) on the Scottish independent filmmaker Margaret Tait is not.

ON THE PERIPHERY OF SCOTTISH CINEMA STUDIES: MARGARET TAIT

Throughout her lifetime, the Orcadian-born film-maker and poet Margaret Tait produced over thirty short films, including the feature *Blue Black Permanent* (1992). After studying at the Centro Sperimentale di Cinematografia in Rome in the 1950s, Tait established Ancona Films with fellow student and film-maker Peter Hollander. Her films were largely self-financed, and distribution and exhibition were largely confined to the festival circuit and various touring exhibitions; eventually many of her films would be distributed by the London Film-makers Co-op and the British Film Institute.

By the time *Scotch Reels* was published, Tait had been making experimental films for thirty years and was also exhibiting on the international circuit. Yet the oversight is hardly surprising when considered within the context previously discussed. It is also worth noting that Tait expressed her own frustration with the Films of Scotland Committee and its narrow remit to fund only certain kinds of film-making.

The lack of critical attention given to Tait in this instance could be explained as a reluctance to engage with non-narrative films which are not classified as documentary and a general failure to ascertain the significance of what might be considered part of the amateur film-making movement. Lack of interest in Tait's work could also be read as part of a more general and problematic history of the critical reception of women avant-garde artists, a reality that has prompted a number of feminist initiatives to recover a somewhat fragmented film history. The material most at risk of being lost is often driven by personal, intimate narratives that deal with issues perceived as having lesser value than those deemed to be of cultural, 'collective' importance (Rabinovitz 2006). As with Tait, these film-makers risked being overlooked because of the failure of their work to be identified within existing genres or film-making practices. Robin Blaetz has criticised the narrow-vision of previous film scholars for:

> not realizing that the play with focus, the haphazard framing, the disjunctive editing, and the often abbreviated length found in the films of Gunvor Nelson, Chick Strand, and others working in the 1960s and beyond were not signs of incompetence but marks of a different vision. (Blaetz 2006: 154)

Like the other avant-garde filmmakers mentioned, Tait's work focused on the particular and the personal. Like other non-narrative films that explore the materiality of the medium, their primary focus is not to attempt to address issues of national identity. Mitch Miller explains the critical oversight of Tait's work in the following way:

> Filmmaking on 'big subjects', big landscapes that excited political and social engagement and educated the masses drove this small northern adjunct of the British film industry. Tait's examination of the minute and domestic, had it been noticed at all, would have seemed indulgent in such a setting. (Miller 2005: 63)

Tait's oversight can be seen as part of a general issue around the invisibility of avant-garde film-makers within studies of Scottish cinema where artists are relegated to an international framework lying outside the radar of the national, and are often marginalised because of their inability to contribute to the debates around national identity (Morgan 2003).

Unfortunately, very little has changed since Tait's encounter with the Scottish Film Council in the 1950s, when it refused to support her work financially. If Tait had been unable to fund her own production activity, it is unlikely that any of her films would have been made. Film-maker Peter Todd, curator of the LUX touring exhibition of Tait's work, blames the lack of support from UK funding bodies for limiting the work of independent and experimental film-makers (Todd 2000: 25). A similar marginalisation of experimental film exists in Ireland (Connolly 2003). Given the strong literary heritage in both Scotland and Ireland, Cousins' argument about the burden of that heritage on the development of an innovative cinema culture is relevant here. The strong links between literary, cultural and film criticism could well explain an unsympathetic view to non-narrative approaches. Ruth Barton blames the literary origins of Irish cinema studies for the lack of attention given to the visual. Speaking of this narrowness (or lack) of vision Barton asks: 'Had

Irish film studies become obsessed with the relationship between the state, the nation and cultural representations thereof?' (Barton 2004: 2). Like the funding bodies that fail to see beyond what is widely deemed as commercially salient, criticism has also suffered from the blind-spot formed by the dominance of debates around representation.

OPENING UP THE DEBATE: GENRE-BENDING AND NEW
REPRESENTATIONS IN RECENT SCOTTISH FILMS (2000–)

While the critics might be obsessed with the exhaustion of this network of causal relationships, Scottish film-makers get on with the business of making films that challenge the relevance of debates around representation or, on occasion, side-step them altogether. The recent rise in films which playfully rework a variety of genres is striking.

The examples are numerous. Richard Jobson transposed the martial arts genre onto contemporary Edinburgh in his film *The Purifiers* (2003). The horror genre has also proved popular. In 2002, *Dog Soldiers* (Neil Marshall) used Scotland as a backdrop for its story about a British squad on a training exercise that goes haywire when they come under attack by werewolves. At the time of writing, Marshall is also set to release another thriller, *Doomsday*, a futuristic depiction of the aftermath of a deadly outbreak of the plague, filmed around Blackness Castle near Linlithgow. David McKenzie mixed the horror genre with the road movie in *The Last Great Wilderness* (2002). His latest film *Hallam Foe* (2007), produced by Sigma Films, is billed as a thriller narrative tracking the activities of a young peeping tom in Edinburgh. The multi award-winning *Red Road* (Andrea Arnold, 2006), also developed by Sigma Films as part of their Advance Party project with Zentrope, has been marketed as a thriller for its suspenseful narration, which plays with notions of voyeurism through the point-of-view of its central character who works as a CCTV operator.

Comedy has also proven to be a successful platform for playing with genre. As in the films of Bill Forsyth, humour provides a way to explore myth and stereotypes that distances itself from the 'serious' debates of representation. Annie Griffin's 2005 mockumentary, *Festival*, which takes the fictional camera behind the scenes of the Edinburgh Fringe, astutely employs comedic form as a way to explore a number of cultural and national stereotypes. *American Cousins* (Don Coutts, 2003) playfully engages with stereotype and issues of representation through its story of the reunion of two diasporic Italian communities (Scottish and American) cast through the generic lenses of the romantic comedy and thriller. Although critically it provides a rich text worthy of further analysis, it suffered from distribution problems. Ultimately, its inventive approach to genre made it a challenging film to market.

Despite the discouragement of critics, a host of films continue to engage with the more distant Scottish past, and the heritage genre remains a commercially successful one in both local and overseas markets (Neely 2005). Narratives of damaged masculinity, often within an urban setting, also continue to substantially define the Scottish cinematic landscape. These include films such as *Orphans* (Peter Mullan, 1998), *16 Years of Alcohol* (Richard Jobson, 2003), *On a Clear Day* (Gaby Dellal, 2004), *Sweet Sixteen* (Ken Loach, 2002) and *My Name is Joe* (Ken Loach, 1998), but there has also been a noticeable rise in films which engage with multicultural representations of Scotland. In addition to the aforementioned film exploring the Italian diasporic community, *Ae Fond Kiss* (2004) is Loach's insightful take on love across the cultural divide, where the star-crossed lovers are an Irish-Catholic school teacher and a Scottish Pakistani man. Another film, *Nina's Heavenly Delights* (Pratibha Parmar, 2006), set in an Indian restaurant in Glasgow, tells the story of a Scottish Asian woman who returns home from London after the death of her father and then falls in love with a woman working in the family shop. And finally, *Gas Attack* (Kenny Glenaan, 2001), borrowing from real-life issues, uncovers the acts of violence carried out against Kurdish refugees on a Glasgow estate.

Other film-makers have looked outside Scotland to consider Britain and Scotland's role in the wider, global community. *The Last King of Scotland* (Kevin Macdonald, 2006) offers a studied portrait of the Ugandan dictator Idi Amin told through the eyes of Nicholas Garrigan, a fictitious young Scottish doctor who becomes one of Amin's personal advisers. Along similar lines, but perhaps less successfully, Michael-Caton Jones's *Shooting Dogs* (2005) revisits the 1994 Rwandan genocide through the viewpoint of two British workers, a Catholic priest and a young school teacher who are marked by the same optimism as the Scottish doctor in Macdonald's film. Unfortunately, the narrative-structuring device results in the marginalisation of Rwandan points-of-view. Perhaps most interesting, in terms of its reframing of the representation of damaged masculinity through its relationship to wider global issues, is Scott Hudson's *True North* (2006). The story follows the fate of a small fishing boat run by a father and son and facing hard economic times. Unbeknown to the father, a crew member, Riley, played along the familiar lines of the hard-man stereotype by Peter Mullan, hatches a money-making scheme to stow away Chinese immigrants – a decision which ultimately endangers both the future of the boat and the lives of those on board. In one poignant scene, issues of culpability come to the fore, when Riley, faced with the consequences of his actions, refuses to handle the dead body of one of the stowaways, leaving the skipper's son to deal with his mistakes.

Other critics have praised Peter Mullan's *Orphans* (1997) for its skilful subversion of social realist narratives and potential to serve as a metaphor for post-devolutionary Scotland. David Martin-Jones argues that *Orphans'* deployment of a variety of European Art cinema styles – social realism, magical realism, expressionism, and surrealism – works to destabilise the documentary-realist tradition, ultimately characterising it as 'a somewhat arbitrary way of defining Scottish national identity' (2004: 240). Although these types of readings are in danger of overplaying the assumed links between criticism, culture, politics and film that Barton questions in relation to Irish cinema studies, there is no doubting the significance of Scottish film-makers' look to other cultures in order to counter the somewhat dominating influence of British social realism. As Alan Riach has argued, the referencing of other cultures has long served as a strategy to bypass England (1996: 84). More positively, this might be read as actual cosmopolitanism. However, as Martin McLoone has remarked in relation to Irish identity, it has often defined itself against its 'other' (England). He explains: 'Whatever its positive attributes, crucially Irish identity was not British' (McLoone 2000: 12).

In addition to its referencing of European film-makers, Scottish cinema has also drawn from American traditions. Citing *Shallow Grave* (Danny Boyle, 1994) and *Rob Roy* (Michael Caton-Jones, 1995) as examples, Jonathan Murray has argued how in 'both institutional and representational senses, 1990s Scotland can be asserted to have spawned a "devolved" *American* cinema as much as it did a "British" one' (Murray 2005: 218). On the other hand, the appropriation of alternate cinematic traditions can also signal the type of subversion that Martin-Jones refers to in his analysis of *Orphans*. His argument, drawing from Deleuze and Guattari's work on minor literature and its later application to cinema by Deleuze, is that the film 'makes a minor use of a major voice, ensuring that it exists as both a work of devolved British cinema *and* of new Scottish cinema' (2005: 240). Similar claims have been made for other Scottish films such as *Dreaming* (Mike Alexander, 1990) and *Trainspotting* (Danny Boyle, 1996) and also Irish films like *The Butcher Boy* (Neil Jordan, 1997) and *When Brendan Met Trudy* (Keiron Walsh, 2000). In particular, their inventive employment of the voiceover in relation to conventions of classical Hollywood cinema or European art cinema resonates with Deleuze and Guattari's work (Neely 2004).

What this brief overview of recent film productions emanating from Scotland reveals, especially when considered alongside the growth in co-productions – Denmark for *Breaking the Waves* (Lars von Trier, 1996) and *Wilbur Wants to Kill Himself* (Lone Scherfig, 2002) and Ireland for *The Magdalene Sisters* (Mullan, 2002), *Blind Flight* (John Furse, 2003) and *True North* (2006) – is that Scottish cinema is increasingly less bound to issues of representation; there is an opening-up of discourse and a freedom of movement across both genre and subject.

Continuing with the 'orphans' theme, Alan Riach, referring to recent trends in Scottish literature, cites the growing 'self confident use of cultural models' as evidence that 'late twentieth century Scotland flourishes, culturally distinct, but [. . .] also an absent political entity in search of its own statehood, an heroic ideal, orphaned from itself and travelling in a world without closure' (1996: 79–80). Scotland's current unresolved issues around sovereignty are in fact more and more characteristic of the contemporary world.

Likewise, Riach's comments also ring true in relation to the rise in film narratives engaging with displaced identity. Several critics have identified films like *My Way Home* (Bill Douglas, 1978), *Carla's Song* (Ken Loach, 1996), *Morvern Callar* and *Dear Frankie* (Shona Aurbach, 2004) for their concern with the diasporic and migratory experience (Petrie 2000). In many instances, recent Scottish cinema provides fruitful terrain for both the metaphor of the orphan and that of the drifter, but it is also important to note the surge in narratives that are highly personal and individual representations of identity rather than aimed towards the collective.

PERSONAL FILM-MAKING AND A SCOTTISH ART CINEMA

In *Screening Scotland*, Duncan Petrie describes the formation of a Scottish art cinema, citing film-makers like Bill Forsyth, Bill Douglas, Ian Sellar, Margaret Tait and Timothy Neat as key figures. As Petrie explains, notions of art cinema have traditionally been described as emerging in response to the dominance of Hollywood (2000: 148; Higson 1995). In this regard, art cinema mobilises the nationally specific, and often that which is associated with 'high culture'. The strategy assumes that even if a film is not commercially successful within the mainstream, it will be of great cultural importance in its ability to speak to a global audience through its participation in the festival circuit and an international, art-house market. Again, this framework brings us back, full-circle, precariously leaning towards a privileging of national representations and cultural specificity. But as Petrie notes, art cinema in Scotland has evidenced itself in self-reflexive, personal narratives (2000: 151). Although subjective narration is a common feature of art cinema, the recent rise in such styled narratives may not serve as a method of differentiation from dominant Hollywood practices. Instead, it perhaps signals a shift away from the turgid roots of its realist past and a reinvigoration of the cinematic traditions marked by film-makers like Douglas, McLaren or Tait, and other films which reached the universal through the personal – the kind of avant-garde more closely akin to Wollen's 'personal' avant-garde which he linked to the co-op movements (1996).

Margaret Tait was Scotland's first woman feature-film-maker with *Blue Black Permanent* (1992), a film about an artist's coming to terms with the long-ago suicide of her poetess mother. Although a conventional feature funded by the BFI, the film explores issues of the personal in the meditative style characteristic of her experimental shorts. I would argue that other more recent film offerings, particularly those from women film-makers, offer a similar departure from previous styles but also reflect on similar themes around displacement and mourning, usually the absence of a family member, typically the mother. One obvious example is Lynne Ramsay, whose poetic films *Morvern Callar* (2002) and *Ratcatcher* (1999) have been compared in their use of highly charged images to the work of Bill Douglas. But we could also add films like *Dear Frankie* (2004), a moving portrait of a young mother who continually uproots and moves to a new town in order to distance her son from an absent father. The young boy's yearning for his absent father who he believes to be at sea recalls earlier films like Ian Sellar's *Venus Peter* (1989). *Dear Frankie* was written by Andrea Gibb who scripted *Nina's Heavenly Delights*, and *AfterLife* (Peebles, 2003) and has also adapted Louise Welsh's novel *The Cutting Room* which has yet to be produced. Similarly, we might include Arnold's *Red Road* whose psychological exploration of its central character, who faces trauma following the death of her sister, handles complex issues around violence and sexuality with a considerable amount of depth.

Ian Goode has discussed the break from British realism and the challenge to the masculine narratives of Scottish cinema provided by films such as *Stella Does Tricks* (Cokey Giedroyc, 1996) and *Blue Black Permanent* (2005: 239). Goode describes the films as coming-of-age narratives akin to the body of work Phil Powrie categorises as 'rite of passage films', a genre in which Powrie includes films like *Distant Voices, Still Lives* (Terence Davies, 1988) or *Small Faces* (Gillies MacKinnon, 1995). Organised around character subjectivity, these films often result in elliptical, fragmented narratives rather than following a more traditional, linear approach (Powrie 2000: 317). The foregrounding of the central character's inner experience also provides a point of departure for reflections on the past (Goode 2005: 236). Although Petrie has argued that *Blue Black Permanent* lacks the intimacy and observational acumen of Tait's shorter films (2000: 165), a wealth of moments exist where the privileging of character subjectivity breaks with the narrative progression in order to explore the minutiae of detail in a self-reflexive manner. Goode explains:

> Tait's tendency to cut away from the speaker to the artefacts and materials of expression, such as the trace of watered-down paint splashed above a sink, the paintings mounted on a wall, or the books and objects that line a shelf, further underlines her concern with expressive form and its materiality. (2005: 237)

Lynne Ramsay's film *Morvern Callar*, adapted from Alan Warner's novel of the same name and hailed as the 'female *Trainspotting*', provides an interesting point of comparison. It was co-written with Liana Dognini, an Italian film-maker whose collaboration with Ramsay began when they were students at the National Film and Television School. Warner's focus on feelings of displacement and alienation experienced by the central character was emphasised through their choice of casting an English actress. The novel developed its strong characterisation through first-person narrative written in Oban dialect, but unlike *Trainspotting* – which began life as a text constructed as a series of vignettes narrated in the first person by several protagonists, and evolved into the strong, unified narration of the central character, Renton – Ramsay's film forgoes the employment of voiceover and instead largely withholds Morvern's voice. Comparisons can be made between Samantha Morton's laconic performance as Morvern and the character James in Ramsay's first feature *Ratcatcher* (1999).

It might be tempting to read the silencing of Morvern's first-person narration from the original text as undermining her authority within the film. Considering that the voiceover is usually a privilege reserved solely for male characters in narrative cinema (Silverman 1988: 164), the failure to utilise Morvern's strong and vivid narration may seem like a missed opportunity. It may further be charged with diluting the cultural specificity that, in the light of *Trainspotting*, Alan Warner's novel promises to deliver.

Although Morvern's highly developed first-person narration would prove ripe terrain for translation into voiceover, its use, like Renton's narration in *Trainspotting*, would suggest a compliance with established structures of power in classical narrative cinema. Instead, Morvern's silence further articulates a central theme of exile, both personal and cultural. The difference in modes of adaptation, suggests a break in the film's engagement with issues of national identity. T. G. Murray, connecting Ramsay's approach to other film-makers, notes how:

> by with-holding women's voices, physically and symbolically, these film-makers free their true subjects – the cultural, rather than national subaltern – from the overwritten discourses of both politics and economics, making their experience unique to them, and unknown to us – the international audiences who might otherwise attempt to make them up. (2006: 279)

Rather than control the narrative through language, the emotive musical soundtrack – although ultimately dictated by the selection provided by 'His' (her boyfriend's) usurped record collection – allows Morvern to direct the narrative. Again, identity here is more concerned with the personal rather than any larger consideration of cultural identity. A similar argument could be made of Kate Dickie's wonderfully restrained performance as the CCTV operator in *Red Road* and the tension created through the character's point-of-view guiding the narrative.

Shohat and Stam's formulation of a 'poetics of embodiment' provides a useful frame of analysis for these types of narratives of displacement featuring in recent Scottish cinema. Briefly characterised as a general resistance to 'macro-narratives' in favour of stories reflecting a 'diversity of experiences within and across nations', the narratives can also be marked by themes of dislocation within 'a "multinationalized" global economy' (1994: 318).

The alienated relationship between the morbid reality of Morvern's personal life and the sterile environment of the supermarket she works in and the utopian fantasy provided by the mass-produced suburban housing in *Ratcatcher*, are evidence of similar themes of dislocated identity which Shohat and Stam describe. However, in *Trainspotting* the narrative of Renton – hardly an orphan – revolves around his inability to break the strong bonds with his close-knit group of friends. Even when he relocates to London in an attempt to start over, it takes little time for his past to catch up with him in the shape of Begbie. The narrative ends with him heading to Amsterdam with the money, but the film's cyclical return to the structures laid out in the opening sequence suggest the impossibility of a clean break; furthermore, as we learn in Welsh's follow-up novel, *Porno*, Renton eventually returns. *Trainspotting* explores the place of the disaffected within global-capitalist culture, but, conforming to narrative principles of unity, the closing sequence and the cyclical return to the theme of the film's opening voiceover implicate Renton in the lifestyle he originally rejects.

The differences in narration and structure perhaps signal a divergence in the films' infuences: *Trainspotting* can more easily be traced to American independent cinema, whereas *Morvern Callar* draws more clearly from a European art cinema tradition. Additionally, *Morvern Callar* could be seen as part of a recent trend in Scottish cinema, where issues of national identity are dealt with more tentatively. Issues of migration come to the fore, identity is not fixed but fluid, and breaks with narrative convention serve to mirror the fragmentation of experience.

To varying degrees, films like *Blue Black Permanent*, *Stella Does Tricks*, *Ratcatcher*, and also *Young Adam* (David Mackenzie, 2003) could be read in this way. *Young Adam*, an adaptation of a novel with a distinct first-person narrative, like *Morvern Callar*, avoids voiceover in another skilful depiction of estranged identity, the Forth and Clyde canal providing a shifting backdrop for a transient group of drifters. Performing well on the festival circuit, the film's dark subject matter and elusive central character played by Ewan McGregor sit comfortably within established definitions of art cinema, but the film's billing as a noir-thriller pulls it in other directions. *Red Road* serves as another prime example of the complexities continually offered by contemporary film-makers. As with Bill Forsyth's films, which have enjoyed popularity within both art-house and mainstream markets, *Red Road* successfully balances the popular thriller genre alongside an art-house aesthetic.

In this respect, it is better to avoid too neat a categorisation. Although it is appealing to attempt to define a 'New Scottish Cinema', what the project of *Scotch Reels* showed us is the limitations and dangers in this type of analysis. What criticism should ultimately accept is that the films produced are too complex and contradictory to allow for a clear definition of Scottish cinema to be easily carved out (Blain forthcoming).

A comparable situation exists in studies of Scottish literature which fail to address the discontinuities of new work resisting traditional frameworks of analysis. Concerned with similar themes of 'exile or estrangement', Eleanor Bell argues:

> while there has been an impulse within Scottish literature to experiment with these new possibilities of identity, in criticism there has been a repeated recourse to more traditional formulations of identity, an anxiety about potentially losing hold of the bedrock of tradition. (Bell 2004: 138)

Similarly, the opening-up of modes of discourse within Scottish film-making should also be reflected in its film criticism. The fact that many of the recent offerings of Scottish cinema resist easy classification is most certainly an indication of their responsiveness and inventive approach to contemporary issues.

The accessibility of technology provides further hope for the diversification of film-making practices. Films like May Miles Thomas's acclaimed digital feature *One Life Stand* (2000), made on an estimated budget of £60,000 (Petrie 2000: 165), suggest an opening-up of possibilities for new film-makers, allowing for more intimate modes of storytelling. The film, shot in monochrome and following the story of a mother, played by Maureen Carr, who unwittingly encourages her son into the escort business, is testament to what a good production team, skilful cast and powerful script can achieve.

To return to Mark Cousins' argument cited at the start of this chapter, a strong literary tradition does not spell the ruin for a vibrant cinema. Some of the most successful cinemas stem from cultures with rich artistic, musical and literary traditions. An ideal environment would allow for the forms to intersect, overlap and inspire one another. One should not have to cancel the other out. A bad adaptation is one that limits itself entirely to the merits of the text it is drawing on without adding anything of its own. A vibrant cinema is marked by a diversity of influences, the collaboration with and borrowing from other film cultures, and the embrace of a variety of film-making practices, both mainstream and experimental. The potential of smaller-budget or 'no-budget' film-making offers the hope of increasing flexibility and the opportunity for film-makers to choose their own path.

REFERENCES

Allen, D. (1982), 'Workers' Films: Scotland's hidden film culture' in McArthur, C. (ed.), *Scotch Reels: Scotland in Cinema and Television*, London: British Film Institute, pp. 93–9.

Barton, R. (2000), 'The Ballykissangelization of Ireland', *Historical Journal of Film, Radio and Television*, vol. 20, no. 3, pp. 413–25.

Barton, R. (2004), 'Introduction', in R. Barton and O H.'Brien (eds), *Keeping It Real: Irish Film and Television*, London and New York: Wallflower, pp. 1–5.

Bell, E. (2004), *Questioning Scotland: Literature, Nationalism, Postmodernism*, London: Palgrave.

Blaetz, R. (2006), 'Rescuing the fragmentary evidence of women's experimental film', *Camera Obscura* 63, vol. 21, no. 3, pp. 153–6.

Blain, N. (forthcoming), 'The visibility of small countries: the Scottish dimension in film and television', in C. Harvie and K.Veitch (eds), *Scottish Life and Society: A Compendium of Scottish Ethnology*, vol. 8: *Transport, Communications and the Media*, Edinburgh: John Donald.

Caughie, J. (1990), 'Representing Scotland: new questions for Scottish cinema', in Dick, E. (ed.), *From Limelight to Satellite: A Scottish Film Book*, London and Glasgow: British Film Institute and Scottish Film Council, pp. 13–30.

Connolly, M. (2003), 'Excluded by the nature of things? Irish cinema and artist's film', *Circa Art Magazine* (c106) Winter, pp. 33–9.

Cousins, M. (2006), ' ". . . and now, it's over?" The problem with Scottish cinema', *The Drouth*, no. 20, pp. 11–14.

Deleuze, G. and F. Guattari (1986), *Kafka: Towards a Minor Literature*, Minneapolis: Minnesota University Press.

Deleuze, G. (1985), *Cinema 2*, London: Athlone.

Dick, E. (ed.) (1990), *From Limelight to Satellite: A Scottish Film Book*, London and Glasgow: British Film Institute and Scottish Film Council.

Goode, I. (2005), 'Scottish cinema and Scottish imaginings: *Blue Black Permanent* and *Stella Does Tricks*' in *Screen* 46: 2, pp. 235–9.

Higson, A. (1995), *Waving the Flag: Constructing a National Cinema in Britain*, Oxford: Clarendon Press.

Hill, J. (1982), 'Scotland doesna mean much tae Glesca': Some notes on *The Gorbals Story*', in C. McArthur (ed.), *Scotch Reels: Scotland in Cinema and Television*, London: BFI, pp. 100–11.

Hill, J. (2000), 'Failure and Utopianism: representations of the working class in British Cinema of the 1990s', in R. Murphy (ed.), *British Cinema of the 90s*, London: British Film Institute, pp. 178–87.

Lea, D. and Schoene, B. (eds) (2003), *Posting the Male: Masculinities in Post-War and Contemporary British Literature*, Amsterdam and New York: Rodopi.

Martin-Jones, D. (2004), 'Orphans, a work of minor cinema from post-devolutionary Scotland', in C. Geraghty and A. Gray (eds), *Journal of British Cinema and Television*, vol. 1, no. 2, pp. 226–41.

McArthur, C. (ed.) (1982), *Scotch Reels: Scotland in Cinema and Television*, London: British Film Institute.

McLoone, M. (2000), *Irish Film: The Emergence of a Contemporary Cinema*, London: British Film Institute.

Miller, M. (2005), 'Re: Margaret Tait', *The Drouth*, no. 15, pp. 57–67.

Morgan, D. (2003), 'Life on the margins: the Scottish avant-garde film', *Filmwaves*, no. 19.

Murray, J. (2001), 'Contemporary Scottish film', *Irish Review* 28, pp. 75–88.

Murray, J. (2005), 'Kids in America? Narratives of transatlantic influence in 1990s Scottish cinema', *Screen* 46: 2, pp. 217–25.

Murray, T. G. (2006), 'Small voices in the big picture', in T. Hubbard, and R. D. S. Jack (eds), *Scotland in Europe: Scottish Cultural Review of Language and Literature*, vol. 7, Amsterdam and New York, Rodopi, pp. 265–80.

Neely, S. (2004), 'Cultural ventriloquism: the voice-over in film adaptations of contemporary Irish and Scottish literature', in J. Hill and K. Rockett (eds), *Studies in Irish Film 1: National Cinemas and Beyond*, Dublin: Four Courts, pp. 125–34.

Neely, S. (2005), 'Scotland, heritage and devolving British cinema', *Screen*, vol. 46, no. 2, pp. 241–5.

Petrie, D. (2000), *Screening Scotland*, London: British Film Institute.

Powrie, P. (2000), 'On the threshold between past and present: "Alternative heritage"', in J. Ashby and A. Higson (eds), *British Cinema, Past and Present*, London and New York: Routledge, pp. 316–26.

Rabinovitz, L. (2006), 'The future of feminism and film history', *Camera Obscura* 61, vol. 21, no. 1, pp. 39–44.

Riach, A. (1996), 'Nobody's children: orphans and their ancestors in popular Scottish fiction after 1945', in S. Hagemann (ed.), *Studies in Scottish Fiction: 1945 to the Present*, Frankfurt am Main: Peter Lang, pp. 51–84.

Schoene, B. (2000), *Writing Men: Literary Masculinities from Frankenstein to the New Man*, Edinburgh: Edinburgh University Press.

Schoene, B. (2004), 'Nervous men, mobile nation: masculinity and psychopathology in Irvine Welsh's Filth and Glue', in E. Bell and G. Miller (eds), *Scotland in Theory: Reflections on Culture and Literature*, Amsterdam: Rodopi, pp. 121–45.

Shohat, E. and R. Stam (1994), *Unthinking Eurocentrism: Multiculturalism and the Media*, London and New York: Routledge.

Silverman, K. (1988), *The Acoustic Mirror*, Bloomington and Indianapolis: Indiana University Press.

Todd, P. (2000), 'The British film industry in the 1990s', in R. Murphy (ed.), *British Cinema of the 90s*, London: British Film Institute, pp. 17–26.

Warner, A. (1995), *Morvern Callar*, London: Cape.

Welsh, I. (2002) *Porno*, London: Jonathan Cape.

Welsh, L. (2002), *The Cutting Room*, Edinburgh: Canongate.

Wollen, P. (1996), 'The two avant-gardes', in O'Pray, M. (ed.), *The British Avant-Garde Film 1926–1995*, Luton: University of Luton Press, pp. 133–43.

11

Radio and Popular Music

KEN GARNER

INTRODUCTION: ANOTHER COUNTRY, ANOTHER MUSIC

The closure of a country music radio station, which was devised and pro-grammed by an American and only available digitally, and its relaunch two months later under a new name in Nashville, Tennessee, might seem to have little to do with the health of Scotland's radio industry. Still less might it be expected to offer any insight into the characteristics of the Scottish music business. But the sudden switch-off of 3C by Emap plc on 27 March 2007 is subtly indicative of something about the state and future of both these sectors of the creative economy in Scotland.

3C announced on air on 26 March 2007 that the closure was 'the result of a brand review undertaken by our parent company'. Emap had acquired 3C as part of its takeover of Scottish Radio Holdings plc (SRH) for £280 million in cash in August 2005 (Emap 2006: 6). SRH – founded in 1991 from a merger of Radios Clyde, Forth, Tay and Northsound – had launched 3C from Radio Clyde's Clydebank studios in 2000. It was broadcast initially on the Internet and as one of the extra stations on SRH's local DAB digital radio multiplex run by SRH-subsidiary Score Digital, and from 2004 on the Freeview digital terrestrial television platform across the UK as well – thus making it the first national country music service in the history of UK radio and the first UK national radio station to be based in Scotland. The station, devised, programmed and run by Pat Geary, a Californian music business entrepreneur who had moved to Scotland at the end of the 1980s, was oper-ated with just two presenters and a computerised and part-automated playout system. Nevertheless, it won critical acclaim, and was judged Best Country

Music Format in the World by judges at the 2001 International Radio Festival of New York. Its critical success, and loyalty among its (admittedly modest) specialist audience of 100,000 listeners across the UK (Rajar 2006a), derived partly from its boldness. On winning the New York award, Geary said:

> Many stations have trimmed their formats to seek the false security in high rotation of safe songs and artists, claiming that the duration of radio listening is becoming shorter. In order to maximise reach in the core audience, playlists have been cut and rotation increased. Inevitably this becomes a self-fulfilling formula resulting in smaller audiences listening for shorter hours. 3C Continuous Cool Country flies in the face of this current thinking. Our aim is to entertain and stimulate not only short-term listeners, but also those who want to listen for hours or even the entire day. We feature the best of the fresh new music out of Nashville, choosing user-friendly tunes that sound familiar the first time you hear them yet have sufficient originality to stimulate the senses. (UK Digital Radio 2001)

There is some evidence to support Geary's contention, regarding those listeners prepared to seek out radio stations on digital platforms. 3C's listeners stayed tuned for longer (5.8 hours per week) than listeners to Emap's other digital-only national stations, Q, Mojo, Smash Hits and The Hits. On the other hand, those of the group's digital radio formats which share brand names with its traditional UK AM/FM stations, such as Magic and Kiss – rather than with its magazines or music TV channels – continue to do better; and all of Emap's other radio brands have a greater number of listeners than 3C had (Rajar 2006b). In fact, Emap claims that: 'Compared with our competitors in the market we have the largest number of digital listening hours, with 17.8 million' in an average week (Emap 2006: 8).

It is perhaps this which partly explains Emap's 'brand review' decision to close 3C, and it also hints at the future path of commercial radio in the UK, including Scotland. As the group acknowledges, with its core businesses in magazine and radio dependent on advertising revenue for 43 per cent of all group revenue, with its radio stations in particular solely dependent on such income, and in the light of the freefall of radio's share of advertising spend in the UK – 6 per cent just before the millennium, 3.3 per cent in 2005 – it hardly has any option but to 'target resources towards faster-growing platforms' (Emap 2006: 6, 20). After the boom years in the UK of the 1990s – new licences, new advertisers and investors, new formats, new listeners, all leading to corporate and financial growth – the commercial sector of the medium is now struggling. While the total time the UK population spends listening to radio has increased since the early 1990s – from 875,000 hours to 1.05 million hours per week – the percentage tuning in has not changed, at around 90 per cent of the population. The lion's share of any increased time we spend tuned in across the UK as a whole has gone to the BBC. Commercial radio, after briefly overtaking the BBC in share of all listening in the late 1990s – 51.1 per cent in summer 1998 – by the end of 2006 had seen its share fall to 43.2 per cent (Rajar 1998, 2006b). And radio's advertising revenue is now migrating to the Internet even faster than that of newspapers. The only option for traditional media organisations would appear to be corporate belt-tightening: cost-cutting, rationalisation, mergers.

The sad story for commercial radio in Scotland today is that it has ridden the expansionary wave like everyone else, but has done so from a rare, possibly unique position of established, original local programming and business strength. Blessed with personable local voices, a strong journalistic tradition, generally sound financial management and a commitment to investment, and a ready supply of successive waves of ground-breaking Scottish popular music and entertainment stars and styles to stimulate programming, Scottish local radio was a popular and commercial (if not always critical) success story from the mid-1970s till the century's end. But now times are hard, the mergers and acquisitions genie cannot be put back in the bottle. Irrespective of any local character or strengths, the fate of mass-market commercial radio in Scotland is now wedded to UK corporate agendas.

Hence the bad news for 3C. But that story, at least, is not quite over yet. Pat Geary relaunched the format in May 2007 as a web-only station called www.voiceofcountry.com, relocated to Nashville. 'We thought, why not go where the artists are? There are other web-based country stations, true, but none focussed on presenting new music to the international listenership,' he says (Geary 2007). It is this faith in local musical innovation and newness, wherever that 'local' might be, and an international outlook in terms of style and audience, that has echoes of the most creative areas of the Scottish pop music-making scene, and its own route to continued success. Today, as we shall see, this means Scottish pop has very little to do with its seemingly logical media partner, Scottish commercial radio.

COMMERCIAL MUSIC RADIO IN SCOTLAND: 1973–2007

It was not always the case that commercial radio in Scotland had at best a tangential relationship with Scottish pop music-making. As Sean Street has observed, 'the first era of Independent Local Radio (ILR) was a curiously Reithian affair' (Street 2002: 118). Regulation by the Independent

Broadcasting Authority (IBA) meant stations had rigid programming obligations, including community and religious programming. In this period, for music programming, the Musicians' Union had secured a compulsory investment by every station of 3 per cent of net advertising revenue annually in 'live' or 'locally-recorded' music. By 1981, when all the major Scottish city stations were on-air (see Baron 1975: 117–36), the IBA was able to trumpet that 'well over £4 million has been spent on providing employment for musicians' across the UK (*Television & Radio 1981*, 1981: 155). But while music already accounted for 'about half of all broadcast airtime on most ILR stations', most of this was UK and US commercial chart music, playlisted and programmed, with varying degrees of rigidity, in 'format' rotation during daytime hours (see Starkey 2004: 89–93; Hendy 2000: 168–77). In other words, the Scottish ILR stations, like their counterparts elsewhere in the UK, never chose to interpret this 'live-or-locally-recorded' stricture as an encouragement to give daytime playlist exposure to new Scottish bands.

Instead, they invested heavily in staging minority taste musical events, constructing music-recording facilities, and operating mobile studios, and they built evening and weekend programmes and special events based on the resulting taped output. Radio Forth had a £35,000 outside broadcast unit and set up the Radio Forth Youth Orchestra. Radio Clyde had two mobile recording studios, and it created and staged an annual Festival of Scottish Popular Music (though this was decidedly light entertainment and traditional in character). When it moved to its purpose-built complex in Clydebank in 1984, it incorporated music recording studios – as well as an indoor swimming pool – into the design. Many mainstream artists had their concerts in Glasgow recorded and broadcast by Clyde, and new commercial bands on tour, or doing promotional rounds of the radio stations for a new single or album, came in and recorded basic studio sessions for evening shows in the 1970s and 1980s which were presented by the likes of Bill Padley, Mark Goodier, and Billy Sloan (the last of these, to the station's credit, is still hosting his Sunday night show on Clyde 1, though the recording studios have long since been converted to other uses). Elsewhere, Radio Forth's Colin Somerville and Northsound's Jim Gellatly, for example, presented weekly evening shows introducing the latest local, Scottish and international acts and pop styles, featuring occasional basic sessions or outside-broadcast recordings of live sets. However, by the late 1980s, the IBA was relaxing its requirements in anticipation of formal deregulation by government, and various restrictive practices involving the Musicians' Union's dealings with public and commercial broadcasters were successfully challenged and abolished in 1988–9. In these final years before most public-service obligations were removed from local commercial radio in the 1990 Broadcasting Act, the 'live-or-local' financial commitment to music was mostly met by securing concert recordings by visiting mainstream pop stars.

It is hard to think of another media industry or sector in Scotland which experienced such a peculiar mix of rapid change after 1990: one of simultaneous, extensive market expansion and competition, combined with corporate failures of nerve and rapid changes of ownership. In 1988 Scotland had just seven local non-BBC stations. By 2001 it had thirty-one, partly as a consequence of the relaxation of simulcasting rules by the old IBA – enabling stations like Clyde, Forth, Tay and Northsound to operate separate services or 'stations' on their AM and FM frequencies from 1988/1989 – but mostly a result of the drive to widen listener choice set by the 1990 Broadcasting Act, leading to the new Radio Authority advertising licences for stations in many areas previously denied them. This has led to perhaps the greatest deregulatory media benefit to the public sphere and quality of life in Scotland, if only for a very small percentage of the population: the halo of more than a dozen small, independent, largely voluntary-based radio stations dotted around the country's islands, coast, highland and lowland communities (see Ofcom 2007a). Heartland FM (Pitlochry and Aberfeldy), Lochbroom FM (Ullapool) and Isles FM (Stornoway) have been among the most successful in becoming central to local life. The most competitive expansion, however, has been in the central belt. First, in the licensing of two new central Scotland FM licences, initially won and operated by Scot FM (launched in 1994, by Border & Grampian Television) and Beat 106 (launched in 1999 by a local consortium of live music and nightclub promoters); and later, after 2002, with the battle to win new city FM stations in Glasgow and Edinburgh, won by Saga 105.2 (Glasgow) and Talk 107 (Edinburgh). More recently still, and subsequent to the Radio Authority being integrated into the new UK media regulator Ofcom in 2003, a new tier of community radio stations has been inserted, with three each already on air in both Glasgow and Edinburgh.

But all of these new stations, which have undoubtedly widened listening in Scotland and brought many benefits, have also brought turmoil, instability and in some cases failure, takeover, receivership, or liquidation. Who now remembers the defunct East End Radio, Clan FM and River FM? Whatever happened to the idealism of the original owners behind Q96 in Paisley and Beat 106? Partly as a consequence of the troubles brought on by rapid expansion – Q96 has changed hands and been re-formatted three times since 1994 – the corporate ownership map of commercial radio in Scotland now has a shape unthinkable just ten years ago (see Table 11.1).

Several things are immediately obvious. All the major stations in the major

Table 11.1 Scottish radio station ownership 2007

Owner	Stations	Former owners / notes
Emap plc	Clyde 1 Clyde 2 Forth 1 Forth 2 Tay FM Tay Am Northsound 1 Northsound 2 Moray Firth Radio Radio Borders West Sound West FM South West Sound CFM (Carlisle)	All formerly SRH, now each part of Emap's 'Big City Network' (sold to the German publishing group, Bauer, in December 2007)
GMG (Guardian Media Group)	Real Radio 96.3 Rock Radio Smooth Radio	Central Belt, formerly Scot FM Paisley, formerly Q96 Glasgow, formerly Saga Radio
G-CAP Media	XFM-Scotland	Central Belt, formerly Beat 106
UTV	Wave 102 Talk 107	Dundee Edinburgh
Local Radio Company	Central FM	Falkirk/Stirling
Independent	All other small-scale commercial and community stations	

centres are owned by one or other of the UK's leading radio groups, and are no longer owned in Scotland. Furthermore, notice how the stations owned by two of those groups are now labelled solely as one of those group's national UK radio format 'brands'. The next major step would seem obvious. While it is hard to imagine Emap's 'Big City Network' attempting anything so reckless as to abandon the familiar geographic, non-brand names of its successful FM stations in Scotland (Clyde 1, Forth 1, Tay FM, and so on), it can surely be only a matter of time before Emap seeks to re-format and re-brand the old SRH's various, less successful AM stations (Clyde 2, Forth 2, Tay AM, Northsound 2) as outposts of its elsewhere ubiquitous and successful 'Magic' format.

But, despite current troubles, commercial radio is still a sector of Scottish media that retains great popular appeal. As far as mass audiences go, radio listening in Scotland since the late 1970s has always meant commercial radio listening, and consequently *music* radio listening. The major stations within SRH inspired loyalty amongst their listeners few stations could dream of (see, for example, Garner 1994a, 1994b). As recently as December 1998, for example, Clyde 1 FM and Clyde 2 AM in Glasgow had a combined share of the total time people in their area spent listening to the radio greater than that spent listening to all other stations put together: that's BBC Radios 1, 2, 3, 4, 5 Live and Scotland, plus Scot FM, Classic FM, Virgin, Talk Radio and 96.3 QFM (Paisley). In June 1997 Forth FM and Forth AM in Edinburgh had a greater share of all local listening than all the BBC stations added up (*UK Radio Guide & Directory* 1999). Radio Borders still regularly reaches 58 per cent of its population, Moray Firth Radio 43 per cent, West Sound 42 per cent, and Northsound One in Aberdeen 41 per cent. The only other radio stations anywhere in the UK that consistently break the 40 per cent threshold are local BBC or commercial stations on islands: Guernsey, the Isle of Man, and the Isle of Wight (Rajar 2006b).[1]

BBC RADIO SCOTLAND AND SCOTTISH BANDS: *ROCK ON SCOTLAND, BEAT PATROL, AIR, THE SESSION*

By contrast, BBC Radio Scotland, launched in 1978, four years after Radio Clyde came on air and three years after Radio Forth, has struggled until recently to maintain its traditional benchmark of regularly reaching approximately one million listeners, equalling about a quarter of the adult Scots population. Of the BBC's four national/regional services (Scotland, Ulster, Wales, Radio Cymru), it has traditionally performed the worst in listenership (although in 2007 Radio Cymru is doing less well); however, to be fair, it has to try and serve the largest geographic area and population of them all, and, in its main conurbations, is up against strong commercial competition which beat it to market. In most Scottish cities, either BBC Radio 2 or BBC Radio 1 is normally the second or third most popular station, after the local commercial leader(s), and BBC Radio Scotland comes third or fourth at best (*UK Radio Guide & Directory* 1998, 1999, 2000). However, its Saturday afternoon national football show *Sportsound* has for over a decade been the second-most-listened to radio show in the country after the Radio 1 chart show on Sunday afternoons (BBC Scotland 1996), partly thanks to now having the exclusive radio rights to broadcast live Scottish Premier League football commentaries.

One area in which Radio Scotland has consistently had difficulty is with young audiences. Apart from the football coverage, and its long-defunct weekend morning show with Scots comedian Andy Cameron, most of its programmes have failed to attract listeners under the age of twenty-one. Throughout the 1980s various 'youth audience' programme initiatives were attempted, including a Friday teatime twenty-minute entertainment show *Nightlife;* and in 1988, a summer-holidays-only, two-hour Wednesday evening comedy, live bands and feature reports show, initially entitled *Not The Archie MacPherson Show*, and latterly *Bite The Wax* (see Garner 1988b). Today the show is chiefly remembered and celebrated as being where Radio 4 news presenter Eddie Mair, comedian and satirist Armando Iannucci, and electronic dance-music DJ Mark Percival all began their BBC careers.

The one programme that consistently did get young Scots to tune in was the weekly show that championed new Scottish and international bands, *Beat Patrol*, and its predecessor *Rock On Scotland*. Launched late on Friday nights in November 1984, *Rock On Scotland* was initially programmed, produced and presented, respectively, by three BBC Scotland staffers in their spare time: Sandy Semeonoff and Stewart Cruickshank (later a staff senior producer) of the record library at Broadcasting House Glasgow, and Radio Scotland head of presentation Peter Easton (see Garner 1988a, 1988c). At least a third of every one-hour show was devoted to Scottish bands, and over the years – retitled *Beat Patrol* and moved to Sunday teatime in 1990 – it won loyal listenership and acclaim for having been the first radio show to play acts like The BMX Bandits, The Bachelor Pad, Baby Lemonade, and others from successive generations of local musicians. In November 2000, in a drive to give Radio Scotland's coverage of Scottish pop a broader appeal, *Beat Patrol* was replaced by an energetic two-hour Monday evening show called *Air*, presented initially by Amanda Mackinnon, of the Glasgow band Bis, and produced by Claire Pattenden, formerly executive producer of specialist music at Radio 1. Despite its best efforts, however, *Air* never quite managed to retain the critical acclaim and listener loyalty built up by its predecessor over the years, nor did it develop a significantly larger audience. Both Mackinnon and Pattenden departed in 2002, and the Monday evening slot and new music format is now occupied by Vic Galloway.

Beat Patrol, however, had a wider legacy than merely securing a regular slot for new bands on Radio Scotland. In its heyday in the mid-1990s, it recorded numerous concerts and original sessions, and this led to several of its debut live session scoops by new Scottish bands – made by the likes of Uresei Yatsura (1994), Pink Kross and The Delgados (both 1995) and Adventures In Stereo (1997) – being picked up for a UK network repeat a few weeks later by BBC Radio 1's globally-influential *John Peel Show*. Scottish bands such as these went on to enjoy huge popular acclaim from Peel's listeners, appearing regularly in his annual end-of-year 'Festive 50' poll of listeners' favourite songs of the year; The Delgados, Mogwai and Belle And Sebastian memorably took the top three places in the 1998 poll. All this no doubt contributed to the confidence with which new Radio 1 controller Andy Parfitt decided in July 1999 to launch a weekly series of regional opt-out new music shows on Thursday nights, entitled *The Session In*, from Wales, Northern Ireland, and, most notably, Scotland – the last to be presented from Glasgow, originally by Gill Mills and Vic Galloway, and more recently by Galloway on his own. The commissioning of the show from BBC Scotland also built on the short-lived success of John Cavanagh presenting Radio 1's Sunday-night, heavy rock show from Glasgow, from 1995. Subsequently the music production department at Radio Scotland went on to win many documentary and special feature music programme commissions from BBC Radio 2, and continues to do so, as well as producing regular jazz shows for Radio 3. It has even sometimes proved easier for creative producers to win airtime and enthusiasm for their programme ideas about Scottish and international music and entertainment trends from London network controllers, than it has been to find a secure home for them on BBC Radio Scotland itself. Partly this is a consequence of the station's mixed format, its obligation to carry much news, speech, sport and other programming. But it could also be viewed as a public-service broadcasting equivalent of the difficulties Scottish bands have faced in getting their records played, post-1990, on local commercial stations: bands and radio producers alike have at times found greater media interest in their work outside Scotland.

SCOTTISH POP AND ROCK IN 2007: BANDS, LABELS, CLUBS, GIGS, PROMOTERS, MEDIA

Whatever its critical and creative achievements, Scotland's music industry remains 'under-developed and highly fragmented', constituting mostly very small, even one-person record companies or studios, and 'volatile', with new businesses launching every year and old ones going bust (see Symon and Cloonan 2002: 101–3). The exception to this is the live music industry, where, on top of the 'vast array' of sole-trader and freelance operators, there are several sizeable and profitable companies – such as DF Concerts, Regular Music, and CPL – who put on concerts in venues ranging from tiny clubs, to open-air festivals with major sponsorship, most often from brewing companies: 'live

music is one of the most successful sectors in the music industry in Scotland'
(Williamson, Cloonan and Frith 2003: iv, 27–37). And while the artists and
record companies based in Scotland might be small economically, and certainly could neither survive financially from earnings in Scotland alone, nor
command the commitment of international major record companies, they
punch far above their weight internationally in terms of critical acclaim. If in
these ways only, the popular music scene and industry in Scotland is in a very
different state to that which persisted until the mid-1990s. Since the 1960s
there have always been successful Scottish pop and rock acts (see, for primary
popular history, Hogg 2007, Kielty 2006, Wilkie 1990), but until the late 1980s
most had to leave Scotland to succeed. There was then a brief period of multinational confidence in Scottish acts, and it was even claimed that, by the end
of the 1980s, about forty-five acts were signed to major labels, and most
remained based in Scotland. These numbers had shrunk to just ten such major-
label signed acts by 2002, and several of these have been subsequently dropped,
split up or retired. But at the same time many more acts were signed to Scottish,
UK or international independent labels (see Williamson, Cloonan and Frith
2003: 12–14).

For most acts, their major source of income has now become not advances
on royalties from record companies, but live performance. International
acclaim and a licensing deal for records with a large independent record
company in an overseas market can lead to an invitation from local promoters
to headline short world regional tours – a month touring Australia and Japan,
for example – that can produce income sufficient for a four-piece band to live
on back at home for several months, or even a year. This has meant Scottish
bands now have the option, not available before, to contemplate narrowing the
scale of their commercial ambitions – 'let's face it, we'll probably never make
millions or play stadium gigs' – yet being able to scrape a living while retaining the luxury of artistic freedom and critical acclaim. If superstar status means
leaving Scotland and/or compromising with a major multinational label, they
will now more often than not choose not to do so – not that the majors are
exactly beating a path to new acts' doors. It is the boom in live performance
income that has made this alternate career structure possible. This heady
bohemian and seemingly egalitarian mix of the prospect of a modest but sustainable income, combined with being lauded to the skies in the hip American
music mags, has even percolated down to the manner in which the smallest
live-music clubs are now run in Scottish cities. While 'pay-to-play' still exists –
under which new bands pay the promoter for the privilege of getting the
bottom slot on a bill at a known venue – it is becoming common for new
club nights, or one-off events in the smallest venues, to be created by networks
of friendly bands who then work out a collective, shared costing and

remuneration deal so everyone gets something back from the 'take' on the door. No band is going to become rich or famous this way, but equally each is potentially being rewarded with at least some of what it seeks, in financial, critical and moral return.[2]

This curious state of artistic and economic sustainability, combined with lack of mass-market commercialism, is reflected in the music's relationship with Scotland's music media. While the major Scottish newspapers, music magazines, freesheets, tipsheets and fanzines cover the national music scene extensively (Williamson, Cloonan and Frith 2003: 48–52), the same is not at all true of the broadcast media. The two locally managed TV stations, BBC Scotland TV and STV, have minimal coverage of pop groups, and, as we have seen above in detail, BBC Radio Scotland has 'struggled to determine a coherent structure for its music output with frequent changes to both policy and programming' (Williamson, Cloonan and Frith 2003: 48). But Scottish bands look in vain to what one might imagine to be their natural medium of coverage – commercial format music radio – for any kind of systematic engagement. Scottish pop groups have always grumbled about not getting enough airplay for their singles, whether on BBC Radio 1 or local commercial stations, but in the 1980s this was unreasonable whingeing because it was simply not true. You could not turn on Radio 1 or Radio Clyde in the late-1980s without hearing Simple Minds, Texas, Hue and Cry, Wet Wet Wet, Deacon Blue and Danny Wilson at any time, day or night. But in the last decade some of their successors could be forgiven for becoming paranoid. The regulatory environment for the musical content of commercial stations has become ever looser over that time. The Radio Authority's 'Promise of Performance' for every station replaced previous specific public service requirements after the 1990 Broadcasting Act, but still specified music-speech ratios during peak times, and expected stations to define their musical format, most commonly via indicative lists of artists for each genre featured. This has been replaced since 2003 by Ofcom's simplified, one-page 'format' statement, which can be amended by application at any time. Of the metropolitan FM stations, Clyde One and Forth One make an identical, minimal commitment to Scottish music in their format, both stating that 'the main mix should be spiced with Scottish pop or rock and/or other hits'. Real Radio hints that its music schedule 'should include a sprinkling of Scottish artists', and Radio Borders and Central FM each say their specialist programmes might include Scottish music. No other urban Scottish radio station mentions Scottish musical content in its format statement (Ofcom 2007b). There has been some discussion by the music industry in Scotland since devolution about whether to seek some form of 'Scottish-content' regulation on local broadcast media, requiring that a certain percentage of music played on radio stations meet defined criteria for 'Scottish' content, as applies in countries such as France and Canada (see Hare 2003; Henderson 2007). The problem here is an intractable one, however: broadcast and copyright regulation remain powers reserved for the Westminster Parliament, not Holyrood. The fact that corporate ownership of all the major stations now resides outside Scotland would also make any such change practically and politically almost impossible to implement, even if desirable. Many Scottish musicians themselves find such special pleading distasteful and meddlesome, but it cannot be denied that such a policy has stimulated economic and artistic sustainability where applied.

CONCLUSION

Commercial music radio in Scotland, the overwhelmingly popular first choice for the majority of Scottish radio listeners, has a curious non-relationship with the nation's music-makers. Its music formats are very popular with Scots listeners, but only occasionally feature Scottish acts during the daytime. Stations are under no regulatory obligation to do so, and anyway their listening figures, despite falling, are still sufficiently strong (unlike commercial radio elsewhere in the UK) for them to argue that their listeners are evidently not bothered.

The one station which has, by contrast, recently experienced a critically successful relaunch by basing its new identity largely on local bands and the aggressive promotion of live music, nevertheless chooses to make no mention of Scottish music in its declared format. In January 2006 G-Cap Media relaunched the central Scotland regional dance and indie station Beat 106 under its XFM new music brand, under which it already operated stations in London and Manchester. Led by head of programming Claire Pattenden, the new station erupted onto the air overnight with a raft of familiar but re-focused presenters, and displaying an extraordinary dynamism and coherence of guitar-based musical content. In its exuberant celebration of the vibrant Glasgow and Edinburgh gig-going culture, this rebranding, prompted by UK corporate group promotional interests, was ironically closer to the aspirations of Beat's original independent owners, DF Concerts and a night club operator, than the station had ever achieved in practice. But as might have perhaps been expected of a change which replaced dance music with guitar bands, this presentational, marketing and critical success was not matched by popular acclaim. From 367,000 listeners to Beat 106 in December 2005, just before the relaunch (constituting a 14 per cent reach and 4.9 per cent market share of all listening), XFM Scotland by the fourth quarter of 2006 had declined to just 294,000 listeners, or an 11 per cent reach and 4.4 per cent market share (Rajar 2006b). In May 2007 the declining state of advertising revenue in radio prompted G-Cap Media to announce that, from the end of the month, it was doing away with its daytime presenters between 10am and 4pm on all XFM stations, including XFM Scotland, instead allowing listeners to vote for tracks and shape the format via text messaging (Morgan 2007).

What the recent events at 3C and XFM Scotland demonstrate unequivocally is that commercial radio in Scotland is driven by UK corporate interests and national advertising and audience trends. And while live music in Scotland is booming overall, indigenous bands have to look internationally for a welcome that will sustain them economically, if founded on local and international artistic credibility. The three industries operate in distinct worlds and have distinct business models. Radio still targets aggregations or substantial segments of a mass audience based on familiar programming in which any Scottish content is constituted primarily by the presenters, news, advertisements and competitions. Live music seeks to satisfy a specialist youth demographic resolute in these times in its determination to go out and see a band every other night. Musicians and bands, however, look for their survival to a combination of local critical approval, and international taste communities. The live music industry alone seems primarily dependent on the Scottish economy. For innovative bands and creative would-be radio programmers, producers and presenters alike, it appears that once more they find they have to look for their future beyond their own doorstep, to the global marketplace for taste and ideas.

NOTES

1. Rajar defines market share as the percentage of all radio listening hours over the course of a week that a station accounts for within its transmission area; weekly reach percentage is defined as the number of people aged fifteen-plus who tune to a radio station within at least one quarter-hour period over the course of a week, expressed as a percentage of the population within the transmission area (see www.rajar.co.uk). Thus, share could be viewed as a measure of listener loyalty; reach as an indicator of a station's centrality or otherwise to the public sphere in its area as partly constituted by broadcast media consumption.

2. I am indebted for the formation of my ideas in this paragraph to conversations over the past decade or so with my friends Raymond McGinley, Stewart Cruickshank, Craig Tannock and John Williamson, and former students Julie Whiteside (née MacCaskill), Lee Beattie, Davy Hughes and Carrie MacLennan.

REFERENCES

Baron, M. (1975), *Independent Radio: The Story of Commercial Radio in the United Kingdom*, Lavenham: Terence Dalton.

BBC Scotland (1996), 'Radio Scotland's coverage is a big hit with football fans', press release, 15 March.

Emap plc (2006), *Annual Report & Accounts 2006*, London: Emap.

Garner, K. (1988a), 'Pop goes FM', *Cut*, April, p. 32.

Garner, K. (1988b), 'Turn it up!', *Cut*, August, p. 45.

Garner, K. (1988c), 'It's only Rock 'n' Roll radio, but they like it', *Radio Times*, 6–12 August (Scottish edition), p. 82.

Garner, K. (1994a), 'Radio Review', *Scotland on Sunday*, Spectrum section, 6 February, p. 19.

Garner, K. (1994b), 'Radio Review', *Scotland on Sunday*, Spectrum section, 7 August, p. 19.

Geary, P. (2007), telephone interview with author, 27 April 2007.

Hare, G. (2003), 'Popular music on French radio and television', in H. Dauncey and S. Cannon (eds), *Popular Music in France from Chanson to Techno*, London: Ashgate, pp. 57–76.

Henderson, S. (2008), 'Canadian content regulations and the formation of a national scene', *Popular Music*, 27, 2

Hendy, D. (2000), *Radio in the Global Age*, Cambridge: Polity Press.

Hogg, B. (2007), *All That Ever Mattered: The Birth of Scottish Rock and Pop: Beat, Punk and Beyond*, 2nd revd edn, Edinburgh: Justified Sinner.

Kielty, M. (2006), *Big Noise: The History of Scottish Rock 'n' Roll as Told by the People Who Made It*, Glasgow: Black and White.

Morgan, J. (2007), 'Radio station takes its DJs off the air', *Glasgow Herald*, 18 May, p. 10.

Ofcom (2007a), Analog Commercial Radio Ownership – Ownership, http://www.ofcom.org.uk/radio/ifi/rbl/formats/acrm.pdf.

Ofcom (2007b), UK radio station details and formats, http://www.ofcom.org.uk/static/radiolicensing/amfm/analogue-main.htm.

Rajar (1998), *Quarterly Summary of Radio Listening: Survey Period Ending June 1998*, London: Radio Joint Audience Research.

Rajar (2006a), *Quarterly Summary of Radio Listening: Survey Period Ending June 2006*, London: Radio Joint Audience Research, available at www.rajar.co.uk.

Rajar (2006b), *Quarterly Summary of Radio Listening: Survey Period Ending December 2006*, London: Radio Joint Audience Research, available at www.rajar.co.uk.

Starkey, G. (2004), *Radio In Context*, Basingstoke: Palgrave Macmillan.

Street, S. (2002), *A Concise History of British Radio, 1922–2002*, Tiverton: Kelly Publications.

Symon, P. and M. Cloonan (2002), 'Playing away: popular music, policy and devolution in Scotland', *Scottish Affairs* (40) Summer, pp. 99–122.

Television & Radio 1981: Focus on Independent Broadcasting (1981), London: IBA.

Television & Radio 1986: Focus on Independent Broadcasting (1985), London: IBA.

Television & Radio 1987: Focus on Independent Broadcasting (1986), London: IBA.

Television & Radio 1988: Focus on Independent Broadcasting (1988), London: IBA.

UK Digital Radio (2001), 'The world's best country station from Glasgow, not Nashville', press release, 25 June, available at www.ukdigitalradio.com/news/display.asp?id=76.

UK Radio Guide & Directory (1998), Rothwell: Goldcrest Broadcasting, Edition I.
UK Radio Guide & Directory (1999), Rothwell: Goldcrest Broadcasting, Edition II.
UK Radio Guide & Directory (2000), Rothwell: Goldcrest Broadcasting, Edition II.
Wilkie, J. (1990), *Blue Suede Brogans: Secret Life of Scottish Rock Music*, Edinburgh: Mainstream Publishing.
Williamson, J., M. Cloonan and S. Frith (2003), *Mapping the Music Industry in Scotland: A Report for Scottish Enterprise*, Glasgow: Scottish Enterprise.

THEMES AND FUTURES

12

Gender, Spaces, Changes: Emergent Identities in a Scotland in Transition

JANE SILLARS AND MYRA MACDONALD

Scotland, in common with many small or stateless nations, has struggled with its history and identity. Representation, whether on page, stage or screen, has played a crucial role in that struggle. There are two key trends in the construction of Scottish identity which can be seen as particularly problematic in terms of representations of gender: firstly, the turn to a static past as the guarantor of separate identity (McArthur 1982; Craig 1996); and secondly, the search for a single, unified national identity, whose emphasis on masculinity sees femininity relegated to a supporting or symbolic role, and which neglects to account for other kinds of diversity.

Our analysis focuses on the moving image and predominantly on fictional narratives, arguing that this is the key cultural ground where ways to imagine and re-envisage identity are explored. This chapter makes no pretence to be comprehensive in its references, but signals some of the emerging processes that offer new models of gendered approaches to a nation in transition, despite continuing limitations. In this chapter we identify dominant trends, and traces of alternative imaginings. We pay particular attention to the representation of historical change, arguing that gendered representations play a highly symbolic role as bearers of moments of transition, as well as functioning in more traditional ways as markers of ossified difference, whether national or gendered.

REPRESENTING SPACE AND CHANGE

This chapter moves beyond considering gender as an attribute of character to trace gender mappings across the imagining of space. We draw attention to the figuration of the space of the nation as not just a physical space but also a psychic space, invested with meaning, which can be imagined as bounded or porous, as limited or liberating. We will concentrate on two aspects of post-modernity which have transformed the space of contemporary Scotland – globalisation and de-industrialisation. The complex movements of globalisation have reshaped ideas of nationhood as well as other forms of identity. The migration of people and ideas has intensified the spread of modernity and diversity (Harvey 1990), whilst new technologies have altered transnational communications and the relations between centres and peripheries (Soja 1989). All these shifts are bound up with a re-imagining of different kinds of spaces: geographical space, cyberspace and the space of internal subjectivities (Massey 1994).

De-industrialisation has trapped Scottish political and cultural life in a rear-guard action. The move away from heavy industry has conjured the spectre of male redundancy (real and symbolic) and a forced reshaping of masculine identity. This move, alongside a service-economy re-branding can be argued to have created a re-gendering of Scotland's civic space. The 'hard city' of industrial labour, tribal loyalties, drink and violence is re-imagined as a place of leisure and consumption – a 'soft city'[1] which offers feminine spaces of pleasure, social and sexual possibilities (Raban 1974). Within Scottish representation this soft city can also be visualised as a place of escape from the surveillance and social repression of the kailyard (Law and Law 2002).

The following sections will highlight some of the dominant ways in which representations of Scotland have figured femininity and masculinity; they then move on to identify emergent forms which seem to re-articulate gendered, sexual and national identities in ways which respond to a society in transition.

SCOTLAND AND THE ETERNAL FEMININE

What Colin McArthur (1996) has identified as the 'Scottish discursive uncon-scious' produces a vision of Scotland as existing outside time. Across a range of popular cultural forms, Scotland is shown as a place of the ancient and the uncanny. The Loch Ness monster may have become an icon of Scottish kitsch, but Nessie, as the archaic feminine, speaks of a vision of Scotland so physically distant from the centres of modernity that history is unable to reach it.

Despite Scotland's relatively under-developed indigenous moving-image culture, Scottish scenes and stories, as noted elsewhere in this book, have featured heavily on screen from the earliest days of cinema (Petrie 2000). The dominant perspective has come from outwith its borders: Scotland is imagined as embodying remoteness, escape and perhaps redemption. Notions of Scotland as a restorative space, existing beyond the reach of modernity, are frequently figured in film through the form of the romance: a romance with place as much as between individuals (Martin-Jones 2005). Female characters and the land itself are mapped across one another, both functioning as backdrop to the journey of the male protagonist.

Across a series of twentieth-century films, Highland Scotland is used as the location for a voyage of discovery. A refugee from the modern world finds there respite and a reconnection with the natural world, often brokered by a feminine spirit of place. MGM's 1954 musical fantasy *Brigadoon* offers the *locus classicus* of this mythology and the construction of Scotland as other, feminised, magical and timeless (McArthur 2003). *The Maggie* (1954), *Local Hero* (1983) and *Loch Ness* (1996) all repeat this narrative form, structured around the experience of the American hero (as a reminder of the dominant economic power relations of film production; *Local Hero* is perhaps the most knowing in its reflection on how and why identities become constructed from and for elsewhere – 'You can't eat scenery'). Within these narratives Scotland becomes the place at the end of the road, the space where modernity breaks down. Cars, boats, phones – all lines of communication – cease to function. The trappings of modern civilisation are undermined by a mix of natural and supernatural elements: mists, winds, tides, mermaids and monsters. The gendering of these mysterious and wayward elements as feminine is clear, and mirrored in the characters' encounters with women who are presented as rooted, and as authentic in their connection with the ancient rhythms of home and hearth (Sheena in *The Maggie*, Peggy and Catriona in *Whisky Galore*, Stella in *Local Hero*, Laura and daughter Isabel in *Loch Ness*); or as carrying the magic of the land within them (Fiona in *Brigadoon*, and mermaid Marina in *Local Hero*).

Within the moving image, Scotland is seen as a space where older patterns of social organisation still hold sway – whether of the community, celebrated in the obligatory ceilidh scene of so many films, or, more specifically, as a set of entrenched relations between the sexes. In another cathexis of Scottish space and time, highly traditional, and often regressive, images of gender relations are shown to be licensed not only by the weight of history, but by nature herself. William Wallace announces in *Braveheart*, 'I came home to raise crops and, God willing, a family'. Heterosexual relations are paralleled with, and sanctioned by, the laws of nature. To underline the point, Wallace and Mirin's marriage ceremony is conducted in a wood and, in a toe-curling slow-motion scene, consummated there as well. Wallace in this film is of course a peace-loving sort, and his latent, violent, head-splitting masculinity is only awakened by the threat to his womenfolk. The leering, dribbling rapists of the English occupying forces offer a schematic opposition of bad masculinity against which the sanctity of both women and the land must be defended. In case the gendered symbolism of land and purity were not sufficiently laboured, Mirin's emblematic thistle embroidery fuses Scotland, 'freeedom' and the feminine.

Rob Roy, released in 1995, the same year as *Braveheart*, again centres its narrative exploration of nationality around violent rape and disputed paternity. Blood and seed become the tokens of masculine national dispute, spattered across the contested bodies of women and the land. Rape is used as a weapon of war, and also (alongside Wallace's romance with the Princess in *Braveheart*) as a token of homosocial aggression, an act perpetrated on women but whose communicative force lies between men. Despite these similar thematics, *Rob Roy* offers a more ambiguous exploration of the relations between nationality, gender and sexuality. The film also celebrates the time-honoured union of man and the land in another scene of vigorous, outdoors, marital heterosexuality, showing Rob and Mary cavorting by the standing stones which Mary teases 'make men hard and women fertile'; nonetheless, there is a sense by the end of the narrative that Rob's heroic values of honour, clan and family may be as monolithic and as stuck in the past as the stones thrust into the landscape. The film is explicit about its historical moment with an opening title card that delineates the politics of the early eighteenth century. *Rob Roy* shows a man marooned by the incoming tides of modernity: the decline of the clan system, the advent of mercantile capitalism, and voluntary migration are all shown to be as significant as Jacobite politics (or crude English/Scottish antagonism).

In this telling of the story, Rob's opponent, Archibald Cunningham (played by a fabulously camp Tim Roth), initially appears as a painted fop and is denigrated by other Scots as an effete Englishman and 'a buggerer of boys'. (This crude equation of Englishness with effeminacy is deployed more offensively in *Braveheart*, which appears not only to record homophobia but enact it in its treatment of Prince Edward.) Neither designation is proved correct. Archie is a seducer of women, a tactical rapist and a ruthless and talented fighter. He is also, through the disavowed paternity of Montrose, at least half-Scottish. Much of the film's initial use of *mise-en-scène* deals in the oppositions that are the stock-in-trade of McArthur's 'discursive unconscious'; Scotland's untutored wilderness is set against (English) civilisation. The figure of Archie, however, confounds these essentialised oppositions. Archie's nationality, his sexuality, his class and his identity are in dispute and in disguise. When Archie strips off his clothes and his powdered wig to reveal the skinhead below, he displays his identity to be little more than costume, a series of masquerades. As Rob apparently abandons honour and embraces trickery to defeat Archie in their final battle, the question of the paternity of Mary's baby remains unresolved – not simply whose child, but what sort of inheritance will a changing Scotland require?

WOUNDED MASCULINITIES

If historical heroes have dominated imaginary conceptions of Scottishness in recent decades, they have been shadowed by men in crisis, driven by an obsessive search for assured identity. The 'crisis in masculinity' (Beynon 2002) has, within Britain, been seen as a 1980s phenomenon, emanating from a collapsing industrial base, a populist distillation of feminist ideals, and a growth in women's non-domestic identities. In the Scottish context, male angst, male dislocation, unstable masculine identities incapable of emerging into maturity have acted as rich metaphors for the dilemma of the stateless nation, haunted by anxieties about identity and a secure 'place' in the world. Within this trajectory, the feminine has been portrayed both as a source of functional service provision ('Maws are great machines' proclaims Dancer in Peter McDougall's television drama *Just a Boy's Game*) and as the absent stabilising force that would enable maturation. It is not accidental that atrophied forms of masculinity (the perpetual 'boy', incapable of reaching manhood, the cyclical reproduction of violence in the 'hard city') co-exist with the marginalisation or absence of women (Scullion 1995).

In many 1990s fictions (such as *Trainspotting* or the television drama *Looking After Jo Jo*), drink and drugs provide the sole means of alleviating the enveloping misery of the post-industrial landscape, enabling momentary escape into psychic spaces that merely intensify masculine isolation. Other texts from that decade and beyond (Peter Mullan's *Orphans*, the BBC comedy series *Still Game*), by drawing attention to the masquerade implicit in performances of Scottish masculinities, open up different possibilities for renegotiating stagnant discourses. The sterility of cultural constraints that have insisted on particularly caricatured polarities of 'masculinity' and 'femininity' are also, we argue, adumbrated in the unlikely terrain of Bill Douglas's *Trilogy*, with its poetic evocation of a masculine subjectivity, capable, however temporarily, of eluding its repressive environment.

The traditional 'hard man' appears both as a victim of a hostile and dehumanising world, and as an active perpetuator of violent misogyny. In attributing 'cause', the absent mother and the ineffective father (the former failing in nurturing, the latter in achievement and positive role-modelling) act as tropes of historical inadequacies that set limits on present agency. Peter McDougall cites the frequent assumption that the 'hard man's' pathology resulted from his positioning in a matriarchy, where the 'wee woman' with the rolling pin (immortalised in comedy from *The Broons* to *Rab C Nesbitt*) was capable of terrorising grown men (in interview on Channel 4's *The Media Show*, 13 May 1990). This mythology owes as much to class as to gendered presuppositions (as *Andy Capp*, for example, testifies), reversing locations of

power in order to legitimise aggression.[2] If the matriarch appears as one manifestation of warped attributions of blame, the 'absent mother' forms another.
In a culture that, as we have seen, attributes both national spirit and the capacity to heal to femininity, the malfunctioning of the maternal is especially
pernicious.

In Bill Douglas's *Trilogy* (1972–8), the absent mother plays a key role in the
evolving consciousness of the central character. Jamie's single visit to his
mother in the asylum in *My Childhood* (1972) accentuates the acerbity of the
withdrawal of feminine care through condensed visual signifiers: the nurse
who steals the boy's apple prefigures the paternal grandmother who lays a
mousetrap to forbid access to the forbidden fruit in *My Ain Folk* (1973). Jamie's
mother gestures her withdrawal from both her son and her own sobbing
mother by pulling the bedclothes over her head, underlining the inarticulacy
of any capacity for care within the family circle.

The community within the *Trilogy* is governed by a vigilant policing of
female desire (women who give way to it end up dead, in the asylum or, in the
grandmother's words, 'hoors') but its surveillance does not extend to care for
bastard children, carriers of a shame so intense it cannot be spoken about. This
sense of wider context means that Douglas avoids centring blame for incapac-
ities in female nurturing on the women themselves (McMillan 1993: 221–5).
Instead, his vision of a scarred landscape and corrosive attitudes to sexuality
(especially female sexuality) suggests forces that intrude into the deepest
recesses of everyone's psychic spaces (male and female).

Jamie can escape from this space devoid of feminine comfort only through
his fleeting relationships with other men (McMillan 1993: 225–6). Although
absent fathers in the *Trilogy* shoulder some of the blame for child misery, they
can be at least partially substituted; the absent mother cannot. An early wistful
shot from Jamie's point of view of fathers picking up and embracing their children as they make their way home from the pit is compensated for in later
scenes of his (rare) joyful interaction with the German prisoner-of-war,
Helmut. The centring of their pleasure on reading and on the flying of a kite
situates both as what novelist Jessie Kesson evocatively calls 'ootlins' – living *in*
a place but not *of* it.[3] It takes a journey out of Scotland to Egypt, and an
encounter with the cultured Robert, to enable Jamie to move beyond his atrophied childhood. The barren landscape of Newcraighall, the mining community featured in the *Trilogy*, and its de-humanising of men, captured in their
herd-like movements and the descent into the dark that Douglas visualises so
acutely, ensure that hints of masculine nurturing, evinced in rare and fleeting
moments, cannot be permitted any development in this Scottish context.

Where Douglas's work suggests nuanced interactions between men's stunted
growth and the curtailment of female desire, the more routine construction of

Scottish 'hard men' involves a fetishising of masculine angst that eclipses any notion of a complex, troubled or resistive feminine consciousness. Marginalised as service-providers or as harridans, articulating rage against a masculine world that ignores them, women are viewed almost entirely through arrested masculine eyes. As Peter McDougall's *Just a Boy's Game* (BBC1, 8 November 1979) emphasises, machismo is a recyclable commodity: from grandfather to grandson, repetition replaces development (Mathieson 1987/8). In caricaturing Jake McQuillan and his gang as 'just boys', McDougall can suggest something insidiously appealing about their game-playing. Anticipating techniques adopted by 1990s 'lads' mags', Peter McDougall excuses machismo behaviour through witty banter and racy action sequences. Jake's absent mother provides a shadowy excuse for his magnetic attraction to the only kind of life that ensures status in a landscape dominated by the vestiges of decaying shipyards and blighted council housing estates. 'Real men' in this world may be expected to shoulder family responsibilities, but it is their incapacity to fulfil this role that is stressed.

The recycling of machismo reappears in the four-part drama *Looking After Jo Jo* (screened on BBC2 in January 1998, scripted by Frank Deasy and directed by John Mackenzie). Jo Jo McCann (Robert Carlyle), in an effort to become the key player in his community's petty-gangster culture, remains enclosed within the dynamics that ruined his childhood (the killing of his alcoholic father when he was a child left him in the care of an absent and ineffective mother). When his ambition fails, thanks to his envelopment in drug-taking as well as trafficking, the line of male continuity in gangster lifestyle is further underlined as his nephew takes his uncle's place as the local 'big man'.

In this respect *Looking After Jo Jo* replays a trajectory familiar from McDougall's work, but it moves beyond it by constructing a parallel feminine fantasy. Men are shown as confined within the peripheral Edinburgh housing scheme they have grown up in (their faces, as Jo Jo comments, would not 'fit' anywhere else). Feminine transformations of costume and make-up may enable women to pursue their fantasies elsewhere. Jo Jo's girlfriend, Lorraine, cultivates the appearance of Marilyn Monroe to pursue a career as a look-alike in London. While other women characters are stuck with the job of supporting fractured families, Lorraine's desires propel her out of the derelict environment and indeed into a different time-frame, that of the postmodern world of celebrity consumer culture, with its confusing simulacra and decentred identities. Lorraine appears at least partly conscious of the distance between the material space she inhabits and the psychic space she desires, while Jo Jo's performance of machismo masquerades as the 'real thing', refusing to acknowledge change and silting past and present in a cycle of violence and despair.

Peter Mullan's *Orphans* (1997) offers a far more interrogative approach to the exploration of masculine identities. The orphans of this film are not children but supposedly grown adults, yet each suffers from arrested development. Within this context, Mullan's decision to visualise immediately the physical disablement of the one female sibling appears less uncomfortably reminiscent of conventional delimiting of 'the feminine', and more an index of the film's evolving paradox: Sheila is shown to be best able to cope with her mother's death, and least in need of a cure. It is her brothers who require to undergo rehabilitation from their psychic paralysis. Sheila's cerebral palsy also inhibits any expectation that she will become the replacement mother. Instead, the 'feminine' role of carer is adopted by the oldest son, Thomas, who insists 'we're still a family, even after death'. His failed attempts to lock the family in the past are repeated when he refuses to allow his sister to leave the church where he stands vigil over his mother's coffin. Enraged by his consecration of dead femininity over her needs, Sheila charges towards him in her wheelchair, shattering the altar statue of the Virgin Mary. In a powerfully comic and symbolic moment, the living woman makes her own way out of the church, leaving her brother to his painstaking but doomed restoration of the ruined icon of the idealised mother.

The character of Michael offers a particularly sustained figurative treatment of post-industrial masculinity (Murray 2001). Hurt in a pub brawl, he spends most of the film leaking blood and attempting, unsuccessfully, to mask his wound. In a heavily symbolic narrative device, Michael determines to disguise his damaged body long enough to claim an industrial injury, receive the compensation he believes he is entitled to, and repair relations with his estranged wife and children. In an image of outrageous symbolic overload against the frozen cranes and rusting machinery of a near-derelict shipyard, he eventually falls, both crucified and baptised, into the Clyde. In a narrative that condenses violence, performative masculinity, family breakdown and industrial labour, the cry 'I want compensation' carries layers of meaning. As it transmutes into the emotionally explosive 'I want my mammy', it raises the possibility that pain, and the acknowledgement of need, might break through the masquerade. The contrast between this solution to the 'hard man's' future in the post-industrial age and Vincent Diver's implosive self-immolation in John Byrne's *Tutti Frutti* (BBC1 1987) (Sillars 1999: 250) is sharply delineated.

Thomas's increasingly grotesque clinging to established rites leaves him to struggle alone under the weight of the past (and his mother's coffin). Michael and his brother John's dishevelled appearance at the funeral, held in a rubble-filled and roofless church, reveals them as marked but not destroyed by the processes of change that have laid waste the structural institutions of religion and industrial labour.

EMERGENT IDENTITIES: RECONFIGURING LANDSCAPE ECONOMIES

As *Orphans* indicates, the representation of gender in an urban context can draw from readily visualisable metaphors of post-industrial change. In imaginings of small-town or rural Scotland, historical stasis and the shadow of the 'eternal feminine' are more robust. Yet, as screen texts from *Local Hero* to BBC Scotland's 1996 drama *A Mug's Game* (scripted by Donna Franceschild) have indicated, the movements of global capital impact powerfully on 'peripheral' communities, rupturing relationships and traditional gendered roles. Capitalism, in *A Mug's Game*, also reveals its ugly capacity to exploit the guise of protestant ethics when the asset-stripping McCaffrey cites Biblical verses in self-defence against the vain attempts of the central character, Kathy, to persuade him to save local jobs at the fish-processing plant. Residual fishing, in this threatened community, carries none of the romantic associations of the picturesque. The fish are mass-produced, cheap female labour turns them into saleable produce, the workforce are housed in council estates not cottages, and the only attempt to reinvent the past for tourist consumption, by turning a clapped-out fishing boat into a tourist vessel, ends in predictable disaster. By intertwining Biblical references, community disintegration and transnational movements of money, *A Mug's Game* revisits powerful players on the Scottish stage: religion, capitalism and exploitation in a global economy.

Movements of capital also carry in their wake movements of people. Three very different texts – Lars von Trier's *Breaking the Waves* (1996), Sana Bilgrami's *Across the Waters*, a small-budget documentary (screened on BBC2, 7 March 2005), and Lynne Ramsay's *Morvern Callar* (2002) – set issues of migration and belonging at the heart of Scottish landscapes more familiarly associated with unchanging traditionalism. In reworking notions of 'self' and 'other', 'inside' spaces and 'outside' places, present conjunctures and past memories, these texts, in their differing ways, open up possibilities for re-imagining 'community' and 'home'.

Lars von Trier's extraordinary *Breaking the Waves* is set in a remote Highland village, home to a community bound by an unforgiving religious doctrine. It marks a shift into transnationalism, in its production history and narrative content. Although determinedly traditional and indeed insular in its customs, the village finds itself penetrated by modernity – in this instance, the oil industry which brings incomers and with them their exciting and unsettling music. The film's glam-rock soundtrack locates it in the 1970s but is seen, by the elders at least, as an interloper from another place.

The narrative is driven by female sexual desire which is constructed as transgressive. Bess's marriage to outsider Jan initiates a series of disruptions to tradition and community, but also, in the film's provocative finale, to the very laws of nature and the limits of realist film-making. The presbyterian way of life in this film is shown as rigidly patriarchal: women are forbidden from speaking in church or from attending graveside committals. However, the film's narrative offers a deeper and more complex exploration of the ways that women can be not only victims but also agents of emotional and sexual repression. It is Bess's mother who insists that she, like generations of women before her, must control her grief at separation; and it is her mother, rather than her distant grandfather or wavering minister, who most implacably prosecutes Bess's exclusion from the community. The film is striking both for its unflinching exposure of the oppressive weight of the religious and cultural practice of repression (a topic seldom attempted in Scottish film outwith Bill Douglas's coruscating *Trilogy*, discussed above), but also for the ways it insists that repression is not simply imposed from the outside but something that comes to structure and misshape the interior life of individuals. It is Bess who speaks the words she hears from God, in the tones of her punishing mother.

Fearfulness about 'outsiders' is not, of course, unique to Scotland, but is nuanced in specific ways within the representational economy of the Highland landscape. Metaphors of rape speak to a penetration of religious exclusiveness: physical place becomes sacrosanct space, and the body of the woman the symbolic site of desecration. In the imaginary of a Scotland embedded in past traditions, the Outer Hebrides have conventionally occupied the farthest outpost from modernity. It was thus a brave decision, on Bilgrami's part, to situate her exploration of migrancy, identity, community and memory on the island of Lewis, and to focus on women, and women's bodies (not now as symbols, but as interacting with the landscape and reflecting on origins and transitions). *Across the Waters* traces the connections and discontinuities between the imminent departure to the mainland of a young Lewis woman of Pakistani descent and her grandmother's journey to Scotland from Pakistan fifty years earlier. By interweaving the reflections of three generations of women within this family with the reminiscences of a Gaelic-speaking native islander, 'othering' of the family of Pakistani origin is avoided. Shared experiences emerge, whether of small-scale agriculture, or the exchange of Gaelic lessons in return for favourable terms from the Pakistani door-to-door salesmen in the 1950s. At the same time, romanticism is avoided. The impact of 9/11 on the Muslim women, and the potential fracturing of community along religious divides are recognised. Gaelic psalm singing, introduced diegetically across shots of women in a presbyterian church, segues into the scene of a social gathering, inclusive of the Pakistani grandmother, but potentially disrupted by the continuation, now extra-diegetically, of the symbolically exclusive music.

Despite the familiar sea- and skyscapes associated with tourist discourses of Hebridean islands, it is the landscape's paradoxical signalling of permanence and impermanence, and its interactions with migrant livelihoods that are emphasised in Bilgrami's documentary. Its subtle modulations of space and time cut across any clichéd narrative of 'escape' from a 'repressive community'. The young woman embarking on her journey has the regretful blessing of the older women, and her own lyrical evocation of the island's beauty and her reluctance to leave makes this a necessary, not rebellious, transition. Migrancy and journeying are presented here as part of the inevitable ebb and flow of contemporary living.

In *Morvern Callar*, Bilgrami's lyricism is replaced by a harsher vision of relations between migrancy and identity in a postmodern world. Much of this film is a wordless exploration of the relation between individual and place, the inside of subjectivity and the beingness of out there. Tension between the rooted and placelessness is signalled in the first words in the film – half of an exchange between Morvern and a stranger on the station phone. Morvern spells out her name, that of a specific West Highland place, then explains her flattened, anonymous accent 'I'm not from round here'. One of this film's fascinations is the way it offers up new conceptions of gender and identity which are nonetheless located in a highly specific place. The Scottish port, where Morvern's story opens, is not a tourist destination, but a lived landscape of council houses, rowdy pubs and McJobs in featureless supermarkets. As Lanna and Morvern giggle and pee by the road on the long walk home from the lochside rave, the film achieves a de-romanticisation of wilderness and a cheeky undercutting of the imagined union of nature and femininity (this mimics a scene in Jane Campion's *The Piano* (1993), where the women shield one another with crinolines, again suggesting that adventure is not impossible for women but may be complicated by conventions of feminine propriety). Morvern takes to the mountains, not to commune with nature, but to bury her boyfriend's dismembered corpse.

The over-determined meanings of the Scottish landscape are remade through the soundtrack that accompanies Morvern's hike, filling her head and speaking to the audience of different kinds of spaces and meanings. As with Bess's transistor under the bedclothes in *Breaking the Waves*, Morvern's ever-present earphones connect music with feminine interiority. Morvern's internal soundtrack transforms the space she inhabits – a transformation rendered through shifts in aesthetics, lighting and colour (*Breaking the Waves'* digitally manipulated and hyper-real chapter settings can be seen as representing Bess's vision of the world). Morvern glides through the overlit supermarket, as if floating on the unworldly drone of Lee Hazlewood's 'Some Velvet Morning'.

The film offers a tentative and always provisional remapping of traditional power dynamics. The death of the male author is not symbolic here but a plot motor of the film. Morvern's adoption of what he leaves behind (the novel, his bank card, lighter and mix-tape) grants her a new kind of autonomy and mobility. She journeys, not to the metropolis, but to another edge of Europe, Ibiza (ironically, the London publishers who want her novel have to travel there too). With its celebration of music, partying and drug culture, the island has become a destination and a state of mind (as countless Ibiza-mix CDs attest). Here again the film holds in balance the pleasures of hedonism with the darker side of drugs come-down, commodified sex and joyless 18–30 fun. Following her boyfriend's suicide, Morvern is a free-floating figure, a nomad able to redefine her identity and her place in the world, but also haunted, as the personification of the postmodern migrant, by anomie.[4]

EMERGENT IDENTITIES: RECONFIGURING THE CITY

The texts considered in the previous section reconfigure the kailyard, traditionally imagined as a bounded and parochial space, by drawing attention to the porousness of both place and identity in the new globalised economy. Similar reworkings of the 'masculine' space of the post-industrial city are currently in progress in both television and film representations.

Annie Griffin's Channel 4 series *The Book Group* (2001) attends to the complexity and ambivalence that attaches to processes of change in the post-industrial city, and their consequences for the performance of gender. This sitcom centres on the attempt of a migrant American, Claire, to build her own community in Glasgow by setting up a reading group. The notion of Claire as cultural shopper, keen to consume and even assume the native culture of her new home, is flagged through the use of costume and *mise-en-scène*: she is clad in Fair Isle knitwear; books and Timorous Beasties wallpaper fill her West End flat. However, her desire to be a *metteur en scene* is derailed when she unearths not a group of like-minded 'artists and writers' but an array of entrenched stereotypes of Scottishness, as her flat is invaded by footballers' wives and a shell-suited ned. Claire's Glaswegian guests, native and adopted, use football as a lingua franca, and resist her attempts to impose her own meanings on them.

While the transnationalism of the characters may speak of a renovated Glasgow of cosmopolitanism and cultural exchange, the faltering progress of Claire's project suggests that any embrace of this new brand identity may be premature. The way football is elbowed centre-stage in the book group reveals that, despite a shift from manufacturing to leisure and consumption, residual passions and gender identities still dominate. The programme does introduce some sly undermining of football's cultural hegemony and unreconstructed gender politics, showing Dirka furiously masturbating next to a footballer husband saving his energy for practice; and, in Rab and Jackie's affair, queering two icons of Scottish masculinity – the international footballing legend and the ned – whilst exposing the disavowed homosocial relations between fandom and fantasy. The footballers, as part of a traditional masculine economy of power, money and pleasure, have the right to live out their fantasies. Other characters must struggle to imagine and invent their own identities and spaces. However, as with many other cultural critiques, the programme proves unable to determine whether this ironic framing of identity reconstructs or simply reinforces existing power relations (Murray 2005).

Shifting power relations and the representation of gender and sexuality lie at the heart of the very different Glasgow that features in Andrea Arnold's *Red Road* (2006). This film, a Danish/Scottish co-production, tells the story of Jackie, a CCTV operator in Glasgow, who spots on screen Clyde, a character from her past, and is drawn into what, for the viewer at least, appears to be a series of puzzling and potentially dangerous entanglements. This film situates its representations of masculine and feminine relations in a very particular social, historical and economic space: the de-industrialised and impoverished late modern city. *Red Road* is about individuals and a city haunted by the past as they eke out existence in a hollowed-out present.

Clyde's name evokes the lost space of labour underlying contemporary marginalised working-class masculinity. Clyde is unemployed and lives in poverty; his flat is furnished with salvage from skips; his clothes remain unchanged throughout the film. When Jackie attempts to make Clyde reveal himself, she tells him 'You live on the edge'. Toying with notions of transgression and excitement, this is also a flat statement of his peripherality and social exclusion. The Red Road flats, initially a utopian experiment in high modernism seen as an escape from the slums below, are now known as a place where the abandoned, the lost and the dispossessed wash up. The shocking locations around the flats look almost post-apocalyptic and, along with the prevalence of CCTV cameras (now accepted as a way of life in Britain), led many European viewers to interpret the film as science fiction. As well as offering an urgent call for social change, these spaces serve as a fierce corrective to lazy notions of the spread of postmodernity. There is not a Starbucks to be seen here. As Jackie stalks Clyde across windswept and empty plazas, the sense of the urban uncanny (Vidler 1992) is enhanced by a rare use of non-diegetic sound. Dissonant clanks and wheezes evoke nails being hammered, trains shunting, machines clanging – the ghost sounds of vanished industries.

It is this mix of naturalist and expressionist techniques in soundtrack and in *mise-en-scène* that enables the film to extend its reach beyond the individual to operate on a more symbolic level. Whilst the film's surface may speak of an everyday realism, with its bleak inner-city scenes, limited and opaque use of dialogue and non-diegetic music, and repeated use of the flat affectlessness of the CCTV screen, this masks a highly expressionist element. The title of the

film points to this mix of modes. Red Road is a real place, but also signifies
Jackie's journey into danger, often explicitly coded as sexual danger.

Clyde's redness, his red hair and colouring, is repeatedly shown and
described as what is other, unknown but also dangerously seductive about
him. He is figured onscreen as animalistic and linked with the foxes that
roam the wasteland around the flats. He is a scavenger, dragging furniture out
of skips and lumps of wood back to his lair. As he laps at his plate in the café
(prefiguring the later scene of cunnilingus) the waitress with a mix of desire
and disgust tells him 'You're a fucking animal'. Stevie too comments
on Clyde's ambivalent appeal: 'He's charmin – for a ginger cunt'. The
camouflage of sexual predator gives way to a shifting dynamic of power and
vulnerability.

The Clyde that Jackie sees is coded as diabolic (like the medieval fox): at the
party he glows redly, is wreathed in smoke, his eyes black and closed off,
opposed to the lighting scheme where close-ups show Jackie's eyes as clear,
lucid and receiving. Part of the unease created by the film is generated by the
readiness with which we ascribe victimhood to female and brutality to male
characters. These cultural framings, alongside the ways this film (radically, and
not just for Scottish cinema) is focalised through Jackie's perspective, lead to a
viewing experience of misdirection and misreading. Jackie may be in charge
of the machinery of vision, but there is no simplistic reversal of power relations here. *Red Road* rejects the crude equation of looking with control,
making us recognise the partial and compromised nature of all single visions,
whether masculine or feminine.

Jackie is trapped in a past and a moment of trauma which she cannot let go.
While Clyde may be out of jail, the city remains a prison for him and, in
different ways, for Jackie. She is dressed in a drab warder's uniform and works
in a panopticon-like structure of surveillance. The repressive social control of
the CCTV machinery is mirrored in Jackie's withholding self-control, betrayed
only by her twitching mouth and tapping fingers. In tamping down the past,
Jackie cannot gain access to the parts of her history which might nourish and
sustain her. While her parents-in-law live in a home filled with photographs,
Jackie's mementoes are shut up in a box under the stairs. As her quest devel-
ops, she is forced to let go of her control – of her body in orgasm, her temper
in rage, and of her plans. Jackie's journey takes her not towards the revenge she
hoped for, with its continuation of the cycle of violence and abuse, but towards
a forgiveness that leaves her emotionally raw and exposed. The condition of
living in the present is not forgetting the past, but reaching some kind of
accommodation with it. In letting go of some of the things she thought defined
her, Jackie is able to let in the potentially dangerous and different, she is finally
able to change.

CONCLUSION

Traditional representations of Scotland oscillate between romanticised visions of an idealised masculinity and femininity and a darker realm, stalked by repression, religion and trauma. We have identified emergent representations, showing attempts to break free from the sclerotic grip of discourses locked in the past. New forms of Scottish identities are in the process of being imagined 'at the unstable point where the "unspeakable" stories of subjectivity meet the narratives of history' (Hall 1987: 44). However, change (at a structural and an individual level) is not a painless process. Those narratives of 'emergent identities' we have discussed all acknowledge ambivalence, and the provisional nature of their gestures to the future.

Both the narratives and the production contexts of *Breaking the Waves*, *Across the Water*, *Morvern Callar*, *The Book Group* and *Red Road* signal a Scotland of diverse identities opening up to the outside, but informed by a distinctive sense of place and cultural history. They show a receptiveness to the possibility of change and also some ways in which developing femininities and masculinities might attempt a fresh accommodation with the past. Just as Morvern Callar has to leap over the dead body that fills her living room, so Scottish cultural representations are discovering a range of sidesteps and tactical jinks to work around (if not always through) the problems of identity and history.

NOTES

1. We are grateful to Jan Law for illuminating this concept.
2. Parallels exist in other cultures (bell hooks, for example, notes the blame attached to black 'matriarchy' (hooks 1992: 99)).
3. Kesson comments that, despite spending much time in Skene, she could never, as an 'outsider', be described as '*of* Skene' (Murray 2000: 83).
4. The combination of sensual immediacy and detachment in the portrayal of the central character in Alan Warner's novel *Morvern Callar* (on which Ramsay's film is based) has been compared to Camus' *L'Etranger* by Petrie (2004: 98) and Watson (2007: 272).

REFERENCES

Beynon, J. (2002), *Masculinities and Culture*, Buckingham: Open University Press.
Craig, C. (1996), *Out of History: Narrative Paradigms in Scottish and English Culture*, Edinburgh: Polygon.
Hall, S. (1987), 'Minimal selves', in ICA Documents 6, *Identity, The Real Me: Postmodernism and the Question of Identity*, London: ICA, pp. 44–6.
Harvey, D. (1990), *The Condition of Postmodernity*, Oxford: Blackwell.

hooks, b. (1992), 'Reconstructing black masculinity', in *Black Looks: Race and Representation*, Boston, MA: South End Press, pp. 87–113.

Law, A. and J. Law. (2002), 'Magical urbanism: Walter Benjamin and Utopian realism in the film *Ratcatcher*', *Historical Materialism*, 10: 4, pp. 173–211.

Martin-Jones, D. (2005), 'Sexual healing: representations of the English in post-devolutionary Scotland', *Screen*, 46: 2, pp. 227–33.

Massey, D. (1994), *Space, Place and Gender*, Cambridge: Polity Press.

Mathieson, K. (1987/8), 'Peter McDougall: an endless boy's game', *Cencrastus*, 28, pp. 1–4.

McArthur, C. (ed.) (1982), *Scotch Reels: Scotland in Cinema and Television*, London: BFI.

McArthur, C. (1996), 'The Scottish discursive unconscious', in A. Cameron and A. Scullion (eds), *Scottish Popular Theatre and Entertainment: Historical and Critical Approaches to Theatre and Film in Scotland*, Glasgow: Glasgow University Library, pp. 81–9.

McArthur, C. (2003), *Brigadoon, Braveheart and the Scots: Distortions of Scotland in Hollywood Cinema*, London: I. B. Tauris.

McMillan, J. (1993), 'Women in the Bill Douglas Trilogy', in E. Dick, A. Noble and D. Petrie (eds), *Bill Douglas: A Lanternist's Account*, London: BFI/SFC, pp. 219–26.

Murray, I. (2000), *Jessie Kesson: Writing Her Life*, Edinburgh: Canongate.

Murray, J. (2001), 'Contemporary Scottish film', *Irish Review*, 28:1, pp. 75–88.

Murray, J. (2005), 'Straw or wicker? Traditions of Scottish film criticism and *The Wicker Man*', in B. Franks, S. Harper, J. Murray, and L. Stevenson (eds), *Constructing 'The Wicker Man': Film and Cultural Perspectives*, Dumfries: Crichton University Press, pp. 11–36.

Petrie, D. (2000), *Screening Scotland*, London: BFI.

Petrie, D. (2004), *Contemporary Scottish Fictions: Film, Television and the Novel*, Edinburgh: Edinburgh University Press.

Raban, J. (1974), *Soft City*, London: Hamish Hamilton.

Scullion, A. (1995), 'Feminine pleasures and masculine indignities: gender and community in Scottish drama', in C. Whyte (ed.), *Gendering the Nation: Studies in Modern Scottish Literature*, Edinburgh: Edinburgh University Press, pp. 169–204.

Sillars, J. (1999), 'Drama, devolution and dominant representations', in J. Stokes and A. Reading (eds), *The Media in Britain*, Basingstoke: Palgrave Macmillan, pp. 246–54.

Soja, E. (1989), *Postmodern Geographies: The Reassertion of Space in Critical Social Theory*, London: Verso.

Vidler, A. (1992), *The Architectural Uncanny: Essays in the Modern Unhomely*, Cambridge, MA: MIT Press.

Watson, R. (2007), *The Literature of Scotland: The Twentieth Century*, 2nd edn, Basingstoke: Palgrave Macmillan.

13

Race and Ethnicity in the Media

ANTHEA IRWIN

INTRODUCTION

The bulk of this chapter will analyse in detail two examples of recent press coverage: one of asylum and in particular unrest in detention, and the other the voluntary flight/abduction of Misbah Rana from Scotland to Pakistan. The two case studies are interesting in and of themselves, but they also throw up more general questions.

Before embarking on the case studies, the chapter starts with some general thoughts on other aspects of the topic. The definition of race and ethnicity is complex, and certainly no less so in the Scottish context than elsewhere. Although the two words are often used interchangeably, it is generally agreed that while race is a biological, physiological attribute, ethnicity is broader and takes in other aspects of identity such as shared language or shared religion. Key to this difference is the fact that ethnicity takes in one's own experience or identity, that is, we could say that while race is an objective phenomenon, ethnicity is to some extent a subjective one. This renders yet more problematic the fact that so much of what is written in the press and elsewhere about people who are members of ethnic-minority communities is written from an apparently objective stance by members of majority communities.

Ethnicity has in recent years become the more common term, which shows a certain awareness of the complexities of groups' identities. That said, Sarah Isal points out that, while discrimination in the 1960s to the 1980s tended to be based on skin colour, in latter decades it has also been based on other factors such as cultural practices and religious beliefs. So awareness of such factors has not been wholly positive; one product of it has been a move from racism to 'racisms' (Runnymede Trust 2000, cited in European Network Against Racism 2002: 8).

In relation to this, it is important to remember that applying the label 'ethnic' to people and artefacts from ethnic minority communities is a misnomer. As with so many other aspects of identity, those that are less dominant become 'othered' and, via this process, they also become a 'marked' category. It is the case, however, that every individual is 'ethnic', that white British and white Scottish are ethnicities as much as any other. Indeed, a fuller discussion of ethnicity in the Scottish media would be lacking if it did not consider the various 'white' ethnicities that are present in Scotland, for example the Irish and English communities, and the extent to which these, historically and currently, could be considered to be dominant or minority groupings (in the symbolic as well as the numerical sense).

RECENT WORK ON RACE AND ETHNICITY IN THE UK MEDIA

Rosa Tsagarousianou has recently argued that it is more useful to think of ethnicity in the media in terms not of portrayals of individual ethnic groups, but as 'construction of difference' which works 'along the lines of a majority/minority divide, establishing a binary and not uncommonly antagonistic relationship' (Westminster Media Forum 2007: 9). There are echoes here of Edward Said's (1979) theory of 'Orientalism' which explores how the West has constructed an identity for the 'orient' that has more to do with constructing a dominant identity for the West itself. Tsagarousianou also suggests that we should not only analyse representations but also absences of representation, a point also raised by Norman Fairclough (1995) about more general analysis of the media.

Rachel Morris, in an essay about gypsies, travellers and the media, warns that it is not simply a case of providing more 'positive' representations: these may be constructed by dominant groups and may not necessarily equate with the representations the group in question would choose, so what is needed is a range of representations and input from that group (Morris 2000: 217–18). In a similar vein, Karina Horsti (2007: 29) explores the fact that 'unexpectedly, marginalisation and recognition can co-exist. The minorities can be recognised and marginalised at the same time'. She is referring to the fact that, whilst multicultural media initiatives are to be welcomed, multicultural newspaper pages and series of stories are generally backgrounded in relation to more traditional material.

Writing about mainstream media content, Sarah Neal provides an interesting illustration of a 'changing same' (Gilroy 1993, cited in Neal 2003: 71) in relation to media discourses around the Brixton Inquiry and the Scarman

Report in 1982, and the Lawrence Inquiry and the Macpherson Report in 1999. Neal observes that the focus in 1999 was on social justice while in 1982 it had been on avoiding further unrest. However, this social justice element was for the most part specific to the Lawrence family, and in a wider sense more normative discourses, for example the critique of political correctness, prevailed. Poynting and Mason (2007) make a similar point in a paper warning against simplistic analyses that postulate a dramatic rise in Islamophobia post 9/11, viewing this instead in a context of existing tendencies in what they term 'everyday racism'. The transformation of the 'other' from Asian or 'Pakistani' to 'Muslim' was, they claim, 'already under way since the Rushdie affair in 1989, and arguably since the Iranian Revolution in 1979' (Poynting and Mason 2007: 81).

ASYLUM AND THE MEDIA IN SCOTLAND: THE GENERAL PICTURE

The detention case study I shall explore formed part of a project undertaken with the Oxfam UK Poverty Programme (Oxfam 2006), which monitored three months' press coverage (mid-July to mid-October 2004) of asylum in a range of Scotland-based papers and Scottish editions of London-based papers, including tabloids and broadsheets, and papers with different editorial viewpoints.[1] In common with other reports (Oxfam 2001; Welsh Media Group 2002), this report found that press coverage that was Scotland-based was relatively more favourable to asylum seekers than that which was UK-based. Furthermore, the study suggested that coverage in Scotland had become more favourable than it was at the time of the previous studies.

This is illustrated by the main themes covered in the stories. There is an interesting trend when we differentiate according to whether the stories focus on Scotland or the UK more widely, which also illustrates a difference between Scottish-based and UK-based papers, given that the former include more stories about Scotland while the latter include more stories about the UK in general. In the former category, the order of emphasis is detention (close to 50 per cent), crime, policy; in the latter category, the pattern is policy, crime, detention. This suggests two things: firstly, Scottish-based reporting of asylum has a more 'human' face; secondly, the fact that the Dungavel detention centre has been a hotly debated issue in Scottish politics has fed through to news discourse, thus accounting partly for the continued increase in favourable coverage.

The political system in Scotland could also be seen to have had a bearing on the voices which were heard in the coverage. Whilst the vast majority of these were political ones, as other studies have found, there was some differentiation between stories with a Scottish focus and those with a UK focus. In the stories with a Scottish focus, individual members of the Scottish parliament (MSPs) had higher visibility than was evident for the UK as a whole, where the debate appeared to be dominated by central government spokespeople. A number of campaigning voices could be heard in stories that focused on Scotland, including the Children's Commissioner Kathleen Marshall, trades unions and groups such as Glasgow Campaign to Welcome Refugees. Such voices were largely absent in stories with a UK focus. The proportion of asylum-seeker and refugee voices in both categories of story was low, but this must be considered in the context of asylum seekers often feeling uncomfortable speaking to the media and being worried about the consequences of doing so (Article 19 2003).

All of that said, favourable coverage or even campaigning coverage is not the same thing as proactively positive coverage. Almost without exception, the stories dealt with the 'problem' of asylum, that is, asylum seekers or the asylum system depending on their stance. Stories that contextualised the reasons why people had sought asylum in the first place, or which explored aspects of asylum seekers' lives other than the fact that they were asylum seekers, were virtually non-existent. This lack of context is reminiscent of the three reports already mentioned. ICAR (2004) also raises lack of context in asylum reporting as having implications for readers' understanding. This, of course, is in keeping with the general 'news values' of any newsroom, which tend to favour simplicity and negativity, but it is worth pointing out nonetheless.

DISCOURSE ANALYSIS

The analysis which follows identifies press coverage as a site of struggle where competing discourses vie for dominance and a simplistic distinction between positive and negative portrayals is problematised. It is indebted to the work of Michel Foucault on ideology and power, and to a number of analyses of lexical representation and narrative structure. Fowler (1991) draws our attention to the implications of word choice for how a news actor is viewed, and the implications of transitivity – the verb processes employed – for where responsibility is seen to lie. Fairclough (1995) talks about 'degrees of presence', the fact that different aspects of an event can be foregrounded, backgrounded or presupposed. Van Dijk (1998), whose previous 1989 work is one of the seminal texts on how race and ethnicity are treated in the media, brings in a relational aspect when he observes a common relational pattern in news discourse that he labels the 'ideological square'. This consists of an 'us' group and a 'them' group with the 'good' and 'bad' acts of each being variously highlighted or mitigated. Bell (1991), who has been a working journalist, points out that news narratives, unlike most informal oral narratives, are not chronological, and that it is therefore possible for the order in which events have occurred, and by extension the cause-and-effect relationships between different events, to be 'lost'.

CASE STUDY I: UNREST IN DETENTION

The bare facts were that in the summer of 2004 when a detainee at the Harmondsworth detention centre outside London committed suicide, there was some violence at the centre; some detainees were moved to Dungavel detention centre in Lanarkshire; a few days later a detainee in Dungavel committed suicide; and some detainees were then moved from Dungavel. It is not possible to examine the coverage of these events in full here, so a sample of stories which illustrate key patterns has been discussed.[2] The focus will mostly be on headlines, key sample sentences and any related material that appears alongside the report in question. I have italicised some words to aid the reader in following the analysis.

Harmondsworth: contesting causes and contexts

The Glasgow *Evening Times* is the only paper in the sample to carry the story on Tuesday 20 July. The story appears at the top of page six. The headline reads: '*Riot* after asylum seeker's *death*'. This is the only headline that includes any reference to the suicide and thus suggests any kind of link between that and the violence occurring. The word 'death' rather than 'suicide' is used however. The paper may have taken the decision to use this label because the full facts of the case had not yet been released by the police. The chief inspector of prisons, Anne Owers, is quoted as saying that Harmondsworth detention centre was 'failing to provide a safe and stable environment' and that 'this was reflected in increasing levels of disorder, damage and escape attempts', the implication being that these problems could have caused the suicide.

The *Evening Times* continues the story on 21 July. It appears on page four in the 'Britain today' section with the headline '16 in asylum riot *quiz*', suggesting there were unanswered questions about the event and therefore not attributing blame. The lead sentence reads: 'Sixteen men are today being quizzed by police about *riots* that rocked a refugee centre'. Simple though it seems, to label the asylum seekers 'men' allows them more complex identities than they are afforded by the more regularly used label 'asylum seekers', the latter having a narrow focus on one aspect of identity. Although the word 'riots' is an emotive one and perhaps questionable in the circumstances, the syntactic construction 'riots that rocked a refugee centre' puts the abstract noun 'riot' in the position of agent rather than placing the asylum seekers there, and again does not attribute blame.

The Herald carries the story on Wednesday 21 July on the bottom half of page four. The headline reads: 'Arrests after violence at detention centre'. The first reference to the death/suicide is in the following sentence: 'The tornado unit, a squad of prison officers with a formidable reputation for swiftly bringing control back into the hands of the authorities, was *deployed* early yesterday to *quell* the disorder which broke out within hours of the death.' The military discourse is striking here with the use of the words 'deployed' and 'quell', reinforcing the stereotype of the asylum 'problem' as a two-sided 'battle'. The nuances of meaning in this sentence appear to be rather critical, however, and suggest heavy-handeness on the part of the tornado unit.

The *Scottish Daily Express* also carries the story on 21 July, on page three, taking up the full page. The headline reads: '£500,000 cost of riot at the asylum "*hotel*"'. The focus is on cost and the story is rather decontextualised in that most of it talks about the violence as a 'stand alone' issue rather than in relation to what preceded or followed it. The use of the word 'hotel' in the headline, later sourced to Mr Kehra, one of the centre's chaplains, arguably *re*contextualises the situation by suggesting the asylum seekers had no reason to 'riot' given their favourable conditions, which redoubles the negative connotations applied to the detainees.

War metaphors are present in the *Express* story as in *The Herald* story, but in the *Express* story the blame lies squarely with the asylum seekers: 'Riot *forces* fought a 16 hour *battle* to *quell an uprising* by asylum seekers yesterday at the UK's leading detention centre'. The 'us and them' differentiation is further reinforced by the following sentence: 'Rapid-response "Tornado unit" prison officers were called in to *corner* 80 rioting inmates . . .'. Using a word normally associated with the hunting of animals dehumanises the asylum seekers involved.

Dungavel: reproducing discourses and repositioning 'us and them'?

The Herald carries this story at the bottom of page one and continues it on page two. The headline reads: 'Death inquiry to *expose* Dungavel', implying that there are negative things about Dungavel that are not known to (and may even be being kept from) the public. An immediate link is made with events at Harmondsworth, from which the man who died was moved, and the death in placed in the context of other deaths, the figures suggesting a steep rise in deaths and suicide attempts.

The story states that Home Secretary David Blunkett believes conditions in Dungavel to be satisfactory and says, 'the announcement astonished Dungavel's many critics, but they may not have to wait long to *return fire*.' This is an interesting reworking of both the military metaphors and the 'us and them' pattern we have seen previously. The image is one of Dungavel's critics battling with David Blunkett (and by extension the Home Office/government as a whole) not over details but over the very existence of the detention system. Whether such discourse is reproduced consciously or not, there is evidence that the asylum situation as battle is both a dominant motif and a site of struggle.

The *Scottish Daily Mirror* also carries the story on 26 July, discussing it in its editorial on page six and placing a story about it on the top half of page twelve. The editorial, headlined 'Asylum shame', is of particular interest to the discussion in hand, notwithstanding the more emotive tone found in editorials. The piece states that prisoners should not be treated like cattle and goes on to say, in italicised type, '*it is even worse when we do this to people who have not committed any crimes at all*'. The italic type sets this out as the main point of the story, suggesting that this is the *Mirror*'s main critique of Dungavel, and the reference to cattle, consciously or otherwise, reproduces the animalistic metaphors we saw in the *Express*'s use of 'cornered' to very different effect. Writing '*we* do this to people . . .' sets up an 'us and them' pattern of all non-asylum seekers versus asylum seekers. The *Mirror* itself and presumably most of its readers are not people who are either involved in the detention process or advocate it, so this use of 'we' suggests that people should take responsibility even if they are not involved themselves, that is, they should campaign against Dungavel.

CASE STUDY 2: MISBAH RANA

The flight of a young girl from Scotland to Pakistan in the summer of 2006 and the ensuing custody battle threw into question the Scottish media's approach to race and ethnicity. This story ran on and off in the Scottish press for five months, culminating in reports of Misbah (I will refer to her by this name as this is the name by which she has said she wishes to be known) remaining with her father in Pakistan after an out-of-court settlement. The case study will analyse the first week of reporting as it is in some ways a microcosm of the coverage as a whole. It illustrates in two ways that imbalance or prejudice do not have to be conscious to be problematic. Firstly, the information that came to light from day three onwards caused journalists and audiences to reassess how they had 'read' the situation and as such provides a good argument for the existence of dominant discourses, and different ones in different societies. Secondly, within a week of the beginning of the coverage, parts of the press had embarked on a kind of 'metareporting' about *how* the case had been reported and whether/how this was problematic, and as such is an example of that which was backgrounded being forcibly foregrounded (see Fairclough) in order to make sense of it. Again a comprehensive analysis of the full coverage is not possible, so I have chosen to focus on Scotland-based papers due to the relative prominence of the story and the fact that the interplay between Scottish national identity and other aspects of the story is one of the most striking elements of the analysis.

Day one: identities

The first time the story appears in the Scottish press is on 28 August on the front page of the *Evening Times* with the headline 'Girl, 12 *"stolen"* from *Scots home*; world wide hunt amid fears youngster was kidnapped and flown out to Pakistan'. Although the word 'stolen' is placed in quotation marks, we are never told who the source of this description was, thus allowing it to 'stand alone' and potentially have greater implications for how the reader engages with the story. Although having a Scots home is not synonymous with being Scots, that national identity is certainly implied and is placed front and centre by appearing in the headline. We find out over the course of the coverage that Misbah has dual citizenship of the UK and Pakistan, and does not consider *herself* Scots. Her name, 'Molly Campbell', appears in the fourth sentence and in a highlighted box of text. It is not until the seventh sentence that we are told that she 'is also known as Misbah Iram Ahmed Rana'. This pattern of giving Misbah the name 'Molly Campbell' and including 'Misbah' later as an alternative occurs for several days across papers.

Day two: generalisations

The Scotsman carries the story on 29 August. Different stories appear in the first and third editions of the paper. The first edition story also uses a claim in the headline: 'Girl of 12 taken to Pakistan by father for arranged marriage, says family'. The claim is sourced in this story, but the 'family' is in fact one person, Misbah's maternal grandmother. We do read in the lead sentence that she was '*allegedly* abducted', but this pattern of portraying as a fact in the headline that which is alleged later in the report is repeated in many of the stories. The headline in the third edition is 'Hunt for girl, 12, taken from school and flown to Pakistan by father' and the arranged marriage claim does not appear in this story, suggesting that it may already be in doubt.

On 29 August the *Evening Times* and the *Daily Record* also use the grandmother's claim for headline material. The *Evening Times* headline reads '*Child bride fears* over "kidnap" girl'. Although 'kidnap' appears in quotation marks, 'child bride fears' does not and is arguably given more gravity than it deserves as the fears too are based on the opinion of one person. The *Daily Record's* headline is 'Girl of 12 *kidnapped to wed man, 25*; Exclusive: gran *tells* of Molly's abduction'. Both the abduction and the alleged plan for Molly to enter an arranged marriage appear in this headline, and in the first two sentences of the story, as fact. The use of the word 'tells' is also problematic as Molly's grandmother was not an eyewitness to her granddaughter leaving Lewis. In the sixth sentence we read that Molly's 'given name' is 'Misbah Iram Ahmed Rana', which arguably gives the Islamic name more status than it has had in other coverage.

The Herald runs with the story on the same day with the headline '*Abducted island girl* may now be in Pakistan; Pupil vanishes with sister'. The abduction is presented as fact and national identity is once again front and centre as she is referred to as an 'island girl'. Indeed, focusing on the fact that she lived on Lewis could be seen to reinforce the 'us and them' pattern: there is arguably more symbolic distance between Pakistan and a 'traditional' Scottish location such as Lewis than there is between Pakistan and Scotland in general. This description is surprising, given that the highlight box tells us 'they had moved to Lewis recently'. Having the adjective 'abducted' modify the description of Misbah presents it as fact. Both of these elements of description are somewhat contradictory to the fact that this is the first story to place Misbah's Islamic name in the same sentence as her Scottish one, albeit the Scottish name comes first and the status of the Islamic name is perhaps lower than it has been in other stories as we are told she was '*previously* known as Misbah Rana'.

The only paper not to have the possibility of abduction, emotive or otherwise, in its headline is the *Press and Journal*. The headline on 29 August reads 'Police hunt for missing girl leads to Pakistan'.

Day three: contradictions

The focus of the story shifts on 30 August. *The Scotsman* again runs a slightly different story in its first and third editions, with both headlines focusing on Misbah's mother Louise Campbell's plea for the return of her daughter. This is an interesting choice of focus for the headlines, given that it begins to become apparent on this day that Misbah may have travelled to Pakistan willingly, which is arguably more newsworthy. This suggestion comes both from friends of her father who speak to the media *and* from her mother's statement which includes the words, 'I would like to say to Molly that we miss her so much and we beg her to come home to us. She has to know that she is not in any trouble and we are not angry; we just want her home.' There is a nuanced shift away from the suggestion of abduction from the first-edition headline to the third-edition headline: they read '*Bring* my daughter home to me, begs mother' and 'We miss Molly so much, we just *want* her home'.

The *Evening Times* of 30 August contains two contradictory stories on the subject. The first, on page two, has the headline 'Mum in tearful plea over *abducted Molly*'. Once again we see the abduction presented as fact in the headline, by using the adjective 'abducted' to modify 'Molly', and a shift to saying it is 'alleged' in the lead sentence. The second story, on page six, has the headline 'Girl, 12, "begged" to be taken to Pakistan; Glasgow friend tells of pleas by youngster to dad'. It covers the claims of former Glasgow councillor Bashir Maan, a friend of Misbah's father Sajad Rana. It seems odd for the paper not to have conflated these two stories, or placed them on the same page. The practicalities and time constraints of producing a newspaper notwithstanding, these editorial choices do not shift the focus as far as the content itself would suggest it could have been.

The first time the possibility that this is not an abduction is explicitly stated in a headline is in *The Herald* on 31 August. It reads 'Pakistani father "did not abduct daughter"; New claims by friends over island girl's disappearance'. The story is based on Bashir Maan's claims and introduces for the first time the information that, after her parents' split, Misbah had lived with her father until 2002.

Days four and five: heroes and villains

On 31 August and 1 September a number of stories focus on Glasgow Central MP Mohammad Sarwar having agreed to meet with Misbah in Pakistan, but again the framing is rather different in different papers. The *Daily Record*'s headline is 'I'll *find* Molly; Exclusive: MP Sarwar *pledges to help* mum of girl, 12, *snatched* to Pakistan'. This headline has echoes of traditional narratives (Propp 1968), with Mr Sarwar portrayed as a hero figure being sent out on a quest by Louise Campbell to win Misbah back from the villain who has 'snatched' her. This is rather at odds with *The Scotsman's* coverage which once again includes different headlines in the first and third editions, 'MP hopes to *meet missing* schoolgirl in Pakistan today' and 'MP in Pakistan as an "*honest broker*" to *meet missing* girl'. The second of these shifts the tone to neutral as regards the conflict between Misbah's parents, as does the Aberdeen *Press and Journal's* 'MP flies to meet Molly as *row rages*'. Contrary to Mr Sarwar going on a quest to 'find' Misbah, we hear of a 'private meeting' having already been arranged. Sarwar also dismisses the arranged marriage claims, which leads to the headline in *The Herald*: 'Sarwar to meet "abducted" girl in Pakistan; Child bride claims rejected'.

Days six and seven: battles

The *Press and Journal's* use of 'row' foreshadows the next shift: on 2 and 3 September, a large proportion of what is written frames the situation in military discourse, as a 'battle'. Some examples of headlines are: 'Custody *war* as Molly begs to stay with dad; *Tug-of-love* girl, 12, insists she wants to stay in Pakistan' (*Evening Times*, 2 September, p. 6); 'It was my choice. I like it here and want to stay with my father'; 'Parents prepare for *international custody battle* over daughter' (*The Herald*, 2 September, p. 5); 'Molly wins *battle* to stay with dad; judge says girl remains in Pakistan till custody is decided' (*Sunday Mail*, 3 September, p. 2).

'Battle' is of course a common metaphor to use for custody situations, but the front-page coverage in the *Press and Journal* on 2 September extends the discourse in an interesting way. The lead sentence following the headline 'Call me Misbah – and I was not kidnapped' reads 'Schoolgirl Molly Campbell sat *shoulder-to-shoulder* with her father yesterday as she faced the world's media in Pakistan and insisted: I was not kidnapped'. 'Shoulder-to-shoulder' has immediate echoes of its high-profile use during the Iraq war and adds gravity to the situation.

CONCLUSIONS: EMPOWERING, DISTANCING, METAREPORTING AND HISTORICISING

It is apparent from the above that many of the news headlines on these two days following Misbah's press conference are presented as direct quotes from Misbah herself. In the headline of its story on page nine on 2 September, the *Daily Record* reinforces this by using upper case and referring to Misbah 'speaking out': 'MY REAL NAME IS MISBAH . . . I DON'T WANT TO GO HOME; SNATCH PROBE GIRL SPEAKS OUT'. There are two ways to view this trend: does it empower Misbah and give her the voice she has not had thus far? Or does it allow papers to avoid deciding on the wording for headlines that, at least for some of them, are in blatant contradiction to what they had been reporting just a few days earlier?

September 2 and 3, a Saturday and Sunday, see various opinion pieces alongside the latest news reports. The opinion pieces display a range of reporting strategies: distancing strategies similar to the use of Misbah's own words (for example, the *Sunday Mail*'s 'Opinion: Molly must have a say in her future'); discussions about the complexities of the story and Misbah's identity; and a strategy I have labelled 'metareporting', that is reporting which critiques how the press covered the story when it initially broke. It is interesting to view these opinion themes in relation to the previous and current coverage in the papers in which they appear.

On 2 September *The Scotsman*'s comment headline contradicts its news headline somewhat. On page four we read the headline 'I was *not kidnapped*, I just want to live with my family', while on page twenty-three we read

'*Abduction* leaves a trail of heartache in its wake'. Closer scrutiny demonstrates that the news story is very quote-led, drawing on both Misbah's press conference and an interview with her brother Omar, thus avoiding the need to take a stance on the issue. The paper instead positions itself in a broader sense by using a discourse of traditional family values. The comment piece frames Misbah as a 'victim of marriage breakdown' and paints her as a rather fickle child whose statement must be 'taken with a pinch of salt'. This disempowerment of Misbah continues with the final words of the piece, which play down the gravity of the situation and focus squarely on the centrality of the mother/daughter relationship: 'there will likely come a time, in the not too distant future, when she will want her mum. And what will happen then? Because Lahore is an awfully long way from the Isle of Lewis'. The focus on the personal and the emotional arguably allows the paper to take a position on the issue in a roundabout way: it empathises with Louise Campbell's heartache at the 'abduction; or at least seeming abduction' and likens Louise's situation to that of Lady Catherine Meyer, wife of the former British ambassador to the US, whose sons *were* abducted. The traditional family values discourse is continued in one of the more general comment pieces, 'Word of the week', which focuses on 'family' and frames the Misbah story as shattering a family unit.

It is notable that many of the pieces over these two days, both news and opinion, focus on the contestation about Misbah's name. It has become a metaphor for the whole case, and the papers cement its place in public discourse. *The Herald*, which takes a 'metareporting' approach to its coverage over these two days, highlights the name issue in the headline of almost every story it runs on the story. Its front page headline on 2 September is 'Girl wants to stay with her father; MY NAME ISN'T MOLLY, IT IS MISBAH', and the lead sentence of a feature on page fourteen is 'For Molly Campbell of Stornoway, read Misbah Iram Ahmed Rana of Lahore'. The feature is headlined 'A child caught in the middle; Custody decisions do not belong in press conferences', an example of 'metareporting' in that it critiques media involvement in the case, both invited and uninvited. The *Sunday Herald* on 3 September carried an openly critical piece on page six headlined 'Kidnap claim "shows media bias"; RACISM: PRESS UNDER SCRUTINY; Anger at newsrooms' treatment of Misbah Rana case' and an opinion piece on page thirty-nine headlined 'Molly Misbah; A story of our times; When a young girl went missing from her mother's home in Scotland and turned up with her father in Pakistan, the world jumped to conclusions. The wrong ones. Neil Mackay separates fact from fiction'.

This final headline is interesting on several levels and provides an appropriate conclusion to the wider discussion. Firstly, its word choice and structure provide a microcosm of the case as a whole: the two names and the two parents are given presupposed equal status and it is pointed out that 'the world' has thus far not given them this. Secondly, it positions the *Sunday Herald* in opposition to 'the world' suggesting that it did not engage in jumping to 'the wrong conclusions'. And thirdly, the words 'a story of our times' historicise the Misbah case and present the case as a metaphor for the press treatment of race and ethnicity in this country. This is perhaps unfair, given some of the good practice we have seen in the discussion of asylum coverage, or at least good practice relative to the UK more widely, but undoubtedly the case of Misbah Rana has and will continue to cause journalists to be conscious of the discourses they employ. It also reminds us all of the ideological force of language, and the responsibility which comes along with that.

Although it has not been possible to explore broadcast coverage of both cases here, certainly as far as Misbah Rana is concerned, it would appear to have followed a similar pattern to press coverage, in that it began with a suggestion of abduction, then called that into question and finally moved into 'metareporting' about its own coverage of the story. Further analysis in this area would be welcome.

NOTES

1. The newspapers monitored were the *Press and Journal, The Herald, The Courier, The Scotsman,* the *Daily Record,* the *Evening Times, The Scottish Sun,* the *Scottish Daily Mail,* the *Scottish Daily Mirror,* the *Scottish Daily Express,* the *Sunday Herald,* the *Sunday Mail,* and *Scotland on Sunday.* The same papers were examined in the Misbah Rana case study.
2. Refer to Oxfam 2006 for further discussion of the coverage.

REFERENCES

Article 19 (2003), *What's the story?: results from research into media coverage of refugees and asylum seekers in the UK.*
Bell, A. (1991), *The Language of News Media,* Oxford: Blackwell.
European Network Against Racism (ENAR) (2002), Shadow Report, *Racism and Race Relations in the UK,* http://www.justice.org.uk/images/pdfs/enarracism.pdf.
Fairclough, N. (1995), *Media Discourse,* London: Edward Arnold.
Foucault, M. (1980), *Power/Knowledge: Selected Interviews and Other Writings, 1972– 1977,* New York: Pantheon Books.
Fowler, R. (1991), *Language in the News: Discourse and Ideology in the Press,* London: Routledge.
Horsti, K. (2007), 'Celebrating multiculturalism: European multicultural media initatives as anti-racist practices', Proceedings of International Association for Media and Communication Research (IAMCR) Community Communication Conference.

Information Centre about Asylum Seekers and Refugees in the UK (ICAR) (2004), *Media Image, Community Impact*, London: International Policy Institute, King's College London.

Morris, R. (2000), 'Gypsies, travellers and the media: press regulation and racism in the UK', in *Communications Law* 5:6, pp. 213–19.

Neal, S. (2003), 'The Scarman Report, the Macpherson Report and the media: how newspapers respond to race-centred social policy interventions', in *Journal of Social Policy* 32:1, pp. 55–74.

Oxfam (2001), *Asylum: The Truth Behind the Headlines*, Oxford: Oxfam UK Poverty Programme.

Oxfam (2006), *Asylum and the Media*, Oxford: Oxfam UK Poverty Programme.

Poynting, S. and V. Mason (2007), 'The resistible rise of Islamophobia: anti-Muslim racism in the UK and Australia before 11 September 2001', in *Journal of Sociology* 43:61, pp. 61–86.

Propp, V. (1968), *Morphology of the Folktale*, Austin: University of Texas Press.

Said, E. (1979), *Orientalism*, New York: Vintage.

Van Dijk, T. A. (1998), 'Opinions and ideologies in the press', in A. Bell and P. Garrett (eds), *Approaches to Media Discourse*, Oxford: Blackwell, pp. 21–63.

Welsh Media Group (2002), *Welcome or Over-reaction: Refugees and Asylum Seekers in the Media*, Oxford: Oxfam UK Poverty Programme.

Westminster Media Forum (2007), *Ethnicity and the Media*, Bagshot, Surrey.

14

Gaelic, the Media and Scotland

MIKE CORMACK

When *Headlines: The Media in Scotland* was published in 1978, Gaelic received only the most fleeting of mentions (Hutchison 1978). This was not surprising given the minimal amount of the language on television, and the merest outline of a radio service (see Cormack 1993 for an account of Gaelic broadcasting before the 1990s). Since then, however, much has changed in the Scottish media, and Gaelic provision is no exception. This chapter describes the changes and sets them in the international context of minority language media. In doing so, it seeks answers to two questions: How important are the media to Gaelic? How important are the Gaelic media to Scotland?

MINORITY LANGUAGE MEDIA

Since the 1980s, minority language media have gradually emerged as significant parts of provision, particularly in Europe. The inception of television channels in Welsh, Basque and Catalan in the early 1980s marked this change. There had, of course, been minority language media in earlier times and in other places (see Browne 2007 for a short general history), but in the European context it was the development of television in the Celtic languages and the Iberian 'regional' languages that most firmly put the issue on the map. Before then, minority languages were typically regarded either with complete distrust or with a condescending paternalism. That paternalism was evident at the BBC. The Corporation's *Handbook* of 1942 noted that 'For the Highlander there were the regular weekly broadcasts in his native tongue – the news and a postscript in Gaelic' (BBC 1942: 31). The implication was that the Gaels should be pleased that there was *any* weekly broadcast in Gaelic. It was a gift handed down, rather than something that the Gaels might have expected as a right, given the principles which the BBC was supposed to embody.

These attitudes partly stemmed from the idea of the nation-state – a state whose legitimacy was based on the claim that its citizens, or at least, the great majority of them, formed a single nation. One of the ways in which this was supposedly demonstrated was through the use of a single language which both united the people and demonstrated their homogeneity. This was particularly important in Italy and Germany which used language as a prime unifying principle when they became nation-states in the nineteenth century. In France the importance of the national language was even written into the constitution, despite the many linguistic minorities which had always existed in that country. Although attitudes in Britain were not quite so blind as in France, nevertheless it is not difficult to find 'establishment' voices who wanted nothing less than the complete abandonment of the Celtic languages. The surprise then is that these languages have lasted as well as they have. Welsh survived better than Gaelic, partly because in more recent centuries it had always been spoken by a higher percentage of the Welsh population than Gaelic had been by the Scottish population. In addition, Gaelic, like Irish, was associated with rebellion in the eighteenth century, and when education developed in the Highlands, Gaelic was seen as part of the problem, rather than as part of the solution. In Wales, the language did not have these associations, and so 'Welsh was never alienated from religious life and education as were the Gaelic and Irish languages' (Durkacz 1983: 81).

From one point of view, the opposition to these languages is not surprising. The existence of indigenous minority language communities raises questions as to how the nation is defined. Within Scotland this is reflected in the arguments for and against the claims of Gaelic and Scots to be 'national languages'. Most Gaelic speakers will have encountered fellow Scots who are, at best, reluctant to see Gaelic as having any role in modern Scotland, and, at worst, display a sometimes ferocious antipathy towards the language. This may be explained as the reaction of those ignorant of Gaelic but who, in seeing themselves as 'real Scots', feel threatened by claims that Gaelic has, in some way, a role to play in Scottish culture and identity.

The change since the 1980s – not least the creation of the European Charter for Regional or Minority Languages, adopted as a Convention by the Council of Europe in 1992, and gradually ratified by member states subsequently, which contains an explicit call for media provision in minority languages (Grin 2003 contains a full discussion) – does require explanation. One obvious factor is the rising current of political nationalism in many parts of Europe (although the relationship between nationalism and minority language media is not as straightforward as might at first be thought – see Cormack 2000). However, it is important to look at the broader changes that were happening. Three in particular need to be noted – the expansion of the European Union, the process of globalisation, and the development of multiculturalism.

As far as the European Union is concerned, the important dates in its development post-1970 were the accession of the United Kingdom, Ireland and Denmark in 1973, the first direct elections in 1979, the Maastricht Treaty in 1992, along with the various accessions of new member states to the EU. This expansion affected the status of minority languages in two ways. First of all, it brought a greater awareness of what was happening in other countries, allowing minority communities to feel less isolated than they had typically felt before this. Secondly, it created an institutional structure which recognised minority language communities. Alongside this, organisations such as the European Bureau of Lesser-Used Languages were created (in 1982), and, as already noted, the European Charter for Regional or Minority Languages appeared. In effect, the EU created a political context in which it was easier for minority languages to gain recognition than it was within many traditional nation-states.

Globalisation took matters a stage further, particularly since it made the proponents of many official state languages aware of their own weaknesses against the international power of languages such as English, Spanish and (increasingly important today) Mandarin/Putonghua. Similarly, although multiculturalism has recently become a rather contentious term for some, there can be no argument concerning the existence of the changes which the term describes, with different cultures, religions and languages existing alongside each other, particularly in the larger European cities. The old mythology of the unified nation-state was under attack from all sides.

Out of all of this, minority languages became an accepted (if often still controversial) part of European life. And the mass media could hardly ignore the changes. Furthermore, by the later 1990s, particularly following the popularisation of the Internet and the development of multichannel digital broadcasting, media space was suddenly not the scarce resource, to be carefully husbanded by governments, which it had been for most of the twentieth century. There were still arguments to be had about the funding of production, but governments could no longer plead spectrum scarcity as an argument against providing space for minority languages in the broadcast media, just as they could no longer plead ignorance of the claims of their minorities.

MINORITY LANGUAGE BROADCASTING POLICY

For minority languages, radio and television have been crucial. Print media depend on literacy, and most minority languages have suffered educationally – the result often being lower-than-average literacy rates in the minority language community – while film has usually been too expensive for minority communities. The Internet is still finding its feet, in terms of what it can add to or replace in other media, and it is only in recent years that minority languages have established a more secure presence on it (Cunliffe 2007). Broadcasting, as generally the most regulated part of the media, has been the area in which minority language media policy has developed most explicitly. The central issues in such policy concern funding and accountability. Minority communities are usually too small to fund a television service – help is needed from the majority language community and usually comes in the form of some kind of grant from the national government. Accountability raises two issues – political control of broadcasting, and the relation between the broadcasters and their community, in other words, accountability 'upwards' (in terms of power) to the government, and 'downwards' to the audience. Although upwards accountability is the most obvious sort, particularly when it is related to questions of funding, downward accountability is crucial in minority communities in which most people are bilingual and can easily change to channels in other languages if they are unsatisfied with the minority offer.

Another issue lurks behind these two – what is minority language broadcasting for? Is it to fulfil some combination of public service and commercial aims? Or is it explicitly to help in the maintenance of an endangered language? If the latter, it is worth noting that it is not at all clear exactly how broadcasting, and in particular television, does help a language. A Gaelic television programme may be popular among Gaels but that does not *necessarily* mean that it encourages them to speak the language more often (Cormack 2006; 2007). Minority language television policy usually just assumes the necessity of television, and does not look too carefully at the impact it might have.

GAELIC IN SCOTLAND

The history of Gaelic in Scotland over the past 1,000 years has been one of gradual decline. In the tenth century, the Scottish court spoke Gaelic and the presence of Gaelic place names (for example, those with the prefixes Inver-, Bal-, Kil-, Dun- and Ach- or Auch-) make clear that the language was spoken then in most parts of modern Scotland. By the fourteenth century it had retreated to the Highlands, the Western Isles and Galloway (where it persisted at least until the seventeenth century). By the first census which asked questions about Gaelic (in 1881), there were 231,594 speakers (6.2 per cent of the Scottish population) who said they 'habitually' used Gaelic, these being mainly within the Highlands and Islands. By the most recent census in 2001, the figure for Gaelic speakers was down to 58,652, although 92,000 claimed some Gaelic skills (for example, reading).

However, numbers do not tell the whole story. Since the 1970s there has been a contrast between declining numbers overall and rising numbers of those learning Gaelic as a second language, along with a slow increase in institutional support – from the Western Isles bilingual policy starting in the 1970s, through the development of Gaelic-medium, higher education at Sabhal Mòr Ostaig on the Isle of Skye and Lews Castle College in Stornoway, to the passing of the Gaelic Language Act by the Scottish Parliament in 2005, under the provisions of which the Bòrd na Gàidhlig (Gaelic Board) has responsibility for planning Gaelic developments.

Alongside the question of numbers, there are important issues of identity and culture. Gaelic makes clear how contested is the notion of Scottishness. Much of the traditional symbolism of Scotland is related to Gaelic culture – Highland landscapes, typical Scottish place names and surnames, tartan, and identifiably Scottish music. Yet in most displays of 'Scottishness' , official and non-official, the Gaelic language itself is notable by its absence, apart from the odd well-worn phrase (such as 'ceud mile fàilte' and 'slàinte mhath'). In a move which goes back to Sir Walter Scott's romanticising of the Highlands, aspects of the culture have been cut loose from the language, to create symbols of a Scottishness which is clearly distinct from the identity of other English-speaking countries, but which is easily accessible to the non-Gaelic speaking majority of Scots.

Despite this adoption of the more accessible aspects of Gaelic culture in place of the language itself, there is a general appreciation of Gaelic's role in Scotland, as the strongest signifier of Scottish difference. For many Scots, a Scotland without Gaelic would not only be culturally poorer, but would also be a less distinct place, with a less distinct identity. Gaelic also establishes links with the past, and, through place names, with the landscape itself.

BROADCASTING BEFORE 1993

Although Gaelic writing has regularly appeared in some newspapers (in particular *The Oban Times*, established in 1866; the *Stornoway Gazette*, established in 1917; and the *West Highland Free Press*, established in Broadford on the Isle of Skye in 1972), it is broadcasting that has had the major impact (at least as far as public awareness has been concerned). Gaelic radio had begun as early as 1923 but was only sporadic for many years. Indeed, the BBC did not appoint its first Gaelic producer until 1935, and the first Gaelic television play did not appear until the 1960s. During the 1970s, however, a gradual expansion took place, alongside an increased vociferousness amongst Gaelic activists. Despite this activity, Scotland never experienced anything like the campaign for Welsh-language television which, beginning as early as 1968, went from rallies through civil disobedience to Gwynfor Evans MP's threat of a hunger strike in 1980, and finally to Mrs Thatcher's government agreeing to set up a Welsh television channel – Sianal Pedwar Cymru (S4C) – which began in 1982. The BBC in Scotland reorganised Gaelic radio broadcasts in 1976 when *Radio Highland*, based in Inverness, was established, and then again in 1979 when its Gaelic programming was increased and brought under the name *Radio nan Eilean* (Radio of the Islands), with a studio in Stornoway. During this time too, Grampian Television gradually developed its Gaelic programming.

The BBC reorganised and expanded its radio services once again in 1985, using the name *Radio nan Gaidheal* with three categories of broadcast – some to the whole of Scotland; some to most of the Highland area and the Western Isles, but not beyond; and some only to the island and western coastal areas. Gaelic television also began to change significantly at this time, with the BBC beginning regular broadcasts of short programmes for young children. Meanwhile, not only had Grampian been steadily increasing its output, but, at the end of the decade, Scottish Television (STV) (which broadcast not just to the central belt but also to a large part of the southwest Highlands and Islands) began regular broadcasts in the language, based on a rather different approach from that of the other companies. In 1991 its Gaelic programming went out at primetime, and general light entertainment programmes along with some documentary features were broadcast, all with English subtitles.

In the late 1980s it became clear to many Gaels that in the reorganisation of broadcasting which was then being discussed, Gaelic would need to have a role, otherwise it would be left behind completely. A vigorous campaign followed in 1989 (based on the economic advantages that an expansion of Gaelic television would bring, rather than on arguments about rights or cultural defence), and Mrs Thatcher's government was persuaded to invest in order to increase the annual amount of programming from 100 hours to 300. The legal framework was set out in the 1990 Broadcasting Act which established a Gaelic Television Fund, with money being allocated by the Treasury to the Independent Television Commission (ITC). The amount was to be decided by the Secretary of State for Scotland and was set initially at £9.5 million per annum. The ITC established a management body, the Comataidh Telebhisein Gàidhlig (CTG, Gaelic Television Committee) to administer the fund, and to channel money into programme-making.

TELEVISION, 1993–2007

The new programmes funded by the CTG began to appear in January 1993. At first these showed a clear and coherent pattern. The main strands were the daily news service *Telefios*; a weekly half-hour drama series broadcast in prime time, *Machair*; a weekly BBC current affairs series *Eòrpa*; and a learners' series *Speaking Our Language*. This gave a relatively strong structure to Gaelic television, at least compared with what had been seen previously, even though the programmes were scattered across different channels at different times. In the following years, however, the structure gradually unravelled, not helped by the fact that in 1996 the CTG was changed to the Comataidh Craolaidh Gàidhlig (CCG, Gaelic Broadcasting Committee) with its remit expanded to include radio but with no extra finance. In 2003 the name was changed once again, this time to Seirbheis nam Meadhanan Gàidhlig (GMS or Gaelic Media Service – the English acronym is usually used to avoid confusion with SMG, the Scottish Media Group), in anticipation of the changes which the Internet and digital technology would bring. Such constant modification suggests an uncertainty (at least among the politicians) about the organisation's role. This uncertainty was reflected in the reasons behind the failure to retain a coherent scheduling structure.

Firstly, the CTG/CCG was never given funding to match the expectations resting on it, and indeed the allocation was reduced in real terms over the years. The level of funding was not linked to any other factor, such as ITV advertising revenue, as was the case with S4C in Wales, but has simply been decided by the UK government. This left the service extremely vulnerable and on more than one occasion funding was reduced unexpectedly. The result was a decreasing average budget for programmes and the inability of the CCG to keep to its original target of 200 extra hours per year. The number of hours of funded television steadily diminished, reaching ninety-one in 2005–6 (Gaelic Media Service 2006). From 1999 to 2006 the grant remained at £8.5 million (apart from 2002 when the Scottish Executive added £450,000 to the Treasury allocation), and so, with steadily rising costs, the funding was, in effect, decreasing, year by year.

A second problem was related to scheduling and in particular the actions of STV. There seems little doubt now that when STV started making Gaelic programmes in the pre-CTG period, it saw this, at least in part, as a way of bolstering its regional credentials and thus fighting off the threat of rival bids for the Central Scotland television franchise. In the first years of the CTG, STV was receiving significant amounts of CTG funds, particularly for *Speaking Our Language* and *Machair*. However, under pressure from advertisers and some anti-Gaelic audience reaction, the programmes began to slip from primetime slots. The CTG, when it entered into arrangements with programme-makers and broadcasters, did try to establish schedule slots as part of the agreement but this proved impracticable since unforeseen events might result in schedule changes, and so only broad time-bands were agreed. *Machair* (which, with English subtitles, had initially reached audiences of over 300,000) was subsequently scheduled against BBC1's *EastEnders*, and then moved to Sunday evenings where its ratings improved again, without getting back to the original figures.

By the new millennium, STV's weekday Gaelic programmes were regularly being scheduled after 11.30pm. The overall situation had been made worse in 1997 when Scottish Media Group (SMG), the owners of STV, took over Grampian Television, so that the company then had control over scheduling in the north of Scotland as well as in the central belt. More generally, SMG was perceived as being unsupportive of Gaelic television, and in August 1998 the CCG announced that the contract for *Machair* would not be renewed; the last episode was broadcast in April of the following year. Then, in October 2000, following criticisms of the quality of the news service and, once again, unfavourable scheduling changes, the CCG announced that Grampian's television news contract would not be renewed; *Telefios* ended in December 2000.

A problem related to scheduling was the lack of coherence in Gaelic programming as a whole. Despite the CTG/CCG's attempt to oversee the service (starting with its list of desired programme-types which it drew up as one of its first acts), the reality across the BBC and two commercial regional broadcasters created an impression of chaotic scheduling. Given that both SMG and BBC Scotland also made Gaelic programmes not funded by the CCG, the inherent weakness in the CCG's position in relation to Gaelic broadcasting as a whole became clear. As compared with the strands of news and current affairs, drama and learners programmes of the early years, by the mid-2000s drama was only intermittent, with no long-term series (and the most talked about post-*Machair* example – the six episodes of BBC Scotland's *Gruth is Uachdar* in spring 2002 – was funded by the BBC only, not by the CCG). Moreover, there was no regular news programme, and only a weekly current affairs discussion programme *Ceann-Là*, which started in October 2001, broadcast at 11.30pm on STV and Grampian (and not even being transmitted throughout the year). Of the early programmes, only BBC Scotland's muchadmired *Eòrpa* survived. It may well be that a significant factor in its success is that rather than simply being a current affairs programme, it is one which looks at Europe from a non-metropolitan, minority perspective, thus making it different in kind from its English-language rivals. Neither BBC Scotland nor the BBC in London offers any English-language programme with a comparable remit. In addition, its use of English sub-titles has enabled the programme to gain a non-Gaelic audience.

One potential problem was created by devolution. Although the support of Gaelic falls under the remit of the Scottish Parliament, broadcasting remains reserved to Westminster. That there was an advantage to this partial devolution of responsibility was shown in 2002 when, as noted above, the Scottish

Executive gave the Gaelic television service some additional funding. However, as in Wales post-devolution, such a division of responsibilities makes little sense and is likely to cause problems in the future.

It is difficult to be precise about the size of the Gaelic television industry. There are, for example, independent producers who work mainly in English but who have made Gaelic programmes. The annual reports of the CTG/CCG/GMS, however, give some guidance as to what has been happening. They list more than sixty independent production companies which have been involved in making Gaelic television programmes since 1992, but the rate of change is demonstrated by the fact that only one of these – Media nan Eilean – has been present throughout that period. The independent sector has become more important. Up to 1998, the two ITV companies (STV and Grampian) received a greater amount of funding for programmes than either the BBC or the independent producers, but since then ITV has dropped back and the independents have become the largest sector. In the year 2005–6, the BBC received 39 per cent of the funding, Scottish Media Group just 7 per cent, and the remaining 54 per cent went to independents. This has been an important change and has allowed the establishment of a Gaelic television industry which is not wholly dependent on the BBC and SMG, even if the independents themselves are usually fairly small.

Audience opinion has been surveyed since the start of the new service in 1993. In the Gaelic Media Service annual report for 2005–6, John Angus Mackay (Director of the GMS) noted (p. 12) some general points which have arisen from this research.

> While maintaining loyalty to Gaelic programmes the audience became increasingly perplexed about the lack of resources to sustain the anticipated scope of the programming, the erratic nature of the scheduling, lack of programme variety and creativity, the evolving erosion and eventual disappearance of certain programmes and slots.

Not surprisingly in these circumstances, audience reach decreased from 88.5 per cent in 1993 to 65.7 per cent in 2005. Where quality has been maintained, the audience has been retained, but the range of programmes was seen as 'insufficient to appeal to the overall demographic spectrum of Gaelic viewers'. A frequent complaint has been the lack of material aimed at the 'teens and twenties' age group, an age group crucially important for the maintenance of the language. It has to be said too that the quality of Gaelic television programmes has varied somewhat over the years, although this is not particularly surprising, given how small the Gaelic world is. Perhaps more surprising is how such a small community has been able to sustain programmes of quality such as *Eòrpa*.

RADIO NAN GAIDHEAL

During the 1990s Gaelic radio was less controversial than television (for a brief outline of the earlier history of Gaelic radio, see Cormack 1993: 107–8). The BBC's Gaelic radio service, *Radio nan Gaidheal*, was expanded in 1996. However, by the mid-2000s it was not yet a full, twenty-four-hour operation. By 2007 it was broadcasting for just over fourteen hours each weekday, with much less at weekends (usually four hours on Saturday and just ninety minutes on Sunday). Being available both as a digital channel and on the Internet, its importance has steadily increased. Not surprisingly, most of the output is music, news and chat but there have been more ambitious programmes, including, for example, documentaries and occasionally drama, such as the series *Airdanaiseig* (1994–6). It has been argued elsewhere that if the representations of the Gaelic community shown in the different media are compared, radio offers a fuller spectrum of life in the Gàidhealtachd (Cormack 1995: 278).

Following the transition from the CTG to the CCG, radio became part of that organisation's remit, but the CCG had very specific aims in supporting radio.

> The Committee's strategic thrust is to fund programmes that cannot be adequately financed from Radio nan Gaidheal's own limited resources, and particularly ones that involve topics, personalities and communities that are distant from broadcasting facilities or cannot be satisfactorily reflected and represented in studio-based productions. (CCG 2000: 18)

These have most notably included a series *Sruth an Eòlais*, fifty half-hour programmes based on archive material in the School of Scottish Studies, and an hour-long play *A' Ruith Caol* by Angus Peter Campbell. By 2006, 16.3 hours of radio were being funded (Gaelic Media Service 2006: 44). The CCG/GMS has also been trying to support Gaelic on commercial local radio stations. Such programming is already part of the output of several of these in the Highlands, such as Loch Broom FM in Ullapool, Nevis Radio in Fort William and even Heartland FM in Pitlochry, but they tend to broadcast only one or two hours of Gaelic each week, usually based around music. Even Isles FM in Stornoway does little better, and is still a predominantly English-language station, as is Skye's Cuillin FM. All this merely emphasises that the BBC remains the central provider of Gaelic radio.

NEWSPAPERS

Gaelic is still a very weak presence in the press. In an account of Gaelic in newspapers in the mid-1990s, it was noted how little Gaelic was found, even in local newspapers in the Highlands and Islands such as the *Stornoway Gazette*, the *Oban Times* and the *West Highland Free Press* (*WHFP*), and that these newspapers, like others such as *The Scotsman*, tended to use Gaelic more as a display of identity, rather than as a vehicle for news (Cormack 1995). Since then there has been some limited development. Both the *Gazette* and the *WHFP* now use Gaelic more, especially on news stories involving the language. Similarly *The Scotsman* has expanded its Gaelic content: since the beginning of 1998, it has published two weekly columns, rather than one, and the subject matter of these has expanded to include current affairs. The most significant development, however, has been *An Gàidheal Ùr*. This began as a publication of *An Comunn Gaidhealach* (the oldest-established Gaelic cultural organisation, most famous for its annual music festival, the Mòd) and from 1998 until 2002 it was distributed as a monthly supplement in the *WHFP*. After a period when it was distributed independently from its base in Stornoway, it is now once more distributed monthly with the *WHFP* and other local newspapers. Most of the content of *An Gàidheal Ùr* (perhaps inevitably given its monthly frequency) has been news specifically to do with Gaelic and Gaelic culture, rather than more general political, economic or social news, but it does contain some economic and political items which are relevant to the Highlands and Islands. To call itself a newspaper ('pàipear-naidheachd neo-eisimeileach nan Gàidheal', independent newspaper of the Gaels) gives a rather inaccurate impression, but it is clearly an important addition to the Gaelic media, although how well it is distributed will be crucial to both its role in Gaelic culture and its long-term survival. Funded by Bòrd na Gàidhlig and some advertising, its financial situation is not fully secure (indeed, it almost closed in 2005). The possibility of a more regular Gaelic newspaper remains remote, but for arguments in favour of a weekly newspaper, see Cormack 2003.

THE DEVELOPMENT OF A GAELIC DIGITAL SERVICE

With the Broadcasting Act of 1996, digital broadcasting appeared as a possible saviour for Gaelic. Under the terms of the Act, one hour a day of Gaelic television has been transmitted on a service called *TeleG* and consists of material already broadcast terrestrially. However take-up of digital television has been slower amongst Gaels than amongst the population in general, with many seemingly waiting to see if a full Gaelic channel will become available before they make the financial commitment (NicNèill 2001: 102; see also CCG 2002: 21). The government initially rejected the idea of providing full funding for a Gaelic digital channel. However, in 2000, following intensive lobbying, it was announced that the CCG would be transformed into a broader organisation with more powers, and that its remit would include working towards the creation of a specific Gaelic channel, although there was no mention of increased funding or when such a channel might be up and running. The final version of the Communications Act 2003 transformed the CCG into the GMS, but it was silent on these two crucial issues.

A solution to the funding problem was developed during 2005–7. Ofcom, the recently established regulator of the electronic media, proposed that SMG should be released from its obligations to Gaelic for a cash payment. The operation of the channel would be the responsibility of the BBC which would contribute additional money to the service. On top of the annual Treasury grant, the Scottish Executive would allocate additional funding. The working plan was that the service would broadcast on weekdays, possibly with weekend repeats, and would include just one-and-a-half hours of new programming each day, alongside repeats. *Radio nan Gaidheal* would transmit on the channel when television programmes were not being broadcast. In fact, the concept is more accurately described as a Gaelic digital service, rather than a television channel, since the aim is to integrate television, radio and the Internet (for more on the future of Gaelic in the new media environment, see Cormack 2008). Initially, the service will be on satellite with terrestrial digital following about six months later.

In some ways, the protracted development of the digital channel reflected the position of Gaelic. Outside of the Gaelic community, there had been a guarded acceptance of the idea of a digital channel, but when it came to putting finance towards it, other issues took precedence. The retreat from Gaelic television by SMG has not been particularly surprising, but again has graphically illustrated the lip-service paid by many to Gaelic, sometimes for self-serving ends.

CONCLUSION

At the start of this chapter, two questions were suggested: How important are the media to Gaelic? How important are the Gaelic media to Scotland? The first is the easier to answer. Since the early 1990s television has given Gaelic a much higher profile than it had before. Broadcasting has created attractive jobs for Gaelic-speakers, enabling them to enjoy an interesting career while staying within the Gaelic world. Broadcast production has also helped the economy of the Highlands and Islands (even if it is difficult to quantify this very precisely). Television has encouraged and presented new cultural products, from drama to documentaries about contemporary Gaelic culture. The presence of Gaelic on the Internet (including the broadcasts of *Radio nan Gaidheal*) has allowed a worldwide development of interest in the language and culture. The series *Speaking Our Language* was very successful in getting many people started at learning the language. However, when we come to the question of how much the Gaelic media have encouraged the actual speaking of the language, it is more difficult to make confident assertions. The fact that the 2001 census figures reflected a continuing decline from the 1991 figures was disappointing to many who had thought that the developments of that decade, including the expansion of Gaelic television, would have stemmed the loss. If nothing else, it emphasised that the media are simply one factor among many when it comes to language maintenance, and also that the impact of the media in this area will only become clear in the longer term.

Concerning the second question, as to how important the Gaelic media have been for Scotland, three points can be suggested. First, Gaelic media have helped the Gaelic cultural and literary renaissance of recent years, which itself has been part of the wider Scottish cultural renaissance. Second, the greater profile which the media, and particularly television, have given Gaelic has reminded many Scots of this component of Scottish culture and helped them to a greater understanding of their own culture (some observers have however expressed concern that putting all Gaelic television on a separate digital channel – the ultimate aim – might well reduce this profile). Third, the Gaelic media can be seen as having a role in the Europeanisation of Scotland. This may seem paradoxical but it can be argued that perceiving Scotland as a multilingual country (which, of course, it has always been), and recognising the links which Gaelic media and culture have developed with other minority cultures, demonstrate the outward-looking, more self-consciously European aspects of culture in Scotland – and of course this culture now includes many other languages, such as Urdu. By emphasising the differences at the heart of Scottish culture, Gaelic – through the media – opens up Scotland to a broader view of culture, one which situates the country firmly within a European outlook.

ACKNOWLEDGEMENT

This chapter includes revisions of material first published in *Scottish Affairs* in 2004.

REFERENCES

BBC (1942), *BBC Handbook 1942*, London: BBC.

Browne, D. R. (2007), 'Speaking up: a brief history of minority languages and the media worldwide', in M. Cormack and N. Hourigan (eds), *Minority Language Media: Concepts, Critiques and Case Studies*, Clevedon: Multilingual Matters, pp. 107–32.

CCG (1996–2004), *Aithisgean Bliadhnail/Annual Reports*, Stornoway: CCG.

CTG (1993–96), *Aithisgean Bliadhnail/Annual Reports*, Stornoway: CTG.

Cormack, M. (1993), 'Problems of minority language broadcasting: Gaelic in Scotland', *European Journal of Communication*, 8, 101–17.

Cormack, M. (1995), 'The use of Gaelic in Scottish newspapers', *Journal of Multilingual and Multicultural Development*, 16/4, 269–80.

Cormack, M. (2000), 'Minority languages, nationalism and broadcasting: the British and Irish examples', *Nations and Nationalism*, 6/3, 383–98.

Cormack, M. (2003), 'The case for a Gaelic weekly newspaper', in J. M. Kirk and D. P. Ó Baoill (eds), *Towards Our Goals: Broadcasting, the Press, the Performing Arts and the Economy: Minority Languages in Northern Ireland, the Republic of Ireland and Scotland*, (*Belfast Studies in Language, Culture and Politics*, 10), Belfast: Queens University Press, pp. 95–9.

Cormack, M. (2004), 'Gaelic in the media', *Scottish Affairs*, 46, 23–43.

Cormack, M. (2006), 'The media, language maintenance and Gaelic', in W. McLeod (ed.), *Revitalising Gaelic in Scotland: Policy, Planning and Public Discourse*, Edinburgh: Dunedin Academic Press, pp. 211–19.

Cormack, M. (2007), 'The media and language maintenance', in M. Cormack and N. Hourigan (eds), *Minority Language Media: Concepts, Critiques and Case Studies*, Clevedon: Multilingual Matters, pp. 52–68.

Cormack, M. (2008), 'Gaelic in the new digital landscape', in G. Munro and I. Taylor (eds), *Gaelic Communities Today*, Edinburgh: Dunedin Academic Press.

Cunliffe, D. (2007), 'Minority languages and the Internet: new threats, new opportunities', in M. Cormack and N. Hourigan (eds), *Minority Language Media: Concepts, Critiques and Case Studies*, Clevedon: Multilingual Matters, pp. 133–50.

Durkacz, V. (1983) *The Decline of the Celtic Languages*, Edinburgh: John Donald.

Gaelic Media Service (2005–), *Aithisgean Bliadhnail/Annual Reports*, Stornoway: GMS.

Grin, F. (2003), *Language Policy Evaluation and the European Charter for Regional or Minority Languages*, Basingstoke: Palgrave Macmillan.

Hutchison, D. (ed.) (1978), *Headlines: The Media in Scotland*, Edinburgh: EUSPB.

NicNèill, M. (2001), 'Gaelic broadcasting: on the threshold of a new era', *Mercator Media Forum*, 5, 99–106.

15

The Scottish Media and Politics

BRIAN MCNAIR

Around the time this chapter was being written, the 300th anniversary of the union between Scotland and England had just been marked, and the third election for the Scottish parliament held. The result of that poll saw the Scottish National Party emerge with the greatest number of votes, and one parliamentary member more than Labour, which thereby lost its political dominance in Scotland for the first time in a generation.[1] This chapter will explore the performance of the Scottish media in post–devolution political life, before turning its attention to the specific coverage of the 2007 election.

INTRODUCTION: THE SCOTTISH PUBLIC SPHERE

The distinctive nature of the Scottish public sphere since the formation of the United Kingdom in 1707, and of Scottish political culture in recent times, has been widely acknowledged (Schlesinger 1998). Scotland, as a recognised nation within a multi-nation state, has always had separate legal and educational systems from those of its larger neighbour south of the border (and also from Northern Ireland and Wales, the other countries of the union). As far as the media are concerned, the different approaches to, for example, contempt of court and defamation north of the border affect their daily operating practices. Scotland also has its own religious institutions and a separate system of local government from that of England. Scotland, in short, has never been merely a region of England, but has always been recognised as a national entity with autonomy in key areas of its political, economic and cultural life. The Union was not a colonial imposition, but an agreement voluntarily entered into, on the basis that the respective national identities of its constituent elements would be preserved.

This status has been reflected in the structure of the Scottish media, which since the eighteenth century have comprised a distinct public sphere within the broader communicative space of the United Kingdom. Scottish publications such as the *Edinburgh Review* were at the forefront of the European Enlightenment (Herman 2002; Conboy 2004), at a time when Scottish intellectuals such as Adam Smith and David Hume were elaborating the principles and values of liberal capitalism for the world beyond their Edinburgh salons. The Glasgow-based *Herald*, launched in 1783 as the *Glasgow Advertiser*, is one of the longest running daily newspapers in the world. As is noted elsewhere in this volume, Scotland now supports an extensive range of home-grown newspapers, and Scottish readers also enjoy access to the full range of London titles, many of which have in recent years editionised north of the border.[2]

Historically, the circulations of these titles have lagged far behind those of indigenous publications such as the *Daily Record*, but in recent times the gap has narrowed. In particular, the traditional dominance of the *Daily Record* in the Scottish red-top market has been challenged by the Rupert Murdoch-owned *Sun* (Reid 2006). When in 2006 the Scottish edition of *The Sun* finally overtook its rival in sales, there was much speculation about what this meant for Scottish politics and culture. Here, after all, was 'Scotland's paper', as the *Daily Record* called itself (although it had long been owned by an English-based company) – traditionally left-of-centre and pro-Labour in its editorial line – being usurped by the flagship tabloid title of Rupert Murdoch's News Corporation, associated with the political right. For fifty years Scotland had been dominated electorally by the Labour Party, and for longer than that had been perceived, both within and without, as a bastion of traditional left politics, founded on a large, industrial working class. The west of Scotland was the world-famous home of shipbuilding and the Red Clyde, a region where the electoral map had been coloured red for decades. For most of the twentieth century Scotland's politics were steeped in the rhetoric and mythology of blue-collar, cloth-cap socialism. Glasgow's Saltmarket was occupied by tanks in January 1919 to forestall a feared Bolshevik-style putsch. More than anywhere else in the United Kingdom, Labour and its collectivist, social democratic values were hegemonic in Scotland, or at least its central industrial belt where the *Daily Record* held sway for so long.

That the Tories 'ruled' Scotland for the eighteen years between 1979 and 1997 was no reflection of their electoral strength in the country, but a consequence of the pre-devolution constitution, which allowed the Westminster government of the day to impose its preferred Secretary of State, irrespective of the wishes of the Scottish people as expressed at the ballot box. The perceived arrogance with which the 1979–97 Conservative governments of Margaret Thatcher and John Major did this, and the fact that they then used

Scotland as a testing ground for the hated poll tax, contributed greatly to the emergence of a pro-devolution mood in Scotland in the 1990s, and the establishment of a Scottish parliament by the New Labour government which came to power in 1997.

The rise of the Murdoch-owned *Sun* in Scotland, then, a newspaper forever associated with the excesses of the Thatcher era, when Murdoch was the Iron Lady's most vociferous cheer leader, was perceived to be more than merely a circulation trend. *The Sun's* rise was assisted by the familiar News Corporation approach of ferocious competitive tactics which even the wealthy *Record* found hard to match, although this was not enough to explain the former's success in the land of the Red Clydesiders.

What the trend reflected, it might be argued, was precisely the decline of that Labourist, collectivist, working-class culture of the post-World War Two era, precipitated by the decline of shipbuilding and other heavy industries on the one hand, by the 1960s decanting of communities from Govan and other inner-city, working-class districts to the new towns on the other (a process driven by Labour itself, in local government), and by the general de-ideologisation of Scotland which occurred during the 1990s, just as it occurred elsewhere in the UK. As the left-right divide which had structured British politics for generations dissolved under the influence of Tony Blair and New Labour in the 1990s, as working people bought their council homes, acquired shares in privatised utilities and invested in holiday homes overseas, the culture of dependency and deference which had been a hallmark of 'old' Labour and municipal socialism in the post-war era gave way to something much more volatile and apolitical. There were still socialists in Scotland, and the country was one of the few in the world where a politician such as Tommy Sheridan could in 2003 win parliamentary seats for his Scottish Socialist Party by condemning the 'boss classes' and threatening to 'tax the rich until they squeak' (an electoral achievement made possible by New Labour's introduction of proportional representation for the Scottish parliamentary elections. In the 2007 election, following the spectacle of the Sheridan-*News of the World* libel case, which will be discussed later, and the subsequent disintegration of the SSP, all its seats were lost.)

The SSP and its fellow-travellers were the remnants of the dependency culture, feeding on the sense of entitlement felt by many Scots to public subsidy, and hanging on to a mythical past of (largely) male class warriors. For most Scots, as for most Britons, the 1990s and into the 2000s were periods of rapid economic advancement, which inevitably meant the decline of the collectivist paradigms of the past. The decline of the *Record* and the rise of *The Sun* reflected this change in the country's political culture. Away from the smoky committee rooms of the SSP and Old Labour, most Scots cared little about who owned *The Sun*, as long as the paper guaranteed a good read, which by comparison with a tired and rudderless *Daily Record* during this period, it increasingly did. By the standards of the red-top tabloids by which it should be judged, *The Sun* was a good product, and its Scottish edition no less so.

The Sun's rise was consolidated by opportunistic gestures towards local public opinion. Thus in 1992, as the UK *Sun* enthusiastically backed the Thatcher government in that year's election, the Scottish edition urged its readers to back the SNP and 'be a nation again'. In the Blair years, it backed Scottish Labour, reflecting not just Murdoch's general approval of New Labour in Westminster, but the continuing (if eroding, for the reasons suggested) allegiance of the Scottish working class to the party.

SCOTTISH BROADCASTING

In broadcasting the Scottish audience is served by BBC Scotland (TV and radio), the commercial Scottish TV – since 1997 incorporating Grampian, which covers the north east of the country – and Border TV which serves the rural south, and a variety of commercial radio channels.

BBC Scotland produces 500 hours of TV news and current affairs annually, including at least 100 hours of current affairs and political coverage. The latter is concentrated in the weekly magazine *Holyrood Live*, and in *Newsnight Scotland*, which broadcasts twenty minutes of Scottish current affairs four nights a week, cutting into the London-produced *Newsnight*. This programme was introduced, not without controversy, as a direct result of devolution and the perceived need for BBC Scotland to enhance its political coverage at a time of rising nationalism. For some commentators, especially those of a nationalist persuasion, it was perceived as too little too late, a token gesture of little real value to the Scottish public sphere. For others, including *Newsnight* presenter Jeremy Paxman, it was a messy fudge, breaking a successful format into two unwieldy bits.

Newsnight Scotland was indeed a gesture, in so far as it was introduced with the approval of BBC managers in London to forestall the demand for a 'Scottish Six' which emerged after devolution[3] (see Schlesinger, this volume). The contrary view of then Director-General John Birt, reportedly shared by the UK government, was that such an innovation would, by removing the unifying influence of a London-produced, UK-wide BBC news flagship, exacerbate separatist tendencies in Scotland. In 2003 BBC Scotland announced that there would be no Scottish Six after all, a position confirmed by Director-General Mark Thompson at a speech in Edinburgh in 2006. The Scottish National Party, however, continued to support the idea, and seemed likely to put it back on the political agenda in the lifetime of the 2007–11 parliament.

BBC Scotland also produces some 2,200 hours of radio news and current affairs annually, in formats such as *Scotland At Ten* and phone-in based public participation shows. Radio Scotland's news programmes draw on the BBC's correspondents worldwide in order to offer listeners a similar diet to that offered on Radio 4 but ordered according to an agenda which takes account of the Scottish, the UK and the international dimensions, but is determined in Glasgow.

These then are the main locations in the Scottish public sphere where ordinary citizens engage in debate about politics.

In the case of the commercial broadcasters, public service broadcasting (PSB) obligations have lessened in recognition of the forthcoming switch to digitalisation, and the adverse impact of this on audience share, advertising revenue and profitability (McNair 2006). News and current affairs coverage of quality, including at peak time, continues to be a requirement of the Scottish commercial television PSB sector, as it does in the English regions, Wales and Northern Ireland, but at a less onerous level which recognises the financial constraints imposed by the post-digitalisation erosion of analogue subsidy. Surveys by Ofcom and others have shown, however, that Scottish audiences desire and value local broadcast journalism, and wish to see it continue in commercial form as well as on the BBC. In response, Scottish Television has pledged to maintain local coverage of quality. In addition to its daily news coverage in *Scotland Today* and *North Tonight* (for the Grampian region), Scottish produces the weekly *Politics Now*.

The economic climate which will accompany the post-digital future is uncertain, however, and there are justified concerns as to the ability of the commercial broadcasters to maintain this level of commitment beyond digital switchover, assuming that they wish to do so.

Commercial radio channels such as Forth, Clyde and Real Radio have lighter obligations with respect to content, but still carry regular news bulletins and often feature late-night talk shows in which political matters are discussed.

BROADCASTING AND POLITICAL BIAS IN SCOTLAND

As at the UK level, both the commercial and licence fee-funded public service broadcasters are, under the terms governing their operation, prevented from being anything other than neutral in relation to Scottish party political debates, and also on the issues driving public discussion north of the border, such as the merits or otherwise of devolution and independence. This has not prevented them from being involved (or dragged into) those discussions from time to time (for example, a live, London-produced TV debate show featuring prime minister Tony Blair and broadcast on ITV in 2001 was accused of breaching the impartiality rules by the SNP, which was then fighting a by-election in Scotland; in 2006 concerns were raised about the relationship of BBC presenter Kirsty Wark to then First Minister Jack McConnell – see below). As a rule, however, Scotland is similar to the rest of the UK in that newspapers have been and remain the partisan, editorially committed voices of the Scottish public sphere, while broadcasters have striven to remain as detached and impartial in their political coverage as possible.

ONLINE

In recent times, as in all countries, the traditional print and broadcast media in Scotland have been augmented by Internet and online channels. Every newspaper and broadcast organisation has its website, as do most official and public bodies, lobby and campaigning groups, and others with a desire to influence or shape public debate. There is a growing Scottish blogosphere, comprising the usual mix of politics junkies, citizen journalism enthusiasts and obsessive techno-heads.

As in other countries, too, the rise of the Internet has eroded the market share of the traditional print and broadcast outlets over time. Print circulations in the UK as a whole declined on average by around 5 per cent in the year to April 2007, continuing a longer-term decline which can be attributed to the initially slow but now accelerating infiltration of the Internet into the everyday lives of the general population. Slowly, but surely, newspapers and traditional broadcast outlets are being replaced, especially amongst the younger demographics, by the consumption of news and other content on computers, mobile phones and MP3 players. In Scotland, as elsewhere, there is more news and journalism available to the average person than ever before, but it is migrating from the print and broadcast platforms to a much more varied and flexible range of media. Media consumption patterns are changing, and media organisations in Scotland, like their competitors and counterparts everywhere, continue to seek the business models which will guarantee their long-term futures.

SCOTTISH POLITICAL JOURNALISM – BEFORE AND AFTER DEVOLUTION

The distinctiveness of Scottish culture and politics has always been reflected in Scottish political journalism. It may reasonably be argued that the restrictions placed on Scottish politicians by the pre-1997 settlement – principally, that far too many aspects of Scotland's administration were the responsibility of a Westminster-appointed Secretary of State – robbed Scottish political journalism of the urgency and saliency attaching to the work of journalists in a fully independent country, even one of similar size such as Norway. But it was always an important element of the national life, and a breeding ground for illustrious careers beyond Scottish borders. Many Scottish journalists have achieved UK-wide and international reputations (Alastair Hetherington, Neal Ascherson, Andrew Neil, Andrew Marr, John Lloyd, Kirsty Wark, Kirsty Young, Shelley Joffre and Mark Daly, to name but a few). Devolution, however, has further enhanced the status of, and resources devoted to, Scottish political journalism. The establishment of a Scottish parliament in 1999 was accompanied by the establishment of a Scottish lobby system, and greater priority being given to coverage of Scottish affairs by print and broadcast media (Schlesinger et al. 2001).

Brian Cathcart notes that 'by embracing devolution a decade ago, Scotland devolved its news, giving its own papers a lot more home-grown, kitchen-sink political stuff to write about'.[4] Indeed. Both press and broadcast media in Scotland were presented from the election of the first devolved parliament in 1999 with an entirely new tier of government to cover. Scotland's political journalists now had a parliament of their own to report, an Edinburgh-based government with devolved powers to scrutinise and watch over. All the opportunities and challenges faced by the Westminster lobby were reproduced, if on a smaller scale, with the establishment of the new parliament. The Scottish media, like the newly elected Scottish political class, took on greater responsibility than ever before in the history of the Union. If devolution was going to work, then the overseeing role of the media was going to be central.

Press and broadcast media organisations responded to this challenge by boosting the editorial resource devoted to politics. Money was invested in reporting facilities at the parliament, which became the home base for an expanded cohort of political journalists reporting on debates in the chamber, committee proceedings and other business. The Holyrood Parliament's Freedom of Information (Scotland) Act of 2002, the provisions of which have been robustly upheld by the Information Commissioner, Kevin Dunion, provided a further source of material for Scotland's political journalists. The *Sunday Herald*'s Paul Hutcheon in particular, armed with the fruits of hundreds of disclosure requests under Freedom of Information rules, emerged as a thorn in the flesh of officialdom's side.

The Scottish media as a whole developed a habit of intense criticism of the Scottish Parliament, the Scottish Executive and its activities. Stories about alleged expense-account fiddling and other corruption brought down not only the first minister Henry McLeish, but Tory leader David McLetchie. The papers were full of stories about ministers' dodgy relatives, and alleged cronyism in the Labour hierarchy. This pattern of coverage paralleled trends in political journalism south of the border, criticised by John Lloyd and others as inducing widespread and unjustified cynicism amongst the electorate (Lloyd 2004). I have addressed the debate about the appropriate limits of adversarialism in political journalism elsewhere (McNair 2000), and simply note here that the same pressures on journalists to find stories, to obtain scoops, to gain a march on rivals, meant that the first eight years of Scottish devolution were, if Scotland's political journalists were to be believed, a dispiriting succession of low-level scandals, corruption and mediocrity. Whether this pattern of coverage contributed to the disappointingly low turn-outs at the elections of 2003 and 2007 is a question which remains to be answered.

SCOTTISH STORIES IN THE UK NEWS AGENDA

Before devolution, one frequently heard complaint of many Scots was that the London-based media tended to ignore or downplay events north of the border. Football fans regularly condemned the real and perceived slights of BBC commentators such as Jimmy Hill, while cultural commentators noted the relative lack of newsworthiness attaching to Scottish events in the UK media. There was undoubtedly truth in this perception, which arose not merely from the smallness of Scotland (smaller than some of the English regions, after all) but the London-centric structure of the UK media. With the majority of the UK media and their employees based in the southeast of England, not just Scotland but the entire UK outside of that zone tended to be de-prioritised. Why interview a Geordie about inflation rates for a vox pop if your reporter can simply step out of the London office and find an endless supply of opinion? Why go to the trouble of tracking down a Scottish academic to talk about a UK issue when the southeast is brimful of international-class universities?

Not necessarily a conscious anti-Scottish bias, then, but organisational features of the UK media, and the inevitable metro-centrism of media workers in the London area, meant that before devolution Scotland rarely appeared in the UK media in anything other than the most dreadful or dramatic contexts – the Ibrox disaster; the Piper Alpha disaster; the Dunblane massacre. After devolution, this pattern of coverage continued. In January 2007 journalism professor Brian Cathcart observed that Scottish stories had 'all but vanished' from the London-based newspapers. 'It is as if', added Cathcart, 'now that the Scots have a parliament where they can air views and discuss events among themselves, the English don't want to know them any more, and so, as far as political news value goes, Scotland now has a standing on a par with a middle-sized English local authority'.[5] Some research to substantiate this claim was carried out by Douglas MacMillan of Aberdeen University in 2005. His six-month content analysis of BBC TV news found that only 2 per cent of coverage was devoted to Scotland, and he concluded from this that Scottish licence-fee payers were not receiving value for money.[6] Welcomed by the SNP and others as evidence of the need for a Scottish Six, the study certainly supported the view that Scotland was not in itself of major interest to UK news-makers. Then again, why should it be? If the establishment of the parliament gave the Scottish media much more to write about than previously, they also furnished the UK media with a reason to write less about Scotland. Do the Scots read regularly about the politics of northeast England, or the Midlands? Do they know the name of even one local politician in these vast and important regions of the UK?

A number of Scottish stories have made the UK news agenda in recent times, however, many of them as a consequence of devolution. The scandal of the Parliament building project, for example, could not be ignored by the UK media, and was often reported in the context of the similarly afflicted Millenium dome (vast overspend, controversial design, allegations of Labour cronyism).

Associated with this story was the Wark–McConnell scandal, in which BBC journalist Kirsty Wark was revealed to have a close friendship with Labour First Minister Jack McConnell. She was photographed with him and his family at her holiday home in Mallorca. Given Wark's traditional front-line role in the BBC's coverage of Scottish political events such as elections, this raised questions about her impartiality. Could she, for example, present an election-night special and be relied upon to exercise due impartiality between the parties competing for power? It might have been possible to argue that she could – can journalists not have friends in political life, under any circumstances? – but the story was given 'legs' by the additional pertinent fact that Wark's TV production company, Wark-Clements, had been commissioned by the BBC, at a cost of £3 million, to document the building of the parliament. Moreover, she had been a member of the committee which controversially chose the Spanish architect Enric Miralles to design the building.

All of this added up to a picture of a Scottish media and political elite which was rather too close for comfort. By the end of the wave of stories, Wark had been required to withdraw herself from future coverage of Scottish elections. Other stories of alleged cronyism in the first eight years of the parliament included the resignation of Donald Dewar's successor as First Minister, Henry McLeish, after corruption allegations; and 'lobbygate', in which inappropriate connections were alleged between Labour politicians and lobbyists (these involving UK government minister John Reid and his son among others). Also receiving UK-wide coverage was the bizarre tale of Lord Watson, the Scottish Labour peer who attempted to set fire to a hotel curtain during a drunken binge and had the misfortune to be caught on CCTV, before being sent to prison for a year.

Even more exotic, if richly entertaining, was the saga of the Sheridan–*News of the World* libel case and its aftermath, which fascinated the Scottish media and then the UK in the summer and autumn of 2006. As is well known, the Scottish edition of the *News of the World*'s allegations of sex orgies, attendance at swingers' clubs, and vicious SSP infighting were contested by Sheridan, whose assertions of innocence were accepted by a jury in the Edinburgh High Court. Sheridan's messianic comparisons of himself to Mandela and Martin Luther King, allegations of secret service conspiracies, feuding within his own party ranks over who had told the truth in court – all provided the Scottish and UK media with a rare cocktail of ultra-left politics and celebrity scandal which was irresistible to editors both inside and outside Scotland. Since, at the time of writing, an appeal by the newspaper against the verdict is pending, and a police investigation of alleged perjury by witnesses is underway, the story clearly has a long way to run.

By far the biggest Scottish story in the UK media since devolution, however, was the rise of the SNP in the opinion polls as the 2007 parliamentary election approached. At times in the past, including the previous 2003 election, the nationalists had commanded early leads in the polls before settling back to their traditional 25 per cent of the vote (a figure roughly corresponding to public support for independence in recent decades). This time, however, as the May election approached, the SNP's support held up, and even increased. It is not the remit of this chapter to address in depth the reasons for the SNP's ascendancy. One could cite the lacklustre nature of the Labour-Liberal Democrat coalition since 1999, and its failure to sell what was a good economic record; or the desire of a significant proportion of the Scottish people to give Tony Blair and New Labour a kicking because of the invasion of Iraq; or even the collapse of the SSP following the Sheridan libel case (the migration of SSP voters to the SNP was identified by many observers as a contributing factor in the outcome of the election). Whatever the explanation, and even though support for the SNP was not necessarily support for independence (overall, almost 70 per cent of voters in the 2007 election supported pro-Union parties), the growing likelihood of an SNP victory as polling day approached raised the issue of Scotland's relationship to the United Kingdom in unprecedentedly stark terms.

An SNP government in Edinburgh had always been a possible outcome of devolution. Now, for the first time, it looked like it was going to happen, raising debate not just in Scotland but in the wider UK media about the sustainability of the constitutional status quo, and the merits of Scottish independence. All of this took place at a time when, because of the imminence of Gordon Brown's succession as prime minister, and the lingering dilemma of the 'West Lothian question' (why should Scottish MPs be allowed to vote on matters such as education and health which affect only English voters, since the devolved parliament has responsibility for these and other matters in Scotland?), relations between the English and Scottish political spheres had already become more tense. The fact that the 2007 election coincided almost exactly with the 300th anniversary of the Act of Union merely added to the newsworthiness of these issues. Although they declined in visibility in the immediate aftermath of the election, as Salmond succeeded McConnell and Brown succeeded Blair, they resurfaced in the following months, and were likely to be a major issue in the next UK general election.

The rise of Scottish nationalism became a UK story not just about Scotland, but England too. Did England benefit from this Union that was apparently held in such contempt by so many north of the border? Did the Barnett formula, which determines the level of resources allocated by the UK government to Scotland, represent an unfair drain on the English electorate?

THE POLITICS OF THE SCOTTISH MEDIA AND THE UNION

Even although the Scottish press has reflected, and indeed promoted, a recognisably Scottish identity for centuries, that has nearly always been within the broader context of support for the Union. Scotland was in the vanguard of the Enlightenment project, as already noted, and by the late eighteenth century hosted one of the most vibrant and intellectually sophisticated public spheres in Europe. The voices contributing to that public sphere, and to the periodicals and newspapers which comprised it, believed wholeheartedly in the economic, cultural and political benefits of the union with England, even if they spoke with a distinctively Scottish voice.

Later on, as mass literacy and education developed in Scotland, and with it a popular press, newspapers such as the weekly *People's Journal* of Dundee, which by the 1914–18 war was selling 250,000 copies, participated in what David Goldie, William Donaldson and others refer to as 'the construction of a vernacular culture' in Scotland – a print culture recognisably different from that of the London-based press, though rarely conceived in terms of nationalist separatism. As the *People's Journal* newspaper became more popular, reaching out to a broader Scottish audience, 'it stripped itself of most of its recognisable markers of nationality'(Goldie 2004: 140). Goldie points out that the founder of the *People's Journal*, John Leng, was an Englishman. Likewise, Charles Cooper, editor of *The Scotsman* between 1876 and 1905 came from Hull.

The content of these papers was largely driven by Scottish events, as one would expect, but they were at the same time 'solidly Unionist' in their editorial standpoint (Goldie 2004: 141). Neither independence, nor devolution, were on the agenda of the Scottish media as the popular press expanded in the late nineteenth and early twentieth centuries. On the contrary, Scotland's people and press were enthusiastic participants in the British imperial project, and pursued an unashamedly integrationist agenda. Scotland's soldiers, entrepreneurs, scientists and philosophers were among the shock troops of the expanding British empire, and saw no contradiction between that role and their ownership of a distinctively Scottish identity.

Scottish cultural historians such as Goldie would assert that this integrationist consensus peaked in the Edwardian period and during World War One, but it has remained the default stance of the Scottish media more or less until the present day. Even as the Scottish nationalist movement began to develop in the 1920s and after, there was no corresponding shift in the presumption of the Scottish press that the Union was a good thing. Titles have differed in their party political affiliations, but in so far as – until relatively recently – all the main parties in Scotland have been pro-Union, the integrationist consensus cut across the lines of left and right which divided the media on many other issues. *The Herald* and *The Scotsman* may have had different views on the management of social or economic policy, but they agreed on the fundamental correctness of the Union. Under the leadership of Andrew Neil, indeed, *The Scotsman* opposed even devolution on the grounds that it would undermine the Union and encourage collectivism and parochialism in the country.

What changed to make this consensus appear anachronistic, even anti-democratic, was the collapse of the Conservative Party as a major electoral force in Scotland, and its replacement by the Scottish National Party as the second-largest party after Labour. As was observed earlier, the Thatcher/Major approach to governing Scotland fed the desire for self-government north of the border. The Scottish press reflected this desire, and punished the party which opposed devolution, the Scottish Conservatives. In the 1997 general election campaign, wrote John Lloyd at the time, 'In Scotland, the media has been vehemently opposed to a Tory party with only 25 per cent of the vote and with a policy of opposition to devolution, the issue which more than any other has had the attention of the media and political classes'.[7] The Scottish Conservatives' support fell further after the introduction of devolution, reducing the party to one Scottish seat at Westminster, and eighteen MSPs following the 2007 Scottish election. The Scottish press, one might say, has lost interest in the Conservatives, a bias which is likely to remain until such time as the party north of the border regains some of its traditional influence and popularity.

If the recent Scottish press bias against the Conservatives is explicable in terms of electoral trends, the same cannot be said of the relationship to the SNP. Although, as previously noted, Scottish newspapers have displayed a pro-Union consensus for centuries, this has become harder to explain in the context of an ascendant nationalism, and the decline of the Conservatives. Prior to the break-through campaign of 2007, the SNP could lay claim to around 25 per cent of popular support in Scotland, and a little more or less than that in Westminster and Scottish elections. While SNP representation at Westminster has been less than its support would suggest, because of the first-past-the-post electoral system, the adoption of proportional representation in Scottish elections has meant that since 1999 the SNP has been the second most popular party, both at the polls and in terms of seats. And yet, until the 2007 campaign, the party had no unambiguous editorial support amongst the Scottish press. Newspapers retained their pro-Union and anti-SNP positions, despite the apparent growth in support for them at the polls. Former political editor of the *Herald* and self-confessed nationalist Murray Ritchie complained in 2004 that:

> most Scottish newspapers are downright hostile to independence and those which are not are mainly indifferent. This is an auld sang, and an affront to democracy and free expression. Indeed it is more than that because it amounts to a conspiratorial denial of the existence of a polit-ical ambition which is attractive – sometimes obsessively so – to a significant section of the electorate.[8]

On the eve of the 2003 parliamentary campaign, an attempt was made to launch a pro-SNP newspaper, and to reduce this deficit. *The Scottish Standard* was a failure, however, achieving a peak sale of only 12,000 before closure after a mere seven weeks. As of 2003, there was still apparently no public demand for an explicitly pro-SNP title, although it could also be argued that the paper in question was simply not of the quality required to compete effectively in the Scottish market. Run on a shoestring, with a skeletal editorial resource, the title was never going to compete seriously with *The Sun* or the *Record*. Nevertheless, its failure to sell copies even amongst SNP voters was striking, and suggested to some observers that the demand for a pro-SNP editorial voice in the Scottish press had been overstated.

By 2007, however, the environment had changed. As the election campaign gathered steam in the first months of the year, and an early SNP opinion poll lead was sustained, suggesting the growing likelihood of a victory in the May poll, a number of titles began to move towards a pro-nationalist stance, if not one of pro-independence. On the Sunday before the 3 May election, many of the Scottish newspapers backed the SNP in their leader columns, albeit while striving to distance themselves from support for independence. The *Sunday Herald* qualified its position by stressing that it opposed the SNP's key policy of separation from the union, and remained 'a staunch supporter of devolution',[9] but stated that in its view, Scotland had underperformed under the Labour-Liberal Democrat coalition of 2003–7, and that on these grounds above all Jack McConnell did not deserve to be re-elected as first minister. In criticising the lack of diversity of the Scottish press on the devolution/ independence issue (see above), the *Sunday Herald* appeared to be recognising that a significant proportion of its readership was shifting to the nationalist camp, and that both democracy and the preservation of market share made a pro-SNP shift in its own editorial stance timely.

More surprising than the *Herald*'s stance, perhaps, was that of *Scotland on Sunday*, which announced in its eve-of-poll editorial that while 'we believe the Union has served Scotland well, and that devolution can evolve further, with new powers for Holyrood, to meet the new ambitions of the Scottish people', an SNP-led coalition 'offers the best chance of restoring public confidence in our democracy'.[10] The title had not long before been bought from the Barclay Brothers by Johnston Press, which had clearly permitted a relaxation of its hith-erto staunchly pro-Union position. The daily sisters of both titles followed suit with pro-SNP editorials, and even *The Sunday Times* Scottish edition advised its readers that it was 'a time for change'.[11]

Both *The Scottish Sun* and the *Daily Record* stayed loyal to Labour, however. For *The Sun*, urging readers to 'stop the chaos' which would unfold with a nationalist government, 'it is a time for unionists to put political differences aside and join together to stop the nationalists'.[12] The *Daily Record* editorialised against SNP 'pipe dreams' and 'the romanticism of independence', as well as SNP leader Alex Salmond's 'breathtaking arrogance'.[13]

CONCLUSION

Such declarations were not enough to prevent the SNP's victory on 3 May 2007, which appeared to have little obvious relationship to media coverage of the contest. There had been overwhelming pro-Union bias in the Scottish press for years leading up to the poll, but still the SNP won the election. It is arguable, though it cannot be proved, that the pattern of critical media cover-age of the parliament from its inception, in print and on the airwaves (see above) undermined popular support for the governing coalition by focusing on sleaze, cronyism, and the kind of 'hyperadversarialism' frequently identified in political journalism at the UK level (Lloyd 2004). This, combined with an inept Labour campaign, may have encouraged the electorate to believe that it was indeed 'time for a change'. At another level of influence, *The Guardian* suggested, with its tongue not entirely in its cheek, that 'It was the *News of the World* wot lost it', because of the impact of the Sheridan libel case on the Scottish Socialist Party. Because of that case, pointed out media correspondent Matt Wells, the SSP split and many of its supporters jumped ship for the SNP. This small shift in allegiance may have made all the difference in what turned out to be a very close race indeed. For Wells, 'the collapse of the SSP was a significant factor in the success of the SNP'.[14]

So was a Rupert Murdoch-owned red top tabloid ultimately responsible for the rise of the SNP as a governing party in Scotland? It is unlikely that we will ever know for sure. In the meantime, and for the lifetime of at least one parliament, the *Scottish News of the World* and the rest of the Scottish media face a transformed political environment full of opportunities and challenges. Due to the SNP's electoral success, it is likely that independence will be higher on the agenda of national debate than at any time in the country's political history. Although the narrow margin of the SNP's victory, and the fact that the vast majority of the Scottish electorate voted for pro-union parties[15] reduced the likelihood of a parliamentary majority for a referendum on independence within the lifetime of the 2007–11 parliament, it was widely assumed by most observers that the election of a government with a stated long-term agenda of separation from the United Kingdom would inevitably raise the issue with greater force than ever before. The Scottish media will play a key role in shaping the development and the outcome of that debate. They will, by their choice of which stories to cover and how to cover them, exert substantial influence on how the SNP are perceived to have fared in office, and thus will influence too the prospects of any further move towards separation.

NOTES

1. The Scottish National Party won 32.9 per cent of constituency votes, to Labour's 32.1 per cent. The SNP won 31 per cent of regional list votes, to Labour's 29.1 per cent. Labour won forty-six seats (35.7 per cent share) to the SNP's forty-seven (36.4 per cent). (Source: www.scottish.parliament.uk/msp/elections/2007/analysis.htm.)
2. See Hutchison, D.: 'Ownership, control and cultural policy', *Edinburgh Review*, 116, pp. 35–45 for a discussion of recent trends.
3. A 2004 Scottish Consumer Council survey found 40 per cent of respondents in favour of a Scottish Six, and a further 29 per cent 'registering some support' (http://news.bbc.co.uk/1/low/scotland/3544071.stm).
4. Cathcart, B. (2007), 'Forgotten friends in the north', *New Statesman*, 29 January.
5. Cathcart, B. (2007), 'Forgotten friends in the north', *New Statesman*, 29 January.
6. Money, R. (2005), 'BBC evening news guilty of bias', *Sunday Herald*, 16 October.
7. Lloyd, J. (1997), 'The Scottish media cannot see that Tony Blair is selling devolution to the English', *Prospect*, May.
8. Ritchie, M. (2004), 'Politics and the press', Saltire Society Newsletter, issue 2.
9. Editorial, *Sunday Herald*, 29 April 2007.
10. Editorial, *Scotland on Sunday*, 29 April 2007.
11. Editorial, *The Sunday Times Scotland*, 29 April 2007.

12. Editorial, *Scottish Sun*, May 2 2007.
13. Editorial, *Daily Record*, May 2 2007.
14. Wells, M. (2007), 'It was the *News of the World* wot won it', *The Guardian*, 7 May.
15. Labour, Liberal Democrat and Conservative between them secured seventy-nine seats, as compared to the fifty seats won by the pro-independence SNP, the Greens and the non-aligned but nationalist Margo MacDonald.

REFERENCES

Conboy, M. (2004), *Journalism: A critical History*, London: Sage.
Donaldson, W. (1986), *Popular Literature in Victorian Scotland: Language, Fiction and the Press*, Aberdeen: Aberdeen University Press.
Franklin, B. (ed.) (2006), *Local Journalism and Local Media: Making the Local News*, London: Routledge.
Goldie, D. (2006), 'The British invention of Scottish culture: World War I and before', *Review of Scottish Culture*, 18, pp. 128–48.
Herman, A. (2002), *Scottish Enlightenment: The Scots' Invention of the Modern World*, London: Fourth Estate.
Lloyd, J. (2004), *What the Media Are Doing To Our Politics*, London: Constable.
McNair, B. (2000), *Journalism and Democracy*, London: Routledge.
McNair, B. (2003), *News and Journalism in the UK*, 4th edn, London: Routledge.
McNair, B. (2006), 'News from a small country: the media in Scotland', in B. Franklin (ed.), *Local Journalism and Local Media: Making the Local News*, London: Routledge, pp. 37–48.
Reid, H. (2006), *Deadline: The Story of the Scottish Press*, Edinburgh: Saint Andrew Press.
Schlesinger, P. (1998), 'Scotland's Parliament: devolution, the media and political culture', Arena working paper 3, 1998 (www.arena.uio.no/publications/wp98_3.htm).
Schlesinger, P., D. Miller and W. Dinan (2001), *Open Scotland? Journalists, Spin Doctors and Lobbyists*, Edinburgh: Polygon.

16

A View from Westminster

BRIAN WILSON

Parliamentary reporting, in the straightforward form of placing on record what was said in the House of Commons, is an honourable form of journalism that is now close to extinction.

Unless one dips into the columns of *Hansard*, it is very unusual to read an unvarnished summary of Parliamentary proceedings in which the views expressed by ministers and MPs are allocated a few succinct lines and the occasional ringing phrase or significant sentiment is placed on record.

Nobody, we are told, wants to read it, and this may be true. However, the demise of Parliamentary reporting contributes to one of the great contradictions of modern politics: while the media purport to despise 'spin' as a substitute for some purer flow of information, they have themselves opted to cover Parliament and politics in terms that are overwhelmingly 'spun' rather than merely reported.

Whatever the cynics might wish us to believe, issues of substance which affect the lives of every citizen in the United Kingdom are raised and discussed at Westminster on every day that Parliament sits. The vast majority of these matters go unreported. In Scotland, that reality is compounded by the desire in some quarters to minimise the significance of Westminster in comparison to the Scottish Parliament at Holyrood.

Devolution has undoubtedly removed many of the distinctively Scottish elements from the Westminster mix. There are now very rarely debates on uniquely Scottish legislation in the chamber. There are therefore no standing committees on Scottish business. Scottish Questions is usually a perfunctory occasion. The Scottish Grand Committee scarcely lives up to its name while the Scottish Select Committee struggles to find subjects within its remit to investigate.

None of this means, however, that Westminster is irrelevant to Scotland. The performance of our fifty-one MPs still requires scrutiny. Their contributions to debate merit reporting, whether favourable or otherwise. The great majority of Westminster legislation still applies as much to Scotland as to the rest of the United Kingdom. Failing to report any of this in a distinctively Scottish context creates a democratic deficit which, in terms of Westminster's supposed irrelevance to Scotland, is not so much a reflection as an objective.

This trend is reflected in the Scottish media presence at Westminster. I reckon that it is no more than half of what it was when I became an MP in 1987. To some extent, this reflects more general cutbacks in the numbers employed by Scottish media organisations but it is also a product of the media's reaction to devolution. However unfavourably Holyrood may be reported, the Scottish media have a substantial vested interest in building it up as the main font of Parliamentary activity relating to Scotland, whether or not that is true.

The Scottish press corps at Westminster now consists of two from *The Herald* whereas, in the 1990s, there were four. *The Scotsman* is down from three to two. There is one each from the *Press and Journal*, the *Daily Record*, *Scotland on Sunday* and the *Sunday Herald*. BBC Scotland has two while STV and Grampian have one between them. Their regular political programmes centred on Westminster coverage have long since disappeared. In addition, the London-based general reporters of the self-styled Scottish 'heavies' have gone, so there is no back-up for the Parliamentary teams, either for big events or when stories spill out of the Palace of Westminster into wider developments. For good measure, there are now no Scottish correspondents in Brussels.

Such a small band of reporters at Westminster simply does not have the time, even if the demand from newsdesks existed, to provide much in the way of straight reporting from the House of Commons chamber, never mind from the Committees and other entities within the Parliamentary structure. The vast majority of Parliamentary reporting – in both the London-based and the Scottish media – now comes from briefings or press releases. In other words, it is about what is going on around the Westminster village rather than in Parliament itself. It is about the stories that are being promoted rather than ones which emerge through questioning or debate.

The problem with this is not one of absolutes. Verbatim Parliamentary reporting may well be boring and of little interest to most readers, though I suspect that this view has been arrived at through very little consultation! But there was a lot to be said for the mix which previously existed. I am certain that there is market for – as well as an obligation to provide – more straightforward reporting of proceedings at Westminster, particularly where they feature Scottish interests, and less subjective reporting based on briefings and spin.

The media's attitude towards these sources of stories is truly wondrous to behold. Spin could not exist unless journalists were willing to be spun. This is particularly true where the sources of supposed stories insist on retaining their anonymity. I have always taken the view that an off-the-record briefing which attacks someone is the political equivalent of the poison pen letter. The only story worth telling is about the source of the story but that is the one which is never told. Journalists play the game because it is a lazy way of getting 'exclusives', or else for fear of deviating from the wisdom of the pack, whether the story on offer is well founded or merely self-serving.

Thus the pendulum has swung too far the other way. Verbatim Parliamentary reporting may be unfashionable to the point that it has virtually been squeezed out of newspapers. But the diet which has replaced it of stories based on briefings, press releases and Westminster gossip has little to commend it. Throw in the additional marginalisation of Scottish material emanating from Westminster and you have a dilution of serious coverage to the point at which the Scottish public and the cause of informed debate are poorly served. That is no reflection on the handful of Scottish journalists at Westminster who strive to maintain standards.

At least as significant a trend is the Whitehall machine's corresponding loss of interest in the Scottish media. There is an assumption, which compounds in-built metropolitan attitudes, that 'they (the Scots) have gone off to do their own thing' through devolution. This is a particularly dangerous way of thinking for a Labour government which relies, and will continue to rely, for its existence on substantial support within Scotland. In the past, politically astute Labour professionals like Peter Mandelson and Alistair Campbell understood very clearly that the Scottish media were 'different' and that a close eye had to be kept on how issues and actions would play in Scotland. That level of attention and sensitivity is now very difficult to find within the Government's media operation.

One senior Scottish journalist at Westminster said:

> Time and again, the Government is caught flat-footed in Scotland because nobody is thinking in terms of the Scottish media. A good example was Dungavel (immigration detention centre) where a huge story was running in Scotland without anyone in the Home Office realising it. The story was exaggerated out of all proportion but until somebody says that, it takes on a life of its own – and then it is too late.

At the time of writing, there has been another excellent example over the 'Libya prisoner transfer' controversy where a moment's thought about the potential for mischief in Scotland would have pre-empted the story in the first place, while there was then nobody capable of responding effectively to it once it did break in the Scottish Parliament.

Neither is it guaranteed (again at the time of writing) that matters will improve with the advent of Gordon Brown's premiership. One Westminster correspondent said, 'Gordon has never had an adviser around him with any interest in, or understanding of, Scotland'. Labour is now paying a heavy price for this cavalier attitude which has developed over the past decade. The repeated 'own-goaling' over stories which have both a Westminster and Scottish element is proving corrosive. In a situation where political power is so finely balanced in Scotland, the collapse of a competent Scottish-orientated Government media operation in Whitehall has been a significant factor – and one which political common sense suggests should be addressed.

When I became an MP in 1987, the House of Commons was still not televised live. Indeed, one of my first Parliamentary tasks was to serve on the Select Committee which recommended on how this innovation should be made and managed. Clearly, the televising of Westminster has had an impact on other forms of Parliamentary reporting. Coverage of such gladiatorial occasions as Prime Minister's Question Time has to compete with the immediacy of television; hence the increasing reliance on sketch-writing as opposed to straightforward reporting. At first, Scottish proceedings were widely used as the basis of domestic television and radio coverage, including the live reporting of Scottish Questions. This too has receded to the point of near non-existence.

The most conscientious media outlet in Scotland, in terms of traditional Parliamentary reporting and also recognising the interests of its readers rather than trying to shape them, is the Aberdeen *Press and Journal*. It is a newspaper often derided for its parochialism but it is also a newspaper that sells more copies each day than either *The Herald* or *The Scotsman*! It is a reasonable certainty that any event or debate within the Palace of Westminster that involves MPs from the *P and J*'s circulation area or impinges specifically upon the interests of that area will be reported in a thorough and balanced way. It is a model that others should re-visit. The assumption that the interests of readers, viewers and listeners in Scotland are limited to the reporting of great events, political intrigue or interpretative coverage remains unproven. Maybe they would also like to know a bit more about what their MPs are saying and doing, whether for good or ill.

The natural instinct of politicians is to try to control the flow and nature of media coverage which they receive. The duty of journalists is to resist rather than facilitate that desire. Equally, while it should be expected that politicians will try to draw attention to what they are involved in if they think it reflects positively upon them, the issuing of press releases – whether by Government departments or individual MPs – should not be the sole or main criterion for obtaining coverage. Many of the best stories at Westminster have to be sought out while some of the most interesting and diligent MPs are also the least media-savvy.

But by far the most urgent and pernicious trend surrounding Scottish coverage of Westminster lies in the determination of large sections of the Scottish media, for a variety of reasons, to marginalise it while building up Holyrood as the more relevant institution. That assessment does not have the status of objective truth and it is possible to make a strong counter-argument, based on the breakdown of reserved and devolved powers. The essence of devolution must be that both Parliaments are of generally equal relevance based on their respective spheres. That is the spirit in which they should be reported. It is dishonest of the Scottish media to marginalise Scottish coverage of Westminster and then attribute this decision to the wishes of their readers, viewers or listeners.

It is this trend that makes many of us so resistant to the pressure for the main BBC news bulletin of the day to be generated from within Scotland, the so-called Scottish Six. The fear is that for reasons that are political rather than objective, Scotland would be pushed further into a world of introspective media coverage in which disproportionate attention was given to Scottish politics as conducted within Scotland, as opposed to the broad range of issues that affect Scotland irrespective of where they arise or are debated. It is on the basis of exactly the same expectation that those who want to separate Scotland politically from the rest of the United Kingdom are so keen on the idea.

17

A View from Holyrood

MICHAEL RUSSELL

On election day I always vote early at home in Argyll before hotfooting it to the South of Scotland and my own constituency. On 3 May 2007, having exercised my choice as MSP in favour of my friend and colleague Jim Mather (who won) and my choice as First Minister in favour of Alex Salmond (ditto), I set off to cross the Clyde and stopped at a newsagent's in Sandbank near Dunoon. Scanning the counter I felt a thrill of excitement – could it really be that *The Sun*, which had become the most hostile of cheerleaders for Gordon Brown's 'nat bashing', was suddenly re-converted to the cause of independence, which it left fifteen years ago? Surely it must be so, I thought, as I looked at the huge SNP symbol on its front page?

Reality dawned quickly. The symbol was indeed there, but cleverly altered to resemble a noose. A number of other small symbols, redrawn in the same way, emphasised the point. Voting SNP today, the paper was telling its readers, would be an act of individual and collective suicide.

Such a brutal lack of subtlety was hardly surprising. The day before the paper had carried a double page spread which encouraged voters in a range of marginal constituencies to cast their ballots tactically in order to defeat every significant nationalist candidate. Labour, Tory and Liberal voters were urged to put country before their party (that country being Britain of course) in order to see off the subversive, impoverishing and no doubt scrofulous nationalists.

This type of propaganda had been running in *The Sun* for many weeks. Certainly the other tabloids – most notably the long-term Labour-supporting *Daily Record* – had also been hostile to the SNP but neither so virulently nor so creatively. Of course the paper's London supremo, Rebekah Wade, was known to be close to Gordon Brown. So, apparently, it had fallen to her to ensure that the Scottish edition did as it was told, plugged Brown at every opportunity and worked in his interests by distorting and mis-representing anything a nationalist said.

Allegedly, however, this cosy arrangement was almost derailed early in the campaign when Wade came to Scotland to ensure that all was going to plan. Calling on the then First Minister, Jack MacConnell, to assure him of the paper's support, she was bemused to be offered tea, only to be told that there was no milk available so she would have to wait until a special advisor could nip out for a pint. She is said to have confided later that the atmosphere in Bute House seemed like the last days in the bunker. Which of course it was, despite her best efforts.

The fact that the SNP won in such circumstances is, of course, not really the point. The point is that despite a strong showing for several months the SNP poll lead was being eroded at the very end of the campaign. Furthermore, it is probable that some part of that erosion at least can be attributed not to any successes in a lacklustre and confused Labour campaign (despite Labour pollster Lord Gould's assertions to the contrary) but to the influence of the tabloids, and particularly *The Sun*. It was, in fact, *The Sun* which tried hard to win it for Labour even if – in the media world of swings and roundabouts – it may well have been the *News of the World* which lost it for Solidarity and the SSP, shepherding home to the nationalists many votes that in 2003 had drifted off to Tommy Sheridan, whose star having risen fast had now fallen with greater speed.

Given that the SNP did emerge as the largest party, it might be thought that this is all water under the bridge. But the issue is of future importance for two reasons. Firstly, the tabloids have power and will continue to have influence. They will continue to wish to guide voters and accordingly – for the sake of democracy – the way they do so needs to be better understood. Secondly, the tabloids presently sit awkwardly and with a distorted prominence (particularly at election times) in a media landscape that has, to a great extent, diminished the type of vigorous political debate which might have guided or shamed them into a more constructive role. Bringing the ecology of the Scottish media back into balance – first of all by shining the clear light of inquiry on it – would be a desirable objective.

Within that ecology, of course, it is broadcasting that plays the biggest part, and it is fair to admit that by and large the broadcasting media are neutral in political terms. That neutrality was of importance when the party leaders came (eventually) to debate each other face to face, for quality will out and the dominance of Salmond was clear in every programme.

But the broadcasting companies still suffer from a level of institutional bias. In particular BBC structures are centrist and utterly metropolitan, not to say

London-centric. This problem has been exacerbated in recent years because the current BBC Scotland management is weak and lacks the ability and the organisational muscle to assert itself within the wider organisation. That issue needs addressing, particularly as the lack of a strategic and distinctive Scottish vision of excellence in broadcasting within BBC Scotland becomes ever more damaging in terms of services provided and audiences served.

The Scottish broadsheets (and the Scottish editions of English-based papers) have traditionally been hostile to nationalism, independence and the SNP. Even when editors and journalists have wished to explore matters more constructively, it has proved difficult because of ownership patterns and because of a decade long stranglehold on free opinion imposed by New Labour in the person of Gordon Brown. Stories of his constant interference are legion and there are a number of well documented examples that other pressures may have been applied: for example, Harry Reid, editor of *The Herald* during the first Holyrood election campaign in 1999, believes that advertising monies were withheld from his paper by New Labour in order to attempt to force a more anti-SNP line.[1]

That vice-like grip loosened significantly, however, in the run-up to, and during the 2007 elections. A combination of factors may have been responsible but primarily the clear failure of Labour's campaign to offer a constructive vision of the future – in other words the relentless negativity of Labour's campaign – appears to have convinced a number of editors that it was time to encourage a different type of politics.

The regional and local press was and is more varied. Key regional papers like the *Press and Journal* and the *Courier* usually reflect accurately the on-the-ground politics of their areas which – as they are largely dominated now by the SNP – means setting and keeping a fairer balance. In addition, local newspapers and local radio have also been utilised more effectively by the SNP in recent years, very much as a result of the Salmond emphasis on direct political communication.

Yet overall the amount of serious political debate – during elections but particularly between elections – has declined. The tone of the coverage has also changed over the past two decades with even the broadsheets – and particularly the Sunday broadsheets – increasingly wedded to a tabloid style of coverage which promotes personality above policy and which seeks to expose rather than illuminate. Endless coverage of expenses issues illustrates that point well.

Only in the new media in Scotland – ranging from blogs through commentary sites to the postings on newspaper websites in reaction to stories – is political coverage and interest both increasing and becoming better informed. Whilst some of this clearly verges on the obsessive, most is positive and engaged. It is also, it is worth noting, often strongly nationalistic and often clearly allied with the SNP, though frequently in the stance of a critical friend. Whilst the influence of this form of media is still small, it is of increasing significance particularly amongst those most likely to vote and it may well have had some effect on the national vote. The SNP itself clearly thought so, devoting considerable resources to what was widely agreed to be the best online presence of the campaign which included an Internet TV service in the last week.

The shape of the media landscape, in so far as it relates to politics, is therefore flatter and less interesting than it was even a generation ago, except in those areas which have developed since that time. Consequently when volcanoes erupt at election time – when the tabloids decide to re-engage in the political battle and to do so in a highly partisan fashion – they can assume a prominence which might otherwise be beyond them. They can also exhibit prominently certain failings which may diminish public confidence in the media.

During the 2007 Scottish Parliament election there were occasions on which the *Daily Mail* published stories favourable to the SNP, and even the *Express* managed to avoid hysterical condemnation (unlike in previous years). But as ever it was *The Sun* and the *Record* – by far the largest circulation dailies – which exhibited the greatest prejudice against nationalism and the SNP and which showed the poorest journalistic standards whilst so doing.

The issue of standards is important. When a political journalist on a tabloid tells a politician that there is 'no point in commenting, because we are now just making our stories up', there are real causes for concern. When stories are 'made up' during an election with the sole purpose of promoting one party and denigrating another, then the public have a right to ask whether they are, when purchasing papers which behave in that way, being deceived and abused.

Of course a newspaper, owned by a private citizen or a private company, is entitled to print what it wants, within the general laws of decency and defamation. But perhaps, in the interests of public knowledge and with a view to informing citizens, papers should be required to indicate with prominence which political party they support and what contacts exist between their proprietors, editors, and senior commentators, and those parties. Annual declarations of affiliation, financial connections and other significant facts by key figures in each newspaper and media group would be useful, and no more, in terms of transparency, than those demanded of politicians themselves.

Gordon Brown's dinners with Rebekah Wade are no doubt pleasant social occasions. But if they are also occasions on which decisions are made about the information to be provided to the paper's Scottish readers and how it should be provided, those readers deserve to be told that this is and was a determining factor with regard to what they are offered on a daily basis.

To succeed consensual politics requires positive, confident, outward looking journalism, though no one should ask for, or expect, patsy treatment. Part of the present process of change in our country must be about encouraging constructive debate within newspapers and by journalists. Another part is ensuring that we move away from a blame culture, to a 'can do' perspective. A third priority would be to emphasise policy over personality and illumination over exposure.

But a final one would be to let the public know whether murky influences lie behind some of the stories they read. Of course – to be fair to journalists – this would not be so necessary if the gradual poisoning of the well of public life had not been accelerated by interfering and paranoiac New Labour politicians and their spin doctors who – with increasing vitriol – go on trying to force the media to present a distorted and commingled brew of opinion and prejudice masquerading as information and fact.

We must return to a world of informed choice and open discussion and that requires a new transparency in both the media and politics. Informed choice and open discussion are things that Scotland wants and has shown it wants. They are essential for the new politics and the making of a new nation. Accordingly politicians and the media, working together, should now try to deliver them.

NOTE

1. Harry Reid (2006), *Deadline:The Story of the Scottish Press*, Edinburgh: Saint Andrew Press.

18

Media Sport

RICHARD HAYNES AND RAYMOND BOYLE

Our first and last objection to the League is that they exist. The entire rules stink of finance, money-making and money grabbing. (*Scottish Sport*)[1]

INTRODUCTION

The comment quoted above has a familiar ring to it, drawn as it is from a belief that commerce and greed are somehow to blame for despoiling the nature of sport. This particular quote comes from the *Scottish Sport*, part of a burgeoning sporting press of the 1890s railing against the formation of the Scottish Football League and the rise of professionalism in football. To any regular consumer of Scottish sports journalism – print and broadcast – the critical, almost self-righteous tone serves as a reminder that the Scottish media have rarely shirked their role as the arbiters of how sport in Scotland is meant to be organised and managed. The entrenched feel for the meaning of sport in Scotland's cultural history and among Scots is well documented (Jarvie and Burnett 2000) and its public consciousness is laid bare in its media. Above all, the passion for football, mainly but not exclusively among working-class men in the central belt of the country, has been ritualistically reflected in the voluminous coverage it receives on the pages of newspapers and the hours of coverage it warrants across broadcasting schedules. The national passion for sport, and the social and cultural cleavages that are pervasive within and through sport in Scotland, are – to use Michael Billig's phrase (1995) – 'flagged' on a daily basis by the Scottish media's similar obsession with covering the latest news, scandal and gossip for a ready and willing audience.

As the outlets for sports news and coverage have expanded, so too have the complexities in the media and their audiences' relationship with sport. The arrival of digital broadcasting in radio and television, dedicated sports supplements and associated newspaper websites, fan websites, discussion forums and blogs, and the delivery of sports-related content to mobile phones have meant the communicative space of Scottish sport – its media ecology – has never been greater. Yet, as we plan to explore, the economic cost of these new developments means that media sport in Scotland is not as ubiquitous as some might expect; and this arguably has wider social and cultural implications for how media sport is produced, distributed and consumed.

WAY BACK WHEN

In 1996 we reviewed the ways in which these emerging patterns of extended media coverage, allied with processes of globalisation and hyper-commercialisation of mediated sport, were having complex and contradictory influences on the political economy of sport in Scotland and how it was being organised and governed (Boyle and Haynes 1996). We had been keen to critique the theoretical argument that global sports events were eroding more localised aspects of sport as popular culture, thereby effectively chipping away at notions of national identity and sentiment around sport. We felt that much of the rhetoric that surrounded the arguments about globalisation and sport was too heavily dependent on generalised observations of emergent, new media sport practices, such as the rise of the BSkyB-fuelled English Premier League from 1992, and the television-led innovation of the UEFA European Champions League from 1993.

Our empirical evidence showed that while there certainly were new transnational relationships in the media coverage of sport, some of these developments needed to be contextualised in a national frame. More crucially, in terms of televised sport in Scotland, we argued that 'Scottish audiences are seen to identify with television programmes and broadcasters which appear to address their specific locale, interests and culture' (Boyle and Haynes 1996: 562). More than a decade on, we want to revisit the interplay of the specific political, economic and cultural circumstances of media sport in Scotland, particularly given some of the distinctive changes in the set of technologies, organisations and media practices that have been used to deliver a wide range of mediated sports to Scottish audiences and readers since the mid-1990s.

Our original analysis presented a snapshot of televised football in Scotland at an interesting conjuncture in the evolution of sports broadcasting in general. This process, prompted by an increasingly deregulated television market and new distribution channels, was characterised as moving from a 'cosy duopoly' between the BBC and ITV to intense rivalry and cut-throat competition for the rights to broadcast sport in an era of dedicated sports channels. BSkyB and other niche sports channels around the world were, by the mid-1990s, transforming televised sport into highly marketised, glossily packaged entertainment.

In Scotland, where the spoils from professional sport were relatively small in comparison to the competitions of its larger, immediate neighbour, the economies of scale and scope to expand interest in the country's professional leagues and competitions were very limited, and the globalising tendency of media-driven sport was viewed as a threat. The response was a series of reactive and protectionist policies on the part of Scottish sports administrators at a time of major upheaval in the British media sport landscape during the early 1990s, including attempts to ban the screening of live, English club football on Scottish screens during the 1993–4 and 1994–5 football seasons (Boyle and Haynes 1996). The next decade saw immense upheaval in the governance and economic viability of football in Scotland, with the formation of the Scottish Premier League (SPL) in 1998; changes in the structure of the Scottish Football Association Council in 1999; a planned and aborted SPL-led, pay-per-view television channel in 2002; and an increasingly outward economic turn of both Celtic and Rangers, the 'Old Firm', who planned for success in Europe and beyond, in the context of what they clearly viewed as the restrictive practices of the Scottish League and Cup competitions (Boyle and Haynes 2004: 118–37).

In what follows we aim to map this terrain further and analyse the manner in which the age of multi-channel television and the Internet has opened up new vistas and commercial opportunities to Scottish sports organisations to market their sports to recently disaggregated audiences. After a review of technological advances in the coverage of sport, highlighting the analytical tools with which to understand these processes, we concentrate our attention on specific empirical studies of key changes and developments in Scottish media sport in the areas of the press, broadcasting, the Internet and mobile telephony. We conclude by suggesting renewed ways of understanding the changing relationship between the Scottish media and sport.

SHRINKING SCOTLAND: SCOTTISH SPORT ON TELEVISION

For a country supposedly obsessed with sport, one of the most striking aspects of the terrestrial television schedules in 2007 is the invisibility of Scottish sport. On free-to-air television, a substantial amount of sport is given airtime. For example, in an average week in late March, early April of that year across BBC1, BBC2, STV, Channel 4, Five and ITV 4, there was a mixture of live and recorded material. Live television sport included rugby league Challenge Cup action featuring the Warrington Wolves, Hull Kingston Rovers, the Widnes Vikings and the Wigan Warriors; World Track Cycling from Majorca; the US Masters golf from Augusta; the Davis Cup tennis match between Britain and the Netherlands; and UEFA Champions League football from Milan and Eindhoven. Highlights packages included the World swimming championship from Melbourne; the Cricket World Cup from the West Indies; two programmes of football highlights from the English Premiership; and a range of football preview programmes focused on English football and the UEFA Champions League. Although Scottish athletes featured in some of these contests, the framing of such events was distinctly British and produced from a largely English perspective.

For sporting insomniacs, Channel Five ran a night-long sports schedule from about 1am to 6 am which that week predominantly featured highlights of American-based sports events: NHL ice hockey, golf from Texas, speedway from Virginia, IndyCar racing from Florida, NBA basketball from Memphis; and live major-league baseball. It also carried highlights of French, Dutch and Argentinian football, boxing and even a European poker tournament. Domestic Scottish sport enjoyed a 90-minute highlights package of SPL football broadcast at 11pm on a Monday night on STV, the main Scottish commercial television franchise of the ITV network. Aside from material broadcast on BBC and STV/Grampian news bulletins, this was the sum coverage of Scottish domestic sport on terrestrial television.

Such is the invisibility of live Scottish football on free-to-air television that most non-football fans would probably be hard-pushed in 2007 to name a dozen players from outwith the Old Firm playing for other clubs in the SPL. These players may get discussed in the sports pages of newspapers and perhaps in football phone-in programmes, but their absence from mainstream television means, as far as the wider viewing public is concerned, that the players of Bolton or Aston Villa in the higher-profile English Premiership are likely to be better known in Scotland than those playing in the lower echelons of the SPL.

What is striking looking back at some of the regulatory arguments regarding the broadcasting of live sport that we discussed in the mid-1990s is how obsolete many of these now are. Technology has simply driven a coach and horses through the vain attempts by the SFA and UEFA to prevent live matches being beamed into other national territories and impacting on attendances at live football in the home countries. In 2007, unless you have access to pay TV, you cannot watch any live Scottish Premier League football, but you can throughout the year see live English FA Cup matches and UEFA Champions League games (which can include Scottish teams) scheduled for primetime evening slots. Many of these games coincide with Scottish football games. So, on the night in April 2007 that STV was showing live coverage of the UEFA Champions League semi-final between Manchester United and AC Milan (watched by up to 9.4 million viewers across the UK), just over 8,500 people were turning up for the Scottish Cup semi-final reply between Hibs and Dunfermline at the national stadium, Hampden Park. Live Champions League football on STV attracts on average up to 700,000 viewers and in some cases can boost its audience share in Scotland to nearly 40 per cent.

You can also watch regular preview and highlights packages of English Premiership football scheduled at reasonable times as opposed to the late-night, limited highlights coverage of the Scottish game on STV. It is worth noting that this is not a reflection on the *Scotsport* programme itself, which is the longest-running sports programme on UK television and celebrated its fiftieth anniversary in 2007. Rather, STV is highly restricted in what it can schedule in its own highlights package by the rights owners, the SPL. That in turn took the view that a live pay-TV deal with Setanta Sports would need to be protected by limiting the exposure given to football on terrestrial television.

As a result of its shambolic attempts to create its own television channel (Boyle and Haynes 2004) at the height of the boom in sports rights at the turn of the century, and its subsequent capitulation to the BBC as it eventually struck a deal, the SPL felt that an exclusive Setanta deal in 2004 was its only option if it was to attempt to generate serious revenue through selling its rights. An initial four-year deal to screen thirty-eight games worth £35 million was extended a further two years in April 2006 to include sixty live games per season. This brought the total investment in Scottish football from the Irish broadcaster to £71 million to the end of the 2009–10 season. By way of comparison, individual clubs finishing bottom of the English Premiership in 2007 will receive in the order of £20–25 million for that season alone (a figure which will rise to £30 million in 2008). Never has the competitive financial advantage of English over Scottish football been greater.

THE RIGHTS MARKET

Interestingly, the extension to Setanta's deal in 2006 occurred at the same time as the blind-auction for Premier League rights which was being heavily monitored by the European Commission's Competition Directorate in an attempt to bring plurality to the licensing of television rights in football, and to break BSkyB's grip on exclusive live coverage. Similar pressure had been placed on football television deals across the major leagues of Europe. Here, Setanta stole a march on its competitors, picking up two of the six Premier League packages available from 2007–8 to 2009–10 for £392 million. However, the SPL's exclusive dealings with Setanta and the marginalisation of terrestrial coverage failed to appear on the Commission's radar screen. Despite the heady economic developments in the media sports market since the early 1990s, the value of Scottish sports rights has stagnated by comparison.

Therefore, any regulatory interest in balancing plurality and public interest in Scottish television football deals has also been negated. In a libertarian sports market, some of the reasons for this are simply down to economics. Scottish-only sport does not have the economies of scale afforded to England due to the size of its population. In March 2005 *Scotland on Sunday* ran the headline 'Setanta fails to match BBC as viewers desert live SPL coverage in droves' (Wilson 2005). Although Setanta has remained coy over its viewing figures since its entry into Scotland, the newspaper reported that with 70,000 subscribers the channel had an average 161,000 household viewers which peaked at 450,000 for Old Firm games when group viewing in pubs was taken into consideration. Such figures are not wholly reliable, but if taken as a general trend, and compared to the coverage of sport on mainstream or terrestrial channels, they do suggest a proportional decline. Old Firm games on BBC Scotland attracted nearly 700,000 viewers in households alone, without taking into account any public viewing figures across Scottish pubs and clubs. Setanta Sports aims to compete with Sky through securing English Premiership football rights and hopes to have a subscription base of one million by the start of the 2008 football season. It will need substantive growth, given that in June 2007 it was estimated that its UK and Irish subscription base was about 200,000 (*Media Guardian* 18 June 2007) and its Setanta Sports 1 channel had an audience share of 0.1 per cent (BARB, 5 June 2007).

Even the consumption of domestic Scottish sport outwith Scotland is arguably limited chiefly to two clubs. The value of clubs such as Celtic and Rangers, both with an undoubted large support across and beyond Scotland, remains limited because of the overall value of the league that they play within (Moorhouse 2002). One of the ongoing stories since 1996 has been the recurring threat, currently in abeyance, that the Old Firm would leave Scottish football and play in either the English Premiership or some form of European league. In the foreseeable future, the former is unlikely because English clubs will not want increased competition, the latter because national associations and UEFA are unwilling to sanction structures likely to weaken their powers.

So while the English FA enjoys a £425 million four-year deal to show the FA Cup and England internationals from 2008 on ITV and Setanta Sports, the Scottish FA's four-year deal with Sky from 2006 to 2010 is worth only £26.5 million and includes live coverage of the Scottish Cup. What is significant about this deal is not only the relatively low value placed on the rights, but the fact that it includes all home Scottish internationals. While the BBC has rights for a number of away games, the Scottish national team playing at Hampden

Park has disappeared from free-to-air television and we would argue that the impact on public consciousness more generally has lessened as a result – maybe not among the self-styled Tartan Army of Scotland supporters, but certainly among those non-football fans who engage with big national and international sporting events when they are available for all to watch and participate in. Therefore, one of Scotland's most memorable performances in the past twenty years – a one-nil victory at home over World Cup finalists France in the Euro 2008 qualifying round – was missed by the majority of Scottish viewers. While Scotland has failed for a decade to qualify for a major tournament since 1998, the absence of the national team playing at home from the majority of television screens has contributed to a growing invisibility and lack of recognition of many of the stars of the team, something unthinkable throughout the 1970s and 1980s.

Ironically, one of the reasons ITV's Chief Executive Michael Grade was so keen to secure England matches was that in the digital multi-channel ecology with a fragmented and segmented audience, sports events like this are among the most watched broadcasts. So, for example, six of the top rated programmes in 2006 were football matches from the FIFA World Cup (*Broadcast*, 21 December 2006). These sports transmissions are viewed as 'event TV', part of a small group of programmes that cut across demographic audience profiles and pull an increasingly disaggregated audience together.

What is interesting in a country that supposedly places such importance on the cultural and national impact of sport in general and football in particular, is that the absence of live SPL football from Scottish screens, and its general invisibility, have largely passed unremarked by critics and politicians alike. Although the Scottish Parliament has instigated reviews of Scottish football and its sustainable development (Enterprise and Culture Committee 2005, and Scottish Executive 2006), its lack of remit in the area of media and communications means that there is little scope for a national debate on public access to the broadcasting of key Scottish sporting competitions. Broadcasting remains a reserved power located squarely within the Department for Media, Culture and Sport, with the only concession to civic national pride being the protection afforded to the Scottish Cup Final on the A Listed Events in the 1996 Broadcasting Act.

Professional Scottish club rugby has also endured increasing economic strain in comparison to its English counterpart. From the origins of professional rugby and the launch of the Celtic League in 2001, the governing body; the Scottish Rugby Union (SRU), has struggled to make professional rugby in Scotland sustainable and credible among Scottish fans. The financial pressure of running a professional game – the SRU was £23 million in debt in 2007 – came to a head when the SRU decided to close one of Scotland's three professional clubs, the Border Reivers, after only five years of existence. The decision was met with dismay in the Borders region, traditionally viewed as the hotbed of rugby union in Scotland and with a large amateur club membership that had produced household names such as coach Jim Telfer and long-time BBC rugby commentator Bill McLaren. The fear was that the loss of a top-flight professional club with wide European exposure would impact on the profile and development of the sport in that region among future generations.

Although the Borders had a thriving local club scene, including clubs like Melrose and its internationally renowned Sevens tournament, the commercial power of the sport resides in the SRU offices at Murrayfield in Edinburgh. That body's decision to focus resources on the two remaining professional clubs in Edinburgh and Glasgow smacked of central belt bias against the Borders region, but it also raised the question of why professional rugby in Scotland was floundering. Part of the answer, at least, had been a perceived lack of marketing of the Borders club to the region.[2] But more importantly, it could be said that, much like top-level Scottish football, professional rugby in Scotland had a very marginalised presence in terms of television coverage. In spite of the Celtic League obtaining a titled sponsor in 2006 from the brewers of Magners Cider, and the SRU signing a deal with Setanta to show Scottish professional games, the wider identification of rugby fans with the sport has been found wanting.

This predicament highlighted the problems of launching new professional league competitions without any historic embedded spectator base, a fact revealed by the marketing director of the SRU, Dee McIntosh. In a letter to the online magazine *Scrum*, McIntosh explained why there was no terrestrial television coverage of professional rugby in Scotland in contrast with the rights deals struck by BBC Wales which showed eleven live games during the 2006–07 season:

> I suspect this contrast of broadcasting priorities between BBC Wales and BBC Scotland reflects the fact that rugby is the number one sport in Wales, whereas football dominates life in Scotland and the Scottish TV schedules as a result. (*Scrum* 2006)

The statement is revealing, not only in terms of BBC Scotland's lack of desire to cover the professional game, but also in the lack of confidence the administrator has in the appeal of rugby to a wider Scottish audience.

The crisis in Scottish professional rugby had the potential to deepen further in spring 2007 with the threatened boycott of the European Heineken Cup by English and French clubs over a dispute with the European Rugby Union about commercial shares in the competition. While this crisis was averted, it highlighted through the potential loss of revenue for Scottish rugby – reportedly

£2 million, an amount which would have jeopardised the whole fabric of the professional game – the extent to which Scottish rugby is beholden to the commercial imperatives of its English counterpart.

Here we have an example of the potentially destabilising force of commercial sport, driven by profit rather than grassroots development, and a misplaced perception that pay TV can deliver financial security. Miller et al. (2001) have argued with respect to other national sports leagues that such pressures represent the invidious power of global market forces and what they term the New International Division of Labour (NICL). In a relatively small European nation, professional rugby is drawn upward by the potential economic rewards of transnational capital and television rights fees, but does not have the indigenous audience to sustain the initial investment required to realise this value. Unfortunately, as is evident from the threatened withdrawal of bigger market players in England and France, it is the domestic clubs in smaller nations that will be hit hardest.

Globalisation does of course have complex rhythms, and the economic reasons for axing the Border Reivers created a groundswell of localised support in defence of the club which also raised wider cultural politics of identity and difference within Scotland. Rugby, often defined as a 'way of life' among some communities in Border towns, became a terrain for political campaigning and petition, interestingly, aided and supported through local media such as the *Border Telegraph* and Radio Borders. The importance of local media to represent local and regional sporting cultures should not be underestimated, and it is to radio coverage of sport we now turn.

RADIO TALKS BACK

Radio figures prominently in Scottish sporting culture. Radio phone-ins and irreverent sports-related talk programmes are important features of the Scottish media environment and are key elements in the branding of stations and the building of audience ratings. The dominant force in sports coverage in Scotland is BBC Radio Scotland, with a weekly audience of just over one million listeners. In the west of Scotland it receives stiff competition from the two dominant commercial radio stations Radio Clyde (1 and 2) owned by Emap, and relative newcomer Real Radio Scotland owned by Guardian Media Group. It was Radio Clyde which introduced the sports radio phone-in to the UK by developing the programme *Saturday Super Scoreboard* in 1978. The programme was created by producer Richard Park after a trip to the United States where the format of sports phone-ins had taken off in the early 1970s. Park, along with the now managing director of Clyde, Paul Cooney, used the programme with great effect to exploit a well established tradition of talking about sport, especially 'fitba', to build interest in commercial radio in Scotland (Boyle 2006: 64–5). The football phone-in is now a staple diet of Scottish football fans.

New entrants have increased their pressure on established commercial operators like Clyde which lost ground to Real Radio after the latter launched in 2003. Both carry phone-ins through the week and at weekends which form the mainstay of their sports output. This is largely because BBC Scotland has had exclusive rights to the SPL since 2004. The Scottish radio environment is also characterised by a large number of intra-media performers. At BBC Scotland the irreverent programme and chat show *Off the Ball* is presented by Stuart Cosgrove and Tam Cowan. Cosgrove, Director of Nations and Regions with Channel 4, also hosts BBC Scotland TV's *Sportscene Results* at Saturday teatime. Cowan, a food columnist for the *Daily Record*, also presented BBC Scotland's light entertainments review of football, *Offside*. Finally, Jim Traynor, sports editor with the *Daily Record*, hosts the Saturday post-match phone-in *Your Call* for BBC Radio Scotland. Scottish sports media can thus be seen to be populated by a select range of 'actors' who have increasingly enjoyed popular status in Scotland as minor celebrities. The insular nature of Scottish football coverage has itself been the focus of comic parody in BBC Scotland's intermittent, long-running television comedy sketch show, *Only an Excuse*, written and produced by Philip Differ, himself a journalist for the *Glasgow Evening Times*.

Wit and humour provide the key elements of most radio output outside live commentaries and match reporting. Through the playful and sometimes subversive use of Scottish football vernacular, radio is both a centrifugal and centripetal force in Scotland's sporting culture. By this, we mean that it both draws upon the wider subcultures of football fan practices and, at the same time, plays into the 'sports chatter' (Eco 1990) of Scottish society, setting agendas and circulating gossip. In an analysis of language used by fans and presenters in Radio Clyde's *Super Scoreboard*, Hugh O'Donnell (2002) has suggested that football radio programmes provide rare outlets for variants of Scots dialect. Crucially, O'Donnell sees the debates and discussions of the phone-in as having 'much broader social, economic and political significance' (O'Donnell 2002: 223). Radio phone-ins, comic reviews and light entertainment formats that centre on sport can therefore be seen to have dialectical or 'porous' relationships with wider political debates on Scottish sport and culture.

NEW COMMUNICATIVE SPACES FOR SPORT

The political undertones of this now well established form of Scottish sporting popular culture and a willingness to share experiences and raise contemporary issues have now been transported to the Internet through e-zines, discussion forums, blogs and, increasingly, online multimedia spaces. These include social networking sites such as MySpace and Bebo, digital photography sites like Flickr, or personalised video clips and mash-ups of famous televised moments in Scottish football on YouTube or Google Video.

While mainstream media outlets, including broadcasters and newspapers, have integrated online material and interactivity into their programming and output, the new communicative space of sport is driven by fans for fans. Again, these new spaces of debate around sport have their precedents. The fanzine phenomenon that mushroomed in the mid-to-late 1980s carried features now found in radio programmes and online communication. The issues raised in forums are perennial talking points around sport, particularly football, in Scottish fan culture: television and other media coverage; club ownership and stadium development; players and managers, especially the relationship between wages and performance; ticketing policies and other commercial 'rip offs' like the cost of replica kits; other fans and rivalries; the governance of the game by the SPL, SFA and the Scottish League; and the national team, who is in, who is out, and what the tactics should be.

This typology is not exhaustive and indeed could be broken down further to reveal some of the more nuanced issues and debates that circulate among fans at different times and places. But the list does stand as a firm reminder that talk around sport, especially as it proliferates in online discussion forums, does enable debate and political probing of issues *through* sports cultures.

There is also something important about the changing social relations of fandom and the media which online communication and digital technology have brought to Scottish sporting cultures. The web and associated technologies have enabled a level of disintermediation in Scottish sports media. Both fans and sports that once found the barriers to entry into media production too high or editorially exclusive (in a mainstream media dominated by football) have now been able to circumvent the dominant channels of media production to create websites, online radio stations such as Scottish Rugby Radio (scottishrugbyradio.com), podcasts like Aberdeen fan site AFC Podcast (afcpodcast.co.uk) and streaming video from fans' travels and viewing experiences on YouTube and social network sites which meet their needs to communicate to their specialised audience. There are important issues raised by these new forms of sports content, not least the fact that they are niche productions for niche audiences. Gauging why fans create such material, for whom it is created and how it is consumed requires further empirical research. Analysis of online sports content by Sandvoss (2004) emphasises the ways in which these new spaces provide greater scope for communication, but by and large they merely reflect the wider rationalising processes of global popular culture as 'the fan' becomes just another form of sports consumer. It is certainly the case that Scottish football fans' online activity mimics much within wider media consumption.

However, we might also suggest that the creative empowerment of digital technologies – with ease of production, manipulation, copying and distribution to pre-ordered communities of interest – raises interesting questions about the experience of sport and how fans make sense of it in a Scottish context. As noted above with regard to radio phone-ins, the discursive accounts of football, and for that matter other Scottish sport, in online media suggest that media sport does not only operate in a top-down fashion. Again, this is something O'Donnell (2002) noticed in phone-ins, but we could make an even stronger case for it in terms of the proliferation of content and messages seen on the Internet.

At the same time as the Internet has grown, the past decade has also seen a major growth in newspaper space devoted to sports journalism. This has been particularly clear in the broadsheet/compact market, where editors feel that expanded sports coverage is a driver of sales and speaks to a changing, more literate sports readership (Boyle 2006). UK national newspapers such as *The Guardian* or the *Daily Telegraph* have also extended their sports journalism brand identity onto the web successfully, although both give minimal coverage to Scottish sport. Indeed, in any discussion of the representation of Scottish sport in the media, it is hard to disentangle debates about cultural and national identity from those of political economy and the endemic structural weaknesses of the Scottish media industries. Put another way, Scottish-based national newspapers such as *The Herald* and *The Scotsman* simply cannot compete in terms of journalistic resources with their UK national rivals when it comes to sports coverage. They survive in the market because the attention given to Scottish sport by London-based newspapers is relatively poor, but it is not uncommon to find *The Herald*'s daily sports supplement carrying multiple pieces from the same journalist as its small team try to cover the waterfront of Scottish sport. By way of comparison, *The Herald*'s supplement looks flimsy and lightweight when set against the substantially better resourced daily sports supplement in, say, *The Guardian*.

If *The Times* does invest in a distinctly Scottish edition scheduled to be launched in 2007, coverage of Scottish sport and football in particular will be a key element of its pitch to attract readers away from *The Herald* and *The Scotsman* (it signalled its intent by poaching the top sportswriter of *The Herald*, Graham Spiers, early in 2007). In many ways this is an extension of a longer process by which editionised tabloids have eroded indigenous newspaper sales. To this end, if London-based, upmarket newspapers ever got really serious about moving into the Scottish market, investing in sports journalism would seriously weaken the position of the current dominant players, in much the same way as *The Scottish Sun* has eroded the position of the *Daily Record* since the 1980s. Economics matter, and attempts by Newsquest Scotland, owners of *The Herald* and the *Sunday Herald*, to cut £2–3 million in their budgets in 2007 can only weaken their sports – and other – journalism (*Press Gazette*, 4 April 2007). In the next decade, expect the debate about merging the Glasgow-based *Herald* with the Edinburgh-based *Scotsman* to re-emerge.

CONCLUSION: BACK TO THE FUTURE

The most striking aspects of the media sport environment over the last decade have been the pace of technological change, the struggle of regulatory bodies to keep pace and the establishment of a new culture and tradition of watching sport on television. There is also an ongoing process of continuity and change in how Scotland engages with, reports, mediates and represents Scottish sport.

By and large, key events have migrated to pay-TV from free-to-air digital television. While major international events such as the FIFA World Cup remain available to all, Scotland's inability to qualify for the final stages of such events serves to enhance the invisibility of the national team for the non-sporting Scottish audience. In the age of the market, Scotland, like other small countries, simply cannot compete financially, yet other relatively small countries such as Holland and Portugal both operate within limited television markets and still enjoy marginal and sporadic footballing success, so clearly wider and deeper problems remain to be addressed in the ongoing process to re-juvenate Scottish football (Banks 2002; Morrow 2003).

Of course, Scottish sporting success does exist and sporadically gains national and international media attention. Often these successes are focused around individual sports stars such as Andy Murray in tennis, John Higgins in snooker, or Dario Franchitti, in Indy car racing. In some cases these individual athletes are partly defined by their 'Scottishness' (for example, Andy Murray with his saltire sweatbands or comments about his lack of support for England in the 2006 FIFA World Cup), at other times less so. Even the most evergreen Scottish sports stars like golfer Colin Montgomerie only receive intermittent attention from the Scottish media, usually around major tournaments like the Ryder Cup (where there is a strange ellision of national pride into pan-European collectivity) or the Open Championship, which is frequently hosted in Scotland but packaged as a global sports event. In a book celebrating more than 100 years of reporting from the Open, *The Herald* proudly noted that of the 128 championships staged by the year 2000, the paper had carried reports from 123 of them (Lowe and Brownlie 2000). While this reflects a clear pride and natural interest in golf, rarely is the sport given much prominence in

Scottish-based television. Most golf is on pay-TV channels or covered by the network BBC Sports department. In an age of event television, however, it is the global team sports such as football and rugby which become vehicles for wider expressions of national identity on an international stage, and here, of late, Scotland simply has not turned up on the big night. Ironically, while the media may claim this structural failure in football is more to do with the ineptitude and lack of long-term vision among those who run the game, the role played increasingly by television as the financial underwriter of a sport left to find its place in the cultural marketplace cannot be underestimated. Nationally, other indigenous sports such as shinty remain largely invisible in the central belt, and, for a range of historical, political and cultural reasons, Scottish Gaelic sport has never enjoyed the countrywide grassroots support and extensive media coverage which, say, Gaelic sport has in Ireland.

Sport still matters to the collective sense of identities that exist in modern Scotland, but these also co-exist with a range of other sporting and cultural identities. Regional and local rivalries are the staple diet of a sporting culture and they continue to be served via a range of local, regional and national newspapers, the Internet and increasingly radio coverage of the live event. At the same time, Scots are happy and keen to watch the best that international televised sport has to offer.

The media have always played a central role in creating the myths which surround the national narratives which countries tell about the role of sport in society. Often these stories are linear in nature and have tended to have any complexities airbrushed away through repeated telling over time. The 2007 Cricket World Cup, best remembered for the extraordinary death of the Pakistan coach Bob Woolmer (not least since his 'murder' subsequently appeared to be a fiction), was also an example of the new more commercial world of international sport. As the ICC attempts to extend the rather limited world map of international cricket-playing countries, so (rather like the recent FIFA football world cups) a number of 'minnows' are allowed into the event in order to encourage the process of extending the international cricket community. In the 2007 tournament both Scotland and Ireland competed. The former displayed all the aptitude associated with their footballing and rugby counterparts when competing at the highest level of international sport: they failed miserably. By way of contrast, Ireland made it to the quarter-finals before being beaten, but far from humiliated, by England. Indeed, the relative closeness of the contest would have been unimaginable even five years ago.

The Scottish and UK media informed us that cricket fever was gripping Ireland as the team progressed in the tournament. In reality, interest was shown during the matches, but the mainstream sports of Gaelic games, rugby and (English) football all continued to command the attention of the sporting Irish.

No doubt had Scotland fared better and reached the latter stages with a match against England, all sorts of traditional stereotypes (and some strange anomalies, such as the unusually high number of cricket clubs once to be found in Aberdeen) would have been dusted down by the media as cricket became invested with elements of a longer historical symbolic battle with Scotland's larger neighbour. The point we want to make is that simply reading media discourses of sport as accurate indicators of wider attitudes is becoming more problematic in a 24/7 digital media environment. As the way people engage with media changes, as the media themselves become more commercially orientated, so the level of trust invested by people in the ability of the media to accurately reflect what is going on in and around sporting events and their hinterland begins to be eroded. At key moments sport retains its ability to give articulation to expressions of collective and national characteristics and feelings, but it is an increasingly complex process as the media themselves struggle to provide a forum for such expression in a crowded marketplace.

For most of the time, we are addressed as media consumers rather than citizens – something not unique to Scotland and increasingly given a UK institutional voice through the communications regulator Ofcom – and the implications of this approach extend well into all areas of cultural life. If the governing bodies of sport, and football in particular, view supporters as simply consumers, and sport as 'product' rather than cultural activity, then they should not be surprised that an erosion of trust and commitment, often associated with emotions not generated solely by the market, continues apace as a younger generation view sport as just another consumer product.

Going forward, it will be interesting to see how a nationalist government in Holyrood may impact on this situation, and longer term, how an independent Scotland – should it come into being – might involve a substantive re-calibrating of the Scottish media industries, and broadcasting in particular. Evidence from the election campaign for the Scottish Parliament in May 2007 suggests that strategic thinking about what broadcasting would look like in an independent Scotland is substantially underdeveloped at this stage. However, given the relative structural weakness of much of Scottish sport, and the dominance of the market-driven discourse across the sporting and media industries, changing the existing media sport ecology may prove to be more difficult than some might anticipate. That said, of course, politics is concerned with the art of the possible and a dramatic re-positioning of the role of sport in Scottish life and an attendant rethinking of the role, impact and importance of the media in society cannot be completely discounted.

Now that Glasgow's bid to host the 2014 Commonwealth Games has proved successful, then the aim of the organisers will be to offer a distinctively Scottish version of the relationship between sport and society (more than may have been on show at the London-based 2012 Olympics). A major sporting event – and the Commonwealth Games becomes more important for smaller nations, offering as it does the opportunity to compete successfully at international level – held in Scotland, with a Scottish team competing under the country's flag, will focus attention on the wider relationship between sport, society and the media.

Our point of departure was revisiting the 1996 landscape; no doubt, ten years on from now there will be another story to tell. But it is striking just how different things seem now. Mainstream Scottish league and international football has withered away from free-to-air television. The policy debate on whether or not live coverage of English club football matches should be screened in Scotland looks somewhat ridiculous. Indeed, as noted earlier, it is easier across a season for Scottish viewers to watch the likes of Manchester United and Chelsea on free-to-air television than Celtic or Rangers. In 1996 we were witnessing the emergence and consolidation of a new broadcasting power in the UK, BSkyB, largely driven by sports subscription channels. Even after EU and UK government intervention, BSkyB continues to dominate the rights market for sport, and even where it is not the key rights holder, as is the case with Scottish domestic football, it has still prospered as the principal carrier of rival television sports channels like Setanta. All of this means that televised viewing of sport is far more of a niche activity than in previous decades and we would argue that this has had a detrimental influence on how sport is perceived in the wider culture. It could be argued that the overall coverage is far superior, a view with which we would concur, but in a small nation like Scotland the current provision dramatically reduces the number of people engaging through television with top-level sport.

The Internet did not really figure in Scottish sports coverage in 1996, but has clearly evolved to become an important communication tool in terms of reportage and marketing while providing a new communicative space. The most active agents in this new communicative space have been grassroots sport and football fans. Both provide evidence of thriving sporting cultures in Scotland. However, these disintermediated success stories remain marginalised from the wider public consciousness of sport in Scotland. The Internet works best at creating and consolidating niche audiences and communities of sports fans. Until it becomes a mass medium on which live sport is watched, then it is television that remains the crucial vehicle for mediated sport. While the coverage of football continues to fill the back pages and sports supplements of Scottish newspapers and provide hours of debate and discussion on Scottish radio stations more broadly, Scottish sport is crucially absent from the two dominant television channels, outside of news programming. Where it does feature, it is invariably pushed to the margins of the schedule. This cannot be advantageous to the long-term health of Scottish sporting culture. The political debate is about how to balance the commercial interests of elite sport in Scotland with the role of the media – and television in particular – in providing a public forum through which citizens engage with sports culture.

It is time that debate started.

NOTES

1. The quote from *Scottish Sport* is taken from the Scottish Football League website at http://www.scottishfootballleague.com/scottish_football.cfm?curpageid=971.
2. With the announcement of the closure of Border Reivers, BBC Scotland hosted an open forum in Kelso (12 April 2007) to discuss the issue among local rugby fans and administrators. A strong feature of the discussion was the lack of support for the Borders team from within the region, largely due to the lack of marketing of professional rugby to local fans whose allegiance was firmly with local amateur club rugby.

REFERENCES

Banks, S. (2002), *Going Down: Football in Crisis*, Edinburgh: Mainstream.

Billig, M. (1995), *Banal Nationalism*, London: Sage.

Boyle, R. (2006), *Sports Journalism: Context and Issues*, London: Sage.

Boyle, R. and R. Haynes (1996), ' "The grand old game": football, media and identity in Scotland', *Media, Culture & Society*, vol. 18: pp. 549–664.

Boyle, R. and R. Haynes (2004), *Football in the New Media Age*, London: Routledge.

Eco, U. (1990), *Travels in Hyperreality*, London: Harvester Books.

Enterprise and Culture Committee (2005), *Report on Reform of Scottish Football*, Scottish Parliament Paper 456, EC/S2/R13.

Jarvie, G. and J. Burnett (2000), *Sport, Scotland and the Scots*, Edinburgh: Tuckwell Press.

Lowe, D. and A. Brownlie (2000), *The Herald Book of The Open Championship*, Edinburgh: Black and White Publishing

Miller, T., G. Lawrence, J. McKay and D. Rowe (1991), *Globalization and Sport: Playing The World*. London: Sage.

Moorhouse H. F. (2002), 'The distribution of income in European football: big clubs, small countries, major problems', in C. Baros et al. (eds), *Transatlantic Sport: The Comparative Economics of North American and European Sports*, Cheltenham: Edward Elgar, pp. 69–82.

Morrow, S. (2003), *The People's Game: Football, Finance and Society*, Macmillan: London.

O'Donnell, H. (2002), 'Fitba Crazy? Saturday Super Scoreboard and the dialectics of political debate', in A. Bernstein and N. Blain (eds), *Sport, Media, Culture: Global and Local Dimensions*, London: Frank Cass.

Sandvoss, C. (2004), 'Technological evolution or revolution? sport online live Internet commentary as postmodern cultural form', *Convergence*, vol. 10, no. 3, pp. 40–54.

Scottish Executive (2006), *Calling Time on Sectarianism*, Edinburgh: Scottish Executive.
Scrum (2006), 'Scrumbag – give Scotland fans a break', http://www.scrum.com/2444_1299.php, 15 September 2006.
Wilson, M. (2005) 'Setanta fails to match BBC as viewers desert live SPL coverage in droves', *Scotland on Sunday*, 20 March 2005, http://scotlandonsunday.scotsman.com/business.cfm?id=298612005.

Select Bibliography

Barr, B. and R. McKay (1976), *The Story of the Scottish Daily News*, Edinburgh: Canongate.

Bonnington, A. and R. McInnes (2008), *Scots Law for Journalists*, Edinburgh: W. Green.

Bruce, D. (1996), *Scotland the Movie*, Edinburgh: Polygon.

Burnett, G. (1938), *Scotland on the Air*, Edinburgh: The Moray Press.

Couper, W. J. (1908), *The Edinburgh Periodical Press*, Stirling: Eneas Mackay.

Cowan, R. M. (1946), *The Newspaper in Scotland: a Study of its First Expansion 1815–1860*, Glasgow: George Outram.

Craig, M. E. (1931), *The Scottish Periodical Press 1750–1789*, Edinburgh: Oliver and Boyd.

Dick, E. (ed.) (1990), *From Limelight to Satellite*, Glasgow/London: Scottish Film Council/BFI.

Donaldson, W. (1986), *Popular Literature in Victorian Scotland: Language, Fiction and the Press*, Aberdeen: Aberdeen University Press.

Douglas, F. M. (2008), *Scottish Newspapers, Language and Identity*, Edinburgh: Edinburgh University Press.

Hardy, F. (1990), *Scotland in Film*, Edinburgh: Edinburgh University Press.

Hetherington, A. (1992), *Inside BBC Scotland 1975–1980: A Personal View*, Aberdeen: Whitewater Press.

Hutchison, D. (ed.) (1978), *Headlines: The Media in Scotland*, Edinburgh: Polygon.

McArthur, C. (ed.) (1982), *Scotch Reels*, London: BFI.

McCrone, D. (2001), *Understanding Scotland: the Sociology of a Nation*, London: Routledge.

McDowell, W. H. (1992), *The History of BBC Broadcasting in Scotland, 1923–1983*, Edinburgh: Edinburgh University Press.

Murray, J. (2004), *That Thinking Feeling: A Research Guide to Scottish Cinema 1938–2004*, Edinburgh: Edinburgh College of Art/Scottish Screen.

Petrie, D. (2000), *Screening Scotland*, London: BFI Publishing.

Petrie, D. (2004), *Contemporary Scottish Fictions*, Edinburgh: Edinburgh University Press.

Reid, H. (2006), *Deadline: The Story of the Scottish Press*, Edinburgh: Saint Andrew Press.

Schlesinger, P., D. Miller and W. Dinan (2001), *Open Scotland? Journalists, Spin Doctors and Lobbyists*, Edinburgh: Polygon.

Smith, M. (1994), *Paper Lions: the Scottish Press and National Identity*, Edinburgh: Polygon.

Notes on Contributors

Neil Blain is Professor of Media and Culture and Head of Department of Film, Media & Journalism at the University of Stirling.

Raymond Boyle is Senior Lecturer in Media and Cultural Policy at the Centre for Cultural Policy Research at the University of Glasgow.

Kathryn Burnett is Senior Lecturer in Media and Culture at the University of the West of Scotland.

John R. Cook is Reader in Media at Glasgow Caledonian University.

John Corbett is Professor of Applied Language Studies in the Department of English Language, University of Glasgow.

Mike Cormack is Senior Lecturer at Sabhal Mòr Ostaig, the Gaelic College on the Isle of Skye, part of UHI Millennium Institute.

David Bruce is the former Director of the Scottish Film Council (now Scottish Screen) and was Director of the Edinburgh International Film Festival in the mid-1960s; he is currently Chair of Glasgow Film Theatre.

Ken Garner is Senior Lecturer in Journalism and Media at Glasgow Caledonian University.

Richard Haynes is Senior Lecturer in Film and Media and Director of Stirling Media Research Institute at the University of Stirling.

David Hutchison is Research Fellow in Media Policy at Glasgow Caledonian University.

Anthea Irwin is Lecturer in Mass Media at Glasgow Caledonian University.

Myra Macdonald is Reader in Film and Media at the University of Stirling.

Brian McNair is Professor of Journalism and Communication at the University of Strathclyde.

Ian Mowatt is Lecturer in Media at Glasgow Caledonian University and has contributed many sketches to *Naked Radio, Naked Video, Scotch & Wry* and *Spitting Image*.

Sarah Neely is Lecturer in Film and Media at the University of Stirling.

Hugh O'Donnell is Professor of Language and Popular Culture at Glasgow Caledonian University.

Michael Russell is an SNP MSP for the South of Scotland and was appointed Minister for Environment in May 2007. He has worked as a commentator, author, broadcaster and film-maker.

Philip Schlesinger is Professor in Cultural Policy and Academic Director of the Centre for Cultural Policy Research at the University of Glasgow.

Jane Sillars is Teaching Fellow in Film and Media at the University of Stirling.

Maggie Sweeney is Lecturer in Media Studies at the University of the West of Scotland.

Brian Wilson is a former Labour MP and Government minister who is also an award-winning journalist.

Index